D0855074

LÉON BLUM / THE FORMATIVE YEARS

LÉON BLUM

THE FORMATIVE YEARS
1872–1914

WILLIAM LOGUE

NORTHERN ILLINOIS UNIVERSITY PRESS
DE KALB

Library of Congress Cataloging in Publication Data

Logue, William, 1934–
    Léon Blum: the formative years, 1872–1914

    Bibliography: p.
    1. Blum, Léon, 1872–1950.
DC373.B5L64   944.081'5'0924 [B]   72–7515
ISBN 0–87580–030–0

The translation of "Extracts from *Le Petit Lannionais*" appearing on pages 20–21 is from the book *Léon Blum, Man and Statesman* by Geoffrey Fraser and Thadée Natanson. Copyright 1938 by J. B. Lippincott Company. Renewal © 1964 by Geoffrey Fraser. Reprinted by permission of J. B. Lippincott Company.

DC
373
B5
L64

© 1973 Northern Illinois University Press

Published by Northern Illinois University Press,
DeKalb, Illinois 60115

Manufactured in the United States of America

All Rights Reserved

To My Parents

CONTENTS

ACKNOWLEDGMENTS

The author would like to express his gratitude to all the individuals and institutions who helped make his work possible. I want to thank first of all Professor S. William Halperin of the University of Chicago, who directed the doctoral dissertation on which this book is based and who encouraged me throughout the many revisions necessary for its publication. I want to thank also the University of Chicago, the Fulbright Commission, and the French government for the financial assistance which made possible my research in the invaluable collections of the Bibliothèque Nationale and the Archives Nationales.

Among the many people in France who were generous with their knowledge and advice, I am especially grateful to Robert Blum, the son of Léon Blum, whose recollections were invaluable and who provided many helpful introductions. Others who were most helpful through interviews or correspondence were Marcel Blum, brother of Léon Blum, André Blumel, former *chef de cabinet* of Léon Blum, M. and Mme Paul Grunebaum-Ballin, and Joseph Paul-Boncour.

Most valuable of all has been the help of my wife Carol, skillful editor, patient critic, and indefatigable optimist.

LÉON BLUM / THE FORMATIVE YEARS

INTRODUCTION

Léon Blum is famous as the leader of the French Socialist party in the 1920s and 1930s and as the head of the Popular Front government of 1936–37 which strove to save the Third Republic from the Depression and the threat of fascism. Outside France it is less well known that before 1914 he was a respected literary critic, an influential drama critic, a controversial essayist, and a distinguished jurist. Even those aware of his multiple early careers commonly underestimate their importance and understand them only superficially. It is the aim of the present work to contribute to a fuller understanding of Léon Blum through the study of these early careers.

While still virtually unknown to the rank-and-file French worker, Blum emerged in 1919 as a leading defender of the policies and record of the Socialist party since its unification in 1905. He especially sought to carry on the tradition of Jean Jaurès, the party's great tribune and martyr. Seeking to preserve French socialism from Bolshevik inroads, Blum became the spokesman for the minority which at the Congress of Tours (1920) refused to choose between the dictatorial methods of the Third International and the revisionism of the party's right wing. After the newly formed

French Communist party carried off the majority of the socialist militants, the party apparatus, funds, and newspaper—*L'Humanité* —Blum devoted himself to rebuilding the Socialist party. Though he must share the credit for the remarkable success of that effort with many others, especially party secretary Paul Faure, Blum's contribution as the public leader of the party was vital. An intellectual with little apparent experience in politics, he became a political journalist to be reckoned with through his editorials in the new party paper, *Le Populaire*, and a parliamentarian whose ability was respected by all sides.

The successes of the party, plus the crises of the 1930s, made it possible for Blum to become the first Socialist and first Jewish premier of France. During the Depression, the republic once again appeared threatened from the right. The riots of February 1934 motivated efforts at republican defense, which led to the formation of the Popular Front movement, linking Communists, Socialists, and Radicals behind a common program. Blum entered the movement with misgivings about the reliability of the Communists, who had previously treated him as one of their most dangerous enemies. With the victory of the Popular Front in the 1936 parliamentary elections, the Socialists became the largest party and the central element of the new majority. Blum was the obvious choice to direct the first Popular Front government.

The record of that bold experiment has remained a subject of controversy. Historians of all persuasions have tended to dwell on the disappointments and failures of the Popular Front and Blum has had to bear a large share of the responsibility for them. He did not shirk that responsibility before the Vichy court at Riom in 1942; nor did he disguise his pride in the measures by which his government improved the daily lives of working men, such as the introduction of paid vacations. Sympathetic scholars have shown that Blum's "exercise of power" was consistent with his long-established convictions, but they have felt that at best he was the right man in the wrong time and place. While paying homage to his great personal courage in the face of the Vichy regime and the Nazis, they have found his intellectual qualities, his humanism, to have been shortcomings in facing the menacing irrationalism of

4

the fascist 1930s. Without denying that Blum made mistakes—e.g., in his reluctance to devalue the franc—it seems that his assessment of the situation in France and its potentialities was more realistic than that of his critics, past and present.

Blum's qualities—one is tempted to say, his wisdom—would be better appreciated if he had had the good fortune to govern in more tranquil times, for those qualities developed in an era of outward calm and complacency retrospectively called *La Belle Epoque*. But the gulf between the 1890s and the 1930s was less profound than appears on the surface; the roots of the social, intellectual, and moral crisis that disrupted European civilization in the thirties were already visible in the years when Blum was maturing. The Dreyfus affair first made him aware of the dangers which threatened democracy and freedom just below the surface of society. In a sense, he fought those threats all his life.

The events of the summer of 1914, which brought an end to the world of the nineteenth century, also caused a sharp break in Léon Blum's life. Saddened by the assassination of Jaurès and the outbreak of the war, he abandoned his literary career to enter the government as *chef de cabinet* to Marcel Sembat, the Socialist Minister of Public Works. When Socialist participation in the government ended after two years, Blum returned to his judicial career on the Conseil d'Etat, where he remained until his election to the Chamber of Deputies in 1919. He did not, however, resume his literary career for he had been drawn into the internal struggle which was destroying the hard-won unity of the socialist movement. Thus Blum's life would never be the same after 1914. But he was forty-two when the war started and the ideas, attitudes, and inclinations he would follow for the rest of his life were already largely formed, outside the battleground of politics. That Blum had the quality of character to become the leader of the French Socialist party in one of its most difficult moments can be understood only through examination of his earlier careers.

The historian can only regret that there are, for all practical purposes, no unpublished materials to shed new light on the pre-1914 careers of Léon Blum. Blum was always reticent about himself, even in private, and his personal papers were lost after they

were confiscated by the Germans during World War II. Fortunately, he published a great deal, beginning at an early age, and a
thorough study of these published works gives us an illuminating
picture of his formative years. Blum was an intellectual *par
excellence* in a nation of intellectuals, who wanted to be known
through his words, the vehicles of his thought, and it is fitting that
we should know him thus. This study, which will often confirm
opinions already widely held about Blum, has been guided not by
a search for novelty but by the belief that a man of nuance and careful distinctions can be accurately known only when he is fully
known.

The desire to increase our understanding of Blum's later political
career has been the primary motivation for studying his earlier
life; the relevance of that life, in its own right, has not been
adequately recognized. In spite of James Joll's warning that
"concentration on his political career should not obscure the
considerable merits of his literary work," most studies have done
just that. Even before 1914, Blum had made himself well known in
two distinct fields, literature and administrative jurisprudence.
This breadth of interest, and the remarkable vitality which
enabled him to give rein to it, are enough to stimulate our curiosity
about the man. Relatively few men pursue different careers
successively; even fewer successfully pursue different careers, as
Blum did, simultaneously.

Léon Blum was sharply attuned to the literary and intellectual
currents of the two prewar decades, and this, combined with the
breadth of his concerns, makes his life and work a good device for
viewing the intellectual history of the time. Certainly he was not
one of the literary giants of the turn of the century—though he
was a friend or acquaintance of most of them—but he was a
significant figure in the literary world. His talent as a critic was
recognized at an early age and his work reached an important
audience. He was much more than the *homme-reflet* portrayed by
the hostile Julien Benda, but he was in many ways representative
of his generation. Thus the present study hopes to make a modest
contribution to the intellectual history of the age as well. Inadequate
attention to the intellectual—and especially the literary—life of

the prewar world has been one of the weaknesses of even the best studies of Blum.

Only the most hostile observers have failed to see the great honesty and sincerity of Léon Blum, the French patriot as well as the socialist internationalist, the Frenchman and the Jew; but even the most hostile have had to recognize his great intelligence. Those studies of Blum which have concentrated on his political career have usually done justice to these qualities, but this biographical study of his earlier careers is required to present some of the other basic qualities which are essential to a full understanding of the man. The two most important qualities were his commitments to self-knowledge and to the present. From his earliest years, Blum exemplified French devotion to one of the most demanding maxims of ancient moral philosophy: Know thyself. This commitment led to his individualism, since the first corollary of the duty of self-knowledge is the duty of self-realization. Self-knowledge cannot be realized in the abstract, and the young man understood that the self must be known in action as well as thought—the potentialities an individual harbors must be tested in the light of experience. As Blum later testified, there is something particularly appealing to intelligent young men in individualism, something almost intoxicating in the assertion of one's value before the world. Gradually, during his youth, Blum came to realize that self-assertion also implies obligations to recognize the worth of others, to grant them the same rights to self-realization as oneself, and to work for a world in which all men have the opportunity to develop in harmony. Blum's quest for self-knowledge endured throughout his life, although it took a new form after 1914.

Blum's self-conscious commitment to the present was evident in his legal and literary careers. It led him both to champion his own generation in its struggle for recognition in literature and—a much rarer quality—to admit that succeeding generations have the same rights of self-expression. Thus, in spite of his unwillingness to become a literary historian, he developed a sense of history which not only gave a valuable perspective to his literary criticism but helped shape his socialist attitudes. In life, as in literature, Blum was aware of the limitations on what can be achieved in any period or by any generation. He knew the vanity of millennial expectations—of expecting a great moral regeneration of man or society in anything but the long run or of expecting a great new age in literature that, by its genius and energy, would surpass the accomplishments of earlier generations. But this knowledge did not make him a cynic or lessen his commitment to the progress of literary art, the improvement of relations between the sexes, or social justice. He approached these causes with a lack of dogmatism and with a deep concern for means as well as ends. He would not sacrifice the present in exaggerated respect for the past; neither would he sacrifice the present for some idealized construct of the future. This, more than anything else, made Blum the kind of literary critic he was; it would also make him the kind of socialist leader he became.

After a thorough consideration of Blum's dual career as man of letters and the law, it should no longer be possible to think of him as "a gentle dreamer and idealist in an age of harsh practicality" (Louise Dalby); he was both a realist and an idealist. However one may choose to judge his appreciations of this or that author, book, or play, or his strategy as Socialist leader, or his tactics as parliamentary leader, one must recognize that Blum was a man of considerable practical sense as well as abstract intelligence. Even the most sophisticated studies of Blum, those by Joel Colton and Gilbert Ziebura, tend to see him as dominated by an abstract intellect and to explain his failures as a political leader in terms of the presumed qualities of his intellect. That Blum was an intellectual, as well as a man of considerable intelligence, is unquestionable, but close study shows that his education, philosophical orientation, and legal training—when filtered through his experiences as literary critic, essayist, and jurist—did not make him a man of abstract intelligence who "tended to confuse ideas with reality" but a man of very practical intelligence who was not afraid of abstract ideas or speculative thinking.

But for the events associated with World War I, Blum might have continued the dual careers he had managed with such distinction since the 1890s. It is certainly hard to imagine any process by which he might have left them for a career in politics. But when the brutal shock came that would transform his life, Blum was prepared by experience and his self-awareness. Had that shock not come, he might not have achieved political fame; but his life, even so, would still be of interest to those who seek to understand the intellectual life of modern France or appreciate the struggle of an acute intelligence and fine sensitivity coming to grips with life.

CHAPTER ONE

THE EDUCATION OF LÉON BLUM

IN JANUARY 1896 Léon Blum began his functions as *auditeur de deuxième classe* on the Conseil d'Etat, and in February he also assumed the post of regular critic of novels for *La Revue blanche*—judicial and literary careers that were to prosper until the coming of war, in the summer of 1914, turned his thoughts and energies in new directions. These eighteen years were a period of maturity and fulfillment, with which this study will be primarily concerned. Although a lack of evidence compels us to treat the preceding twenty-four years of his life more briefly, we can learn much about the man from his youth. The self-knowledge and self-assurance which enabled Blum to embark on dual careers were developed in his secure and stable family life and his thorough classical education.

Blum's most deeply rooted qualities became apparent early in life: a high order of intelligence and emotional sensitivity. A willful child yet one who needed affection, Blum learned within his family life the necessity of restricting the play of his ego, not simply because of the resistance of the world but primarily because of the moral obligation to respect the rights of others. Concern for justice and an effort to combine the search for self-realization with respect for others were to mark his life. In the family, too, his intellectual potential was recognized and cultivated. His later criticisms of the family as an institution were certainly not based on a rejection of his own experience, any more than his criticism of the institution of marriage reflected personal disappointment. His family life was tranquil and pleasant.

As it does for many young men, separation from his family involved psychological strains for Blum, but he soon found his place in the lycée, which enabled him to enter the literary and intellectual circles of French society. The education he received suited his temperament admirably, giving his intelligence a literary and philosophical orientation. New friends revealed the attraction of the intellectual life by introducing him to a world which had thus far been beyond the scope of his family contacts.

At the lycée, Léon Blum began to take more self-conscious control of the direction of his life. He sought to understand himself: to come to terms with adolescent emotion, to measure the range of his literary and intellectual talents, to find goals worthy of the potential he felt within himself. Literature was an important vehicle for this self-study—and, fortunately so for us as well, since it is through his earliest literary efforts that we can see Blum begin to emerge, see his serious effort to understand himself and the world, see the precocious lucidity of his literary style, and see the qualities of analysis and synthesis he displayed in handling ideas and sensations. By 1896 he was well prepared for the remarkable careers that were opening up before him.

It was on 9 April 1872, only eleven months after the army of Versailles swept past 151 rue Saint-Denis to attack the Communard stronghold at Chateau d'Eau, that Léon Blum was born at that modest Parisian address, in the apartment of his parents.[1] Once the route from Ile de la Cité to the royal city of Saint-Denis, in 1872 the rue Saint-Denis bore no traces of this romantic past, except for the triumphal arch erected by the city in 1672 to commemorate the victories of Louis XIV and to serve as one of the city gates. Now it was a dark and narrow business thoroughfare, whose buildings were given over to a variety of small businesses, mostly wholesale. The upper stories sheltered a not very heterogeneous population of working-class families and the families of small merchants, who, like the Blums, lived frugally above their places of business. It was a depressing urban street, with not even a tree to break the bleakness of its dirty stone walls. But it was not depressing for the Blums, who were looking ahead to better surroundings and whose years of effort were soon to be rewarded.

The families of Léon Blum's parents had moved to Paris from Alsace shortly before the revolution of 1848, and as far back as anyone could remember, they had been French subjects.[2] His father's family had lived in the department of Bas-Rhin in 1808 when French Jews were required to adopt family names.[3] His mother's family, the Picarts, had come to Paris from the Haut-Rhin. Auguste Blum, Léon's father, was born in Alsace in 1842.[4]

The Blum family had not been successful financially, but matters had taken a turn for the better when Auguste opened a wholesale house in Paris specializing in silk ribbons, a trade which attracted many Alsatian Jewish merchants.[5] Progress had been slow until fortune came to the aid of hard work. The two decades following the collapse of the Second Empire were generally a period of slow economic development throughout France, but the evolution of feminine fashions created an expanding demand for ribbons and Auguste Blum prospered. Soon the business was big enough for him to bring in his brothers, and it was reorganized as Blum Frères which, as it continued to grow, moved first to the rue Réaumur and then to the important wholesaling center of the rue du Quatre-Septembre, close to the Bourse.[6] After the death of Auguste in 1921, Blum Frères was managed by three of Léon's four brothers, Lucien, Marcel, and Georges, until the Great Depression and yet another change in fashion brought an end to its success.[7]

Léon Blum's early family life had no small influence on his development, but because of his life-long reluctance to talk about himself, little is known about his early years.[8] Though later he moved in intellectual circles far removed from his humble beginnings, he never attempted to cut himself off from his family. Indeed, he was closely attached to it throughout his life and always spoke of its influence with approval and gratitude. Blum's "esprit de famille," as his brother Marcel called it, was one of the more important elements of his Jewish heritage.[9]

Although not religiously inclined, Auguste Blum had retained the moral authority over the family that was traditional among French Jews.[10] Léon was on good terms with his father, and held him in respect, but his father's business life had little fascination for him. Like many a second son of a self-made father, he would never show much interest in money matters.[11] His elder brother Lucien also was attracted toward a literary career, and the two boys spent many hours reciting verse and declaiming speeches to each other. But Lucien would sacrifice his literary inclinations to enter the family business,[12] which allowed the women in the family more freedom to encourage Léon's intellectual interests. Thus it is not surprising that he grew up interested in books but not in ledgers, sensitive but not shy, and possessing a certain graciousness he had learned from the women.

By far the greatest early influence on Blum was that of his mother, an intelligent and in her own way deeply religious woman. It was her respect for the intellectual life that opened that world for Léon. Her ambition for her sons was so great that she even learned Latin in order to be able to encourage and aid them.[13] Her intelligence was accompanied by a remarkable memory, which Léon also possessed.[14] However much he owed to her encouragement of his intellect, Blum was to revere his mother even more for her moral influence.

Madame Blum came from a family that practiced its religion, but her faith was more personal than orthodox. She taught the boys to pray, but she herself preferred to pray at home rather than in the temple. Both she and her husband respected religious faith, and they taught their children that respect, rather than religion.[15] Like the large majority of French Jews, they were on the long road to assimilation, so that Léon did not acquire a sense of being different from other Frenchmen.

It was the tradition of justice, which she considered the better part of Judaism, that Mme. Blum wanted most to communicate to her sons, and she was succeeded in impressing it deeply and permanently on them—perhaps most profoundly on Léon, who later spoke of her, in a frequently cited passage, as the very incarnation of justice:

She was the most just being I have ever known. I have never encountered in anyone else such an intensity of scruple. She carried the sentiment of justice to melancholy extremes. ... Have I ever told you the story of the apples? I was raised with a brother a little older than myself. When my mother gave us apples for a snack, she did not give each of us a whole apple. She cut two apples in half and gave each of us one half from each apple. It was only in this way that the division seemed equal to her.[16]

13

Her example taught Léon that consideration for others should be a part of one's everyday life—never an easy lesson to learn, especially for a willful and intelligent child, but learn it he did.

From his maternal grandmother, Blum recalled, he learned that the ideal of justice had political as well as personal significance. Like many French Jews, she looked upon the revolution of 1789, which brought emancipation and legal equality to Jews, as the earthly embodiment of eternal justice. She maintained the cult of the revolution more fiercely than most of her class, going so far as to sympathize with the moralistic socialism of George Sand and Pierre Leroux. Of an independent temperament, she had run her own bookshop on the Place Dauphine, near the Palais de Justice, before coming to live with her daughter's family around 1883. The republican enthusiasm which had made her hostile to the regime of *Napoléon le petit* had even led her to sympathize with the Commune. It was from this "Communarde," as her sisters called her, that Blum learned to identify his mother's ideal of justice with the revolutionary tradition and believe in the mission of France (rather than of ancient Israel) to bring justice into the world.[17]

At an early age, Léon seemed destined to be the intellectual of the family. He displayed his quick intelligence by learning to read at the same time as his elder brother Lucien, looking over his mother's shoulder as she gave the first lessons.[18] He was indeed "something of a child prodigy"—not in any specific talent but in general intelligence—and willful and difficult on occasion but possessing a charm that made up for his offenses.[19] His early school career, as the family expected, was a marked success. While still in the early grades, Blum was chosen as one of a deputation of Paris schoolboys that visited Victor Hugo on his eightieth birthday and recited a poem of honor, composed for the occasion by the eminent Parnassian Catulle Mendès:

> We are the little thrushes,
> The warblers of mischievous flight,
> Who come to sing our songs
> To the eagle.[20]

Three years later, at the time of Hugo's death in 1885, Blum was one of the schoolboys who carried wreaths in the funeral procession which followed the bizarre night of national mourning.

After beginning his formal studies in an *école communale* near

home, Blum entered the secondary system at the lycée Charlemagne on the rue Saint-Antoine in 1882.[21] About the same time
that he thus embarked on a serious academic program, the family
was able to move from its constricted quarters on the rue Saint-
Denis to the nearby but spacious and tree-lined boulevard Sebas-
topol.[22] The lycées were the only route to the liberal professions in
France, and his attendance marked the young man as a member, or
at least prospective member, of the dominant bourgeoisie. In spite
of the system of state scholarships, few families outside the middle
class could afford to send their sons to the lycées, which, though
subsidized, were not free.

Blum's lycée experience formed the link between his home life
and the quite different circles of French intellectual society, but the
gulf which separated these spheres must not be exaggerated; his
life was not a leap from the ghetto to assimilation. His family had
several generations of necessarily gradual progress toward assimilation, but with Léon this assimilation was to be as complete as
possible. Indeed, it is somewhat misleading to speak of his assimilation for he had always felt himself totally French. Only later did
Blum become conscious of his Jewishness, which, as we shall see,
served only to complement and enlarge his Frenchness. These
qualifications understood, the lycée served as the instrument of his
introduction into French society.

The traditional education which Blum received at the lycée
Charlemagne (and elsewhere) was also a vital intellectual experience. His quick intelligence and wide curiosity soaked up the
culture of past French generations. His home did not stand in the
way of this discovery—indeed, it pushed him outward—but it did
not have the kind of intellectual stimulus that was so advantageous
for some of Blum's contemporaries, such as Elie and Daniel
Halévy, whose home was almost a museum of French culture, or
Maxime Leroy, whose father was a music critic and friend of
Wagner and whose library furnished innumerable volumes of
Sainte-Beuve and Henri de Saint-Simon for the young man's
nourishment.[23] The lycée gave Blum the opportunity to compete
with his more advantaged contemporaries, for which he was grateful. Later, it seemed to him that the lycée came closest to realizing
the ideals of French democracy.[24] If admission was too narrowly
limited, still, within the lycées, it was merit and not family origin
that counted.

The intellectual formation which the lycée imparted was naturally of great importance for a person who all his life, even in politics, was an intellectual. Blum was an intellectual not merely in the sense of a person who earns his living with his brain rather than his hands but in the fuller sense of a person whose main interests are matters of the spirit, the intellect.[25] Like most capable young intellects, Blum would perhaps have pursued, with application and success, whatever subjects were set before him, whatever ideals were proposed as worthy of emulation. Yet, sooner or later, every mind needs to come to a consciousness of its own bent, and sometimes this means the rejection of all it has been taught. Fortunately for Blum, the slant of the late nineteenth-century lycée proved compatible with his deepest inclinations. In an atmosphere that treated the makers of France's literary heritage as heroes as great as kings or generals, Blum proposed to become a man of letters and make his own contribution to that heritage.

France has produced her share of pioneers in the physical and social sciences, but often, it seems, in spite of the orientation of its educational system. The lycée has long been committed to the ideal of the classical literary education. In Blum's schooldays, the compulsion to study Greek as well as Latin was somewhat relaxed, and though the mathematics baccalaureate was recognized, it had not gained equal status with the philosophy *bachot* as the key to higher education and/or government employment. The main emphasis of the curriculum remained literary, with French taking the place of honor and Latin following close behind. Blum found this stress on language and literature congenial, and in the competitions in each term his most consistent successes were achieved in these subjects. He was regularly at the head of his class at the lycée Charlemagne in French and Latin composition, and he did well in Greek and German (though he never acquired real mastery of them). His other major interest was history—especially French history, of course, but also the history of other countries. Mathematics and the natural sciences had a smaller place in the curriculum, and a still smaller place in his interests, but he often achieved more than passable marks in them. Because of the breadth of his abilities, Blum often won the "prize of excellence."[26]

The literary studies which Blum preferred dealt primarily with the art of composition and the reading and analysis of literary masterpieces. During his first two or three years at the lycée, grammar was studied, but never as a subject in itself; it was presented as no more than a prerequisite for self-expression and for understanding others. Simple composition and the memorization and recitation of verse also were part of the program in Blum's first year at the lycée, and the approved book of readings offered a sampling of La Fontaine, Fénelon, Buffon, and various nineteenth-century authors of prose and poetry.[27] The French system stressed a carefully measured increase of difficulty in the works studied and in composition, so that by the time he left the lycée Charlemagne (in 1888) Blum had received a thorough grounding in French literature.

Literary education always tends to concentrate on what are accepted as the eternal masterpieces of a language, with the attendant risk of labeling them "the classics"—the books that everybody talks about but would never read if not compelled. But the French were perhaps more successful than others in avoiding this pitfall. Part of this success was due to the nationally prescribed method of teaching literature, which endeavored to make clear, through the close study of carefully selected texts, just why some books should be considered great, and more deeply than most, Blum acquired the habit of looking critically at works of literature. He also developed concern for moral values in literature. French imaginative writers in all ages have tended to be moralists, and the secular education of the Third Republic was anxious (and not entirely out of fear of Catholic criticism) to inculcate a positive moral tone. School, therefore, reinforced the influence of Blum's home and linked his growing moral concern with his literary interests, which was to be of great importance in almost all of his mature literary work.

The greatest emphasis in French-language and Latin education was on composition, and Blum's teachers believed that practice in Latin composition would also benefit their pupils' French. Clear and precise self-expression was honored as a part of the national character, but the French realized that this was not hereditary and had to be taught. Blum, an exceptionally apt pupil, acquired a life-long devotion to clarity at the lycée, which sometimes led him to a conservative style, but the clarity of his own writing was never a cover for superficiality. At the same time, he acquired the ability to express himself with a sureness and lucidity that must have been .the envy of more than one lycée professor. When his first prose was published, during his twentieth year, Blum's style was already mature, already a sure instrument for the faithful expression of his thought.

His education also helped him decide what use to make of his blossoming literary ability by orienting him toward a combination of literary and philosophical studies. At that time, the final year of the lycée offered students two basic alternatives: the philosophy or the mathematics form. After completing the first part of the baccalaureate in literature in 1888, Blum moved across the Seine to the more celebrated lycée Henri IV, located behind the Pantheon, to pursue the philosophy course.[28] There, in a year of concentrated study, he was introduced to the Western philosophical tradition, from the pre-Socratics to the latest French schools of thought. Such a sweeping survey was necessarily less than profound, but it gave him a fund of knowledge that was useful in his literary career. More importantly, it helped him find his philosophical orientation.

The philosophers he encountered in the lycée Henri IV provided points of reference throughout his life, and he retained respect for his teachers, especially the young idealist Henry Michel, who subsequently became well known for his *L'idée de l'Etat*.[29] The philosophic mood of the late 1880s, among professors and students alike, was a revived form of idealism that was largely a reaction against nineteenth-century materialism and positivism, which had the prestige of modern science. Blum's schoolmates liked to think of themselves as Kantians, although, as a professor remarked to Blum, few of them read much (if any) of the work of the Königsberg philosopher. In this atmosphere, Blum too became an idealist—though of no particular school—and basically he remained one, although his later adherence to Marxism modified his idealism.

More valuable for Blum than any specific knowledge was the framework for self-examination and understanding that his studies provided. Like many of his contemporaries, he tried to understand the present rather than the past. Of necessity, his personal convictions were still vague, but his communion with the philosophers, like that with the literary masters, gave him the tools for building his convictions.

After his year at the lycée Henri IV (1888–89), Blum was successful in the second part of his baccalaureate examinations,[30] but no sooner was this hurdle surmounted (only 40 to 45 percent passed each year) than he undertook an even more difficult challenge.

18

It is likely that Blum transferred to the lycée Henri IV because of its record in preparing candidates for the entrance examinations to the *grandes écoles*, especially the Ecole Normale Supérieure, and after a year of post-baccalaureate studies at the lycée Henri IV, which offered such advanced classes, Blum confronted the fearsome entrance competition for the Ecole Normale and was admitted in 1890.[31] The competition for the two dozen–odd openings in the humanities section was one of the fiercest in France, so that many candidates put in years of additional study between unsuccessful attempts.[32] Blum's success, only a year after his baccalaureate, was a mark of exceptional intellectual accomplishment.

Unfortunately, it soon became clear that Blum was far from certain that the Ecole Normale represented the path he wanted to pursue. Because he had excelled at whatever he attempted, he had been able to defer this important self-interrogation, but now he could do so no longer. He seems to have been aware that the decision to attend the Ecole Normale had been made by those who knew him through his successes in the lycée. The misguided good will of families and teachers has often pushed bright but uncertain young men into paths they did not choose, and Blum may have felt that this was happening to him.[33] He felt a growing need to take the direction of his career into his own hands, but was he yet certain where to steer?

His first reactions seem to have been negative. The Ecole Normale was supposed to lead to a career in teaching (though some of its graduates pursued other paths), and he had decided that this career was not for him.[34] The possible reasons for this decision are many, but though he never made them clear the alternative path he chose sheds some light on them. That his decision was not clear-cut is attested by the method by which he carried it out: he allowed himself to fail twice in his examinations for the *licence* at the end of his first year, because of his lack of application.[35] The Ministry of Public Instruction required that students who did not pass this examination at the end of their first year be excluded from further study at the Ecole Normale, and the rule was not waived for Blum,[36] who was more relieved than aggrieved and apparently not chagrined by the first failure in a career of brilliant academic success. The pressure from without was off, and he could chart his course more freely. His relief was apparent in the mock funeral oration that Blum composed that summer and sent to René Berthelot.

(Extracts from *Le Petit Lannionais*)

Today, Thursday, the young man, M. Blum, whose suicide we announced in our number of yesterday, was buried. After M. René Berthelot, in the name of the deceased's personal friends, had uttered a few moving words on his premature death, M. Georges Perrot, member of the Institute and director of the Ecole Normale Supérieure (did we mention that M. Blum had belonged to the Ecole Normale?) made a speech:

"On August 11th, 1891, from Perros in the department of the Côtes du Nord, where I was holidaying with my daughter and my son-in-law, I wrote M. Blum a letter four pages long in which I seemed to forecast the sorrowful event we are here gathered to weep over. My extensive knowledge of human nature had allowed me not only to follow but to foresee the evolution of that impatient soul. At the time when I wrote to M. Blum I was, of course, unable to ask him to express to his family the share I was to take one day in its sorrow. It is a sad duty which I wish to fulfill in the first place. I will say to this weeping father, to the absent mother, this: 'Console yourselves. The memory of your son that is lost will not live in your hearts alone. He enjoyed the friendship of some, the esteem of many. Of course he had failed twice running in the *licence* examination and would doubtless have failed again in November. But let us not forget that he had been admitted to the Ecole, and that is a difficult examination. Despite the law on compulsory military service, the number of our candidates remains undiminished.'

"I will say frankly that I did not like M. Blum. He had entered our school with a certain reputation. But we had swiftly recognized that it was not justified. One must be very wary of these college reputations. I lost a very dear friend this year: Edouard Young. When he was with me at the lycée Charlemagne he was supposed to be a much better pupil than I. Yet I have had a more brilliant career than his, and, in addition, I have always taken care to prepare myself for a long existence by careful hygienic measures. For to live long is, in a certain sense, equivalent to being of higher value. It follows that M. Blum was not worth much. He had on the general spirit of the school a pernicious influence, though his high and mighty character and his disdainful manner should have rallied the sympathies of but few to him. This is neither the time nor the place to talk to you about the Review [*La Conque*], in the founding of which, last winter, he had a share. It was for suchlike futile amusements, for the pleasure of discussing with the supervisors, or merely that of affecting an ironical smile, that he neglected every serious pursuit.

"The truth is that he had too high an opinion of himself. I do not remember who it was told me that, *before getting his degree* (think of that!), he was positively enchanted with his own essays. Mr. Marthe had not been a week in the school (where we had admitted him in pious respect for the memory of his father), when he asked me: 'What is the name of that big lad who is so obviously pleased with himself?' There is no greater proof of feebleness of mind that the fact of admiring oneself, said Pascal, particularly at the Ecole Normale, where a young man can really find others worthy of comparison.

"This is what I never ceased telling him. People called him intelligent! Perhaps he might have understood if life had given him a few more warnings. But that is all over now. ..."

Editorial Note: The interesting passages from this funeral oration, which in reality has not yet been pronounced, are borrowed from a letter we have recently received from this eminent archaeologist.

Kindest regards,

LÉON B.[37]

The relentless self-awareness of the nineteen-year-old Blum had shown him that his vocation was not academic but literary.

Having decided to become a man of letters, his first step, like that of many others, was to prepare for the *licence ès lettres*. He realized, however, that his chances of earning a respectable living as a writer were slim indeed, whatever his talent. In the quarter century before 1914, only a handful of French authors were able to live from the proceeds of their art, and these few—Anatole France, for example—were forced into overproduction. For the vast majority of writers, journalism offered the only opportunity to live by writing. Such a path seems to have had no attraction for Blum, who perhaps aspired to greater security and a more bourgeois mode of life, but he also feared that his literary production would be harmed by too close an association with mercantile interests. Even later, when he became a part-time but nonetheless professional literary and (especially) drama critic, Blum made a virtue of necessity by insisting that a writer ought to make his living at something else. His generation was one of the last to include many writers who could live on the accumulated capital of their families and not worry about work or sales. This group included some of his friends and acquaintances—Gide and Proust, for example—but this advantage was not open to Blum.

Agreeing with Stendhal that the writer ought to find an occupation which would leave time for his literary activities, Blum was faced with a difficult choice, but he did not take long to make up his mind. Having determined on a literary career, he resolved to turn to law for his living, and in the fall of 1891 he entered both the Faculty of Law and the Faculty of Letters of the University of Paris. His choice was not unusual for a person in his position. Other writers had found that their classical literary education was a sound preparation for law studies, as they were conducted in France at that time. While it was mainly an expedient at first, Blum soon became fond of his work in the law and discovered that it provided satisfactions as strong as those gained in literature. Within three years he earned both his *licence ès lettres* and his *licence en droit*.[38]

Blum's determination to follow a literary career was less the product of his formal education than of his contact with other students at the lycées and the Ecole Normale. It is a commonplace observation—and like many clichés is basically true—that we learn as much outside the classroom as within and as much from our peers as from our professors. It is especially true that we form our estimates of ourselves, and often our ambitions, by comparison with our contemporaries. Blum was perhaps overly sensitive to the influence and ideas of those around him; but though he did not aspire to be a leader, he had an inner strength which prevented him from becoming anyone's disciple. Thus he was able to absorb a variety of influences while molding his own personality. As a literary critic, he was to discover that many writers hated to admit having been influenced by anyone else; but Blum, like Gide, recognized that no one escapes these influences and that men of the greatest individuality are often the freest in acknowledging the influence of others.

From a very early age, Blum had shown his sensitivity to those around him, and especially his sensitivity to their opinion of him. He also had an acute need to feel liked and loved, as his earliest published writings reveal. More than once he returned to this favorite anecdote, here put into the mouth of Goethe, which has a strong autobiographical ring:

Young Wolfgang [Mozart] was then ten years old. But he was already quite celebrated and many came out of curiosity to hear his concerts. He would begin to play only after he had first asked around the room: "Do you like me?" One fine day he was invited to play before the Court. He put the same question to the archduchesses.[39]

Although as a prodigy he could hardly be compared to Mozart, Blum at an early age knew the experience of being the center of adult attention and he felt the need to be reassured of its genuineness:

We have all passed, said Goethe, through that state of sensitivity, and, for a few of the most tender souls, it endures. When I was an adolescent, the desire often came to me to ask: "Do you like me?" of all those whose lives I felt penetrated, however little, into mine.[40]

Blum's attachment to his family was certainly reinforced by the knowledge that its affection was sincere.

This affection was an important compensation for the scholastic efforts that were demanded of him—a haven from the harshness of classroom discipline and the intense competition at the lycée. The young, especially, need such recompense for the premature pressure of French education, and Blum was no exception. When he first went to the lycée Charlemagne, he had not been an "intern"; his parents had settled him in a pension of the quarter which specialized in providing the "correct" atmosphere for lycée students. Its discipline and regimentation, apparently, were as severe as for interns, and Blum detested this from the start. He had to fear punishment if he did not excel and received little or no reward when he succeeded. He seems to have been the most promising pupil the director of the pension, the not-so-genial "Father" Kahn, had in his charge, and this gentleman tried to make Blum a *bête-à-concours* to bring honor (and more business) to his pension. Blum did not crack under the pressure—he had the ability and he succeeded—but he eventually rebelled and ran away from the pension. He was soon found, but refused to return.[41] After some time, his obstinacy prevailed and he was allowed to live at home during the rest of his lycée education. Later, when he attended the Ecole Normale, Blum was compelled, like the others, to live in the rather forbidding edifice that Romain Rolland called the "cloister on the rue d'Ulm," which was one of the things Blum disliked most about that brief experience.[42]

Blum probably needed the security his home and family provided, and his later strictures on the influence of the family hint that he had been more dependent than he wanted to admit. Blum was not emotionally dependent on his home for very long, but he was sensitive about it because his was an especially strong case of the common adolescent desire to be independent. The needs of his sensitive nature were increasingly met among his peers, and the opportunity for this independence and development was one of the by-products—and not the least important—of his lycée experience. The child's desire for affection took the form of a desire for friendship in the adolescent, and the young lycée student developed what must be considered a remarkable capacity for friendship and great skill in all the arts of friendship.[43]

From his schooldays on, Blum was an aggressive collector of friends and acquaintances, and he always had a large number of both. But he sought no satisfaction in numbers; it was quality that interested him—intellect, personality, talent, and sincerity. His outgoing, even aggressive personality was a product of genuine interest in others, as well as his need for friendship. His interest in others was twofold: learning through personal exchanges and observation and simply being useful to others. He was self-effacing in that he preferred to steer conversations to intellectual topics or discussions of the behavior of others, rather than discourse on his own experiences. This tendency was counterbalanced by his readiness to give his opinions on a variety of subjects. Like most Frenchmen, he doubtless enjoyed the stimulation of intellectual controversy, but he always deplored the acridity of literary debate.[44] His desire to be useful to others was certainly motivated in part by the desire to gain affection, but it also derived from a need to give expression to his own affections. He ran the risk of appearing patronizing, especially to a less self-assured, more tormented soul, such as Gide,[45] but most of his friends could not help but accept his obvious sincerity and interest.

Whatever personal interests may have been involved, Blum's affection for his friends was deeply genuine; however, he often displayed a certain "romantic" emotivity in his friendship. A friend of his, the poet Fernand Gregh, who admired Blum's lucid intelligence, also thought he was a highly emotional person.[46] Blum's emotivity was near, perhaps too near, the surface; if he wept freely at the death of a very close friend, tears might also come to his eyes upon meeting an old acquaintance after several years' separation.[47] To an unsympathetic person, it might have seemed that Blum demanded emotional stimulation—that he demanded more than he gave[48]—but those who were not misled by this nervous agitation, so often observed in French Jewish intellectuals, found the real depth of his affection. If Blum's friendship had a defect, it was his propensity to assume a sincerity comparable to his own in others. He was not undiscriminating, but once he had made up his mind his loyalty was strong and he was reluctant to believe the evidence when "friends" betrayed that loyalty.[49]

Blum's capacity for friendship was a significant factor in his intellectual development and ambitions. By comparing himself with his peers and sharing their experiences and enthusiasms, he became convinced of his literary vocation. His ambition took form in the milieu of the lycée Henri IV, where Blum met some other young Frenchmen who had already decided to become writers, the foremost of whom were Gide, Pierre Louys, and Valéry. Some of them had a more exclusive commitment to literature than Blum, who would never have the wholehearted devotion of Gide, but there can be little doubt that their firm convictions helped solidify his own.

The social-literary contacts of his two years at the lycée Henri IV were preserved through his passage to the Ecole Normale; indeed, they contributed a great deal to the social activities that diverted him from his studies. His new acquaintances at the Ecole Normale also broadened his social life considerably and brought him into close contact with a wider variety of minds and ambitions. These included the future philosophers Emile Chartier [Alain] and Léon Brunschvicq, the future historian Elie Halévy, and the future sociologist (and future director of the Ecole Normale) Célestin Bouglé.[50] His roommates, high up under the roofs of the école, were René Beaunier and René Berthelot. Berthelot was the son of the great chemist Marcellin Berthelot, and Blum and René's brother Philippe would long be friends and neighbors on the boulevard Montparnasse.[51] Blum had met René at the lycée Henri IV, and through the Berthelots he was introduced into some of the most distinguished intellectual circles. The Berthelots were related to Ernest Renan, whom Blum was to meet in the salon of Michel Bréal, the pioneering semanticist, shortly before Renan's death in 1892.

Blum's experience in the salons was not, however, purely intellectual and literary; during his year at the Ecole Normale, he became interested in girls. His schooling, of course, had been exclusively among males and the scholastic pressure was intense, so that his introduction to the salons and their young ladies undoubtedly contributed to his failure at the Ecole Normale, as he threw himself into a round of novel activities.[52] During the next three years (1891–94), at the Sorbonne, Blum learned to balance an intense social life with adequate attention to his studies, in which he made steady if slower progress. He seems to have become a man-about-town who was fond of dancing and adept at organizing balls (with the help of his youngest brother René, who was to become director of the Monte Carlo ballet). Blum's biographers, Fraser and Natanson, called these his "Little Bob" days, after a character in a popular novel by Gyp.[53] Blum appears to have been well liked by the young ladies of his social circles; he was "très ami de jeunes filles,"[54] and had many girl friends but as yet no serious romance. He cut an attractive figure in the salons and on the dance floor because of his grace and animation.

Not especially handsome, he was of average height and somewhat slender. His face, long and rather rectangular, was accentuated by a long slender nose and penetrating eyes behind a pince-nez. A strong chin and wide, full moustache compensated for his thick lips. Topped by slightly wavy dark hair, parted smartly on the left, his countenance, like that of many French Jews, had none of the so-called Semitic features. He was a careful dresser and somewhat vain about his appearance—in the way a Frenchman shocks an Anglo-Saxon. His voice was high and thin, but this did not prevent his becoming an effective orator, and his grace of movement gave him a certain effeminacy which led to his playing female roles in theatricals at the all-male lycées.[55] Acquaintances soon found this appearance deceiving, for there was nothing effeminate about his mind and personality.

Blum's somewhat belated adolescence brought the usual problems but without extremes or crises, as one may deduce from his early writings. He enjoyed the company of girls, and had no trouble attracting them, but soon he felt the proddings of physical passion and the vague, uncertain trouble this brings to the adolescent. Why, he asked himself in an early essay, couldn't women be sublimated, put off? Why couldn't there be simple friendship between the sexes? Couldn't there be *amitié* without the constant danger of its turning into *amour*?

Faced with these emotional problems of adolescence, Blum turned to literature for solutions—or, more precisely, to see more clearly into himself. Literature offered two paths to such self-knowledge: through reading, he could study the collective knowledge of others; through writing, he could transmute his problems from emotional questions into intellectual problems. The poets he had studied in class were his first authorities on emotion, and Blum found that he could gain a sort of catharsis by writing verse. In this he was similar to his literary friends, "these young men, of astonishing intellectual precocity, [who] are gauche when faced with intimate feelings and who hide their embarrassment behind a carefully chosen and delicate language."[56]

If the evidence of his early verse is as trustworthy as it seems, Blum's sentimental troubles were relatively mild, for his verses have a fin-de-siècle, adolescent weariness. Their emotional range is narrow, with no trace of profound passion. Sometimes they are pervaded by a timid and not wholly convincing nostalgia:

> The memories of times past remain in us.
> We have in vain prayed and wept on our knees,
> Their rebellious mirage cannot be exorcised.
>
> And it remains in us like a too strong perfume,
> Or like a halting refrain that one spells out. . . .
> —My God! Will we find repose in death?[57]

More often, this nostalgia viewed the past as happier than the present:

> Our hopes are tarnished; our desires are calmed,
> But let me, my eyes closed, see again in dreams,
> The days that have fled, the dead dreams, the old lies,
> And believe that once we loved each other.[58]

The lack of conviction in these lines betrays their bookish inspiration. Blum was quite incapable of living in the past, and it is doubtful that he ever spent much time longing for some lost love.[59]

Inspired by his Latin readings in Marcus Aurelius, he tried for a while to picture himself as a stoic. His last published verse was a set of three sonnets titled *Stoïcisme d'automne*, the first of which ran:

> It is Indian summer,
> It is the season of chrysanthemums.
> We must still our curses
> And smile on destiny's blows.

The rays in the changing sky
Form benevolent systems.
If I am sad, I who love you,
Roses will yet open in the morning.

The joyous universe abandons us.
The heavens laugh at our sadness,
The sun insults our tears.

But we must bend before things,
Deny to ourselves our pains,
Since one can still see roses.[60]

It is less stoicism that one finds in these "rather Sully-Prudhomme-like" verses[61] than a fundamental optimism, which was a dominant characteristic of Blum's personality. He always refused to be discouraged by the turn of events. At the time he wrote this sonnet, Blum had failed his *licence* examinations at the Ecole Normale, and then his first attempt at the entrance examinations for the Conseil d'Etat; but when a friend asked him whether he felt any chagrin, Blum replied that he felt none at all, "for everything that happens to me is for my own good."[62]

Blum's optimism did not lead him to live simply in hope of a better future; the philosophy of the ancient stoics reinforced his feeling that one must accept the present, with its joys as well as its pains. To turn away, to live on hope, was to risk living for an illusion.[63] To live wholly in the present was difficult, perhaps impossible, but he wanted to be strong enough to do so. Early in his career, therefore, Blum formed one of the psychological bases of his humanism. His effort to live in the present would shape the non-dogmatic character of his socialism, which reflected his refusal to put unlimited trust in the future. It was also to shape his literary career, in which he declined to emphasize the accomplishments of the past.

His refusal to follow an academic career was symptomatic of Blum's reluctance to become too deeply involved in the literature of the past. Without being scornful of it—indeed, loving much of it—he was most concerned with contemporary literature, with what young men of his own age were doing. He was deeply immersed in the aspirations of his friends, and an important part of his social life revolved around their literary interests. Through Gide and other school friends, Blum entered the circle of literary salons and aspiring reviews.

Gide and Louÿs were his entry into the salon of José-Maria de Heredia, the outstanding Parnassian poet, whose salon brought together all levels of the literary world; and this Cuban-born master of the French sonnet was especially friendly to young writers, whom he encouraged in their work without regard for their general rejection of his school. Also, he had three lovely daughters, around whom the young writers gathered in the drawing room at 11 bis rue Balzac.[64] It was a joyous circle, full of esprit. Marie, one of the daughters, organized a "secret society" known as the Académie Canaque, of which she was queen and Proust was perpetual secretary. Blum was among the members, along with Louÿs, Henri de Régnier, Valéry, Fernand Gregh, Ferdinand Hérold, and Philippe and Daniel Berthelot.[65] The members mimed their acceptance "speech" and Valéry's was regarded as the most elegant.

While they might thus make fun of the older generation, the young were also anxious to meet its leading representatives. For Blum, the most important contact he made in the Heredia study was Anatole France, who was twenty-eight years his senior and was to be one of his few idols among the older generation.[66] France, for his part, appears to have been attracted by Blum's intellect. Also, Blum became one of the familiars of the salon of Mme de Caillavet, where France regularly shone in the settings arranged for him by the mistress of the house.[67] The Caillavet salon, moreover, became a center for socialist politicians, especially Jaurès, thus adding a political to the literary attraction it exercised for Blum.

It was in these literary salons that Blum came to think of himself as a man of letters, committed to a literary life, and it was in the company of his contemporaries who shared this milieu that he made his literary debut. He was still studying at the Ecole Normale in the spring of 1891 when his first poem appeared in the pages of *La Conque. La Conque*, a slender poetry review of high aesthetic and typographic quality, was the brainchild of Pierre Louÿs, who, even before reaching his majority, had been anxious to establish himself as a literary figure.[68] With assistance from Gide, Valéry, and several members of the older generation, he had finally succeeded. In their prospectus, the young collaborators proudly announced that "*La Conque* will have only twelve numbers, each printed in one hundred numbered copies on deluxe paper. It will be neither continued nor reprinted."[69] The most promising poet revealed by *La Conque* was Valéry, who was already an accomplished artist.

As for Blum, his skill as a versifier was limited, but more than skill, he lacked inspiration and poetic imagination and temperament. Gide, who recognized his own shortcomings as a poet, called Blum "the least poetic brain I know" and, as far as creative potential was concerned, that verdict was not unjust.[70] Blum soon realized that he could not create poetic images and that his skills were better suited to prose. He nonetheless remained sensitive to the poetic qualities of others and not only a lover of verse but a good judge of it as well. If he could not be a poet, he did not regret that he had made the effort, and he considered his experience invaluable training in the discipline of language, making him a better writer of prose.[71]

La Conque was a distinct success and, as its founders anticipated, became a valued rarity. Its financial success was doubtless aided by the support it received from many established poets who contributed an unpublished piece to stand at the head of the eleven issues that appeared: Leconte de Lisle, Léon Dierx, Heredia, Mallarmé, Swinburne, Judith Gautier, Verlaine, Jean Moréas, Charles Morice, Maeterlinck, and Henri de Régnier. The variety of this group—Parnassians to symbolists—reveals much about the attitude of the young poets of *La Conque*. Their review, unlike many, had not been established to promote a particular aesthetic theory.[72] They did not care to be considered rebels, preferring to assert themselves through positive accomplishments rather than negative condemnations. Their tastes tended to be eclectic, guided only by the pursuit of beauty.

Blum was very much at home in this atmosphere, and when he entered the circle of *Le Banquet* the next year (1892), he joined a group whose interests were different but equally diverse. Less aesthetic and aristocratic than *La Conque* (it sold for one franc instead of ten), *Le Banquet* had been founded in March 1892 by Fernand Gregh, Robert Dreyfus, Jacques Bizet, his cousin Daniel Halévy, Proust, and others.[73] This group had originally formed at the lycée Condorcet, and thereafter met principally in the salon of Jacques's mother, Mme. Bizet-Strauss, the intelligent and witty widow of the composer of *Carmen*, whose charm attracted a large circle of writers, artists, and musicians.

Blum had met Gregh, Dreyfus, and Proust at the Sorbonne, where all of them were preparing for the *licence ès lettres*.[74] Dreyfus remembered a day when Blum interrogated him: "You seem to have an extraordinary friend, M. Marcel Proust. Everything that I've heard about him interests me very much. Couldn't you enlighten me even further so that I can grasp totally the originality of his nature, which must be quite exceptional?"[75] Dreyfus confessed that he didn't understand Proust fully—and it is doubtful that Blum ever did either. Proust found some of Blum's work for *Le Banquet* offensive, and Blum probably found Proust not serious enough. They did not become enemies, but neither were they friends. Blum's brother, René, would become much closer to Proust, though not one of his intimates. The circle of *Le Banquet* was sufficiently open to accommodate such diverse personalities as Blum and Proust.

Blum shared fully in the "social, political, historical, and intellectual curiosity"[76] of *Le Banquet* (whose offices were in the second story of the Passage Choiseul), and these contacts helped to broaden his intellectual and aesthetic interests. *Le Banquet* was very interested in foreign literature, and Robert Dreyfus, in particular, did much to invite French appreciation of the flourishing contemporary Scandinavian literature. Blum later had considerable admiration for at least its leading lights, such as Ibsen, Hamsun, and Björnson. German philosophy was another major interest of *Le Banquet*, and Blum may have been involved with René Berthelot in writing a spurious "Entretiens avec Schopenhauer" that Fernand Gregh, the editor, innocently published along with genuine excerpts from Nietzsche.[77] Blum's interest in foreign literature gave breadth to his literary outlook and helped counteract the provincialism that marked so many Parisian literary circles.

Shortly before the demise of *Le Banquet*, Blum had made the most important move of his literary career: in 1892 he began to contribute to the prominent review of the brothers Natanson, *La Revue blanche*,[78] where he was soon rejoined by most of the staff of *Le Banquet*. *La Revue blanche* was to be Blum's literary home for eight years, during which time his thought matured and he made himself widely known.

During the years 1891–94, Blum tested himself as poet, essayist, and *nouvelliste* in the pages of *La Conque*, *Le Banquet*, and *La Revue blanche*. Many of his emotional and intellectual preoccupations show clearly in these works—and they are basically the preoccupations of an intelligent and sensitive adolescent.[79]

Blum's first published prose appeared in *Le Banquet* in June 1892 under the title "Méditation sur le suicide d'un de mes amis." In this essay—in which, as Gregh wrote, "all of his acute lucidity can already be found"[80]—Blum compared the case of his (imaginary?) friend with Goethe's Werther, showing understanding and sympathy for the fatal decision. Despite the topic, there was no convincing emotion in Blum's treatment, which concluded with an idea that may well have come directly from his school exercises in Greek philosophy, for it echoed the words of the skeptic philosopher:

We are unhappy as thou, dear boy; but since nothing can tempt us, Nothingness, Death, and Eternal Repose do not tempt us more than the rest. And that is why we do not think of suicide.[81]

This was one of the very rare occasions on which he wrote of death—an exception to his preoccupation with life.

Blum's views of life, like his view of death, were usually developed through the medium of his literary culture rather than experience. In spite of his failure at the Ecole Normale, there had been no serious crisis in his life up to this time. The ordinary course of growing up furnished abundant challenges to the young man's understanding, and he was constantly engaged in interpreting his limited experience of life in the light of what he found in literature.[82] Typically, much of his effort was devoted to understanding his emerging emotions.

Blum's interrogation of his emotions toward the opposite sex, which he had begun with sentimental lyricism in *La Conque*, took a decisively different turn in *La Revue blanche*, where his vehicle was the short story. His lyrics were essentially expressions of feelings, however tepid, but his short stories were externalized observations on the working of love in young people. Their basic ideas may still have come from his own experience, but not necessarily, for they could also have come from observation of others. In any case, the stories were based on the description or interpretation of an emotional situation rather than the expression of a feeling.

In this early prose fiction, Blum discussed emotions with such lucidity that it is easy to forget he was handling topics that by their very nature tend to resist logical analysis and neat classification. He was by no means unaware of the power of the subconscious and the unpredictable, but he was trying to reduce emotions to manageable proportions. Perhaps only a weak passion would allow itself to be so reduced, but it seemed to Blum that the passions of his era were of that magnitude. One of his *nouvelles*, "Le livre de mes amies," has an epigram from Stendhal: "There are no longer any true passions in the nineteenth century. That's why it's so boring in France." The observation was valid for Blum, as well as for his contemporaries.

Blum's *nouvelles* faithfully reflected the hesitations, uncertainties, and melancholy of adolescent emotion. His themes ranged from the evocation of a past love, brought to mind by a dance ("A propos d'une anecdote sur la danse"[83]) to a description of the involutions of an *affaire manquée* ("La proie et l'ombre" and "Eliane, ou le regret"[84]) and a sympathetic portrayal of a young man ("Le livre de mes amies"[85]) who cannot make himself love a girl who is clearly in love with him (his solution, to become her lover, does not work out as he expected).

The framework of the short story led Blum to think more about the context of the emotions, about the social situation and its effects on individuals. A growing social concern was especially evident in his "Annie, ou les fiançailles d'argent,"[86] in which, while admitting that the grace of a *jeune fille* of thirteen might indeed inspire love, he excoriated the custom of engaging such girls to men past their teens and detailed the emotional evils of the lengthy engagements. His sympathy for the plight of these girls gave his narrative an excessively didactic tone, but the story was nonetheless skillfully handled. The ensemble of his short stories clearly indicates that Blum had the makings of a novelist, though not a great one. His incipient social consciousness and moralizing need not have stood in the way, for the French novelist has regularly been a moralist.[87] However, his concerns were to find different expression in the studies which led to his *Du mariage* of 1907, his fully mature analysis of the problems in relations between the sexes.

The emotions of young love were not the only ones that agitated the Sorbonne student, for Blum was engaged in the typical torment of trying to decide what to make of his life. This was not the same as choosing a career—though the two might be related—for the malaise persisted even after he elected to study literature and law.

33

It was a question of larger goals. He wanted to become immersed in as many facets of contemporary life, the life of his generation, as possible. Life without some higher purpose seemed to him somehow lacking in meaning. But he found that one does not simply say "I will have a purpose in life" and find all difficulties resolved, for purpose is a matter of the will and is not easily, if at all, created by the intellect.[88]

Blum's desire to "do something," his yearning for action, seemed to indicate that action was essential for happiness, and the pursuit of happiness was one of the constant motivations of Blum's life and thought—an aspect of his concern for the present. His deep-seated desire for happiness and, conversely, his inability to find suffering fruitful,[89] perhaps made him realize his lack of a poetic temperament. He found that this desire for happiness was incompatible with the pursuit of beauty, but he was not willing to relinquish either.[90] Characteristically, he refused this sort of clear-cut, logical either/or, and persisted in this refusal throughout his literary career. On occasion, however, he showed greater willingness to sacrifice art to happiness than vice versa. For a young man, he was an exceptional respecter of nuances, who realized that life could reconcile apparent opposites.

Characteristically also, his early prose, while it sometimes indulged in first-person reverie, sought the form of the dialogue. Blum's fictional interlocutors often discussed conflicting points of view without resolving their disagreements, and without the author's weighting one side or the other. Dialogue enabled Blum to voice the conflicting opinions within himself and, in a sense, reconcile them by expressing them simultaneously. His respect for nuances made it difficult to commit himself to any course of action, even when action seemed the source of happiness; as an intellectual, he could find too many objections. As Gide wrote in his journal in 1890: "Léon Blum cannot make up his mind; he seeks, he gropes; he has too much intelligence and not enough individuality."[91]

Blum found a kindred spirit in the hero of Disraeli's *Lothair*:

There it is proved how a young man of the happiest character can find action distasteful, both because his intelligence is real, and because action is too easy for him. And yet who knows! Perhaps without action no happiness is possible, as the Princess of Tivoli affirmed to Lothair one night. Perhaps it is only in action, in precipitate and feverish action, that one can lose the consciousness of action.[92]

Some of Blum's generation seemed to find value in action for its own sake, but such persons were more common in the preceding and following generations. For the generation of 1890, which felt that the world had stagnated and that the times called for new deeds, the temptation to idolize action was strong. A young man of Blum's aesthetic sensitivity could not help but prefer the example of Julien Sorel and Fabrice del Dongo to that of Lothair. The cultists of Stendhal, led by Maurice Barrès and Paul Bourget, professed to find this romantic novelist a preacher of action and force who would inspire the younger generation.

Although he later rejected this view of Stendhal, Blum was strongly influenced by Barrès and looked upon him as an elder brother, guide, and personal friend. He absorbed much of Barrès's *culte du moi*, the anarchistic individualism which he also found in the novels of Disraeli and Georges Clemenceau and which appealed to the intellectual in him. His inclination toward anarchism was reinforced by a variety of anarchists in the milieu of *La Revue blanche*, the most prominent of whom was the managing editor, Félix Fénéon.[93] But despite his sympathy for these individualists, Blum never convinced himself of the virtue of action for action's sake, and he persisted in looking for a better purpose to which he could devote his desire for action.

This desire was not yet oriented toward concern for society; Blum was still seeking paths of action which would lead to full self-realization, to the best use of his capabilities. Once he had forgone his more or less blind plodding along the well-worn academic path, he began a conscious experimentation—in school and out—to develop his self-knowledge. His awareness enabled him to come to rapid decisions about his literary career, and he soon realized that he had little if any potential as a poet. He saw that his mind could not be utilized artistically, as a means of evoking feeling in others, but rather that its value lay in its ability to manipulate ideas and facts. Despite some promise as a short story writer or novelist, he knew that his powers of observation were not matched by powers of creation or re-creation.

If he could not create literature, he could still understand and enjoy it, and perhaps communicate this to others. Blum tested this ability in a pair of lengthy critiques in *La Revue blanche* on Anatole France and Paul Bourget and in another critique in *Mercure de France* (his only contribution to *Mercure*) on Jules

Renard. The response must have convinced Blum that here, at last, he had found the literary vocation for which he had been groping; and France and Renard were enthusiastic about his talent. Blum and France were already acquainted, and now his article led to a lasting friendship with Renard, based on mutual admiration.[94] This, clearly, was a path to prominence in the literary world.

Blum then created a short-lived column titled "Les revues" for *La Revue blanche* while waiting for an opening to become a critic on a regular basis. Though he used this column for a slashing attack on *La Revue des deux mondes*, it did not offer the kind of contact with current literature that he was seeking. Moreover, he was discovering that his critical and analytic intelligence was well adapted to his law studies, that a dual career in law and literature was definitely in accord with his basic talent—and in accord with his interests, too, for Blum found that the law dealt with ideas and problems of the greatest relevance for contemporary society—from a quite different angle than that of the creative writer, to be sure, but in an organized fashion that complemented the more disorderly inspiration of literature.

Along with feeling that the law could be more than a means of earning a living, Blum realized that it was a career in which fulfillment took time, which demanded an apprenticeship. While serving this apprenticeship in the obscurity of the lower ranks of the Conseil d'Etat, he was quickly to make his reputation as a critic. And in spite of the growing complexity of his life, he was to maintain a balance in his varied activities that permitted the full employment of his capabilities.

CHAPTER TWO

THE LITERARY CRITIC
OF
LA REVUE BLANCHE

TO FULLY UNDERSTAND LEON BLUM, it is necessary to study the whole of his work as a literary critic for *La Revue blanche.* Even the casual reader must notice the intelligence displayed in his reviews, his ability to find the essential points and convey his understanding with clarity, but the casual reader tends to miss the depth of his commitment to literature and may not understand that it was not merely an intellectual game for Blum. A more attentive view, but one limited to the highlights of Blum's work, has led historians to concentrate on the ideas he expounded or the qualities which can be deduced from his style and to miss what can be learned from watching him at work fortnight by fortnight. The result is that most recent observers have missed the spirit of his reviewing, and this failure is important because the spirit that guided his critical work also characterized his thinking more generally.[1] The basic ingredients of that spirit were an insistence on sincerity and a commitment to the present. Underlying these was the motive force of Blum's striving for self-knowledge as a means to self-development.

Nowhere better than in his career as a literary critic can one see Blum's integration into his age and his society. *La Revue blanche* attracted him by its openness to the diverse intellectual and social currents of the age and because it belonged to his generation. We can see that he shared many current fashions, such as the reaction against scientistic positivism, but he reacted in a personal way, shunning dogmatic coteries. He was especially compatible with one of the trends in literary criticism, critical impressionism, but he conformed to it very consciously, committing himself not to any literary theory or theory of criticism but to the appreciation and encouragement of literature, and especially the work of his peers.

If Blum fell short of being the ideal critic (someone sought but never found by literary historians and authors), he nonetheless understood the possibilities of criticism and its place in literature. His weakness as a critic did not stem from excessive intellectualism but from excessive modesty and restraint in judgments. In his work as a critic, Blum emerges as a realist, in love with imaginative fiction but aware of its limitations. His sense of the possible, which combined the desire to see progress in the arts and a refusal to raise utopian expectations, found its equilibrium in these years. If the youth may be said to have had a skeptical intelligence, the maturing critic learned to avoid the extremes of Renanian skepticism. Blum raised his sights high, but he learned to control his disappointment and anger when men did not live up to his aspirations. But he knew that sights had to be kept high if man was to progress.

For Blum, this observation applied not only to the evolution of societies but was part of his self-understanding. He was determined to find (and stretch) the limits of his abilities, and in pursuing a career as a literary critic simultaneously with a career on the Conseil d'Etat, he was following what he believed was a rationally conceived course of self-development. He knew that he ran a risk of not being taken seriously in either career, but he was certain that the benefits outweighed the risks and confident that he could show his worth in both fields. The French, it seemed to him, believed that every individual had a dominant faculty and therefore could not be good in more than one *métier*,[2] but he had seen men who demonstrated that they could pursue diverse interests with skill and success—Clemenceau and Disraeli were once again his models— and he felt he could do so too. The very diversity of his interests urged him to make the attempt.

Blum realized very early that the complexity of modern society creates a problem of specialization. He knew that to refuse to specialize—to attempt to preserve, at all costs, the impulse to universal knowledge—was to risk wasting one's life in pursuit of a chimera.[3] But he also refused to accept the conclusion that the only choice was to specialize. This, perhaps, was one reason why he rejected an academic career, and was undoubtedly a reason why a career in science had no appeal for him. To make a contribution, one had to become too narrow. Blum's concession was to recognize that a certain concentration of energy was necessary, and was possible, if one acquired rational self-knowledge. He had to believe in the possibility of a viable compromise between general interests and specialized knowledge. He was not afraid of being called a dilettante, but he did not mean to waste his life and talents.

The self-knowledge needed for a fruitful direction of his energies had long been his goal, and like many of his generation he had been inspired by the *culte du moi* of Maurice Barrès. There was, however, a certain sterility in Barrès's young heroes, a certain narcissism which Blum sought to avoid. Self-knowledge for Blum was not an end in itself but a necessary means toward self-development. Without self-knowledge there could be no rational choice of the paths to pursue, which faculties to cultivate and which to neglect. Rational self-cultivation had a profound appeal for Blum:

One should not grow randomly; it is necessary to have conceived a rational plan, or more simply, to have acquired a rational knowledge of oneself. One can then mature logically, according to the different aspects one has chosen.[4]

Only by rational choice was it possible to "attain the most complete unfolding . . . of oneself."[5] To develop as much of one's potential as possible was a moral imperative for Blum, not a question of amusing oneself. While his main livelihood was the law, he did not merely dabble in literature, he was a professional. He knew that both literature and the law required a professional commitment to effort and excellence, and in all his endeavors Blum was satisfied only with his best.

Blum's distaste for specialization led him to choose careers which were compatible with the breadth of his interests. In his literary career, therefore, criticism was not entirely the negative product of his discovery of his lack of a poetic or creative vocation. On the positive side, criticism permitted him to nourish his wide interests, and within this field he chose to concentrate on the novel, which, like history, treats every aspect of human activity. Even more than history, it can explore the individual as well as the general and enter the realms of psychology and ethics, which deeply interested Blum. He was occasionally to step outside his rubric to review works of nonfiction, but mostly he found abundant material within the novel to satisfy his interest in man and society.

The novelist, Blum knew, is often deeply immersed in the intellectual and moral issues of his time and is often a sensitive interpreter, both consciously and unconsciously, of its problems, and Blum, by reviewing current novels, could maintain contact with the intellectual currents. French critics had seldom limited themselves to the consideration of aesthetic problems. Like many novelists, the critics were often moralists, and it was not unusual for a critic to touch on many fields of thought. The example of Hippolyte Taine shows the broad intellectual range, originality, and influence a critic might have.

Whatever their ability, most critics depended on other occupations for their livelihoods. Typically, they were affiliated with one or more periodicals, including newspapers and literary reviews. Their outlets were rather numerous in the 1890s, as literature and literary criticism received more space in the periodical press than they do today. This was especially true in the popular press, but Blum was not interested so much in the size as in the quality of the audience he might reach. He was most anxious to communicate with his own generation, to continue to move in the same milieu he had known when he entered the somewhat exclusive circles of *La Conque* and *Le Banquet*. He had already begun to write for *La Revue blanche* before he decided to devote himself to criticism, and he had found himself at home there when the opportunity arose to become its critic. The critic of novels for *La Revue blanche*, Lucien Muhlfeld, had long felt uncomfortable in the youthful enthusiasm of that review, and when his inclination was compounded by failing health, he decided to step down. Blum, who had been writing criticism since 1894, was ready to replace Muhlfeld in 1896.

Each of the "little magazines" or reviews in Paris in the 1890s had its particular atmosphere, which was formed by the personality and literary views of its editors and the style and interests of its contributors. Small, independent reviews were the usual outlet for the younger generation and all who were striving for recognition. Thus ambition generally made these reviews anti-establishment, lively, combative, and anything but stuffy, though often overly earnest. Another characteristic was their evanescence: if one of them survived for a year, it could be considered a success; but few of them did.[6] *La Revue blanche*, which had been in existence for fourteen years, was exceptionally successful. Only *Mercure de France*, a new review with an old name, had more longevity. During the 1890s, these two were the most important of the "young," independent literary reviews, though their relatively long lives and larger circulations did not, of course, rival those of such long-established and staid periodicals as *La Revue des deux mondes* or *Journal des debats*.

The milieu of *La Revue blanche* was especially lively, partly because of its location near the area known as the *Boulevard*. The *Boulevard*, running from the working-class districts in the east to the lower slopes of Montmartre, was the center of Parisian theater and café life, the idle elegance that gave pre–World War I Paris its reputation as the gayest, most frivolous capital. The *boulevardier* who flourished in this period no longer survives, even in the romanticized nostalgia of Hollywood, whose pictures of that lost world ignored its undertones of frustration and bitterness, the acrid wit born of the clash of ambition and wealth. *La Revue blanche* was by no means simply a journal of the *Boulevard* but the hubbub of the café set's often purposeless vitality penetrated its offices.

This influence was enough to make the spirit of *La Revue blanche* very different from that of its Left Bank rival, *Mercure*. In the university-dominated atmosphere of the Latin Quarter, *Mercure* was inevitably more "serious," approaching literature with reverence and earnestness, and not so attracted by the social aspects of the literary life. Left Bank and Right Bank, inevitably, tended to look down on each other, to mock each other's concept of the literary career. This intellectual geography did not, however, create an unbridgeable gulf, and the daily life of many writers, like Blum's, spanned the river both physically and intellectually.

There was no lack of serious devotion to literature in the milieu of *La Revue blanche*, but this devotion was not felt to be incompatible with the pleasures of society. As a member of the inner circle reflected many years later, it was a very agreeable life.[7] Blum certainly enjoyed the social side of his literary life and was, from his debut, a member of the inner circle, which included Thadée and Alfred Natanson, Charles Leclercq, Muhlfeld (before his departure), Tristan Bernard, Romain Coolus, Jean Schopfer, and

Pierre Veber.[8] The offices of the review were a daily meeting place, but there were also more or less regular "evenings" at the apartments of Schopfer or Thadée Natanson. The Natanson salon became a favorite gathering place especially after Thadée's marriage to the celebrated teenage beauty Misia Godebska (better known, after her next husband, as Misia Sert). Misia helped attract a diversified literary crowd, which at various times brought together, in addition to the above, Stéphane Mallarmé, Paul Valéry, Félix Fénéon, Henri Ghéon, Jules Renard, Henri de Régnier, Octave Mirbeau, Alfred Jarry, Ernest La Jeunesse, and Colette and her husband Willy.[9]

Another great attraction of *La Revue blanche* was that it also brought together many artists and musicians. Considerable space in the review was devoted to art and music criticism, largely because of the efforts of Thadée Natanson, and the review was in close touch with many artistic currents of the decade.[10] Illustrations were frequently contributed by Pierre Bonnard, Félix Valloton, Edouard Vuillard, and Henri de Toulouse-Lautrec. The stunted, acid-tongued Toulouse-Lautrec was a familiar figure in the editorial offices, and a number of his justly celebrated lithographs advertised *La Revue blanche.*

Appreciative of art, Blum and his wife, whom he married in 1896, were even more deeply interested in contemporary music, and one can imagine their interest in the salons where they could see—and hear—Debussy, Ravel, and Reynaldo Hahn. All three were composers whose music marked a return to the "scale" of the salon, where they often played their latest compositions. Debussy became the regular music critic of *La Revue blanche*—one of the rare composers who could write about music almost as well as he created it. Many of Blum's friends and acquaintances in the circle of *La Revue blanche* continued to populate his social life long after he left the review. Perhaps the longest-lasting friendships from those years were with humorist Tristan Bernard and pianist Alfred Cortot (who married a cousin of Blum's wife). During the construction of their apartment on the boulevard Montparnasse (which they were to inhabit for many years), the Blums lived in the same building (on the boulevard Saint-Michel) as the Cortots. They often spent summer vacations together, renting a house in the country near Paris or at the seashore. Cortot became a celebrated interpreter of Chopin and a member of one of the century's great trios, with violinist Jacques Thibaud and cellist Pablo Casals. Thus Blum became familiar with many of the leading artists of his day.[11]

The companionship of artists and musicians was precious to Blum, not simply because of his wide cultural interests but also because friendship with them was not complicated by professional jealousy and sensitivity. As a critic, Blum could seldom be certain of the genuine friendship of authors, and on one occasion he was even moved to print a lament on the rarity of true *amitié* in the literary world. Blum had genuine friends, however, and he himself seems to have been free of professional jealousy: his need to be liked and admired did not demand exclusiveness. But however sensitive he may have been to the social tensions of the literary world, he found its life stimulating and rewarding.

Blum's eclecticism enabled him to become an outstanding, perhaps *the* outstanding, representative of both the spirit of *La Revue blanche* and the spirit of his age. He felt especially at home in the review's atmosphere because he did not have to commit himself to a particular literary school in order to have an outlet for his thought. With his aversion to doctrines and dogmas, he had the opportunity to pursue his personal inclinations of taste and thought without worrying about an editorial "line." The first condition of honest criticism, he always thought, was freedom, and he wondered whether anonymity might not also be necessary.[12]

The eclecticism of *La Revue blanche* was perhaps its greatest strength, but this could also prove a weakness in the long run if it could not supply the missionary fervor to keep the review alive in difficult straits.[13] The variety of the social circle of the review was indicative of the variety of literary positions that were welcomed in its pages. During its career, the review spanned all the major literary movements, from symbolism to surrealism, but never devoted itself to an exclusive presentation. From its beginning, it was proud to present the works of Mallarmé and Verlaine, but it did not succumb to the cult of Mallarmé, which reigned in some circles. The symbolists, in general, had a large place in its pages, but it never became a symbolist organ in the way that *Mercure de France* did. The literary eclecticism of *La Revue blanche* made it exceptionally representative, and probably no other journal offers the student of this period such a comprehensive literary picture.

The variety of *La Revue blanche* stemmed in part from the fact that it was the most cosmopolitan of the young reviews. It dis-

played exceptional interest in foreign literature and helped contribute to the vogue of Russian, Scandinavian, and Italian works in
France during the 1890s. Even though conservatives had helped
launch this interest (Vogüé's *Le roman russe* was the most influential), admiration for foreign writers never became well established
in France, and the nationalist revival of 1905 vigorously attacked all
foreign influences in French literature.

Blum, like many of his friends, had developed an interest in
foreign literature while in school, and the circle of *Le Banquet* had
included several enthusiasts of foreign literature. Throughout his
career as a critic, Blum showed a generous (if somewhat shallow)
enthusiasm for the masters of foreign literature, and for some of
the lesser figures as well, which enabled him to keep the work of
his countrymen in critical perspective. He even had the audacity to
recognize Tolstoy and Ibsen as greater than any living French
writers. However, this interest was little more than curiosity; nor
did Blum acquire a profound personal knowledge of foreign
literature. In spite of his exceptional memory and talents, he never
mastered a modern foreign language, and was embarrassed by his
lack of aptitude.[14] Thus when he became an admirer of Jane Austen,
it was through reading the translation of *Northanger Abbey* which
appeared in *La Revue blanche*. Despite these limitations, his
enthusiasm for foreign writers was well informed and in only a few
instances—such as that of Gabriele d'Annunzio—would it seem
strange today.

Its literary cosmopolitanism, which was one of the distinctive
features of *La Revue blanche*, was in part a product of the cosmopolitanism of its circle and its origins. The review had begun in
Brussels as a Franco-Belgian effort but had not been especially
successful until it moved to Paris (in 1891), where its publication
was taken over by the three Natanson brothers, Polish Jews who
had brought their family fortune to Paris and become thoroughly
Parisian.[15] *La Revue blanche* thereupon became more or less a
center for young Jewish writers, but not exclusively, for less than
half of its contributors were Jews.[16] Nor was there anything specifically Jewish about its orientation, because all the Jews in its
social circle were, like Blum, highly assimilated.[17] It would seem,
however, that this Jewish element strongly contributed to making
the atmosphere more cosmopolitan than that of most French
reviews.

There were other aspects to the originality and distinctiveness of *La Revue blanche* as a literary review in which Blum had a part. The proximity of the *Boulevard* was most apparent in the humor of the review, which had a biting edge and an irreverent, mocking tone (that special French flavor one finds today in *Le Canard enchaîné*). Despite its ephemeral, topical wit, the review had at least two humorists—Jules Renard and Tristan Bernard—who produced work of an enduring quality. Both were good friends of Blum, who admired their wit, but Renard's oft-quoted remark (in his *Journal*) that Blum was totally lacking in wit was manifestly unfair. Blum was not a humorist, but his sense of humor was sufficiently appreciated by his colleagues that he was published in the humor columns of *La Revue blanche*, which were edited by Bernard and Romain Coolus. Also, some years later, Blum was a member of the judging committee for a humor contest conducted by the theatrical daily *Comoedia*.

Even more original than its wit was the interest of the review in sports. The later decades of the nineteenth century witnessed an unprecedented enthusiasm for sports among all levels of French society, and the contributions of Baron Pierre de Coubertin to the founding of the modern Olympic Games are well known. Less well known is the growth of sports among the populace as a result of increased leisure and such developments as the mass-produced bicycle. Cycling became immensely popular, and Blum and many of his friends cycled for exercise and recreation. Blum's most important exercise, however, and the one that was most popular in literary circles, was fencing. Blum took fencing lessons regularly, perhaps partly as a precaution, as it was not uncommon for critics to be involved in duels.

On the other hand, Blum's greatest expertise was the judging of horses, which he put to literary use by collaborating with Tristan Bernard (who managed a bicycle-racing track on the outskirts of Paris) and producing an intermittent sports chronicle of undeniable elegance and *savoir-faire* for *La Revue blanche*. It is not possible to tell how much of the writing is Blum's, but some of the column's philosophical tone must have come from him, to judge from an essay on horse-racing he published later. Interestingly, he justified this apparently useless sport in pseudo-Darwinian terms of the virtues of struggle—one of his rare instances of the influence of social Darwinism. While the sports column was only a brief diversion for Blum, it is another evidence of his total integration into his milieu; his interest in sports was permanent.

It was, of course, the intellectual milieu that mattered most to Blum, but it is important to remember that he was a man of his society in all its aspects. Although his literary and social activities centered on *La Revue blanche*, he was in close touch with wider currents of opinion. With his sensitivity to the spirit of his age, Blum accumulated an important fund of attitudes and ideas that he brought to his work as a critic. These intellectual attitudes were probably more important than any specific ideas, for it was an age that was struggling to reorient itself toward the world. The exact nature and significance of the intellectual epoch of the 1890s are still in dispute among scholars, but, as even its contemporaries saw, it was an age of change and ferment that was deeply aware of the dissolution of old certainties and the struggle of new certainties to be born. There was little agreement about the "wave of the future."

These uncertainties of philosophy, of *Weltanschauung*, had an upsetting impact on literature. During the nineteenth century, literature was increasingly influenced by the growing prestige of the natural sciences and attempted, like most other intellectual endeavors, to appropriate some of that prestige. Two outstanding examples of this propensity were the critical theories propounded by Taine (but often honored in the breach)[18] and the naturalistic credo of Emile Zola and the Goncourts, who were especially influenced by the importance of genetics and by Darwinism. The progress of biological knowledge, however, seemed to reinstate the irrational element in man and nature, and thus science—the method of thought most clearly born of rationalism—seemed to undermine its own philosophical bases.

The 1890s thus experienced a full-blown—but not universal or triumphant—reaction against the dominance of science over intellectual life, which was certainly, in part, a justified rejection of the simplistic faith in the power of science of some of its disciples. This reaction, naturally, went too far, as some began to speak (with Ferdinand Brunetière) of the "bankruptcy of science."[19] The revived interest in the irrational did not, however, follow Brunetière into traditionalist channels, for when Ernest Lavisse observed the younger generation's "nostalgia for the divine," he saw that it often remained apart from formal religion.[20]

Biological vitalism found its broadest philosophical expression in the work of Henri Bergson, who tried to give the sanction of philosophy to the indeterminate, the felt, and the alogical. Bergson's influence and fame spread with great rapidity; indeed, Blum felt that it had been dominant at the École Normale when he was there in 1890.[21]

It is a commonplace to observe that the influence of Bergson has been exaggerated, but many, and among them Blum, felt that Bergson embodied the prevalent philosophic spirit of the period before 1914. Blum himself was deeply moved by the appeal of the "open universe," and Bergson typified for Blum his own skepticism about the extreme claims of science and his own distaste for the dogmatic and the certain. But Blum could not follow Bergson very far in the latter's long march toward Christianity, for while Blum's sensitivity made him share much of the emotivity of his milieu, his rationalism could not yield to dogma.

Blum realized that the excesses of nineteenth-century positivism did not undermine the validity of science as a means of comprehending the natural world, and his reservations about the powers of science did not diminish his commitment to the primacy of human reason, although he recognized that it was not limitless. Blum had sufficient contact with the scientists of his generation to be aware that they did not view their disciplines as omnipotent or themselves as omnicompetent—that they, more than others, were aware of the limitations of their knowledge and techniques. He saw that science gave no comfort to those who expected it to bring about a renovation of society. Science could put nature at the service of man but could not determine whether it would be used for good or ill; this was a moral question that was beyond its reach.

Blum was especially antagonistic to the attempt to bring science into literature. Art, he would argue, thrives on the uncertain, the unfixed, and thus is not compatible with the mathematical rigor of science.[22] Literature was concerned with interpreting human life, and there were aspects of life which science did not, perhaps could not, clarify. Blum refused to connect the mystery he found in man with the immortality of the soul or a transcendental divinity: mystery was part of life itself. He thought of himself as a pantheist, and frequently referred to the pre-Socratics and Stoics with sympathy. His pantheistic metaphysics does not appear to have been systematically thought out, but it precluded troublesome questions about man's destiny; it enabled Blum to be a determined rationalist who did not close his eyes to the irrational in the human condition.

In the literary world, reaction against the scientific pretensions of the naturalists was not long in coming, and it varied from a withdrawal into traditionalist formalism (the Parnassians) to an esoteric cultism (the symbolists). Naturalism was discredited, though not exterminated, but no new outlook dominated the following age —and in the 1890s the competing literary schools proliferated, reinforced by the discovery that founding an aesthetic was a sure way to attract public attention. Many individuals, however, belonged to no particular school, or drifted from one to another. The literary keynote of this age was individualism, for a certain "romantic" confidence in one's own value seems essential to literary productivity, even if one's values are not highly individualistic. The youth of 1890, experiencing the perennial feeling of liberation from the errors of their elders, were searching for new truths within themselves.

Literary criticism was as confused as creative literature.[23] The reaction against scientism had led to a discrediting of critical approaches that claimed some sort of scientific validity, and especially the criticism of Taine. The "botanizing" approach of Sainte-Beuve, which neglected the writing to concentrate on the author, was also at a discount. Here, too, the rejection of earlier standards did not benefit a particular viewpoint but left the field open to a variety of approaches. In the University, the school of historical erudition led by Gustave Lanson was becoming dominant, but it had little effect on the literary scene. In the literary journals, there were still some flourishing dogmatists, led by the editor of *La Revue des deux mondes*, Ferdinand Brunetière, and by the less dogmatic but often equally wrong-headed Emile Faguet. These established literary powers were generally viewed with undisguised contempt by the younger generation. At the very beginning of his career as a critic, Blum excoriated Brunetière and Faguet with some of the most scathing words he was ever to use.

M. Faguet had formerly put together a rather agreeably odd style: awkward periods relieved just in time by pointed or bounding phrases. He thus balanced against one another the most affected qualities of the style of M. Lemaître and the most ponderous qualities of M. Brunetière. This process was responsible for the success of three volumes of literary studies—mediocre and even irritating volumes, however, because of their gauche effort to be profound, because of their dry and clumsy bad faith. Today the bounding phrases got lost somewhere along the way, and the study which M. Faguet has consecrated to M. Brunetière offers a fine massiveness of conceit and tedium. What distinguishes this generation of critics from the University—except for M. Lemaître—is the combination of the fine airs of philosophers they bestow on themselves and the incredible poverty of their philosophic intelligence.[24]

The pomposity of these self-appointed literary judges offended young authors and critics, who could see through their excessive pretensions.

The reason Blum excluded Jules Lemaître from his condemnation of "university critics" was that Lemaître, whatever his views, had renounced their pretensions to objectivity. The younger generation found the impressionism practiced by Lemaître and Anatole France more compatible with its own doubts about the possibility of objective criticism.[25] France carried the impressionist position to the extreme of denying that there could be any rapport whatever between the intent of the author and the experience of the reader. All the critic could legitimately do, he asserted, was describe what reading a book had made him think or feel—his impressions. Asserting that the value judgments of the critic had no validity, he attempted to avoid expressing his own. Criticism thus became an art in its own right, for which the book being criticized served merely as inspiration.[26] This sort of criticism could make pleasant and even profitable reading if the critic had the literary talent of a France or even a Lemaître, but it ran the risk of lacking purpose and becoming totally divorced from the literature that presumably was its object.

When he began his career as a critic, Blum thought through the impressionist position and made it his own, but he did so with a full realization of its weaknesses as well as its strengths. He expounded his position in the first of a series of ingenious dialogues published in *La Revue blanche* in 1894 and titled "Nouvelles conversations avec Eckermann." His "Goethe" first conceded the logical necessity of the impressionist position:

The judgment brought on a book will never have an objective value, and for a quite simple reason. It is because two men never read the same book. . . . The impression that a work of art makes is not immediate. It is mediate; it is indirect. What we perceive directly is a set of signs behind which we locate the thought of the writer. The aesthetic impression thus always resolves itself into a personal interpretation of these signs, in a sort of endless translation. And the thought of the author, as soon as it penetrates into us, becomes deformed there. It traverses the whole shadowland of the unconscious; it loses itself in a mass of past memories and personal emotions. It is transformed by contact with them. It is difficult for us to understand how much of ourselves we put into the books we read.[27]

Then, recognizing that the conclusions this implied for literary criticism could not be fully applied in practice, "Goethe" continued:

First imagine a critic who would fully adopt the conclusions we have just presented, a truly relativist critic. He would never give his opinion on a work, but only his emotions after reading a work. He would not attempt to determine what there was of good or of bad in this book, but simply what impressions, what memories, what reflections his reading had suggested. And that no one can ever do frankly, completely, not even Sainte-Beuve, not even France. France eradicates his judgments as much as he can, but he judges.[28]

Blum thus recognized that some element of judgment is inescapable in criticism, and therefore the critic must consciously face up to this necessity.

Blum not only felt that judgment was unavoidable but that it was legitimate. He recognized the primitive impulse of the critic to affirm his own value against that of the author. This impulse had been the failing of many critics, usually because it was unconscious, and authors (with a certain inconsistency) have regularly deplored it. But Blum insisted that it was a legitimate impulse because it helped the critic understand himself; by the self-conscious scrutiny of his reactions, he could extend his self-knowledge.[29] Thus Blum was able to see his work as a critic as a useful part of his self-development. As self-development, the critic's judgments acquired no external validity, and Blum interpreted impressionism as opposition to dogmatism, as a counsel to judge with moderation, modesty, and courtesy. He was determined not to be one of those "fault-finders and measurers of books by vocation and by *métier*, and if I may put it this way, hardened magistrates of letters, testy and cutting."[30]

Avoiding this danger, Blum was by and large able to escape the opposite danger of fearing to express strong opinions.[31] When he was afflicted with indecision, he was conscious of his reactions and sometimes made his indecision an explicit part of his review. He avoided, in particular, the paralysis of opinion which sometimes afflicted turn-of-the-century critics who were overly aware of the gross mistakes of critics of the past and feared to open themselves to posthumous ridicule. Blum's impressionism made him prefer to see the good in a work rather than the bad, and fear of ridicule was not decisive in this indulgence vis-à-vis his awareness of the limitations of criticism.

As a result of his impressionist position, Blum's reviews do not give us a systematic or even wholly consistent picture of his stand on literary and intellectual questions. Instead, we get an intimate and valuable picture of a mind at work amid the sort of intellectual problems it enjoys. This picture is not sharply defined, and observers can easily interpret it in different ways, according to their tastes and prejudices. Henri Peyre has justly observed that criticism is "an art in which technique and method count much less than the personality of the one who practices it."[32] One may or may not like the personality that emerges from Blum's literary criticism, but one cannot deny that it is interesting. His contemporaries could not agree whether that personality was bland or strong, but they had little difficulty concluding that its dominant characteristic was intelligence.

Intelligence is often, but wrongly, considered an abstract quality that can be divorced from other aspects of personality, and Blum has often been described as a cold and lucid intellectual rather than as the thinking human being he was. The intellectual Blum, who emerges as a literary critic, appears most distinctly as a man in search of self-understanding and struggling to preserve his moral and intellectual good faith. He did not so much affirm himself against authors as use his confrontations with them so as to see more clearly into himself. And his preoccupation with the new was another aspect of this search for self-knowledge. Blum was well schooled in the literature of previous generations and aware that he owed much of his understanding of human nature and himself to the classics, but he felt that the frontiers of that knowledge could be extended only in the present—by the ideas and sentiments of new generations.

It is largely because of Blum's concern for self-knowledge that his literary criticism yields such a valuable picture of his mind and personality. In the aspects of his criticism that will be examined in the following pages, many of the qualities that began to emerge in the schoolboy and that marked him throughout his later careers can be found. If the process of developing his self-understanding was to be successful, it had to be carried out with sincerity and self-awareness. Thus his effort to maintain his intellectual good faith—his sincerity—is one of the distinctive characteristics of Blum's work as a literary critic—perhaps the outstanding quality.[33]

"Good faith" has acquired almost mystical significance for French intellectuals through the influence of existentialism, but the term was somewhat less awesome in the 1890s. To be sure, good faith had something of the quality of a state of grace, but it also meant something more concrete, more practical. It meant not only the individual's responsibility to himself (or responsibility in the abstract) but also the responsibility to others that arises from one's activities. To Blum, in his function as literary critic, it often meant something as simple—and difficult—as being frank in one's opinions. To be honest with others, it was first necessary to learn to be honest with oneself. The critic, Blum thought, had to be aware of his own attitudes and prejudices to be able to put his reactions to a particular book into the proper context. He felt that the critic could express his thought with complete frankness only if he wrote his immediate impression of the work when he was most free of the vagaries of recollection and prejudice.[34] Blum's reviews show his special effort to make sure that he knew what he meant and that he expressed himself clearly.

His view of his obligations to readers and authors meant that it was not enough for him simply to record his impressions or deliver his opinions; he must also make his reasons for them clear. As for himself, he said, he would rather have an unfriendly review that gave explicit reasons than any number of vague eulogies.[35] He made a determined effort to live up to this ideal, moreover, and to say whether it was plot or style, substance or expression, that determined his judgment or aroused his sentiments. However, practical every-day demands sometimes made him depart from the ideal: when he reviewed eight novels in two and a half pages, he could not be very specific. Such brevity or compression sometimes led to an impressionism that was journalistic rather than philosophical and to the use of vague, abstract adjectives that did not satisfy his desire for clarity. The importance he ascribed to a book could not be measured by the amount of space he devoted to it, but certainly there was a correlation. A serious effort by an author generally evoked a corresponding effort by Blum to understand and to communicate his understanding.

Blum's efforts at good faith were most interestingly evident when his judgment was uncertain or his reactions were ambivalent. He did not try to disguise his uncertainty but, rather, confessed it in order to put his readers on guard. Sometimes, if he felt he had not adequately justified his opinion, he would say in effect: This is a purely personal impression, which I think is likely to be challenged and which I am not prepared to defend at length, but here it is and you may make of it whatever you wish.[36] Or, on occasion, he might sketch the pros and cons of a book, indicating that he had great difficulty deciding where his sentiments lay, and even end on a note of unresolved indecision. On other occasions he resorted to the favorite device of the critic who has no strong opinion—description. But description for its own sake was not common in his work; more often he used it to illustrate a point. Only rarely did Blum recount his subjective reactions, but when he did—as in his review of Kipling's *The Jungle Book*—his seriousness did not exclude intellectual playfulness and a sense of humor. His concern with good faith did not become a morbid obsession.

Good faith toward his readers required that Blum warn them of his prejudices or sympathies that might influence a particular review, and he seldom failed to warn them. Especially thorny for the young reviewer was the problem of reviewing a work by a friend or acquaintance. In such cases Blum was usually frank about his sympathy—which did not prevent his being critical—but he occasionally failed to mention that an author was a friend of his. He preferred to concentrate on the work, and he did not exhibit much interest in the author's biography, except to indicate whether the author was young or old or at the beginning or the height of his career[37]—factors he thought the critic should take into account.

More important for the critic's good faith was his possession of sufficient knowledge to situate a work in the context of its author's literary and intellectual development. Blum felt obliged to be familiar with all of an author's output, and he would sometimes confess a deficiency in this regard. And if it might influence a review, he would state his opinion of an author's previous work. On occasion, he used a new book as a pretext for reviewing the body of the author's work. His appreciation of a work also required situating it in relation to other works of the same genre, and Blum was not reticent in making comparisons. He also had a predilection for searching out influences, which he occasionally pushed to excess. Most writers objected to suggestions that they had undergone this or that influence, but the better ones, such as Gide, saw no reason to pretend they had not been influenced by others. Blum was sometimes rash in his attributions, but they were generally meant as compliments.

Frequently, Blum wrote with the author's reaction in mind, but never with the thought of gaining anything by flattery. Rather, he believed that the critic should furnish the author with an enlightened reaction to his work, which would help the author in his own self-appraisal. He did not mean thereby to dictate what authors should do, because he did not think that critics had the power to shape the course of literary development.[38] He might, however, influence an author, and therefore his good faith extended to authors as well as to readers: he must say exactly what he thought to both groups, doing his best to serve as both modest counsellor and encourager. He hoped, most of all, to stimulate authors to develop their talents, even to aid them in that effort with an outsider's view of their strengths and weaknesses. It was futile, he felt, for the critic to chastise: his limited efficacy might best be exerted through sympathy. As a result of his attitude toward the relations between critics and authors, Blum came to be regarded as an indulgent critic—"a benevolent judge, who, from indulgence or sympathy, touches only lightly on the faults of each, retaining, however, a very fine understanding of them."[39]

In retrospect, Blum's indulgence was so ample that he seems to have praised far too many authors, causing the modern reader to accuse him of not having been critical enough. There were times when he appeared to bend over backward to find something good to say, but this was a matter of deliberate policy, a result of the reserve with which he offered his literary opinions.[40] In part, it was also a matter of style, for he knew how to express his criticisms in such a way as to draw their barb. He could clothe criticism in encouragement, but without concealing its sting from the intended recipients.[41]

Blum could certainly be sharp when he thought this was called for. He believed the public had the right to demand that an author meet certain standards of style, labor, and honesty. He did not hesitate to take good writers to task when he thought they had been lazy—this was an unpardonable sin; one must always do one's best.[42] He thought that careless and inaccurate writing was exceedingly common,[43] but he was usually content to denounce careless practice in general, rather than specifically—a generosity for which more than one author should have been thankful. But when he decided to let the ax drop, it fell with a finely honed edge, and when he felt that the language had been outraged, his "executions," as Tristan Bernard has noted, were excruciating.[44] Blum usually reserved this treatment for mediocrity that had been sanctified by official honors: the Marquis de Vogüé and Henry Bordeaux were treated mercilessly, with an irony borrowed from the humor columns of *La Revue blanche.*[45]

On the other hand, he was often deliberately indulgent in his criticism of unknown young authors and tried hard to say something encouraging, if at all possible. One of the most striking features of his work for *La Revue blanche* was that, as a young critic and friend and colleague of young writers, he constantly sought to encourage the development and acceptance of new writers. After he became the regular critic, the amount of attention paid to young writers in the critical columns of *La Revue blanche* increased markedly.[46] In part, this emphasis followed from the natural affinity of the young for the young, and in part it followed from intellectual conviction. Blum constantly repeated that it was necessary to love life, and especially to love one's own generation. His commitment to the present was a categorical imperative, a good in itself, an attitude that made life worth living.[47] As a critic, Blum was very close to his time.[48]

Blum's orientation toward youth was also an expression of his fundamental optimism. In every aspect of life, the older generation was necessarily compromised by its adjustments to an imperfect world. The younger generation, on the other hand, had a purity that enabled one to be optimistic. But even when Blum asserted the "moral superiority" of the younger generation, his optimism was tinged with reserve and the knowledge that they would one day be the self-satisfied elders, that the young enthusiasts of today would become the staid members of the Academy.[49] Nevertheless, he asserted that each generation had the potential, even the duty, to create something original. His knowledge of literary history told him that each generation, in ignorance of the past, thinks that it has a whole, new world to offer,[50] but he knew that such originality is fragile and limited and has to be discovered and encouraged, because the originality of each generation—"the bit of novelty, of something not yet said"—was never great. For that very reason it had to be defended all the more.[51] Blum was acutely interested in whether a writer had anything new to say, or a new way of saying old truths. This often meant that Blum had to search for fine nuances, but the search was worth the effort because his self-knowledge could best be expanded by contact with the new, his sensibilities extended only by finding it. Thus Blum found the deepest rewards in the difficult task of reviewing.

Blum's lack of interest in an academic career stemmed in part from his refusal to concentrate on the literature of the past. The literary historian has great freedom and is subject to fewer pressures than the reviewer of current books, but Blum preferred to face the perils of the massed volumes issuing from the publishers— almost overwhelming in their numbers and offering few guidelines for the critic. Instead of discouragement he found challenge in the exceedingly delicate task of evaluating a first novel by an unknown author. He made a determined effort to give a hearing to as many authors as possible, and the only conspicuous exceptions among the scores of books he reviewed during his four years at *La Revue blanche* were the established and popular mediocrities. Blum thought it unlikely that a new genius would pass unnoticed, and his efforts to make sure this did not happen were so thorough that very few works by authors of either subsequent or future distinction escaped him.[52]

As a defender of the young and the new, Blum even argued the necessity of a systematic defense against corruption by the older generation; he called for each generation to protect its fragile originality by waging war on its elders—by distrusting even their friendship, so freely offered in their salons; by closing ranks against them. He thought it was especially perilous for a young critic to have friends among the writers of the older generation, for he would be apt to be overly lenient because of friendship.[53] Although his friendship with Anatole France shows that Blum did not entirely follow his own advice, he kept the other half of his commandment and showed a consistent partiality for writers of his own age.[54]

Blum's enthusiasm for the efforts of the young to make a place for themselves in literature was especially evident in his reception of the manifestos of the group that called itself the naturists (not to be confused with the naturalists, although they professed great admiration for the naturalist leader, Emile Zola). The naturists, reacting against symbolism, called for a literature that would be in closer contact with both nature and social life but would not be committed to any particular ideology.[55] The manifestos of naturist leaders Maurice Leblond and Saint-Georges de Bouhélier moved Blum to his highest level of enthusiasm,[56] for they seemed to combine respect for the past with devotion to the vital forces of the present, which Blum hoped to find in the writers of his generation. He was doubly pleased because the naturist leaders were even younger than himself, and he offered them his support without reservation:

If I have properly understood, I say it loudly: I am a Naturist, and the hope and life of our literature is in Naturism. I have developed or defended here—though only incidentally and from day to day—almost all of the ideas which M. Leblond expounds in such a lively manner and with such gracious ardor, by affirmation or by criticism.[57]

Most of all, Blum saw the naturists as the potential romantics of the coming century. Their approach to language was not revolutionary; they were inclined to view themselves as the heirs of the varied traditions of the French language, and as heirs they did not wish to reject any of their patrimony. Blum applauded their affirmation of the primacy of the vital forces of life—their respect for emotions, even everyday ones, their emphasis on the whole spectrum of society and not just the life of the artist. The emotivity of the naturists was especially congenial because of its this-worldliness, its detachment from traditional religion. A whole social as well as artistic attitude was implied in their explicit choice of Victor Hugo as their patron saint and their recognition of descent from the Romantics. Their explicit proclamation of a love of life reflected the spirit of their generation, which can also be seen in similar statements by Blum and in the humanism of his friend, the poet Fernand Gregh.[58] This love of life seemed to Blum the heartblood of literature, and he wrote:

I believe then with the Naturists that, under penalty of decadence and death, literature will become emotive, objective, and pantheistic, and, as it cannot die, it will be such.[59]

Certainly Blum shared fully in the quest of his generation for something vital and living, which they found missing in the literature of the preceding generation.

Blum's enthusiasm for the naturist theory did not lead him to immoderate praise of the literary accomplishments of the naturists. He never meant his indulgence to be taken as a whitewash of the deficiencies of authors. He wanted his readers to put those deficiencies in the context of an author's development and not expect finished perfection in the young. Hence he could legitimately be, and usually was, more severe with older writers. He believed that young writers needed a sympathetic but not uncritical audience to help them develop their talents. He did not mean to hold the door open forever, and in the case of the naturists he soon became impatient with the failure of their work to approximate the expectations raised by their manifestos. In 1898, Blum was still praising the theory, while finding that the works ("deduced rather than inspired") betrayed the theory, and in 1899, he greeted yet another naturist manifesto with open impatience.[60] Despite his enthusiasm for naturism, Blum was not interested in theoretical pronouncements but in living literature.

In the early phases of his enthusiasm for naturism, however, Blum seemed to feel that the naturist theory was not only good but necessarily fruitful. Its correctness was the guarantee of its efficacy. This lapse, into what might be called the intellectualist fallacy, was the strongest evidence during his *Revue blanche* years of the emphasis Blum placed on the role of ideas in literature. Such was his enthusiasm for the naturist idea that he made a blanket condemnation of earlier literature on the grounds that it was philosophically deficient:

It is still true that among the generations that preceded us isolated individuals can charm, seduce, or even dominate, but in its ensemble that literature is without force, without vital sap, without harmony. Why? Because it is an artificial literature which has departed from nature and from simplicity, which has complicated life and turned language out of its true path, and especially because the sole general idea on which it has lived—individualism—is a false and debilitating idea.[61]

These strong words seem to have been inspired more by Blum's adhesion to socialism than by the naturists, whose views were not so antithetical to individualism.

The literary individualism that Blum attacked was mostly that of fairly recent advocates of an elitist, difficult, even hermetic art. The Romantics, for example, did not come under this condemnation because, in Blum's opinion, they exhibited great social awareness. Although it is clear that in 1897 Blum was far removed from the almost purely aesthetic interests of his former colleagues of *La Conque* of 1891, this outburst, if taken alone, would give an exaggerated picture of the importance of socialist ideology in his criticism during these years.[62]

While Blum's literary criticism for *La Revue blanche* was not shaped by ideology, it displayed consistent interest in what he called "general ideas" in literature. He was, after all, drawn to criticism by the intellectual challenge of dealing with ideas as well as by the aesthetic pleasure of works of art. Of all the qualities of his reviewing, it is his interest in ideas which makes much of his work still readable today. The ideas which attracted him most dealt with the social order or religion, and the authors who won his favor were usually critical of the contemporary social order or the dominant social ideas. In literature, his social ideals found expression only as negations during this period. It was certainly negation that attracted him to such works as Zola's *Rome*, whose anti-papal and anti-clerical themes Blum's review supported and amplified while defending Zola's lapses of style.[63] Blum's early enthusiasm for Clemenceau, whom he praised as a romantic, can best be explained by the anti-Christian motif in his works, such as his novel *Le grand Pan*.[64]

Blum's interest in the ideas within a novel was often obvious in his reviews of novelists whose work he also admired on aesthetic grounds, such as Anatole France and Paul Adam. Adam, almost unknown today, received steady praise for his works, in which Blum found "an Ionian vision of a natural harmony ... wherein man is only a moment, a fleeting aspect of Universal Reason."[65] His interest in ideas was restrained from ideological excess by his conviction that even the most revolutionary novel is powerless to change society.[66] He could admire an author like Bernard Lazare, who sought social impact through his art, but he remained doubtful that such efforts would have any effect.[67] The Dreyfus affair made Blum even more receptive to the novel of social criticism, and he welcomed Anatole France's decision to "drop the mask" by moving the settings of his satires from antiquity to the present day.[68] Nor were his socialist convictions offended when France remained the detached *philosophe*, "heir of La Bruyère and Diderot," because, however subversive his novels might be—and Blum rated them highly subversive—they could not change matters.[69] Thus Blum felt that he could not demand social commitment of a novelist, only that he be interested in contemporary society.[70]

In practice, Blum's range of interest was even wider. While many novelists were interested in social problems, the more traditional preoccupation with the psychology of the individual was a frequent source of inspiration. Thus Blum could be serious about novelists whose social views were opposed to his own if they wrote with a psychological flair. His professed anti-individualism was still largely an abstract idea, which was by no means incompatible with intense psychological curiosity. In any case, most of the novelists who had his sympathy were still at the stage of presenting individualistic attacks on traditional society or traditional ethics; there was no new collective ethic he could oppose to the old one. Blum, a part of this literary milieu, shared its concern with individual psychology. For Blum the critic, this concern found a larger outlet in his later work as a drama critic.

Blum did not consider his interest in ideas, which led him to dissect many a novel in search of its motivating principle or in order to criticize or praise the author's opinions, as incompatible with an interest in literary art. He believed that the "general ideas" he sought in the novel could also bring beauty to their subjects.[71] His aesthetic credo came to be "Beauty is truth, truth beauty"—an idea long familiar in France despite its classic English formulation. This aesthetic was nourished by his love of the classics as well as his concern for the present. The "truth" of the novel, the source of its beauty, seemed to Blum to be particular to it; its effectiveness derived from its limitations:

If the novel has a beauty which belongs to it alone, I believe that it is in its truth, and, although my definition might seem strange, I believe that the truth of the novel is nothing other than a weighted and *partial* force of observation, of poetry, of passion, or of reason.[72]

Observation, poetry, passion, and reason are a sufficiently broad palette for the literary artist, and Blum showed himself capable of appreciating highly varied works that concentrated on any of these elements. His highly rationalistic mind was quite capable of responding sympathetically to poetry and passion, though perhaps he never totally yielded himself up, and he never ceased to be appreciative of writers whose concern was almost wholly with the aesthetic quality of their writing, such as René Boylesve and Henri de Régnier.[73]

It comes as no surprise, however, that a number of his contemporaries, as well as most later observers, detected in Blum's criticism a conflict between what they have generally called his taste, on the one hand, and his opinion or intelligence, on the other. Often these writers have asserted that Blum might have become a great critic had he not allowed his ideas, primarily his social and political ideas, to dominate his taste.[74] Among his contemporaries, there was often ambiguity in this criticism. For example, Jules Renard, for whom Blum always had the highest praise and who furthermore was something of a socialist, often differed with Blum over the value of other authors' work, but sometimes he blamed Blum's intelligence for falsifying his taste while on other occasions he praised this very critical intelligence.[75] After the Dreyfus affair, it was likely to be political or ideological rather than literary considerations which determined contemporary opinions of Blum as a critic.[76] These criticisms of his emphasis on ideas, though usually a cover for disagreement about ideas rather than aesthetics, at least raise an interesting question about the art of Blum's criticism. Their mistake is to assume that taste and intelligence are separate faculties, residing in separate compartments of the mind and warring with each other. Taste and intelligence, however, are only "external" categories of classification, which perhaps help simplify the discussion of certain mental activities, but the mind is a totality, an organism, not a committee.

Blum, very much aware of this unity of the personality, was also aware that the mind is full of contradictions and complications, which also are part of the whole man. Blum's personality was a stable blend of rational lucidity and philosophic *sensibilité*, and different parts of this blend were emphasized according to the circumstances. His articles for *La Revue blanche* offer a broad picture of the nuances of his personality, although any one article, considered in isolation, is apt to be misleading. Without a doubt, Blum's intellectuality was a dominant feature of his personality; his criticisms, however, were by no means marked by a cold and rigid logic. Such rigidity would have been incompatible with Blum's impressionist philosophy of criticism, which emphasized the immediate and emotive response to a work and demanded that intelligence clarify this response while taking care not to falsify it. The "intellectual reviewer" applies a preconceived system of values, but Blum dissected a book to find out what made it tick, not to make it conform to a procrustean bed of values in the manner of Brunetière or Charles Maurras. Blum's reviews were explicitly antisystematic, and in practice he remained true to his renunciation of system and artificial consistency:

All systems are inapplicable in criticism. One does not judge with an aesthetic theory; one judges with one's eyes, sentiments, reason. If you prefer, all systems of ideas are mechanical, and all judgment is dynamic.[77]

Because judgment is dynamic, it is exposed to inconsistency, but any imposed consistency could corrupt the act of judgment. Blum's judgment was influenced by his literary and social-political opinions, though he strove to keep it open-ended, and he was so successful that he could respond with freshness to the emotive appeal of something as unusual as Ernest La Jeunesse's bizarre *L'imitation de notre maître Napoléon*.[78] Blum's intellect, at work and at play in his reviews, was dynamic, not dogmatic.

Blum's antisystematic bias might best be described as part of the romantic side of his rationalist nature, for there was a certain conflict between his emotions and his intellect, but it operated within his literary taste, giving it indeterminate contours. His complexity of taste was clearly revealed in an essay published at the beginning of his career as a critic; it was, in form, a defense of what he called the "classic taste" and a plea for its revival.[79] His admiring use of "classic" has been the source of the greatest misunderstanding of his literary outlook, especially among later scholars.[80] Today, all critics and writers tend to shy away from the classic because it carries the connotation of "academic" and hence "dead," and this was also true of the younger generation in Blum's day, when the Greek and Roman languages and their literature formed the central part of liberal education. The complete rejection of the ancient classics was not yet a common pose in the literary world, and the teaching of the classics had not yet killed all interest in them, but youth was hostile to academicism. This was true even though many writers, such as Mallarmé, had to earn their living as teachers. Nor was Blum himself attracted by the academic atmosphere, which seemed to him unfriendly to literary creativity, but there was no sterile academicism in his advocacy of classicism, no premature elderliness in his outlook.[81]

The artificial, cerebral classicism of Voltaire's tragedies was at the opposite pole from Blum's classicism. The stylistic ideal which Blum expounded was in some respects conservative but it was quite the opposite of formalism. His interest in ideas would have prevented him from exalting form above content and his intense interest in the present would have made a sterile admiration of the classics impossible. Blum's admiration for the French classics was deep and his familiarity with them extensive, as his allusions to them reveal. Of the authors to whom he was exposed in school, he especially favored the prose moralists of the sevententh century: Pascal and La Bruyère, and especially Saint-Simon and Cardinal de Retz. Jules Renard was surprised that the "beardless young man with the little girl's voice [could] recite for two hours by the clock from Pascal, La Bruyère, Saint-Evremont [*sic*], etc."[82] Blum also had some acquaintance with the Latin classics and once recalled having passed "a charming afternoon" with André Gide, the two of them taking turns declaiming from Virgil.[83]

But despite this interest, Blum denied that his plea for a revival of the classic taste meant that he wanted to see more Racine and Corneille at the Comédie Française or Euripides and Sophocles in the theaters on the *Boulevard*.[84] Still less did he want to make imitation of the classics the basis for a literary movement; he did not care to be the Du Bellay of a new renaissance. Thus he quarreled with Antoine Albalat, who offered a program for learning to write through imitation of the masters. The masters had qualities worth emulating, but Blum did not think they could be developed by imitation. Imitation was not a classic method; it was Alexandrian, not Athenian. He found the archaic, pseudo-classicism of Jean Moréas and Charles Maurras sterile. Blum's classicism was conservative in the sense that he did not want his generation to lose contact with the traditions of France's national literature, which he felt were threatened less by youthful literary radicalism than by carelessness, indifference, and obscurantism. These offenses aroused his ire more quickly than deliberate (if unhappy) innovation, and he was blunt in demanding correctness:

With care and study there is no one who could not write correctly, and if one does not want to take the time for it, why write?[85]

In defending classicism he was defending what he thought were permanently valid rules for good writing in French, but he did not mean to reduce writing to the following of rigid formulas and avoiding this or that error:

The fruitful work, the difficult work, is not to avoid repetitions, to hunt down and eliminate auxiliaries, to keep watch over the coherence of images; rather, it is to see clearly into what one thinks, and to apply what one thinks to what one writes.[86]

His own style had many valuable qualities, the most important of which was lucidity, and while he expected other writers to be equally lucid, he did not expect their styles to be like his. Correctness could be learned, but style was part of the individual personality and could not be learned. Blum thought it futile to criticize a writer for lacking personality since there was nothing he could do to correct this deficit.[87] Barrès, he would say, was born with a great style; Bourget was not and would never acquire one. Blum placed considerable emphasis on the role of inspiration in the work of a good writer—so much that he feared the wrong kind of classicism could stifle creativity.

In its stress on the continuity of language, Blum's classicism did not oppose change; on the contrary, as he insisted, it meant recognizing the necessity of perpetual change. A language could die from changing too little as well as from changing too much:

Does a language have its culminating degree of beauty which it reaches laboriously and beyond which it goes only to decay? I do not think so. Languages are not like men, who have a youth, a mature age, and then fade away. They are organisms which do not carry in themselves any germ of inescapable death. One sees no limit to their development. Why should people not be speaking the French language twenty centuries from now, or even longer? If this is true, where can its moment of perfection be fixed? We have no reason to think that grammar and vocabulary have not gained in color, in precision of nuances, in richness of detail from Bossuet to Chateaubriand, from La Bruyère to Flaubert.[88]

While he thought that language could not remain static, he believed that its development followed regular laws and an internal logic which had to be respected. This attitude was no doubt influenced by his contact with Michel Bréal, whose influential treatise on semantics Blum received enthusiastically. Blum did not believe that respect for the "laws" of semantic development was harmful to creativity, though it put some limits on the directions in which fruitful innovation could flow. He was most tolerant of innovations in vocabulary because he believed they rarely led to obscurity, but he condemned deviations in syntax as enemies of clarity. His emphasis on communication involved him in a sort of war on two fronts: against the formalistic tendency of the Parnassians, on the one hand, and against the obscurantist tendency of the symbolists, on the other. Blum remained an apostle of *la clarté française*.

As a reviewer, Blum had few occasions to be concerned with the Parnassians for he seldom reviewed poetry, and their influence was limited to poetry. Furthermore, the *Parnasse* was a movement of an older generation, and therefore he had little reason to go outside his sphere to deal with it. Certainly he respected the talents of some of the Parnassians and agreed, for example, that some of the sonnets of Heredia would have a place in any future anthology of French verse. Symbolism, on the other hand, was of more concern to Blum, for it continued to have an impact on the writers of his generation. Although it was basically a poetic movement, it affected prose fiction as well.

His quarrel with symbolism was not so much with its theory as its practice. He rejected all attempts to elevate symbolism into a philosophy and insisted that, properly understood, it was simply an aesthetic technique, which was based on the idea that direct and exact description is artistically inferior to subtle and indirect description by means of symbols.[89] Blum believed that symbolism, thus understood, could be a valid artistic approach, but he also thought that most symbolists had become enamored of the vague and obscure and used symbolic images merely to evoke a loosely "poetic" atmosphere. He complained that they forgot the substance they were attempting to describe through their symbols:

The symbol is a sign; it must be a sign of something, and the best possible sign to represent that particular something for our eyes. If it is a striking image, it may justly be difficult, but if it is meaningless, it does no good to be elegant. I am quite convinced that one may really appreciate a work without seizing anything of the hidden meaning that the author has jealously concealed in it ... But it is an aesthetic contradiction, in my opinion, to see in Symbolism only the poetic and dispersed evocation of images, however agreeable. One must have intended for these images to add to the descriptive knowledge, the detailed knowledge of their object.[90]

It seemed to Blum that almost all the prose symbolists[91] failed to live up to this standard, and he asserted that only Marcel Schwob, a young novelist who was then relatively well known but is now forgotten, exhibited the "love, respect, and science of language" which Blum considered the qualities of a classic author.[92]

Blum's concern with the love, respect, and science of language was only one aspect of his classicism, and perhaps not the most important aspect at that. His classicism was inseparable from his interest in contemporary literature and his advocacy of his own generation. To Blum, the study of the classical writers of earlier ages revealed that the classic attitude was not antiquarian or backward looking. The authors of fifth-century Athens were as deeply immersed in the literature of their own time as Blum was in that of his. They might have admired the literature of an earlier age—Homer certainly—but they had not tried to imitate it. Their concern with the new had been so great that even the masterpieces of the drama were not repeated, however much they were admired. Blum found this forward-looking aspect of the classic writers most congenial, and it was the antiquarian approach of the classical dramatists of seventeenth-century France which caused him to prefer the prose writers of that age. The tragic poets of the seventeenth century, however, had escaped the Alexandrianism of the next century, just as they had escaped that of the Renaissance, through their possession of truly classical qualities. In spite of a tendency toward imitation in form, their works exhibited the "direct sentiments of beauty," which to Blum were the hallmark of classicism.[93] It was genuine feeling and emotion—sincerity—which made a writer classic in any age.

For Blum, then, classicism meant the combination of sincerity and clarity of expression.[94] Clarity and sincerity were the two criteria that were capable of satisfying both his sentiments and his intellect. If he was inclined to admire the skillful and polished (the restrained prose that was commonly called classical), he did not find this adequate; he insisted that these qualities be combined with the expression of truth and life.[95] Blum would have readily accepted the opinion that the "classics" of the past were really the "romantics" of their day, and his affinity for the Romantics is clear in his poetic preferences: his favorite poet was Victor Hugo, not Malherbe—and certainly not Voltaire.

On the other hand, he tended to identify romanticism in prose with the excessive *sensibilité* of the followers of Rousseau and Chateaubriand, which inclined them toward facility and insipidity. Thus the prose writers of his own time whom Blum labeled as classicists were notable for their purity of style, even for a certain dryness, which seemed to him less dangerous than its opposite. Among these modern classicists, Blum said, were Henri de Régnier, Maurice Barrès, Anatole France ("the most perfect writer of this period"), and André Gide; and in the second rank were Pierre Louys, Marcel Schwob, and Heredia.[96] Blum was not unaware that the classical quality of these writers contained an element of artificiality, and he reluctantly admitted that his age was not one of the greatest. His admiration for Louys as a stylist did not prevent his condemning Louys's incipient decadence, which headed toward the insincerity and artificiality that true classicism could avoid. He even admitted that there was more of the Alexandrian in Anatole France than just the setting of *Thaïs*, that France's skepticism was indeed that of Zeno and Epicurus; but Blum felt that his age was in general much closer to Alexandria than Athens.[97] At the same time, he felt that France was at heart a writer of fundamental sincerity and genuine (though often concealed) emotion.

It was to sincerity and disinterestedness that Blum's heart and mind went out.[98] Among the writers who were published during Blum's *Revue blanche* years, it was Gide (the "martyr of sincerity," as Henri Peyre has called him) who embodied most completely the intense respect for his own emotions that Blum admired. His early recognition of the talent of the man he called the "most truly classic" living writer[99] was perhaps facilitated by their friendship, but that friendship was always strained by differences of personality and opinion, and Blum's admiration for Gide the writer probably exceeded their *amitié*.

Almost any of the several reviews Blum devoted to Gide can stand as a treatise on the former's ideal of sincerity, such as the following.

He has minute and almost sad anxieties, the tormented finesses of a casuist who wants to be sensitive and defiant. ... Precisely to see more clearly into the scruples of his conscience, he knows how to inflate them, to enrich them into the material for a novel or a drama. Moreover, he lacks the premeditated concern for building his successive works into a coherent and closed system in which each would take its place. He is not afraid of contradictions. Each moment in his thought has for him the same importance as the rest. This is certainly not the result of a skeptic's taste for deliberately posing antinomies, but the result of sincerity, of respect for the variety of these contradictory emotions, where one cannot determine which is true, or to put it more exactly, where all are true. Nothing is more mobile, more sensitive, more avid before all the sensations with which reality enriches our lives each day than his thought. Avidity for life, a large and gourmand aspiration, is indeed one of the characteristics of Gide; it is this which animates and embellishes his moral concern; it is this which has made a lyricist and a poet of this scrupulous Jansenist.[100]

Gide's mobility and sincerity were not only part of his character, they seemed to Blum to be the necessary ingredients of his art— indeed, the necessary ingredients of all literary art.[101] The sincerity of the Romantics had enabled them to revitalize the literary world at the beginning of the nineteenth century, and Blum thought that Gide and the naturists would accordingly lead the twentieth century out of the wilderness of formalism, symbolism, and scientism.

Blum's literary stand at the beginning of his career as a critic remained basically unchanged with the passage of time. It came, after all, from those depths of personality which are rarely susceptible to fundamental change. In practice, of course, he was anything but rigid, and not always consistent, but if his personality did not alter, his knowledge and self-understanding increased. The years he spent at *La Revue blanche* were critical for his development for they were also the years of his commitment to socialism and his engagement in the Dreyfus affair.[102] The effects on his work as a critic were not immediately overwhelming or clear-cut, and are more evident in his later work in other journals. Even his interest in novels that dealt with social themes, though already evident, was not yet fully developed. His social commitments tended to appear when he reviewed works other than novels, and especially in the articles he devoted to books on the Dreyfus affair.

Blum was seriously rethinking his position, trying to decide what role to play. Although he temporarily abandoned criticism in 1900 to devote his spare time to a socialist publishing venture, he concluded his stay at *La Revue blanche* with a reaffirmation of his critical vocation. Blum had found that his experience as a critic had satisfied his expectations of keeping in contact with the multiple intellectual currents of his time, and he ended his collaboration with *La Revue blanche* with an essay exalting the critic.[103] In this last article of his "Goethe-Eckermann" series, Blum expressed his depression at the all-pervading influence of specialization in modern society, which he saw as a force for dehumanization. At the same time, he realized that specialization was necessary if one was to make a contribution to the advancement of knowledge or art, and he warned the creative artist against dispersing his powers in pursuit of the chimera of universal knowledge. Yet it seemed dangerous to humanity for everyone to engage in partial pursuits, and he concluded that there must always be persons who are capable of taking an over-all view of human activity—men who would not know everything but who could see the general march of progress and thus help orient the rest, who would otherwise be lost in the narrowness of their specialties. These men of vision he called "critics," and he saw them as the defenders of humanist ideals in a world in which those ideals were threatened. Although his invocation of these "men of the race of Herder" was full of evangelistic enthusiasm, it would not be fair to see Blum as a frustrated intellectual assigning himself a premier place in society; certainly his ambition was much less and his self-estimation more modest. But he saw even more clearly than he knew into the mode of his development.

Blum had committed himself to making a modest contribution to the establishment of a distant goal, that of social justice, but he had not yet found a permanent form by which to express his idealism in action. Criticism perhaps best suited his talents, but he foresaw a time when this might no longer be true. Important as art had been in the development of the human spirit it would not lead the way to social justice. Perhaps its chief value was in sustaining hope while man was still in the wilderness. Nevertheless, the reign of justice would not come until the humanistic task of the "critics" was taken over by the political leaders. As Blum's "Goethe" remarked: We call these universal men *critiques* today but they will be *politiques* tomorrow. It was symbolic of the wholeness of Blum's personality that he later traversed this development, which he had abstractly foreseen.

CHAPTER THREE

THE CONSEIL D'ETAT

ANY CONSIDERATION of Léon Blum's career on the Conseil d'Etat makes the energy and breadth of vision that made his dual careers possible appear all the more remarkable. His two careers complemented each other superbly, enabling him to construct a harmonious life style. The intellectual qualities required in literary criticism and legal analysis were not antithetical, and both careers added to Blum's self-development in ways that are discernible in his later political career. Since his work on the Conseil d'Etat is not so accessible or glamorous as his literary or political activities, the importance of his legal experience has often been underestimated.

In France, many lawyers entered politics, but relatively few by way of administrative law. This perhaps helps explain how even when he became absorbed in parliamentary life Blum retained some sense of the limitations of parliamentary action in a highly administered country. His experience on the Conseil strengthened his grasp of public affairs, gave him an inside view of how an important part of French government worked—or didn't work—and helped develop habits of responsibility and decision. His realism and practicality were evident in his legal work. Only by seeing that he was not just an "Aesthet des fin-de-siècle" can one grasp the whole man.

Blum had to consider carefully the question of earning a living; circumstances made a second career necessary, and his search for self-knowledge and self-development led him to seek a career which would make the best use of his talents. His acute analytic intelligence made law a logical selection, and the law was an eminently respectable career in French Jewish circles.[1] Blum lacked the driving ambition for wealth, so necessary for success in private practice, and it is doubtful that he ever seriously considered that kind of legal career. He must, from the beginning, have considered the law as a path to a career in public service which would offer a modest but steady income—status and security, combined with the opportunity to feel that one was serving the general interest rather than one's own. A career in the administration or the judiciary offered the best possibilities, and Blum was to combine them—with a career in the administrative judiciary. This sort of public career would not only give him the time to pursue his literary interests but considerable satisfaction in its own right. Typically, Blum aimed as high as he could by seeking a post on the Conseil d'Etat, whose appeal was undoubtedly augmented by the fact that one of his literary idols, Stendhal, had once been an *auditeur*.[2]

To understand the significance of Blum's career on the Conseil, it is necessary to know a little about this peculiarly French institution, which has no counterpart in the Anglo-American legal tradition.[3] The modern Conseil d'Etat, which developed in the Revolutionary and Napoleonic periods, was the highest administrative court of France. The system of administrative courts had come into existence as a result of a distinctive interpretation of the concept of the separation of powers.[4] This separation was conceived in such an absolute fashion during the Revolution that the ordinary courts were denied all right to interfere in the activities of the administration; thus the administration had to develop its own court system to deal with litigation arising from acts of administration. Gradually, in the course of the nineteenth century, the administrative courts were converted from a somewhat dubiously self-policing agency of the administration into a fully independent judiciary that applied a large body of case law and had as many safeguards for its independence and impartiality as the civil courts. This was especially true of the Conseil d'Etat, the apex of the hierarchy of administrative courts and the first to gain independence. It served both as a court of appeals from other courts in the administrative jurisdiction and as a court of first instance for many types of cases.

The functions of the Conseil varied considerably from regime to regime. Napoleon had used it as a body of experts for the drafting of legislation, and remnants of this function had persisted into the Third Republic. The advisory branch of the Conseil, the Section Législative, was closely connected with the administrative bureaucracy, acting as an advisory body to give opinions on the constitutionality of proposed measures and help formulate legislation. The functions of the administrative court proper were exercised by the other branch of the Conseil, the Section du Contentieux,[5] to which Blum was appointed.

Appointment to all ranks of the Conseil d'Etat was made by the President of the Republic on the recommendation of the Minister of Justice, who was ex officio president of the Conseil, but in practice, the Conseil regulated its own internal organization. Promotion was based on seniority and ability (as judged by the ranking members of the Conseil), and in the 1890s admission to the lowest rank was gained through a competitive examination held in December of every year in which vacancies occurred.[6] Blum, after taking his *licence en droit*, entered the competition of 1894 but was not successful.[7] It was a strenuous examination, and he accepted defeat philosophically.[8] He redoubled his efforts, studied with a tutor, and was one of the three candidates to win a post in the 1895 competition. His appointment as *auditeur de deuxième classe* became effective in January 1896.[9]

Thus Blum began a career in a distinguished branch of public service that from its origin had remained distinctively bourgeois. It required an expensive education, which was beyond the means of the vast majority of French families. In addition to the lycée program, a professional education was necessary since the *licence en droit* was obligatory. This meant three years' study at the Faculty of Law, or more commonly at the private Ecole Libre des Sciences Politiques.[10] An added burden was the very poorly paid first years as *auditeur de deuxième classe*, which was viewed as a kind of internship. Indeed, during the early years of the Third Republic the position carried no salary at all, but by the time of Blum's appointment an annual salary of 2,000 francs had been established— barely enough, in 1895, to support a middle-class bachelor in Paris.[11] It is not clear how much Blum's family, especially his father, encouraged this choice of career, but it is certain that without their support it would not have been possible.[12]

Similarly, his decision to marry early in his first year on the Conseil was made possible more by his prospects than by his salary. Blum's bride, Lise Bloch, was an old friend whom he had known for several years in family and various social circles.[13] Mme. Blum seems to have shared his social and cultural interests, and theirs was one of those tranquil marriages which have no "history"— very unlike the novels the *Revue blanche* critic was fond of. After a honeymoon in Sicily, they settled in an apartment at 38 rue du Luxembourg, near the Senate and the Luxembourg gardens. The *ménage* was always modest and distinctly bourgeois, with a servant who was so essential to social life in the days before electric appliances. Typically for the intellectual professions, the Blums enjoyed a social position above their wealth and their social life was filled with interesting friends and acquaintances. Typical, too, was the decision to have a small family. The Blums' only child, Robert, was born in 1902.[14]

After entering the Conseil d'Etat on the bottom rung, Blum rose slowly and steadily as his talents made themselves known. As *auditeur de deuxième classe*, he was assigned to the Section du Contentieux and he remained with this judicial branch of the Conseil for the rest of his service. This first position was essentially that of a researcher and reporter. He studied the cases assigned to him, usually those of lesser importance or difficulty, and prepared the material—facts in contention, relevant laws and precedents— for the use of the Conseil.[15] Thus his work, in effect, was reviewed by more experienced members, and his position was a sort of apprenticeship in which the young men chosen by the competitive examination were exposed to the reality of judicial practice. Blum's terms as *auditeur de deuxième classe* almost coincided with his "apprenticeship" as the literary critic of *La Revue blanche*. Although this phase of his career on the Conseil has left no example of his work, it is evident that his success was due to the same penetrating intelligence that marked his criticism, and perhaps even more to the well-balanced judgment which enabled him to earn approval in a traditional middle-class institution at the same time he was involved on the anti-establishment side in the Dreyfus affair and becoming more actively engaged in socialism.[16]

Blum's acceptance within the Conseil was marked by his promotion, in 1900, to *auditeur de première classe*. *Auditeurs* who were not promoted to first class within eight years after entering the Conseil were shifted to other branches of the national administration. Blum's promotion now gave him a sort of tenure, and what is more doubled his salary—a particularly welcome advance as he was just at that moment leaving his regular position at *La Revue blanche*.[17] His work as *auditeur de première classe* was similar to his former tasks, but had added responsibilities. He could now prepare reports for all types of cases; he was able to give his opinion in some matters; and he even could vote on those cases for which he had prepared reports.[18] The quality of his work was such that he was also entrusted with the important post of *commissaire suppléant du gouvernement* in a special section which was created in an unsuccessful attempt to reduce the backlog of cases before the Conseil.[19]

Blum's next promotion did not come until after the period of his most active participation in the socialist movement, during the formation of the unified party and the foundation of *L'Humanité*. There is no evidence, however, that his rise was delayed in any way by these outside activities, and his seven-odd years as *auditeur de première classe* appear to have been typical.[20] Furthermore, his promotion to *maître des requêtes* came in the same year, 1907, as the publication of his very controversial book on marriage.[21] Nor did the boldness of his thought stand in the way of recognition of his government service in the form of a nomination as Chevalier of the Legion of Honor in January 1909.[22] As a *maître des requêtes*, Blum belonged to the second-ranking group within the Conseil and could look forward with near certainty to one day joining the ranks of the *conseillers d'Etat*. As a *maître*, Blum had to work closely with the *conseillers*, who formed the varying groups which deliberated and handed down decisions in the name of the Conseil. Unlike the ordinary courts, there was little argument before these judges, who worked largely from written dossiers. One of the most important of these dossiers was the report prepared by a *maître des requêtes* from the preliminary work of the *auditeurs*.[23] As a *maître*, Blum was to have a deliberative voice in the judgment of many cases on which he served as reporter.[24] His reports, always informal working documents, have not been preserved, but it is clear that his judgment was highly respected by his senior colleagues.

This was made evident by his appointment, at the beginning of 1910, to the function of *commissaire du gouvernement*, although he retained the rank of *maître des requêtes*.[25] Blum was to perform this function with considerable *éclat* until his judicial career was ended by his entry into the Chamber of Deputies in 1919. During the period before World War I, Blum was one of from six to eight *commissaires* chosen from among the thirty-seven *maîtres des requêtes*.[26] In each case which came before the Section du Contentieux sitting as a court, after the objective findings of the reporter were delivered, a *commissaire du gouvernement* presented his "conclusions." This presentation was an argument, based on the data of the report, which set forth the decision that the *commissaire* believed the Conseil should make and the reasons for his opinion.[27] The *commissaire*, who was in no sense a prosecuting attorney, could defend any position of his choosing. The dignity of his function, like that of the Conseil itself, came from his total independence. Indeed, his value to the Conseil resulted from that independence, for it provided the Conseil with the carefully considered opinion of an experienced and capable jurist who was sheltered from outside pressure and who worked in the quiet of his study among the dossiers.[28] The *commissaires du gouvernement* were not representatives of the government; as one observer suggested, they should really be called *commissaires de la République*, and others have suggested *commissaires des lois*.[29] When the government wished to express its opinions in a case, it would have the appropriate minister submit a brief.

The work of the *commissaire du gouvernement* was very important for the development of the jurisprudence of the Conseil d'Etat, which was of the greatest importance because French administrative law, unlike the civil code, was case law and was built on precedents. The influence of the *commissaires* was not limited to the Conseil, where they advised on which precedents to emphasize and which to play down, which to retain and which to reverse. The Conseil itself always deliberated in secret and published only a laconic decision, without explaining much of its reasoning, but the conclusions of the *commissaires*, on the other hand, were available to the public. In the more important cases, they were often circulated in the legal press, where they might receive extensive commentary. It was to these conclusions that lawyers and jurists had to turn in order to interpret the Conseil's decisions, and thus the reasoning of the *commissaires* had wide influence, rivaled only by that of the leading commentators, such as Maurice Hauriou. It is only through his published conclusions that much is known about Blum's legal thought, and it was through them that he earned a reputation as an outstanding *commissaire*.[30] On occasion, his conclusions were considered important enough to be reprinted and commented on even after the Conseil had rejected them.[31]

Blum's conclusions do not tell as much about his legal ideas and attitudes or the influence of his legal career on his intellectual development as one would like to know, but some of his deep concerns show more clearly here than elsewhere and thus are important for understanding the man. Had he been able to choose his cases, his interests would have appeared more clearly, but his sense of responsibility led him to apply himself with equal vigor to all the cases referred to him by the Conseil. It is certainly significant that Blum became involved in administrative law rather than some other branch. Practitioners of administrative law in France were the least likely to have an abstract and rigidly theoretical attitude toward the law. Because law tends by nature to be conservative, it is easy to forget that it changes—in practice—constantly and necessarily. It was during the latter part of the nineteenth century that some French legal experts began to take these changes into account, and administrative law specialists were among the leaders in the effort to reform French jurisprudence.

Although he never offered a systematic explanation of his views, Blum, in his various conclusions, appears to have been deeply committed to the idea that law must serve the changing interests of society. The major defect of French law in this respect was a result of its monarchical origins: it regularly put the interests of the government and the administration above those of the citizens. The establishment of the Third Republic brought no immediate and drastic change in this situation, but a significant evolution had begun. By the time Blum entered the Conseil d'Etat, it had become clear that its jurisprudence tended to make the contest between the citizen and the state less unequal. The irresponsibility of the administration and administrators was increasingly challenged by the expanding use of the *recours pour excès de pouvoirs*, which enabled individuals to have illegal acts by the administration annulled. In a country where administrative law was of great importance in daily life, the ability of the average citizen to find redress against arbitrary administration was of great value.[32] The Conseil was steadily broadening the public's area of intervention.

Blum was fully in harmony with the liberalizing trend of the Conseil's jurisprudence, and on some occasions sought to accelerate it. The desire to protect the individual against the arbitrariness, or irresponsibility, of the government appears with great frequency in his conclusions. There is evidence, too, of the influence of his socialist convictions, but his democratic-liberal orientation (which was also the basis of his socialism) is more apparent. His concern for due process of law, as essential to the protection of individual rights, was forcefully presented on many occasions.[33]

He even went so far as to put this concern ahead of certain social ideals, as it was always deeply against his inclinations to be fanatical in the promotion of his ideas. As a politician, he was later concerned with means as well as ends, and this inclination, though it was present at an early age, was reinforced by his judicial experience. His concern with due process was paramount in various cases dealing with the separation of church and state. The separation laws passed under the violently anti-clerical government of Emile Combes in 1905 were in large measure a result of the emotions created by the Dreyfus affair. Blum had shared those emotions, and along with other socialists had backed the program of the Combes government, but he did not allow this commitment to guide him in framing his conclusions. Some administrators—mayors and prefects—had shown excessive anti-clerical vigor in the application of the separation laws, and numerous cases came before the Conseil. Although the Conseil has sometimes been charged with attempting to mitigate the laws by its interpretation, for the most part it held their application close to the letter of the laws.[34] Blum's attitude was essentially similar: the laws were to be applied with scrupulous fairness to the individuals concerned, without straining for a pro- or anti-clerical interpretation.[35] In cases of this nature, the Conseil increasingly annulled administrative acts not simply for *excès de pouvoirs* but, more subtly, for the use of power in ways not intended by the enabling legislation (*détournement de pouvoir*).[36] This judicial theory was one of the most important developments of the Conseil from the point of view of democracy, "by which the Council enlarged the grounds for possible annulment of suspicious administrative acts by taking into account the motivations of public officials—in particular, the subordination of means to the end being pursued."[37]

Blum's concern for due process as a democratizing principle was evident in his treatment of a pair of cases that involved military discipline in the peacetime reserve. Though without the vindictiveness of many Dreyfusards, Blum believed in the necessity of breaking the custom of giving the military a more or less free hand in its internal discipline. Without straying far from the issues of the cases at hand, he argued the necessity of adapting the army to the democratic republic and of introducing the rule of law in place of the army's arbitrary proceedings. His suggestions were not the sweeping gestures a pacifist would have hailed but the cautious steps of a jurist, who was not, however, blinded by the chauvinistic habits of his more conservative colleagues—who rejected his conclusions. Blum was by no means inclined to find the authorities always in the wrong, as he demonstrated in a case of bureaucratic discipline, but he was disturbed by the continued sanction of the arbitrary in the guise of "military necessity."

Questions of due process were not the only ones in which Blum displayed his interest in protecting the individual against the irresponsibility of the administration. In perhaps the most celebrated of his conclusions, in the Lemonnier affair, Blum played an important role in developing the idea that the administration or administrators could be held responsible for the results of negligence in the execution of their duties, as well as for misdeeds. The security of the individual was markedly favored by this progress of administrative jurisprudence.[38]

Because of the regulatory powers the administration exercised over many facets of economic life—and there was a tendency for these powers to grow—the Conseil was often involved in cases which were essentially conflicts between different groups in society, although they took the form of conflicts between individuals (or groups) and the administration. Some of these cases gave Blum the opportunity to show his sympathy for regulation undertaken in the interests of consumers. It was a concern he shared with most French socialists, but which could certainly not be described as a specifically socialist concern, for the Conseil was willing to sanction wide administrative action in the name of the public interest. Blum was particularly proud of his role in a case involving regulation of the Paris Halles to protect small producers (and consumers) against exploitation by certain kinds of wholesale agents who served no useful economic function.[39]

Better known in this field is Blum's contribution to the theory of "lack of foresight" (*imprévision*), which enabled the state to prevent harm to the public interest arising from the rigid application of public service contracts. The Conseil developed this theory because of problems arising from the concession of rights to exploit certain public utilities.[40] Some of these problems resulted from technological advance, as in the development of electric lighting to replace gas lights (which were themselves relatively new); others resulted from social or population changes. Since the Conseil, unlike the Cour de Cassation, had to deal with the data of these issues and not merely with procedural questions, Blum became familiar with the small details of many social problems and acquired a certain expertise in dealing with them—from a practical as well as theoretical viewpoint. His skill in combining social needs and legal theory was illustrated in his handling of the Marseille street-railway case.

In Marseille, the prefect had decided that the public interest required an increase in the number of certain tramway runs.[41] The operators of the tramways contended that they were not required to supply this additional service under the terms of their franchise from the state. Earlier in the nineteenth century, it had been common to treat franchises in terms of private contract law, which tended to make them unalterable, but the development of public utilities made this an increasingly untenable position. Blum showed clearly how the intervention of the state to alter these contracts could be justified:

The State cannot disinterest itself in the public service of transportation once it has granted a concession. It is conceded without doubt, but it remains nonetheless a public service. The concession represents a delegation, that is to say, it constitutes a mode of indirect management; it is not the equivalent of an abandonment, a desertion. The State remains the guarantor of the execution of the service vis-à-vis the ensemble of citizens.[42]

The trend in the Conseil's jurisprudence which Blum supported in this conclusion tended to undermine the theory of contract, which played such an important role in nineteenth-century economic individualism; but again, his view cannot be described as necessarily socialist. In 1893 the individualist theory of contract had been subjected to a thorough critique by Emile Durkheim in his *De la division du travail social*,[43] and in 1910, when the tramway case was settled, even strong defenders of private enterprise, such as Hauriou, recognized that the general direction of the Conseil's jurisprudence was desirable.[44] Blum, and the rest of the Conseil, had at the same time been anxious that individuals should not suffer financially from such governmental action, and he showed that the concessionaire could obtain compensation and damages for any losses. Blum was always to be concerned that the wheels of progress—even the ones he most favored—did as little harm as possible to the individual.

Although in most of these cases there was little specifically socialist content in Blum's opinions, there was at least one occasion in which his conviction appeared openly: in his effort to induce the Conseil to follow a path conducive to the development of "municipal socialism." The ownership and operation of public utilities by the communes was not supported by all socialists, some of whom saw it as merely a diversion, but Blum's socialism welcomed all sorts of reform as useful precursors of the socialist society. It was typical of his approach, and his optimism, that he framed his support for municipal socialism in terms calculated to appeal to his free-enterprise-oriented colleagues. The Conseil had, in general, hindered the growth of municipal enterprise by permitting any taxpayer to bring objections before the Conseil,[45] and such cases took many forms. In dealing with the tax-exempt status of the municipal lighting plant of Mesle-sur-Sarthe, Blum sought to gain acceptance for this operation (and similar activities) by *not* awarding special privileges.[46] He thought that such enterprises would be more economically sound, as well as less frequently opposed, if they were put on the same footing as private enterprise. Under the existing law, only nonprofit enterprises were tax exempt, but the definition of nonprofit caused continual difficulties. Blum proposed to skirt these problems by considering as tax exempt only those activities which it was compulsory for a commune to undertake. This would exclude most activities of municipal socialism and subject them to taxation. While the Conseil agreed to tax the light plant of Mesle-sur-Sarthe, it declined to commit itself to a general policy for the future, and it continued to hamper municipal enterprises until they achieved wider acceptance.[47]

While Blum, in general, had no difficulty accepting the cautious case-by-case approach of the Conseil, he was to urge a more aggressive and positive conception of the judicial function. By nature of their position, the *commissaires du gouvernement* had to take more positive stands than the rest of the Conseil, but in general they also had to see things from much the same viewpoint as the Conseil if they were to function effectively. They were the "pilots of jurisprudence," but they were not adventurers.[48] When Blum attempted to push the Conseil more rapidly than it wanted to go, he usually did so from an inclination to put socially effective solutions above conformity to judicial traditions.

In a case involving the regulation of electoral districts, he urged the court to take upon itself the responsibility for drawing up new districts, after it had repeatedly agreed to void the districtings imposed by the prefect.[49] The Conseil had succeeded in its basic purpose of controlling prefectoral abuses, but its action had been purely negative, leaving the resolution of the muddled situation to the good will of the very parties whose antagonism had caused the original difficulties. Blum agreed with the Conseil's decisions, but in urging it to go further he was violating the current conception of the limits of the judicial function. In favoring social efficiency over preservation of the separation of powers, Blum had perhaps not considered all the ramifications of such a position, but he had the powerful arguments of common sense behind him. While it declined to follow him in this case, the Conseil d'Etat generally displayed healthy respect for common sense, which was perhaps a by-product of its close involvement in the often tangled problems of public administration.

Blum's interest in the social efficacy of the Conseil's decisions led him on at least one occasion into a procedural conservatism which was out of character with his general approach, and where the Conseil's position was more liberal than his. In this case the Conseil had to rule on the right of a third party to appeal one of its decisions. The tendency of the Conseil's jurisprudence had been to extend the power of individuals to oppose themselves to administrative acts. It had originally insisted that a plaintiff must have a positive material *interest* which was being harmed before he could bring action, but at the beginning of the century it increasingly admitted parties who considered themselves harmed in their *rights*, real or presumed.[50] This trend was of considerable importance in limiting the irresponsibility of the administration. Nonetheless, Blum tried to persuade the Conseil not to receive a third-party appeal against the consumer-oriented decision in the Halles regulation case. He was afraid—unnecessarily as it turned out—that the Conseil might reverse its earlier decision, for which he had fought.[51]

Such instances of Blum's concern about the social conservatism of his colleagues were rare, and he was probably pleased that in these and other cases the Conseil tried to pursue a criterion of public interest which did not bow to every wish of the business community.[52] The Conseil did indeed display a willingness remarkable in a judicial body to adapt to a changing world, and this experience undoubtedly reinforced Blum's reformist temper and helped him believe that socialism would not necessarily require violent revolution. Joseph Caillaux was exaggerating when, in 1905, he remarked: "It is the Conseil d'Etat which will make the social revolution."[53] But Blum was learning that what happened in the more glamorous arena of politics and the Chamber of Deputies was not the whole reality of French social reform.

The expansion of social legislation was of direct interest to the judicial branch of the Conseil, as much as to the legislative branch, for the application of new legislation always called forth much litigation.[54] Thus the Conseil had a further opportunity to influence the nature of legislation and its social impact. As a *commissaire du gouvernement*, Blum was in a position to influence a number of issues. On at least one occasion, he handled the first case under a new law and thus proposed guidelines for its subsequent application. His professional skill was nowhere better demonstrated than in his handling of the immense complexities of jurisdiction which arose from the establishment of a peasants' retirement program that was based on a complicated mixture of state and private action.[55] Blum, of course, was enthusiastic about this legislation and therefore inspired to do his best to make its application meaningful. The amelioration of the common man's lot, whether on socialist principles or others, commanded his support.

The pension cases, nevertheless, brought up an important social problem which Blum did not, and perhaps could not, deal with. This problem was the suffering caused to poor petitioners (and most of the pensioners were certainly poor) by the excessive length of time it took the Conseil to return a judgment. Delays of several years had become common as a result of the immense number of issues which were brought before the Conseil, whose popularity had resulted from its willingness to hear an increasing variety of cases against the administration and from the inexpensiveness of its procedures (no lawyer was required and the legal forms were very simple). By the turn of the century, the backlog caused concern, but even a series of reforms did not improve the situation significantly.

Blum was doubtless aware of this indirect denial of justice, but it is not clear how acutely.[56] In retrospect, one is tempted to think that the Conseil was not so hard working as it might have been, for in spite of the backlog it continued to take a lengthy vacation each summer.[57] This apparent insouciance, however, must be put in the context of the customs of the bourgeoisie of the Belle Epoque, which found such vacations perfectly natural.[58] No little portion of the nostalgia for that era stems from the more leisurely pace of middle-class life, in which work often occupied a smaller place than in our own age of leisure. Blum's contemporaries were not lazy; they had a different set of values. Blum himself led a life which would be considered very active in any era, but it was essentially traditional even in its unconventionalities. Had he attempted to devote all his waking efforts to the Conseil, he would have appeared eccentric and would have accomplished little. What is remarkable about Blum is that, although he was so much a man of his class and period, he was developing the potentialities which enabled him to put aside the pleasant life and devote all his efforts (after the World War) to the cause of the less favored.

As he had anticipated, Blum's activities on the Conseil left him with considerable spare time for literary activities. Also, the structure of the Conseil's work gave him considerable control over his working hours. He could prepare his conclusions in the Conseil's library or in his study at home on the boulevard Montparnasse and meet his colleagues in their afternoon sessions to discuss the cases. The formal meetings at which he presented his conclusions averaged only fifteen a year.[59] If less spectacular than his literary work, his judicial work was no less an intensely intellectual activity. Had Blum been merely a *littérateur*, his future career as a socialist leader would indeed have been difficult to explain. It was on the Conseil that he acquired the practical foundations in the realities of government which enabled him to be more than a literary sympathizer with socialism. He gained legal knowledge and ability which enabled him to perform useful services as a follower in the socialist ranks before 1914, but it was a more general and yet more profound knowledge of the workings of government which enabled him to emerge later as a leader.

His work as a *commissaire du gouvernement* gave Blum the habit of public responsibility and also the habit of making decisions. His legal decisions, products of his intense logic, show nothing of the indecision which sometimes appeared in his literary reviews, where questions of taste and not mere reason were involved. He lost none of his sense of nuance or taste for fine distinctions, both of which were useful in the law, but he learned to come to clear-cut conclusions. Perhaps most important for the future was the understanding he gained of the significance of administration in French life and the necessity for the socialist movement to prepare itself for the practical tasks of administering the nation.[60]

Blum was always proud of his career on the Conseil d'Etat, and justly so, for he had earned distinction and the respect of his colleagues. Blum's dandyism—his preference for the large-brim felt hat of the artist and literary man over the *chapeau melon* or topper, which were marks of bourgeois respectability[61]—made him stand out among his more staid colleagues and make his distinction all the more impressive. The satisfactions he gained from his public service, although different in character, were no less deep than those of his literary career. Both careers made good use of his analytic intelligence, and at the same time satisfied his craving for variety and his desire for close contact with the life of his time. His legal career also offered satisfaction for his desire for socially useful action. But it was his participation in the socialist movement that offered the key to his future.

CHAPTER FOUR

THE MAKING OF A SOCIALIST (I)

BLUM'S FIRST AND BRIEF OVERT ENGAGEMENT in the socialist move-ment did not disclose all the possibilities of his future career as socialist leader. In particular, though his interest in politics was at a new high, he showed no signs of ambition for a political career. Aside from a few articles for *La Revue blanche* and *La Petite république*—articles that indicate his talents and reveal his attitudes —he did not lean toward even a career in political journalism. Engaging himself publicly in the cause of socialist unity, and retiring into the background when this was achieved, he saw his role as primarily that of a specialist, putting his knowledge and contacts at the service of his leader—Jean Jaurès.

To be sure, many of the attitudes and opinions which were to shape Blum's socialist career were formed in this earlier period. Gilbert Ziebura and others have rightly emphasized that Blum came to socialism at the moment when unity was the burning question. And unity would remain one of his basic desires, even long after it was broken by the Communist scission in 1920. More has been said about his association with Jaurès than any other aspect of his social thought, and Blum's decision to defer to the memory of Jaurès has made this inevitable. But we must remember that Jaurès and Blum were led to socialist convictions by the same man, Lucien

Herr, and that Jaurès's adherence to socialism, though it took different forms, did not antedate Blum's by much. Blum was Jaurès's friend and collaborator rather than his disciple.

Though most writers about Léon Blum have paid more attention to his socialist activity than to any other aspect of his early life, there is something to be gained by examining it in a more detailed biographical fashion than has previously been done.[1] As we have seen in his literary and legal careers, Blum was very much a man of his age and generation. He needs to be seen in the context of that age if we are to understand the development and the nuances of his thought, if we are to avoid the fallacy of treating him as an abstract intelligence. Blum was no "gentle dreamer and idealist in an age of harsh practicality"[2] but a man of wide-ranging experience in the problems and affairs of his country, as well as its intellectual life.

The humanistic qualities of Blum's socialism, which Joel Colton has stressed, are certainly evident in this period. Blum's conception of socialism, like that of Jaurès, was not inspired by hatred of the bourgeoisie, the oppressors of the proletariat, but by hatred of oppression, from which mankind as a whole had too long suffered. Whether their vision of a mankind gradually liberating itself from ancient servitudes was more utopian than that of the "scientific" prophets of proletarian revolution remains to be seen. If socialism was (or is), as he thought, a moral movement as well as a political and social struggle, it can only be so—in Blum's words—*à l'échelle humaine.*

It was through a slow process of development—a "slow incubation," as he himself called it—that Léon Blum became a socialist.[3] It was also a natural, inevitable process—the perhaps unpredictable but nonetheless inescapable outcome of all that he had learned and thought. He was not so much converted to socialism as made aware that he was already a socialist, without having realized it. That realization came during his apprenticeships at *La Revue blanche* and the Conseil d'Etat and was, as a result, part of the fabric of his intellectual development. Something of the character of his early socialism is revealed by the fact that it did not disrupt the development of his literary and judicial careers. Few traces remain of the steps by which Blum's socialist conviction was forged; he said little about it, and even this was not so illuminating as one would expect. There emerges, however, from his activities and writings in the prewar period, a sufficiently clear picture of the kind of socialist he became, and the kind he remained when events pushed him from the wings and onto the stage of national political life.

Blum rightly traces the beginnings of his "slow incubation" to the experiences of his early home life. He did not acquire specifically socialist ideas there but, rather, certain habits and attitudes which, although they by no means predestined his socialism, were to constitute its psychological bases. The most important attitude was the love of justice which Blum's mother had striven to implant in her sons.[4] Young Léon was awed by his mother's concern, and it became so much his own that it formed the solid foundation of his socialism, imparting its spirit to the whole structure. The most important practical aspect of the sentiment of justice was the habit of respect for others, for the uniqueness of the human personality, which made Blum a humanist in all his concerns.

The idea of justice taught in Blum's home was tempered by the idea of charity.[5] Not that justice and charity were considered antithetical (as in some Protestant thought), but whatever the standards that rule Jehovah's conduct, human justice required charitableness toward the less fortunate. During his school days Blum showed exceptional sensitivity to personal appeals to his charity, often embarrassing his comrades by going out of his way to help a beggar, and once amazing Gide by interrupting an intense conversation to get a handbill from a ragged distributor, explaining on his return that he did it to help bolster the poor fellow's self-respect.[6] On another occasion, Blum and one of his younger brothers, Marcel, were leaving the wedding of a friend when they were approached by beggars. Léon unhesitatingly gave them all the cash he had and then had to borrow cab fare from Marcel to get home.[7]

Blum later spoke of compassion for suffering as one of the sources of socialism, and though it was a factor in his life, compassion need not lead one to socialism.[8] Charitableness is perhaps even more likely to express an anti-socialist position—as Daniel Halévy learned from the redoubtable anarchist Louise Michel, who said: "Those who give charity, when they are doing it, they are proud and they are contented; but us, we are never satisfied."[9] Blum, however, was able to accommodate charitableness as a special part of his personality without becoming self-satisfied or proud, realizing that if it is a duty to relieve suffering, it is even more obligatory to help build a world in which there will be less suffering—a more just world.

His concern for the suffering of others and his feeling for justice were not in themselves enough to lead him to socialism, for he needed certain experiences and ideas before he would come to the conclusion that socialism was the mundane incarnation of those sentiments. Regardless of his later experiences, his values antedated his socialism and governed his conception and practice of socialism. Blum's origins, after all, were bourgeois, even if they were "très-petits bourgeois" (as he said), and his only path to socialism was through social consciousness, since the realities of working-class life remain, to a degree, unknown to those who have not experienced them.[10] As he later claimed, he may have questioned the morality of his father's wholesale business at an early age, but it was not because of observing the lives of the employees (or from a psychological enmity for his father) that Blum revolted against capitalist values.[11] It was not from the "fils des petits artisans républicains" whom he met in the neighborhood schools before going to the lycée that he became convinced of the injustice of the capitalist economic order, but in the realm of ideas.[12]

While his experience in the schools was in many respects decisive for his development, it seems to have had only an indirect influence on his socialism. In one of his rare confidences, Blum told of being awakened to a basic injustice in society by a chance reading (at age fourteen) in the library of the lycée Charlemagne:[13] the third act of *Les effrontés* by Emile Augier, a well-known author of plays on social themes.

Giboyer.—The French people resemble that gentleman who had eight head colds in one month and who had cured them all, except the first. Finish the Revolution of '89 and you won't have anything more to fear.

Le marquis d'Auberive.—Finish '89? You mean it isn't finished?

Giboyer.—That was only the beginning, the demolition work. . . . The old abuses were all wiped off the slate. The task still remains to reconstruct society, that is to organize resistance against the force of circumstances by creating an aristocracy outside that of wealth.

Le marquis.—But what would you found it on in this democratic country?

Giboyer.—On the very principle of democracy, on personal merit.

A banker then assures Giboyer that society has realized this goal, and a newspaper editor adds that wealth, being the result of labor, is the most precise measure of merit.

Giboyer.—I quite agree that effort and intelligence are needed to build a fortune; the faculties one needs to become rich are of the first order. ... But one tiny point remains which destroys your whole argument from top to bottom: wealth is hereditary and intelligence is not. ...

Le marquis (with his Mephistophelian smile).—Touché. And do you know, gentlemen, where your revolutionary theories will lead you if you follow their logic? To the abolition of inheritance: you won't be able to get out of it any other way.

When he read this passage, Blum was perhaps not aware that he was in some ways one of those who are privileged by birth. He was not the only member of his generation to have been stimulated by the now forgotten works of Augier,[14] but it seems likely that this incident had more symbolic than historical significance—symbolic of the importance that equality of opportunity would have in Blum's socialism. The incident also indicates that Blum's socialist conviction was an intellectual as well as an emotional process.

Although, as a child, Blum displayed a precocious curiosity about politics, it was not until his university years that he revealed a serious interest in anything but the intellectual and literary life.[15] His interest in politics seemed out of character to his friends, most of whom were seeking, as he appeared to be, careers in literature. They could accept his turning to the Conseil d'Etat for a living as a practical expedient, not in conflict with his literary ambition, but politics was another matter. Fernand Gregh, his school friend and a colleague at *Le Banquet*, later recalled:

There was, about 1892, at the railroad station at Enghien-les-Bains, a wooden pedestrian bridge which must have dated from the time of the first railroads and which has since burned. I can see myself one fine June morning, descending the steps with Léon Blum, engaged in one of those young men's conversations where one passes the universe in review, with the illusion that it is waiting for you to change many things in it. Blum had asked me what I wanted to make or do in life. "A few beautiful verses," I said to him. "And you?" "Politics." His response astonished me greatly. In fact I did not see, none of us saw then, anything around us except art and literature.[16]

It is most doubtful that Blum was seriously contemplating a political career in 1892; but he had developed an interest in politics, probably stimulated by Maurice Barrès.

Barrès had entered politics as a supporter of General Boulanger, and while Blum did not share his enthusiasm for the new man on horseback, he appreciated the ironic wit with which Barrès attacked the stuffed-shirt mediocrity of the bourgeois Republic, an irony that was intensified in 1892 by the Panama scandal.[17] Blum did not align himself with the right-wing critics of the Republic, but it seems probable that their criticism helped stimulate his awareness of current political life. Traditionalists and socialists have often joined in criticizing the individualism of nineteenth-century bourgeois society, and gone on, of course, to propose different remedies for it. To both groups, the corruption of parliament seemed to be the product of a too exclusive predominance of individual interests over the general interest. This observation inspired Blum's first serious political reflections.

In the summer of 1892 Blum made his debut in *La Revue blanche* with an essay titled "The Progress of A-politics in France" and dedicated to Maurice Barrès, "deputy from Nancy."[18] The twenty-year-old essayist examined what he called the "decline of politics" in France from the time of the Revolution to the present, which he attempted to explain as the product of a weariness with repeated changes in the political order and disillusionment with the failure of all nineteenth-century revolutions to fulfill their promises. This disinterest in the *res publica*, as Blum interpreted it, had a dual result:

This annihilation of all General Will, this torpid languishing where little by little the conscience of the nation is lost and abolished, has not only served to encourage the free development, the spontaneous and unobstructed expansion of individual desires and private wills; little by little the conviction has been fortified that the ensemble of the individual desires and private wills is sufficient to ensure the common life.[19]

Clearly, Blum doubted that this substitution for the general will could be adequate, but he did not yet see the possibility of remedying the fragmentation of society by developing a new concept of the general interest. Ultimately, he would hope to reconcile the individual and the general will without annihilating either of them.

Blum's interest in individualism in politics was reinforced when he found himself in a milieu that was strongly touched by anarchism, for the circle of *La Revue blanche* included such well-known anarchists as Félix Fénéon, Jean Grave, and Zo d'Axa.[20] During the 1880s and 1890s, anarchism had considerable vogue, but it was for the most part a very "literary" anarchism, whose futility was symbolized by the fate of Laurent Tailhade, who shortly after publishing an article praising the violent gesture of an anarchist was himself maimed by an anarchist bomb.[21] Spurred by public anger and fright, the government attempted to strike at anarchist propaganda by erasing the legal distinctions between use of the bomb and use of the pen. Grave and Fénéon, the editorial secretary of *La Revue blanche*, were among the literary figures prosecuted under the new legislation in the celebrated Trial of the Thirty, in August 1893.[22] The prosecution treated the writers, bombers, and common criminals as equally pernicious to society, but the jury acquitted the intellectuals while sending the "propagandists of the deed" to jail. Blum found a certain seductiveness in the ideas of his anarchist acquaintances and doubtless admired their moral courage —all the more as he had had a streak of rebelliousness and distaste for unjust authority since his childhood.[23] But it was unjust authority and not authority in general which repelled him, and his flirtation with anarchism did not go very far.

Blum had already noted, in his article on "a-politics," that— ironically—bourgeois individualism and dislike of government made Frenchmen more susceptible to anarchism than to socialism.[24] Realizing that anarchism, too, was based on an unwarranted assumption that individual wills could suffice for a general will, Blum expressed his first reservations about anarchist ideals as early as 1894.[25] However, he was strongly influenced by the individualist current, and especially by two writers who were not, strictly speaking, anarchists: Barrès and Georges Clemenceau.[26] In their distinctively different ways, both men led Blum to take a critical look at bourgeois society—the critical look of both the literary artist and the political dilettante. Both views touched him closely, for as an aspiring literary artist Blum felt the need to affirm his individuality, and as an intellectual he had to affirm his superiority over the baseness and compromise of the political world. Indeed, both Barrès and Clemenceau served as examples of the intellectually superior individual who, by participating in politics, endowed the political world with a nobility it would otherwise lack. Such examples enabled Blum to imagine himself in politics, but only more powerful influences could transform the intellectual's curiosity into political activism.

The impact of Barrès and Clemenceau would soon seem merely negative—the Revolution of '89, as Giboyer had described it, compared to the impact of Lucien Herr. Herr was the librarian of the Ecole Normale Supérieure, where he exercised a behind-the-scenes influence in pointing a remarkable number of *normaliens* toward socialism.[27] His most important "convert" (perhaps "discovery" is a better word) was Jean Jaurès, who had appeared at the Ecole Normale as a brilliant philosophy student from Castres. Only Jaurès was to stand above Blum among Herr's protégés. During his year at the Ecole Normale (1890–91), Blum had become acquainted with Herr, who was respected for his bibliographical guidance, but their relationship was "sans intimité" and largely confined to academic matters.[28] Herr, a cautious proselytizer, moved only when he was reasonably certain of being well received. Blum, who was not paying full attention to his schoolwork, may have appeared to Herr as merely a literary dilettante and not a very likely candidate for the socialist intelligentsia.[29]

After leaving the Ecole Normale, Blum did not see Herr, although he maintained indirect contact through Professor Charles Andler, a specialist in German studies and a moderate socialist, whom Blum encountered at the home of Tristan Bernard.[30] Then, one day in 1893, Blum and Herr chanced to meet on the Place de la Concorde as Herr was on his way to the offices of *La Revue de Paris*, where he was a contributor. After a long conversation, strolling up and down the Champs Elysées, they became intimate friends, and out of the friendship Blum's socialism emerged.[31] Blum's "Goethe" later reflected on the experience:

Isn't it a strange thing? Humanity raises itself only very slowly to the level of certain ideas which are nonetheless so clear, so imperiously true, that it seems as if they ought to have imposed themselves immediately on any rational mind. ... Then it seems as if suddenly, at a predetermined moment in history, man's intelligence acquires a sort of new sense. ... It seems to me that something similar occurs in the life of each individual. A moment comes when the world appears under a new aspect, illuminated by an unknown and *inevitable* glow. Truly we are alighting on a new world.[32]

Blum was ready for Herr in 1893, as he had not been in 1891. His reflections on society during his first year at *La Revue blanche* had sharpened his critical eye but had not given him a positive framework for interpretation and action. He had rejected the iniquities of the existing order without finding a better replacement.

Herr exposed him to the collectivist solution with such force of conviction that Blum felt as if he had gone through an operation for cataracts, so clear did it all seem now.[33] Blum later said of Jaurès: "Herr led him to become clearly conscious that he was a socialist."[34] He could have made the same statement about himself.

This intellectual consciousness was only a first step in Blum's socialist experience, and by itself would have had only a limited impact on his life. Lucien Herr's reformist Marxism was an activist philosophy, but by itself was not sufficient to lead Blum to action.[35] It was through Herr, however, that Blum had the decisive contact and the decisive experience that transformed a contemplative conviction into a force ultimately capable of changing his life: his friendship with Jaurès and his participation in the Dreyfus affair.

The personal impact of Jaurès was greater than that of anyone else. When Blum first met him, in 1897 at the latter's apartment at 27 rue Madame near St.-Sulpice, Blum was already an intellectual socialist, but the definitive form of his philosophy was to be shaped by his contact with Jaurès.[36] Blum later recalled that first meeting:

At first contact he did not impose an immediate ascendency, as he lacked a commanding appearance. He was a man of short stature, with a massive, bearded head resting directly on his shoulders, and a thickset body. His voice was at first harsh and monotonous, and it was only little by little that it found its modulation, sometimes its power, sometimes its softness. And yet it seems to me that in the course of a very diverse life, where I have been given the opportunity to approach many truly great men, I have never encountered any other—except, perhaps, M. Albert Einstein —on whom the seal of genius was so apparently, so evidently imprinted.[37]

Although Jaurès's intense devotion to his cause prevented him from developing many friendships, a close and life-long association grew up between him and Blum.[38] After the death of Jaurès in 1914, Blum was to place his own career as socialist leader under the aegis of Jaurès. In part, this was a reflection of their common ideals, in part the testimony of Blum's admiration for Jaurès's leadership— as well as a result of Blum's desire to emphasize the continuity of the postwar Socialist party with the prewar party. Blum perhaps thought that Jaurès's qualities of leadership were greater than his own, but when he was put to the test of leadership, he showed that he had learned from Jaurès although he did not attempt to do things as Jaurès would have done them.[39] Before 1914, Blum was content to be of service to the leader of his party—to do those things for which his temperament and abilities best fitted him.

While it was Herr who involved Blum in the Dreyfus affair, it was Jaurès's leadership during the affair which most moved him. The affair would have affected Blum under any circumstances, because of the crucial role of anti-Semitism, but, as it turned out, the affair gave Blum his first taste of some of the harsh realities of public life, his first lessons in the difficulties of attempting to implement his social ideals, his first real contact with the socialist movement. In sum, it was the first involvement in *action* for the young intellectual, who only a few years earlier had debated the relative merits of thought and action with himself. His experience during the affair left such an impression on him that, with the death of Dreyfus almost forty years later, he was inspired to publish a volume of his recollections of the affair (on which the following account is largely based).[40] There can be no doubt that this was "the decisive period in the life of Léon Blum."[41]

From beginning to end, the affair was full of surprises for Blum, and many others like him, who undertook the defense of Alfred Dreyfus.[42] Blum's involvement began in September 1897 when Herr, with whom he often cycled, rode up to the summer place near Paris where Blum was vacationing and exclaimed: "Do you know that Dreyfus is innocent?"[43] Dreyfus—who was he? Gradually, Blum reassembled his recollections of the incident, now three years old, that had sent a member of the general staff to Devil's Island for betraying military secrets to Germany.

When the treason case had broken, in 1894, it had seemed simple and straightforward to most of the public. An officer had been arrested, brought to trial before a court of his peers, convicted on evidence, and punished. The only criticism had come from those who thought the penalty, perpetual solitary confinement on Devil's Island, ought to have been death before a firing squad. The only other byplay had been a brief flurry of anti-Semitism, because the officer was a Jew, but this issue had not generated much interest. Appearances, however, are often deceiving, and what the public did not know was to prove of grave importance. Little was known of the steps by which the espionage had been detected and traced to Dreyfus, because the trial had been held behind closed doors for apparently justifiable reasons of military security. The public did not know—and later proved very reluctant to learn—how slender was the evidence against Captain Dreyfus.

The case had begun with a single scrap of paper (known as the *bordereau*) which was recovered from the German military attaché by the French "deuxième bureau" and which described the communication of certain classified material to the attaché, Schwarzkoppen. Because of the nature of the military information described in the *bordereau*, the group of suspects was delimited, and it was discovered that the handwriting of one of the group resembled that of the *bordereau*. It appears, though no one can be certain, that at this point anti-Semitic prejudice, especially common in high military circles, impaired the critical faculties of the officers involved. Suspicion pointed to a Jew, and that a Jew should be a traitor seemed logical to them; so no further evidence or serious examination was necessary. Even so, the evidence was so meager that, although he was arrested and interrogated in a bizarre manner, Dreyfus might have been released and the matter hushed up had not a virulent anti-Semite in the intelligence bureau, most probably Major Henry, leaked the case to the daily *La Libre Parole*, the major organ of French anti-Semitism. The military now felt compelled to try the case, and Dreyfus was brought to trial.

Someone, however, was afraid that Dreyfus might not be convicted, and so, with the permission of the Minister of War, a secret dossier was conveyed to the judges with solemn assurances that it had been thoroughly authenticated. In violation of even the one-sided rules of French military justice, the defense was kept ignorant of this move, and the judges, impressed by their superiors, voted unanimously for conviction.

Dreyfus was conducted to the parade ground of the Ecole Militaire, where he was stripped of his insignia and his sword was broken. He was shipped posthaste to his island prison—to the cheers of all patriots. Like almost everyone else, Blum had no reason to suspect that an injustice had been committed, nor was he soon to learn. Dreyfus, steadfastly maintaining his innocence, was gone and soon forgotten.

Of the handful of doubters, only his brother, Mathieu Dreyfus, seems to have refused to give up hope for his rehabilitation, and with the aid of Bernard Lazare he patiently gathered evidence and sought to persuade the general staff to reopen the case by respectful petition. After digesting Herr's unexpected message in 1897, Blum recalled that Lazare, a literary critic who was well known at *La Revue blanche*, had tried to convey his convictions to his colleagues but had little success. Blum had also listened to the doubts of Michel Bréal, who was impressed by the lack of plausible motive. But Blum, like the others, had been unable to believe that the court could have been so certain without good reason. Although Blum was not yet aware of it, in the fall of 1896 the defenders of Dreyfus acquired more solid material. A newspaper leak revealed for the first time the existence of the secret dossier, giving grounds for challenging the regularity of the court-martial. Shortly afterward, *Le Matin* published a facsimile of the *bordereau*, which put the Dreyfusards on the trail of the real author of this *pièce de conviction*, Major Esterhazy. Some intellectuals were now beginning to listen to Lazare and Mathieu Dreyfus, who redoubled their efforts to have the case reopened, and Lucien Herr was among the first to join them.

About the time that Herr came to recruit Blum for the Dreyfus cause, his partisans decided to take the offensive by charging Esterhazy with the crime for which Dreyfus had been transported to Guiana. They chose to attack in a rather oblique manner, with bit-by-bit revelations in *Figaro*, which they hoped would induce Esterhazy to "confess" by fleeing the country. But this proved to be an error in tactics. As Blum later observed, the error resulted from their failure to realize what kind of opposition they were soon to face. Herr, Blum, and the rest did not yet realize that there was going to be an *affaire*, that there would be bitter opposition to their efforts to reopen a case which, it seemed to them, once reopened would speedily lead to rectification of an injustice.[44] This optimism began to dim when the Méline government persisted in ignoring the call for reconsideration, but the greatest shock was the appearance of an organized resistance, which the manner of the *Figaro* revelations had given time to develop. Blum was surprised to find himself denounced as part of a "Jewish syndicate" that was conspiring to buy freedom for a "traitor."

Meanwhile, decisive developments, unknown to Blum's circle, had been taking place. In March of 1896 the new head of army intelligence, Colonel Picquart, was given a note (the *petit bleu*) that had been written by Schwarzkoppen and addressed to Esterhazy. After putting Esterhazy under surveillance, Picquart had made the startling discovery that Esterhazy's handwriting resembled that of the *bordereau*. When Picquart informed his superior, General Gonse, of what he had found, he was sternly warned not to attempt to reopen the Dreyfus case. Shortly afterward, Picquart was removed from his post, and in January 1897 was transferred to southern Tunisia. Picquart accepted his fate stoically, but he conveyed his findings to a friend, the lawyer Leblois. Leblois, in turn, passed the information to a respected life-senator, the Alsatian Scheurer-Kestner, who had already been informed by Mathieu Dreyfus of the suspicion against Esterhazy. After vain approaches to the ministers—at which time Herr and his circle learned of the new evidence—Scheurer-Kestner, in November 1897, published an open letter to a colleague in which he called for a reopening of the case. At that point the struggle took on an increasingly bitter and public aspect, and Blum found himself among the combatants in a very small army.

Blum's first militant Dreyfusard activity began in December 1897 in the offices of *La Revue blanche*, where many Dreyfusards gathered to discuss the latest news and rumors and sometimes to plan action. The circle of *La Revue blanche* had been almost unanimously "touched with the Dreyfusard grace," and Blum's social world was little disrupted. Of his friends and acquaintances, only Barrès, Pierre Veber, and Lucien Muhlfeld from *La Revue blanche* and Paul Valéry and Pierre Louÿs from *La Conque* passed into the enemy camp.[45] Thus Blum was spared some of the tension, and especially the personal bitterness, which the affair soon produced, making neutrality increasingly difficult—at least among the middle classes. These tensions, which split families as they were soon to split France, were mirrored in the famous cartoon by the anti-Semite Caran d'Ache, whose first panel showed a family sitting down to dinner over the caption "Above all let's not talk about the Dreyfus affair" and whose second panel was a scene of overturned furniture and broken crockery over the caption "They talked about it."[46]

The substantial number of Jews in the circle of *La Revue blanche* was of less influence in its becoming Dreyfusard than the presence of anarchists who, because they were firm enemies of military authority, had a particular sensitivity to Dreyfus's fate. The Natansons, however, did have contacts which brought them into the affair early. Thadée in particular—who was close to Joseph Reinach, one of the prime movers of the Dreyfusard cause, and also to Dreyfus's lawyer, Demange, whom he had aided during the Trial of the Thirty—was a center of attention because of his sources of information.[47] The pages of *La Revue blanche* were opened to Dreyfusard propaganda, and the review's publishing house brought out a number of works on the affair, including those of Jean Ajalbert, Urbain Gohier, and Gaston Moch. Blum aided the publicity with glowing accounts of the Dreyfusard literature.

The offices of *La Revue blanche* were also a center for collecting signatures on various petitions, and the task of securing signers was assigned to various volunteers. Fernand Gregh proudly brought the signature of Anatole France,[48] and Blum promised to bring that of Maurice Barrès. Blum had known Barrès since he had been an adolescent visiting relatives in Lorraine, and for him—as for his literary generation—Barrès, who was ten years older, was "not only the master but the guide." Blum went to his friend's home confident that "since he was our leader, he would follow us"—only to learn that one can never know another person well enough to be sure how he will react to a new and unforeseen test.[49] Barrès was unable to refuse him face to face, but his ultimate refusal was one of the greatest personal shocks of Blum's young life, and his dismay was deepened by Barrès's subsequent alignment with the nationalists.

Among other surprises, probably the greatest was the vigor with which Anatole France, the elegant skeptic, almost alone among the older generation of literary men, supported the Dreyfusards. At the Caillavet salon, Blum encountered another assembly of Dreyfusards: the inseparable *vaudevillistes*, Gaston de Caillavet and Robert de Flers, Anna de Noailles, Joseph Reinach, Clemenceau, Jaurès, and (later) Aristide Briand.

The enthusiasm of the first months of Blum's Dreyfusard activity was considerably dampened by the outcome of the Esterhazy trial in early January 1898. Mathieu Dreyfus had leveled formal charges against Esterhazy at the time of the Scheurer-Kestner letter, but the Major had apparently been assured of protection and had boldly demanded a trial to clear his name. The conviction of Esterhazy would have automatically reopened the Dreyfus case, and the Dreyfusards thought that victory was almost within their grasp. They still did not realize that they were faced with an opposition that would stop at no dishonesty to keep its prisoner on Devil's

Island. Esterhazy's acquittal struck Blum so hard that hope gave way to despair. The victory which had seemed certain now seemed impossible.

Only four days later, Blum was awakened by pounding on the shutters of his ground floor apartment. It was the corner newsman, who thrust a copy of *L'Aurore* into his hands and said, "Quick, Monsieur, read this." It was Emile Zola's open letter to the President of the Republic, arrestingly titled "J'accuse" by Georges Clemenceau, editor of *L'Aurore*. In a series of bold sentences, each beginning "I accuse," Zola hammered out the Dreyfusard riposte to the acquittal of Esterhazy. He accused the military judges of knowingly acquitting a guilty man on orders from above and he charged various war ministers (and others) with complicity in a plot to prevent revision of the unjust condemnation of Dreyfus. Deliberately, Zola had impugned the code of military honor, which the opponents of revision had so loudly defended.

To fight back, the military would have to move from the closed rooms of the two courts-martial into the full light of a civil court. They hesitated, but Zola had measured his men. His challenge was too strong to be ignored, and a defamation charge was leveled. A furious effort was made to limit the implications of Zola's day in the court: his charges pertaining to Dreyfus were ignored and suit was brought only on the Esterhazy count. The judges, obviously instructed in how to direct the proceedings, rode ruthlessly over every attempt to show that the Dreyfus case was germane to the Esterhazy case.

Blum chronicled the partiality of the judges and the arguments of Zola and his attorneys in an article on the trial which appeared in *La Revue blanche*.[50] Although Zola was condemned by the court (this time the Dreyfusards were sufficiently disabused to anticipate the verdict), Blum was once again in high spirits for he felt that Zola, in spite of all the obstacles, had proved his case. This was the first time that the cause had had a rostrum from which to reach beyond its own circles, and he believed that it had restored the likelihood of victory.[51] It was now his duty, and that of the others, to follow Zola's heroic gesture with a steady reiteration of what he had demonstrated. In addition to signing petitions in support of Zola, which were published in the Dreyfusard press,[52] Blum felt he ought to use his legal as well as his literary training, and he furnished legal advice to Jaurès, a practice he was to continue.[53]

Blum also had played a minor backstage role at the trial, assisting Zola's attorney, the brilliant Fernand Labori, who was well known for his participation in several *causes célèbres*.[54] Blum must have found Labori an interesting, if perhaps too flamboyant, figure. He was toying with political ambitions more seriously than Blum had yet done, and at the same time was very interested in literature. In 1896, Labori had founded *La Revue du Palais*, which in 1898 became *La Grande revue*,[55] and for a time, Blum was a regular contributor to this important review. Labori was assisted in this case by his regular partners, but an exceptional amount of research was needed, and Blum and other volunteers were set to studying obscure points of law or preparing a riposte to an anticipated government argument. There was nothing glamorous about the work, but Blum was satisfied to be helping.[56]

The Zola trial was marked by an outburst of violent passions, and even inside the Palais de Justice Blum could have heard the mob demanding death for Zola and the Jews. Violence was largely confined to Paris, however, and with legislative elections coming up in May, the political leaders who had become involved in the affair turned to other matters. The outcome of the elections appears to have been little affected by the affair, although it may have played a role in Jaurès's defeat. On the other hand, the new ministry, led by Henri Brisson, a Radical, was shaped by fear of the anti-republican reaction which the affair was arousing. Even so, the Brisson ministry was not committed to revision of the case, as the appointment of the ultra-patriot Godefroy Cavaignac to the war ministry showed.

Cavaignac, convinced of Dreyfus's guilt, hoped to put an end to the Dreyfusard agitation by offering definitive proof of that guilt. On 7 July 1898, in a moving speech to the Chamber, he presented the dossier prepared by Colonel Henry. In his anxiety to convince the Chamber, Cavaignac revealed much that had been kept secret, notably a letter signed "Alexandrine" and purportedly sent by the Italian attaché to Schwarzkoppen, in which Dreyfus was named as an agent. The effect was dramatic. The Dreyfusards were stunned into silence.

Blum, who had not gone to the Chamber that day, was sitting in his study in the late afternoon, talking to Lucien Herr, when a friend of Herr brought the bad news. They sat in despairing silence, which was broken when the doorbell rang and Jaurès burst in on them, angry yet radiant.

What now? You, too!? Just now leaving the Chamber I had to struggle against a group of comrades who were surrounding and pressing me. They imagine that it's all over, the simpletons; they begged me to close my campaign. But don't you understand that now, and for the first time, we have the certainty of victory? Méline was invulnerable because he kept silent; Cavaignac speaks, discusses; therefore he is beaten. Our only dangerous adversaries were Mystery and Silence. Now that Cavaignac has given the example they will have to publish everything, expose everything; the General Staff will have to exhaust its reserves. They cannot whisper in our ears any longer: "But, you see, there's a secret document which . . . ." Now we can examine everything and verify that which is authentic and that which is false. Those items which Cavaignac just cited . . . well! I swear to you they are forgeries. They smell forgery, they stink forgery. They are forgeries, stupid ones at that, fabricated to cover up other forgeries. I was certain of it just from hearing them and I'm going to prove it. The forgers have come out of their hole; we've got them by the throat now . . . . Stop looking as if you were at a burial; rejoice with me.[57]

Jaurès proved a good prophet. Colonel Picquart denounced the Alexandrine letter as a forgery and Jaurès undertook the proof in a series of articles in *La Petite république* that came to be titled "Les preuves." The Dreyfus cause was alive again.

Cavaignac, unlike some other nationalists, was an honest man and he ordered an investigation which revealed beyond a doubt that the Alexandrine letter was a forgery. Summoned before the minister, Colonel Henry confessed to the forgery, pleading patriotism as his motive. The next day, 31 August 1898, Blum received the news at his hotel in Zurich, where he was vacationing, that the forger had cut his throat in his cell at the Mont Valérien fortress. Blum now felt the joy of real victory, for revision of the Dreyfus case and his exoneration could no longer be prevented.

It seemed to Blum that after a year of intense conflict, a year in which life had been oriented around the cause of Alfred Dreyfus, the real affair was finally over and a Dreyfusard could become an ordinary man again. The tide had indeed turned, although there were still to be further disappointments and difficulties. The nationalists fought a bitter rearguard battle, but Blum was calm with the certainty of victory.

The remaining *péripéties* of the affair were not without interest for him. As a jurist, he must have been dismayed when the Chambre Criminelle of the Cour de Cassation, convoked to examine the

LIBRARY
EISENHOWER COLLEGE

regularity of Dreyfus's 1894 trial, was disseized by a legislative act that transferred the case to the court sitting as a whole. While the court was carrying out its inquiry, another obstacle to revision was removed by the sudden death of President Félix Faure. Faure's death was followed by a comic-opera episode when various nationalist groups tried to turn the state funeral into an insurrection because the new president, Emile Loubet, was sympathetic to revision. Paul Déroulède, head of the Ligue des Patriotes, seized the reins of General Roget's horse when the long ceremony ended and cried: "Mon général! A l'Elysée!"—only to be arrested several minutes later, after he refused to desist.[58]

In June 1899 the nationalists made another attempt to avenge themselves on the Republic and its president, after the Cour de Cassation ordered Dreyfus returned for a new trial. While attending the steeplechase at Auteuil, Loubet was set upon by an aristocratic mob and struck on his tophat by a cane-swinging baron. The attack brought a stirring reply the following Sunday in a massive demonstration of support for the Republic, which was organized by Dreyfusards, socialists, and labor unions. Crowds poured into the Longchamps race course in the Bois de Boulogne and formed a column to march back into Paris. They were treated roughly by the police (who had failed to protect Loubet) and were attacked by nationalists at various points, most notably in a lively battle near the edge of the Bois (at the Pavillon d'Armenonville).[59]

Blum and Herr had abandoned their intellectual roles to join the front ranks of the marchers. This was the closest Blum came to the physical violence occasioned by the affair, and he must have been impressed by the quasi-revolutionary atmosphere of the great throng.[60] The immediate result was not only that the nationalist specter was exorcised but, on the next day, the vacillating ministry of Charles Dupuy was overthrown and soon replaced by the determined government of René Waldeck-Rousseau.

The retrial of Dreyfus, at Rennes in August 1899, completed the disgrace of the French army when the court, by a 5 to 2 vote, rendered the incredible verdict of "guilty with extenuating circumstances."[61] Blum and Herr were prevented from going to Rennes by illness in their families, but they followed the proceedings through Mario Roques, who was close to the Garde des Sceaux. The government, like Blum, had been counting on the Rennes trial to exonerate Dreyfus and put a formal end to the affair. When it failed to do so, Waldeck-Rousseau asked the President of the Republic to offer a pardon to Dreyfus so that he would not have to serve his new (though reduced) sentence. Some of the Dreyfusards wanted Dreyfus to refuse this offer of a pardon since his innocence had not been legally recognized; but Blum sided with Jaurès, who drew up Dreyfus's statement accepting the pardon—though it was made clear that they would continue to fight for complete exculpation. And indeed, but more quietly, that fight was carried to victory; but it was vastly overshadowed by the political struggles which emerged as by-products of the affair.

Although it has recently been argued that anti-Semitism was a negligible factor in the Dreyfus affair, such a view is meaningful only as a counterweight to the opposite view, which sees anti-Semitism as the sole motivation.[62] In the light of subsequent European history, the anti-Semitism of the affair seems more important than it did to the participants. They knew of course that anti-Semitism, overt and covert, was involved in the campaign to keep Dreyfus on Devil's Island, but only a few (among them Zola) saw it as the main driving force behind the crime of which Dreyfus had been the victim. The affair, to be sure, was never simply a "race issue" to its participants, for there were anti-Dreyfusards who saw it simply as a question of *raison d'Etat* and Dreyfusards who were anti-Semitic—including the man who contributed so much to proving Dreyfus innocent, Colonel Picquart. Even allowing for this, the case, as Hannah Arendt has observed, was more than a "bizarre, imperfectly solved 'crime.'"[63] Had Dreyfus not been a Jew, there might have been a crime, but no affair.

On the other hand, philo-Semitism, or even the so-called Jewish solidarity, was insignificant in the recruitment of the Dreyfusard forces. Blum, although pleased to discover that his dentist, like his newsman, was pro-Dreyfus, was more than a little irritated that the dentist seemed to assume that Blum, because of his name, would be a Dreyfusard. To Blum and the other defenders of Dreyfus, what mattered was not that Dreyfus was Jewish but that he was innocent and illegally and unjustly condemned. Undoubtedly, there were some whose belief in his innocence was at least bolstered by his Jewishness (and not entirely without reason, since many French Jews felt they had special reasons for loyalty to a country that had treated them so fairly); but to enter the affair on the side of Dreyfus took courage, and those—Jews included—who were not fortified by outrage at the injustice were not likely to have that courage. Many Jews, like other Frenchmen, believed in Dreyfus's guilt, and many others, Blum discovered, thought that the attempt to save him would cause a serious anti-Semitic outbreak and preferred to sacrifice him rather than endanger themselves.[64] As Bernard Lazare put it: "For the three dozen or so men in France who are ready to defend one of their martyred brethren, you can find thousands ready to stand guard over Devil's Island."[65]

Many who came to know Captain Dreyfus after his return, and Blum himself, doubted that he would have been a Dreyfusard had he not been the victim. Dreyfus, quite naturally, was concerned only with his own innocence and his desire to have it recognized. Most of the Dreyfusards, on the other hand, while moved by his unjust suffering, were more concerned by the larger implications of the case. They realized that, in a very practical sense, this infringement on the rights of an individual was a threat to the rights of all.[66] It was because of his leadership on this moral issue that Blum admired Clemenceau, and this attitude was not entirely changed by their later clashes. "What moved Clemenceau," he wrote about 1900, "was the morality of a people hesitating before the most paradoxical of all the crises of history."[67] That crisis was nothing less than a threat to the very bases of modern civilization, and the nearly unanimous Dreyfusard sentiment outside France sprang from deep concern for the principle of equality before the law, of equal justice, which the Western world proudly considered the greatest social advance of modern times.[68]

Blum perhaps felt this threat to civilization even more as a Frenchman than as a Jew: if Dreyfus was a "martyred brother," it was as a fellow human being, not simply as a fellow Jew.[69] He felt it too as a rationalist, striving to make reason as well as justice triumphant. The irrationalism on which anti-Semitism is founded would have seemed to him equally pernicious in any other guise, and perhaps for this reason he did not understand all the dangers latent in the new anti-Semitism. Indeed, the anti-Semitism revealed or aroused by the affair did not seem to him to be a real danger in France—in other countries perhaps, even in Algeria, but not in France.[70] He viewed it as essentially a phenomenon of the upper classes which could not reach the masses.

In the nineteenth century, French anti-Semitism was largely a social matter and intellectually "un jeu de salon." Insofar as it was no more than this, Blum's advice that Jews simply ignore social rebuffs and not confuse them with persecution was probably sound.[71] Persecution, he rightly pointed out, also depends on the attitude of its victims, and he thought the Jew would do well not to over-emphasize his difficulties. Blum, however, ought to have been aware of other varieties of anti-Semitism, such as the "Rothschild syndrome"—the tendency to identify Jews with bankers and capitalists—which the affair helped to weaken in most socialist circles. More importantly, the affair brought the first full-scale political attack on Jews in modern French history,[72] but Blum's ex-periences had not prepared him to see the nature of this attack. The impact of the affair on his life and thought was of a different kind.

Long before the affair, Blum had come to terms with social anti-Semitism, and in the effort to understand it had made himself largely immune to it. Part of this anti-Semitism derived, he thought, from envy of Jews' accomplishments. During the late nineteenth century, a rapid increase in the number of Jews in certain profes-sions served as a focus for enmity, and Blum thought that while Jews might diversify their vocations so as to be less conspicuous, they would in any case be accepted if they were patient enough. The important thing was not to be too sensitive to criticism.

Blum also realized that by adopting a profession which would put him before the public eye, such as the law or book reviewing, he was voluntarily making himself a target, and he resolved to remember that much of the criticism he would receive would have nothing to do with his merits.[73] This was a condition which even the most assimilated Jews, such as Blum, had to face, for they could never be sure whether criticism, or praise, was based on personal merit or prejudice.[74] Blum was able to take a detached view of criticism of himself in part because of the same relativistic attitude toward judgments that marked his literary criticism. Able to trust only his own judgment of himself, he learned to look dispassionately at him-self, realizing that his self-knowledge would always be incomplete, that there would always be dark corners and potential surprises. His self-consciousness helped him develop an assurance about his own worth which was sometimes irritatingly obvious to his friends, even when they had to acknowledge that it was well founded. Blum's extroversion was in no way a cover-up for inner insecurity. His writings never betray bitterness at the unjust fate of having been born into an oft-persecuted minority.

Being a Jew complicated Blum's self-awareness because part of self-awareness is an understanding of one's relationships to others. The assimilated Jew, on the margin between different groups, often finds it difficult to be sure of his relationship both to the Jewish groups he has in part left and to the gentile society into which he has partly entered.[75] By education and culture—by almost every standard—Blum was purely French; if he had, as he later said, feelings "of recognition and pride" for his Jewish inheritance, these links were very slender, consisting of not much more than strong attachment to his family.[76] Yet however much he might have been separated from Judaism, many non-Jewish Frenchmen would not admit that he was wholly French and anti-Semites would not admit that he was French at all. Assimilated Jews had largely assumed that this prejudice was gradually disappearing, and it was the affair which revealed how permanent this barrier was. Most, including Blum, chose to ignore the message, and it is significant that among those whom the affair awakened to an interest in Zionism (a feeling that assimilation is not possible) the most important was not a French but an Austrian Jew, Theodore Herzl.[77] Blum was too genuinely French to find any attraction in Zionism, although after World War II he enthusiastically supported Israel as a "worthy, free and equal fatherland for all those Jews who have not had as I have had the good fortune of finding one in the country of their birth."[78]

The affair, certainly, led Blum to think about his relationship to the Jewish community, which he seems to have ignored before that time.[79] At first he overreacted, swinging from indifference to exaggeration. Not believing in the Jewish religion, he tried to explain to himself why he should be considered a Jew, and it was only natural that he discovered a variety of virtues that he willingly associated with the "Jewish race." The affair not only made Blum aware of his Jewishness but somewhat defensive—or aggressive—about it. At a time when the Jews were being attacked as an inferior race, he would defend them as a superior race; but it was not the time to debate the meaningfulness of the idea of race, so deeply ingrained in nineteenth-century thinking. When the pressures of the affair relaxed and its emotions had had time to subside, and when from his academic friends he had learned something of the conclusions of the new anthropology and sociology, Blum ceased altogether to think in racial terms.[80] From the affair, he retained an interest in his Jewish origins. He was attracted by the discovery that he could connect his social ideals with some of the traditions of the Jewish people and their religion. He discovered, perhaps for the first time, that his passion for justice had precedents in the passion of the Hebrew prophets.[81]

Equating those two passions rather too closely, Blum also saw a connection between Judaism and socialism. Writing at the close of the affair, and still under its influence, he argued that the this-worldliness of the Hebrew religion was more appropriate than Christian other-worldliness to the conditions of modern social life. Already critical of the self-centeredness he found inherent in the Christian ideal of personal immortality and in the social conservatism of the Church, he was probably pushed even further in this direction by the leading role of various Catholic orders in the fight against Dreyfus. These sentiments led Blum to put into the mouth of his usually sage "Goethe" the unjustifiable assertion that Jews are not only more receptive to socialism but peculiarly qualified to play leading roles in it.[82] In reality, the social-political attitudes of French Jews were largely those of whatever socioeconomic class to which they belonged, and Blum seems to have been aware of this when he wrote that the "real life of the race" was in the Jewish proletariat and petty bourgeoisie. But even Jewish wealth, he thought, would surrender its privileges more readily than Christian wealth. Blum's knowledge of his fellow Jews was limited at this stage; most Jews whom he knew were intellectuals, like himself, who were assimilated and politically concerned. He probably did not even suspect the gulf that separated them from the bulk of European Jewry.[83] Although there were a substantial number of Jews in the cadres of French socialism after the affair, there were relatively few among the ordinary members.[84]

Blum's discovery of Judaism's concern for social justice was of great importance in reinforcing his socialist convictions. He felt that this commitment, which had been intellectual and hence subject to change, was a deeply rooted part of his nature. The discovery also made him proud of his Jewishness, and henceforth he had little uncertainty about "who he was." He was a Frenchman *and* a Jew, and there was no contradiction in this. The highest ideals of French civilization and Jewish culture became identical for him:

I have the right to consider myself perfectly assimilated. I feel clearly that no element of the French *esprit* is foreign to me, nor any element of French honor, or of French culture, however refined.

Well, I nonetheless have the sentiment of being a Jew. And I have never noted the slightest contradiction, the slightest opposition, between these two phases of my conscience.[85]

This sentiment was to be a great source of strength for the rest of his life, and he owed it to the affair.

Although political life returned to its customary course after the year in which the affair had dominated everything, Blum found it difficult to return to the routine of his previous life. The affair had not only produced discontent but a channel for its satisfaction. His intellectual adherence to socialism dated from his conversations with Lucien Herr in 1893, but it was through his participation in the affair that he came to take an active part in the socialist movement, which was largely the result of his association with Jaurès, whose decision and leadership were decisive in aligning socialism with the Dreyfusard cause. A substantial part of the socialist leadership, headed by Jules Guesde and Edouard Vaillant, although believing Dreyfus innocent and condemning anti-Semitism and the nationalists' campaign, argued that the principle of the class struggle required socialists to avoid involvement in an intramural bourgeois affair. Other leaders, like Alexandre Millerand and René Viviani, who were not so sensitive about doctrinal orthodoxy, were more concerned lest socialism compromise its (or their) vote-getting potential by identification with an unpopular cause.

Despite pressure from both groups of comrades, Jaurès, once he was convinced that Dreyfus was innocent, felt compelled to take up his defense. To the first group, he said that as the oppressed class *par excellence*, the proletariat had a special interest in redressing all acts of oppression; to the second, he admitted that while in the short run the socialists might lose votes, people would eventually realize that they had been right and would respect their courage. Jaurès was unwilling to separate the cause of socialism from the cause of justice, and it was this bold identification that led Blum to more active involvement in socialism.[86] The proletariat, whom Jaurès had hoped to influence, had remained largely indifferent to the affair and the socialists' stand, but Blum and other intellectuals were attracted to socialism by Jaurès's leadership in the affair. Then, with the passage of time and fading emotions, most of them returned to more conservative positions, which prompted Jaurès's observation:

"Fashion had given them to us, and fashion has taken them away." Of those who stayed, Francis de Pressensé immediately became a leader, while Blum's importance lay in the future.

Blum, meanwhile, was acquiring the specifically Jauressian tone that would always characterize his socialist thought. To understand the significance of this orientation it is necessary to examine Jaurès's place in the spectrum of French socialist thought. Its intellectual tradition was of unrivaled richness and diversity, but these qualities had been an obstacle to its political effectiveness, having divided socialist effort and the socialist electorate. In the 1870s, a great force for simplification and concentration entered French socialism in the form of Marxism, which was more in tune with the realities of a society in the course of industrial development than any of the earlier French philosophies. Marxism also succeeded where they had failed: in arrogating to itself the appearance of scientific validity. Even with these advantages, it took the vigorous propaganda efforts of the father of French Marxism, Jules Guesde, and his comrades to establish and defend the new faith.[87] Jaurès had not yet emerged from the Ecole Normale (as a young professor of philosophy) when Guesde was winning his first victory, at the socialist and labor congress of Marseille in 1879.

The Marxist victory at Marseille was over three major opponents: economic trade unionism, the cooperative movement, and anarchism —all of which had a common and basically apolitical orientation. Marxism stressed the primacy of the political struggle and its victory oriented French socialism toward political action. Marxism claimed that its political efficacy depended on the scientific validity of its doctrine, and the slow growth of the movement was in part due to the necessity of defending the purity of the doctrine against pressures to modify it for political expediency. French Marxism was constantly under pressure from its new adherents to modify its doctrine and tactics, and the party was scarcely three years old when its development was delayed for a decade by the schism of St.-Etienne (1882), which revealed that the purists were a small minority within their own movement.

In that decade there grew up between or alongside the doctrinaire faction led by Guesde (the Parti Ouvrier Français [POF]) and the reformist group of Paul Brousse (the Fédération des Travailleurs Socialistes Français [FTSF]) a number of other socialist groupings that were more or less influenced by Marxism.[88] These included the group to which Lucien Herr belonged when Blum came under his influence, the Allemanists or Parti Ouvrier Socialiste Révolution-naire (POSR), which had split from the Broussists because of Jean Allemane's non-Marxist insistence on the self-leadership of the workers. There were also the Blanquists, led by Edouard Vaillant and Charles Longuet, who combined devotion to the insurrectionary tradition of Blanqui with Marxist collectivism.[89] Finally, there was a growing number of independent socialists, too varied to be easily categorized, who ranged from vague humanitarians to self-seeking individualists. The most important intellectual figure among the independents was Benoît Malon. Though not the leader of a group, he published an influential journal, *La Revue socialiste*, which was open to socialists of all schools. Malon's doctrine was known as "integral socialism," a syncretic blend of French and foreign trad-itions. It was an expression of a broad humanistic aspiration, very similar to that later espoused by Jaurès and Blum. All of these groups had in common a critique of laissez-faire capitalism, whose evils they proposed to remedy with some sort of collective ownership of the instruments of production. This collectivism was sometimes the limit of their Marxian inspiration, but it sufficed to distinguish a new era in French socialism.

In 1893, when Jaurès emerged as an avowed socialist in his campaign for a second term in the Chamber of Deputies, he found himself within the unorganized ranks of the independents. He showed a stronger inclination toward Marxism than most of the independents by adopting, in his electoral propaganda, the "mini-mum program" worked out for France by Marx, Engels, Guesde, and Lafargue in 1880. The minimum program, which had remained the basic statement of the POF, had only a brief doctrinal preamble, stating that collective ownership of the instruments of production was the condition of emancipation for the working class and that this could be obtained only through the organization of the prole-tariat into a distinct party for the economic and political expropria-tion of the capitalist class.[90] The remainder of the document was devoted to enumerating minimum (i.e., immediate) political and economic demands, for the most part of a distinctly reformist nature: freedom of the press and association, suppression of the *livret* (a registration booklet required of every worker showing his complete record of employment), amendment of the Civil Code to abolish class distinctions, religious disestablishment, greater local government autonomy, the eight-hour day and six-day week, a minimum-wage law, equal pay for equal work for men and women, care for the aged, workman's compensation, and a progressive income tax. The most radical demands were for suppression of the public debt, abolition of the permanent army and general armament of the people, and a voice for workers in management. While the ultimate aim was clearly revolutionary, most of the immediate steps were not uniquely Marxist in inspiration, and where the hand of Marx appeared it was largely as a revolutionary tactician. Jaurès's adherence to this platform was conditional, as his decision not to join the POF showed, and he quickly emerged as a theoretician and tactician in his own right, acknowledging his debt to Marx but not bound by the dead hand of Marxian authority.

By the time Blum met him, Jaurès had not only established himself as a leading spokesman for French socialism but had worked out his own distinctive social philosophy, in which Marxism was only one of many sources. Both Jaurès and Blum were to insist on the French sources of their socialism.[91] It was natural that this French tradition, with its moralistic emphasis, should have predominated over the economic emphasis of Marxism at the beginning of Blum's socialist life, since moral rather than economic issues were engaged in the Dreyfus affair. Although Blum came to recognize the primacy of economic justice in building a better world, this recognition followed his more general concern for justice both logically and chronologically. Blum and Jaurès were devotees of social justice before they became socialists.

A materialist philosophy could not furnish a satisfying foundation for Blum's concern with justice, and he discovered a more congenial foundation in Jaurès's synthesis of a universal morality with the Marxist interpretation of modern capitalism. The synthesis was the outcome of the combination in Jaurès of a basic philosophic idealism with the pragmatist's taste for an open-ended universe and a feeling for the dialectical quality of historical change. Blum had been thoroughly drilled in neo-Kantian idealism in school, and his idealism preserved traces of its inspiration.[92] He liked to view the world in terms of ideas, and once remarked (in a book review) that it seemed that all conflicts in life could be reduced to conflicts of ideas. Thus it was virtually inevitable that he would admire Jaurès's dialectical skill as a reconciler of ideas. Jaurès showed him that materialism and idealism were not incompatible and that the intellectual's preoccupation with the subtleties of ideas could be carried into the apparently cruder world of politics.

Jaurès probably had a greater familiarity with Hegel than did any other French socialist, and he used Hegel quite independently of Marx. He did not have to choose between the Hegelian dialectic of history and Marx's inversion of its base; instead, he could take a dialectical step beyond both Hegel and Marx. He was not satisfied with the view that the history of man's socioeconomic organization is the product of a series of naturally evolving transcendent ideas or with the opposite view that all of man's ideas are products of an autonomously evolving socioeconomic order. Jaurès saw a part of the truth in each view, and hoped to reach a more complete truth through a synthesis of historical materialism and idealism.

Jaurès defended his synthesis (usually against orthodox Marxists) on numerous occasions, and Blum would have had many chances, in addition to personal contact, to become familiar with it. Perhaps he was at the celebrated debate with Paul Lafargue before a group of students in 1895, when Jaurès gave one of his most complete philosophical expositions.[93] He began by conceding that "one could interpret all the phenomena of history from the point of view of economic materialism" but argued that the idea of justice and right was prior to civilization and to anything that could be called economic life. He described progress as the succession of man's efforts to realize these ideas through successively less unjust economic systems (the Marxists believed in an Eden and the Fall), thereby making the idealist view of history an explicitly moralistic view. Jaurès insisted that any attempt to explain history in either economic or moral terms alone was inadequate because they are inseparable aspects of man's nature and life: historical phenomena are explicable only by the simultaneous use of materialist and idealist viewpoints. Whether or not he heard this debate, Blum testified on many occasions to the impression left by Jaurès's power of synthesis: "On all the essential problems, his special genius was to conciliate, to merge into a living unity, notions, systems, modes of action which before might have seemed directly contradictory."[94]

The substance of Jaurès's synthesis was more important to Blum than his display of dialectical skill. The reintegration of moral meaning in socialism was the aspect of Jaurès's thought on which Blum most frequently dwelt. Repelled by the ineffectual moralizing of the "Utopians," Marx had devised the idea of class morality, which enabled him to scorn traditional concepts of justice as "bourgeois" and to turn the utilitarian concept of the "greatest happiness of the greatest number" into a tool for advancing the cause of the proletariat, which was conceived as the enemy of all other classes. Although Blum also recognized that the moralizing appeals of the utopians had been doomed to failure, he found the concept of class morality repugnant, and could not have joined a body of socialism that espoused it. Jaurès, by synthesizing Marxism with the "best" of pre-Marxian French socialism, seemed to offer a practical solution to the age-old dilemma of the morality of power and the powerlessness of moralizing.[95]

Marxism made socialism something more than a noble ideal:

Marx has taught us that the necessity of things is working for us, that the internal laws of its development are fatally inclining present society toward the new society which we conceive, that the regime of collective property is preformed in the capitalist regime like the child in the belly of its mother.[96]

But the historical necessity with which Marx endowed socialism had to be disciplined by an ideal. That which is necessary, Blum observed, is not *ipso facto* just, and his socialism had to espouse justice as its goal.[97] As Jaurès had said: "There is in human history not only a necessary evolution but also an intelligible direction and an ideal meaning."[98] The ideal meaning—that is, the moral goal—of socialism did not lie, as Marx conceived, in some unprecedented and unpredictable "proletarian morality" but in the eternal laws of man's nature. Jaurès taught Blum that "socialism responds to the most profound exigencies of human nature, to all those sentiments which are as old as man himself, which are so often wounded by life, crushed by societies, but which make up universal morality." For Blum, the validity of socialism depended on this union with universal morality.[99]

Blum's concern with universal morality antedated his socialism and took priority over it, with the result that socialism was more a means than an end in itself. In this tradition, André Philip has written that "socialism is a *technique* for the realization, in a given milieu, of the *common values* which characterize our Western civilization."[100] As a technique, socialism was distinguished by its insistence on the primacy of economic life in the realization of all these values. Blum, from the first, seems to have been inclined to see injustice as social rather than individual in nature—and here, perhaps, the fact that his background was Jewish rather than Christian was of some significance.[101] Although especially fond of the great French moralists, he could not believe that the way to a better society was through the moral reform of individuals; rather, the process was the other way around: the moral reform of individuals was to be accomplished through the reform of society. Blum was thus prepared to be convinced by Marxism that the reform of society is basically an economic problem, that most injustices spring from the basic injustice that—while all working men and women contribute to building the wealth of society—only a few enjoy the benefits.

The observation that the many labor heavily and have nothing while a few labor not and enjoy everything was of course not new to nineteenth-century socialism. What was new was the idea that the solution lay in the elimination of poverty rather than in the elimination of wealth. The French pre-Marxians, as Jaurès pointed out, were the first to discover this potentiality.[102] Marx was to go beyond them by offering a sophisticated explanation not only of how this transformation might take place but of why it was going to take place. Marx added little to the catalogue of the evils of early industrial capitalism, but by linking those evils to the individual ownership of social capital he could simplify their remedy. Collectivism was henceforth the touchstone of socialism.

Blum's collectivism, to which he had been introduced by Lucien Herr, was a pragmatic conviction. It seemed to Blum that a sufficiently radical transformation of society was possible only through collectivism and that collectivism was possible only through the capture of the state by the organized working class. Blum's adoption of the other trappings of Marxism, such as the idea of class struggle (but not without considerable reservation), was largely the result of his conviction that such a position was necessary for political action in the French situation.[103]

It was possible, of course, to believe in the primacy of economic change without being a Marxist, and the degree to which Marxism was an instrument for Blum is revealed in his early emphasis on the concept of the right to existence. If economics is of primary importance, it is because men must have the means of living before they can have anything else.[104] From this it follows that if men have a right to their existence (and many nineteenth-century defenders of capitalism denied this), they have the right to earn that existence through their labor or to receive it from others if they cannot, because of age or infirmity, perform labor. This right to work and right to assistance were spelled out with forceful simplicity by Louis Blanc and others before 1848, and it was these rights which supplied the topic for Blum's first public expression of his socialism.[105] Blum, like Blanc, argued that the intervention of the state is necessary to make these rights meaningful, and if he went beyond Blanc, it was because the latter's program had been shown to be inadequate. Complete socialization of the instruments of production now seemed necessary if society was to guarantee existence, and even comfort and leisure, to all.

Socialism has been in many ways a historical extension, a logical development, of bourgeois capitalist society. Preoccupation with economics is essentially bourgeois, and the right to work is a logical corollary of the bourgeois concept of the duty to work, which had been elaborated as an attack on aristocratic idleness. A bourgeois (like Blum) might therefore become a socialist by divesting himself of (or in Blum's case by never acquiring) emotional attachment to the privileged status which he and his class had come to enjoy. If material comforts, leisure, and economic advantages were good for the bourgeoisie, why should they not be good for all? Blum was more directly aware of the intellectual and moral benefits a life of relative economic security can bring than he was of the emotional and moral degradation of poverty. But socialism, from its origins, has been a philosophy of wealth rather than of poverty, and the viewpoint of a Léon Blum is as significant as that of a Charles Péguy.

Blum was far from scorning the material comforts of life; indeed, he developed a refined appreciation of them, but without becoming the sybarite that enemies on the left and right later charged him with being. His bourgeois origin did not limit his view of socialism to ways of spreading material comforts. Such a socialism would differ from utilitarian individualism, as Durkheim pointed out, only on the question of how best to maximize the wealth of society.[106] Blum was like John Stuart Mill in being unable to divorce himself completely from utilitarianism, while feeling its moral deficiencies too acutely to be content with nothing more. Material comforts could be only a means to higher ends. As Blum's "Goethe" said: "To create a just society it is not enough to dry up marshes."[107]

Economic reform was also necessary for building the just society, because only through such reform could there be an end to man's exploitation of man, the development of equality, and freedom for each individual to develop his potentialities. Blum's diversified career is indicative of the value he put on the development of the individual, and as a young man, when he had sought to justify his right to self-development, he had even been tempted by anarchism. Now he saw that the right of self-development could be justified only by universalizing it. Experience taught him that an individualist philosophy was often used—indeed, was regularly used—to justify the domination of the strong and the privileged and to diminish the individuality of the majority. Because of his optimism about human nature, Blum saw a loss to humanity, an irrational waste of human potential, in contemporary society which helped channel his individualism toward socialism. Liberty for individual development could achieve universal expression only in a society where individuality had come to mean something other than the assertion of the person against society:

Of course the individual ought not to take himself as his own end. . . . He ought to look outside himself, to seek the law of his own perfection in the understanding of the laws of society. His happiness is to be measured by what he contributes to the happiness of the whole of mankind.[108]

Blum did not want the individual to be submerged in the mass any more than he wanted individuals to dominate the mass.[109] Individual freedom, he realized, could be destroyed by either an excessively anarchical or an excessively organized social order.[110] Socialism was the necessary middle way between those two dangers. As Blum remarked apropos of Célestin Bouglé's *Solidarisme et libéralisme:* "One can arrive at socialism by talking about the rights of the person as well as by talking about the needs of society in general."[111] Blum, like Jaurès, had followed that first path rather than the second.[112]

Blum's "socialized individualism" descended from the ideal on which the bourgeoisie had ridden to power at the end of the eighteenth century: the ideal of equality of opportunity. It was well suited to the aspirations of a rising class, which always needs to clear away the entrenched positions of hereditary privilege in order to make room for itself. Once the bourgeoisie had become dominant, however, the ideal was not very comfortable, but it could not be openly repudiated. Indeed, bourgeois apologists continued to speak of equal opportunity as an everyday reality. Blum, as we have seen, was first prompted to take a critical look at society by the revelation of this contradiction, and the desire to make equality of opportunity a reality figured prominently in his socialism.[113] He observed that although someone occasionally rose from the proletariat to the bourgeoisie, or (more rarely) moved the other way, privilege had not been eradicated:

True equality consists in the just rapport of each individual with his task. It is good that the son of a blacksmith, if he has the talent for it, should become a government minister; but what one must envisage as a simple and equitable consequence is that the son of a minister, if he has a talent only for forging, should be a blacksmith.[114]

It seemed obvious to Blum that this equality did not exist, because of the hereditary advantage of property, and thus the only solution was a socialism which attacked at least certain kinds of private property in the name of those who did not have its advantages.

The desirability of equality of opportunity could be argued both on moral grounds and on the practical grounds that it would assure more talented leadership for society. However argued, the issue goes deep, bringing into conflict two fundamentally opposed views of society, which Albert Thibaudet aptly described as the clash between the "party of the heirs" and the "party of the scholarship boys."[115] Blum was to place great stress on education as a force for change and on the school as a model of socialist equality:

The struggle for scholastic success ... knows no privileges. The camaraderie of the schools is egalitarian. Emulation in the schools is the form of true EQUALITY, which is not uniformity but the wholly free development of individual abilities.[116]

Socialism was the triumph of intellect over privilege for Blum, who described socialism as "the result of a purely rationalist conception of society" and as a force for eradicating ignorance and prejudice in society and substituting "clarity of consciousness" and "the action of the reflective will."[117] This socialism of equal opportunity has had a strong and basic appeal for Western intellectuals, not only because it is reasonable but because it promises them a position in society commensurate with their abilities—a position that is often denied them by the holders of power. Such ambition was largely lacking in

Blum's socialism because he had sufficient advantages of birth, talent, and energy to acquire a position with which he was content. Blum believed that the disinterestedness of Jaurès was greater than his own, but this was true only in the sense that Jaurès faced greater temptations. For Blum, the attraction of socialism and politics was not the attraction of ambition.[118]

One of the things Marxism offered Blum was an explanation of why the bourgeoisie could not implement the ideal of equality of opportunity. Marxism told him it is useless to try to reform the individual bourgeois when the system of property holding is at fault. Blum was quick to see, however, that if collectivism removed a major force for the perpetuation of privilege, there were other forces that it did not touch. An absolutely equal start in life would be possible only if all parents were equal in wealth and position, and this condition was possible, if at all, only in the most primitive agricultural societies. In any modern society, there must be differences of position—and even assuming that, at one revolutionary moment, all positions were held by those most qualified for them, parents would almost certainly seek to make access to the better positions easier for their children. Blum was more readily aware of these obstacles because he had not accepted the naïve materialism of most Marxists, who assumed that the transformation of property relationships would suffice to change man's way of thinking. Material transformation was necessary, but not sufficient. A man of strong family attachments, Blum was also aware that family affection itself could be an obstacle to equality of opportunity, and so great that it could be removed only by the utopian solution of the commonalty of all children as wards of the state.[119] Since this was most unlikely, socialism must have a moral appeal which would persuade men to put the common interests of society above those of self or family. Socialism had to be more than an economic doctrine; it had to be "almost a religion."[120]

This social faith, or moral conviction, was also necessary if socialism was to end exploitation (the humanist in Blum realized that there are many forms of exploitation). The modern economy is of necessity complex and the various positions in it are—or are regarded as—of unequal importance. Furthermore, to make such an economy function, orders have to be given and obeyed. Hence the potentiality of exploitation would continue under socialism, if it was no more than a change from private capitalist exploitation to bureaucratic-managerial exploitation (which Max Nomad has charged it with being). A new morale would be needed here too.[121]

Blum saw that if socialism was to provide the material basis for individual freedom and development, it would have to direct itself to industrial development, and indeed exploit the potentialities of industrialism more efficiently than the "wasteful" competitive system. A centrally planned and directed economy would require an elite to manage it, and socialist equality of opportunity would develop the best-qualified elite, Blum thought. But it would have to be an elite unlike any in past societies, a self-sacrificing elite.[122]

Socialism is nothing and will be nothing if it cannot accomplish again that miracle which medieval Christian society partly accomplished, if it does not reawaken in man that sense of disinterestedness and even of abnegation, if it does not show man that higher motives than personal interest exist, even from the point of view of personal happiness. That is what we have perhaps sometimes forgotten and that is what his [Jaurès's] example must always recall to us.[123]

While the complexity of modern society made an elite necessary, that elite would have to be controlled by the people if their liberty was to be secure. If economic government could not always be *by* the people, it must be *for* them. The democratic republic was thus an integral part of Blum's socialism.[124] He realized that the Marxist critique of the bourgeois republic was valid in part—political liberty is of limited value to those who are economically enslaved—but, however faulty in practice, the republic represented values of individual dignity which were important to Blum. He thought the republic was not only a future good but a present advantage as well, being the form of government most conducive to the development of socialism. Ever since the Dreyfus affair, Blum had been aware that "the political health of the Republic is the condition of all social progress."[125] Socialism, in a sense, was inherent in the idea of the republic. As Jaurès said: "All republicans, taking the idea of the republic to its logical conclusion, should come to socialism."[126] Both Blum's socialist idealism and his tactical approach were grounded in this republicanism. Thus even the apparent success of the Bolshevik revolution of 1917 did not tempt him to abandon his republican convictions, though like other socialists he had hailed the 1905 rising and the end of the czarist autocracy. Later, when he used the term "dictatorship of the proletariat," Blum meant the use, by the democratic majority, of the machinery of the state to further its own economic interests, in the same way the bourgeoisie used it.

Jaurès's identification of republicanism and socialism touched Blum deeply, in a way the rather fitful republicanism of a Jules Guesde could not. This basic sentiment, moreover, would frequently separate Blum and Jaurès from Guesde and the Marxists on questions of socialist tactics. To Blum, socialism—by its very nature—had to be the work of the majority and hence could not be accomplished overnight by a dedicated band of revolutionaries. Socialism would bring a revolutionary, new kind of society, but the process would necessarily be gradual. In following Jaurès, Blum tried to take a path between the extremes of the ultra-revolutionary and the reformist wings of French socialism. Jaurès made it unnecessary to choose either extreme by "showing the necessarily reformist element in revolutionary action and the necessarily revolutionary element in reformist action."[127] From this point of view, reforms such as wage-and-hour legislation were not merely ameliorations of the workingman's life but preparation for the new order.[128] Reforms did not strengthen the present order, as the Marxists feared, but forwarded its transformation by introducing contradictions, by showing the advantages of change, by showing that change was possible.

While Blum could not understand the messianic doctrinaires who talked as if they wanted to separate the proletariat from the contamination of the world, he did not completely dismiss the idea of revolution. He saw that the socialist society, if it was to be more than a counterfeit, was a long way in the future, and thus he avoided the dangers of impatience. Revolution would come when the evolution of society had prepared the ground for it; socialism could hasten that day only within limits.[129] When the forces of change burst through those of resistance, revolutionary momentum might carry change beyond the current state of social evolution, and there would have to be some backtracking. To Blum, the political upheavals of the nineteenth century seemed to consist of refighting various aspects of the Great Revolution precisely because that revolution had gone too far for its day.[130] In the democratic republic, the gradual progress of reforms would obviate the violence and bloodshed of traditional revolutions. When the socialist movement was carried to power at the ballot box, the defeated bourgeoisie might decide to resort to violence, but the resulting evils would be on their heads and not on the conscience of the new regime.[131] For these reasons, Blum followed Jaurès in wanting socialism to gain the wholehearted support of the vast majority before it established its rule.

Even though he envisioned a peaceful social transformation, Blum did not want to give up the term revolution; he recognized that it was a necessary symbol in the context of French politics, but he also thought it was meaningful. Acts or events which forwarded the cause of socialism (or its propaganda) seemed to merit the term revolutionary because of their place in a movement whose total proportions were undeniably revolutionary. Thus in 1900 Blum described Millerand's entry into the Waldeck-Rousseau government as revolutionary on the grounds that it was a striking demonstration of the power that socialism had gained: the government of republican defense felt it necessary to seek socialist aid.[132] Of similar propagandistic value was Jaurès's election as one of the vice-presidents of the Chamber. These two events were symptoms of the changing order and, at the same time, promoters of that change. Was this a watered-down idea of revolution? Blum would have said that it was a realistic idea.

The evolutionary character of Blum's socialism was the product not only of his assessment of society and the conditions of its transformation but also of his deep-seated relativism and distrust of the absolute and doctrinaire. It may be true that he wanted a "peaceful and fraternal" revolution because he was a bourgeois who lived among bourgeois, who realized that the bourgeois would not disappear and would have to be converted. But even more he doubted that violence in the name of any doctrine could build a more humane world.[133]

At the height of the Dreyfus affair, Blum felt that he and his comrades would have sacrificed their own lives, and those of their opponents, for the sake of justice; but this was only a vague exaltation, not the kind of ideological fanaticism which Julien Benda discovered in himself during the same epoch.[134] Not only did Blum respect life too much to use violence against it in the name of an idea, his mind was too subtle, too acutely aware of the weaknesses of all doctrines, to be fanaticized. Socialism could be congenial only so long as its doctrine remained fluid and open-ended:

No one among reflective socialists is unaware that Marx's metaphysics is mediocre; no one is unaware that his economic doctrine breaks one of its links every day. I know it; I also know that the doctrine, in renewing itself, will always remain uncertain. But action does not depend on undisputed philosophical principles any more than science or life itself. And this is not skepticism.[135]

Blum was so far from being a doctrinaire that it seemed as if his "turn of mind [was] too full of nuances" for political action, as Joseph Paul-Boncour has observed.[136] Had it not been for Jaurès, Blum thought, socialism would have been dominated by men like Guesde, who in their efforts to fit it into the straitjacket of doctrine were "unwitting priests."[137] In his literary criticism, Blum again and again repeated his conviction that life resists all attempts to pin it down, that it is by nature inconsistent, a perpetual becoming. His socialism shared this humanist quality; it, too, was a perpetual becoming.

The qualities of humanism can be recognized in all aspects of Blum's socialism. Departing not from the proletarian world of want and oppression but from the bourgeois world of the intellect, his socialism aspired to a universalism that would be based on the limitless potentialities of the mind rather than on the numerical mass of an ever-growing working class. Justice could not be circumscribed as either a bourgeois or a proletarian ideal; it was a human ideal, older than classes or the idea of classes. Socialism was the current historical manifestation of justice:

The instinct of justice, solidarity, and human morality which today finds its expression in socialism has throughout the length of history worn other forms and borne other names. It is this instinct which has been the force behind the modern religions, since all of them at birth—in the first phase of their popular proselytism—have addressed themselves to it. An encyclopedist of the eighteenth century, a Jacobin of the Convention, a democrat of 1830, were probably all moved by the same sentiments which are the spring and driving force of our action today. But—and this is the essential point—the socialist faith is the sole form of this universal instinct which corresponds exactly to the present conditions of social and economic life.[138]

Blum felt that whatever the accomplishments of the bourgeoisie had been in the past, they had now lost their moral drive, having been led by economic circumstances to concentrate on preserving their privileges and prescriptive injustices. It was not only to the proletariat, still uncorrupted, that he looked to pick up the age-old struggle, but also to the petty bourgeoisie and, especially, the intelligentsia.

Optimistic as he was about man's potential for realizing justice and the "common happiness," did Blum really believe that the classes and movements to which he looked could succeed where past generations had failed?[139] Perhaps not. He could conceive of the triumph of justice, but he could not for long ignore the innumerable obstacles in its path. The Dreyfus affair had shown him how much struggle could be required for even a small victory, and a mixed victory at that. Whatever the cause of justice was linked to in his own generation, Blum would follow it. This was the human choice—not between absolute good and evil, but among present possibilities. It was a humanist feeling for man, for his potentialities and his weaknesses, which kept Blum from intellectual fanaticism.

The just society would be one in which men lived freely in natural harmony and as individuals innumerable in their variety—not as a faceless, dehumanized mass.[140] Progress toward that society, however limited, seemed possible only through commitment to the present effort, the present generation, and yet nothing was more difficult. Men, he thought, commonly live in either the past or the future, their lives dominated by either regret or hope.[141] But regret and hope, if carried to the point of negating the value of the present, can be dehumanizing as they turn to despair or violence.[142] The human alternative, which Blum constantly urged, was to accept the present for what it is while never ceasing to work to make it better.

CHAPTER FIVE

THE MAKING OF A
SOCIALIST (2)

THE DREYFUS AFFAIR led Blum to resume his contacts with the intellectual world of the Left Bank. His ties with the university quarter had never been completely severed (he lived at that time facing one of the favorite gathering places of the young intelligentsia, the Luxembourg Gardens), but his activities were centered on the Right Bank: the Palais Royal, seat of the Conseil d'Etat, and the offices of *La Revue blanche*. Even his chance renewal of acquaintance with Lucien Herr had taken place on the Right Bank, although it was in the company of Herr that he recrossed the Seine. The catalytic effect of the affair in this transfer was symbolized by Blum's renewed relations with two of the administrators of the Ecole Normale, Paul Dupuy and Victor Bérard, with whom he had been on rather bad terms, only to discover that the common cause of Dreyfus had wiped out all animosity.

During the paroxysm of the affair, Blum's activities were channeled through *La Revue blanche*, but as the affair was transformed from a moral struggle to save Alfred Dreyfus into a political struggle between supporters and opponents of the democratic republic, this literary base of operations offered too little scope for action. Then Herr gave him the opportunity to do something directly on behalf of the socialist movement when he invited Blum to join a socialist publishing and bookselling venture in the late summer of 1899. In a few months, Blum was to leave *La Revue blanche*, because the time left over from his judicial work was consumed in the varied activities which grew out of Herr's venture.

The affair had stirred an unprecedented movement of social consciousness in intellectual circles, especially in the University, and Herr had seized the chance to direct this movement for the benefit of socialism. Intellect in France may be, as Thibaudet says, on the left, but it is not necessarily politically or socially conscious. In modern times, this consciousness can largely be dated from the affair; hence the importance of Herr's efforts to merge intellectual and socialist activity. The opportunity, and perhaps the inspiration, to form a publishing venture, run by and for intellectuals (professors and students), came to Herr in a rather unusual fashion.

Charles Péguy, then a student at the Ecole Normale, had been inspired by the affair, and by his literary ambitions, to go into the publishing business.[1] With the 30,000 or 40,000 francs of his wife's dowry and the name he borrowed from his friend, Georges Bellais, he had bought a defunct bookshop on the corner of rue Cujas and rue Victor Cousin, facing the gray mass of the Sorbonne, and opened it for business in May 1898.[2] Péguy intended to use his bookshop to promote socialism, but his energies were taken up with the Dreyfus affair. He had already shown himself to be one of the most dynamic Dreyfusard leaders among university students, and his shop immediately became a center for activities that were often different from those of *La Revue blanche*, such as providing bodyguards for Dreyfusard professors and engaging nationalist youths in street fights. Such preoccupations, of course, interfered with the commercial aspects of the venture, and Péguy had not yet gained the experience which would later enable him to keep an equally precarious ship afloat. The result was that within little more than a year he was on the verge of bankruptcy.[3]

When he learned of Péguy's situation, Herr decided to attempt to rescue the young publisher. He also intended to take over his business and transform it into a more orthodox socialist venture.[4] The firm was reorganized as a joint-stock company, with the awkward title New Society of Bookselling and Publishing (Société Nouvelle de Librairie et d'Edition), in August 1899. Péguy was given shares in the new company in exchange for his stock, goodwill, and the name Librairie Georges Bellais (now used as a subtitle), but he was excluded from the financial management and reduced to the second-echelon job of "the execution of works, collections, editions, etc., whose publication will have been decided."[5]

Lucien Herr, while drawing heavily on his own resources, also appealed to his many acquaintances for funds to help launch the New Society. Almost all of the new publishers were from the university community—a majority were *normaliens* and a few were still students at the Ecole Normale.[6] Blum, who had rejected a university career, was one of the few "outsiders," and Herr turned to him not only because he could help financially but because the librarian recognized the need for legal expertise.[7] Thus, at Herr's suggestion, Blum was made a member of the five-man board of directors that was elected at the second meeting of the stockholders.[8] Herr, naturally, was elected president of the New Society. The other three directors, all in the University, were Hubert Bourgin, Mario Roques, and François Simiand.

From the first, Blum was active in the affairs of the New Society, dropping into its quarters on rue Cujas nearly every day, perhaps before crossing the river to his work on the Right Bank.[9] He was regarded as one of the mainstays of the operation, but the rather fragmentary archives of the New Society do not indicate his actual functions. The sudden drop in his literary production between 1900 and 1902 suggests that most of his spare time was taken up with the business, as well as with his venture into socialist historiography. In 1901, he even sacrificed his summer vacation to substitute for Simiand, who seems to have carried the major burden of administration.[10] Apparently, Blum's principal activities were editorial, and he participated both in the making of policy and the decisions to publish or decline to publish specific works.[11]

The general line of editorial policy was undoubtedly laid down by Herr when he had recruited support for the venture. Herr and Péguy were in agreement that the purpose of the business was to publish socialist works, but Herr had not rescued Péguy with the intention of publishing the same things Péguy would have published. Péguy's major effort in the socialist cause, a collection of articles by Jaurès titled *Etudes socialistes*, was not a commercial success, which should have served as a warning of the risks the new owners were running. Yet there was reason to suppose that the new owners, through Herr's contacts in socialist political circles, might be more successful than Péguy in their effort to combine idealism and practicality. For Blum, the New Society gave him the opportunity to continue his socialist action, which had grown out of the affair. Also, the idea of a sophisticated propaganda effort must have appealed to Blum, who believed that socialism must appeal to at least part of the bourgeoisie as well as the proletariat. The New Society also intended to assume responsibility for the organizational side of socialist publication, with such projects as the *comptes rendus* of party congresses and official publications. They also handled publication of *La Revue socialiste* (founded in 1880 by Benoît Malon) and, briefly, *Le Mouvement socialiste* of Hubert Lagardelle.[12]

Of the high-level propaganda works issued by the New Society, the most important was a series titled the Socialist Library, issued in the form of 100-page pamphlets, many of which are still valuable for studying socialism at the turn of the century. In 1901, Blum contributed two well-researched volumes on labor and socialist congresses from 1876 to 1900, which, because of their detailed information and lack of bias, are useful references which are often cited.[13] Other volumes in the series were contributed by Herr, the Belgian socialist leader Emile Vandervelde, Anatole France, Albert Thomas, Alexandre Millerand, and many others. But despite its many advantages, this aspect of the New Society was not a financial success.

The other publishing line of the New Society was more remote from Péguy's original intentions: scholarly work, primarily in the social sciences, where the influence of Marx was rapidly growing. During its brief life, the New Society did not reach the prominence in scholarly publication that it attained in the socialist arena. But it made a promising beginning, which, given the number of professors of current and future distinction associated with it, might well have borne fruit had not the financial problems proved insoluble. Among its scholarly works was a series on modern history, which included *Les origines des cultes révolutionnaires* by Albert Mathiez, who had been a roommate of Péguy at the Ecole Normale.[14] The New Society also published, from December 1899 to 1905, *La Revue d'histoire moderne et contemporaine*, which was founded in the spring of 1899 by Pierre Caron.[15] Probably under the inspiration of Caron, who was a bibliographer and archivist rather than a historian, the firm inaugurated a bibliographical periodical called *Notes critiques*, which was devoted to the social sciences and edited by Simiand.

Blum, with his critical intelligence and reviewing experience, was naturally attracted to this project, but though he was listed among the many distinguished contributors, he apparently served in only a minor capacity.[16] More at home in the literary world than in academic company, Blum was nonetheless able to bridge the gap between the two, both in his ability to make friends (and enemies) in both worlds and to gain intellectual sustenance from diverse sources. His wide curiosity and ready intelligence won him the acceptance of academics and gave him the opportunity to learn about ways of studying society that were different from, and complementary to, the insights of a literary critic.

Whatever experience in business management Blum gained was probably of less significance than the expansion of his intellectual contacts, but it was not altogether negligible. As one of the directors of the New Society, he had to face the various difficulties the firm encountered in its efforts to reverse the unprofitable practices of Péguy's management.[17] Very soon after the reorganization, the directors were distracted by a serious quarrel with Péguy himself. That this poet and mystic should have thought he could work easily with his new comrades seems surprising, and it soon appeared that not only were there serious differences of opinion but also that the new managers were much less willing than Péguy to adopt a policy of live and let live. First there was a falling out over editorial policies, and then a more profound dispute over the nature of the socialist movement and the New Society's relationship to it.[18]

Blum was necessarily involved in both disputes, though only once in a leading role. He had become acquainted with Péguy during the affair, and their personal relationship appears to have been cordial but certainly not intimate. Perhaps, at first sight, they might have seemed no more different in personality and origins than Blum and Jaurès, but Blum and Jaurès shared a common rationalism, which separated them from Péguy. At that time Péguy had great admiration for Jaurès, whom he saw as a moral leader, but to Péguy, Blum was a man from another world, a bourgeois world; to Blum, Péguy must have seemed rather provincial.[19] That they should have clashed seems inevitable.

When Péguy submitted the manuscript for *Jean Coste*, a novel by an obscure country schoolteacher which described the misery of his life ("The first schoolteacher's novel was the novel of salaries," remarked Thibaudet[20]), he was enthusiastic and the administrators delegated Blum to look at it. Blum's verdict was, "It's quite long, it's boring, and then it's too black; there is no one as miserable as that."[21] This judgment was undoubtedly influenced by the fact that Blum's knowledge of poverty was more abstract than Péguy's, but *Jean Coste*, although a forceful, even moving story, was not a literary masterpiece.[22] The New Society's refusal to publish it was a major step toward the break with Péguy. Blum was also aligned with the other directors in their last clash with Péguy over publications.

Péguy found the directors' socialist discipline too confining, and though he tried to withdraw from the company as early as November 1899, he was persuaded to stay on.[23] Then, like Blum, he went to the socialist unity congress of December 1899, but unlike Blum he came away profoundly disappointed. Blum and the others, as we shall see, had been working hard for unification, but Péguy was not prepared to accept the degree of conformity demanded and he resolved to preserve his freedom of action by founding a literary and socialist review. When he asked the directors of the New Society to handle the publication, at his expense, they refused. There was a stormy session in the editorial offices, and apparently Blum was the only one who controlled his temper. The administrators decided they had had enough of Péguy, whom Herr called an anarchist. Simiand, whom Jules Isaac called a "future Robespierre," denounced Péguy for wanting to found a "journal for idiots." Blum, as concerned as his colleagues about the unity of the socialist movement, nonetheless shared Jaurès's desire that external unity encompass a wide inner diversity, and thus limited himself to arguing that, with unity still precarious, Péguy's gesture of independence was premature.[24] This, Péguy conceded, was a legitimate point for debate, although he did not agree; but despite Blum's habitual courtesy the time for debate had passed and the rupture was complete. Péguy, on his own, founded *Cahiers de la Quinzaine*. It was characteristic of Blum that, until Péguy turned viciously on Jaurès, he was a regular subscriber to *Cahiers*.[25]

Blum had a smaller role in yet another conflict between Péguy and the New Society—a disagreement over money rather than policy. Blum had been one of the contributors to the refinancing project which had rescued Péguy but the move had been planned and executed almost exclusively by Herr and Simiand, who probably considered the New Society shares they had given Péguy and Bellais as a benefice to bankrupts. Nonetheless, these shares represented legal obligations. By mutual agreement, the shares had been "frozen" for two years, but when this restriction expired in 1901, Péguy, in need of money for *Cahiers*, demanded that the New Society fulfill its agreement and purchase his shares.[26] The financial drain involved in paying off Péguy and Bellais was a heavy blow to the New Society, though by no means fatal.[27] After paying the installments for 1902 and 1903, Herr tried to stop the payments by bringing suit against Péguy for "disloyal competition." The suit was pressed, contrary to the advice of the firm's lawyer, and more money was wasted on appeals.[28]

Although the New Society paid dearly for ridding itself of Péguy, all of its financial difficulties cannot be attributed to this action. From the beginning, Blum, Roques, and Simiand had carried the burden of the firm's commercial management, but none had any experience in this specialized field, as the rather primitive records in the Archives Nationales testify.[29] Unfortunately for the aspiring socialist publishers, they had come on the scene at a time when the entire publishing industry was in the throes of a long crisis that saw the failure of even established firms. In these circumstances, a few unhappy decisions were all it took to doom their efforts. The three amateur administrators were quick to realize that, because of their inexperience and because all of them had other jobs, it was necessary to hire a professional to handle the day-to-day running of the business; but they proved no more judicious in their choice of employees than Péguy, who had hired a cripple as a book "runner." The first manager hired by the New Society was both inefficient and unreliable, but at least he was honest.[30] His successor first talked his employers into paying him a large salary, and then, in 1904, fled to America with most of the liquid assets of the company—a blow from which the business soon collapsed.[31]

The embezzlement, however, merely hastened the end of the enterprise, for it had been in constant difficulty. Although the losses in the first year were "not so much as anticipated," they piled up year after year.[32] Herr, who had invested his personal funds heavily, tried desperately to gather additional capital, and had considerable success, but not enough to keep ahead of the mounting deficit.[33] Blum made further contributions, and Herr raised large sums through Mme. Menard-Dorian and Salomon Reinach. The New Society received strong financial support from the academic community, but that group had rather limited resources for saving floundering concerns.[34] The administrators were finally compelled to recognize that their intellectual success was outweighed by their financial failure; the bookselling part of the business was given up in 1904 and the publishing part in 1905.[35]

During its few years of operation, the New Society was important for Blum's socialist career by serving as the agent of his passage into socialist action. The activities of the publishing house were the most important (though not the only) socialist tasks pursued by the group that gathered there. It was natural, for example, that as propagandists and as intellectuals they should have been attracted by the workers' education movement and felt the responsibility to use their expertise to further the technical and cultural as well as socialist education of the less favored. Organizations, called *universités populaires*, which ranged from rather substantial operations to the modest efforts described by Daniel Halévy in his *Pays parisiens*, were springing up throughout Paris and the group of the New Society was centered in the Ecole Socialiste of the rue Mouffetard, not far from the Ecole Normale.[36] Beginning in December 1899, Blum gave a course on contemporary French socialist doctrines which was apparently well attended.[37] The experience, however, seems to have been relatively unimportant, since he later described the *universités populaires* as ineffective and "incoherent" because they were inadequately integrated into the socialist movement.[38]

This lack of integration must have been particularly distressing to Blum because of his preoccupation with the unity of the socialist movement. One of the first acts by the leaders of the New Society had been to form an organization they called the Groupe d'Unité Socialiste,[39] which was the first organized socialist group to which Blum belonged. Herr was its leader, although its "scientific . . . irreligious, democratic, reformist, unificationist, that is to say Jauressist and Dreyfusard" program, was drawn up by François Simiand.[40] Thus Blum entered socialist politics in support of Jaurès's program for socialist unity through an intellectual rather than labor or proletarian group. Since all the diverse socialist groups were concerned with unity at the time Blum became actively engaged, it is understandable that a special concern for unity would mark his whole socialist career.

131

Throughout the decade of the 1890s the various fragments of French socialism had been groping toward greater ideological and political unity.[41] This reversal of the previous tendency to fragmentation resulted from several factors: the growing strength of the Marxists, the decline of other socialist groups, and socialist success at the polls. The revival of the French Marxist organization led by Jules Guesde, the Parti Ouvrier Français (POF), began with the international socialist congress held in Paris in 1889 under the sponsorship of the POF. At the same time, most rival groups were starting to wane as a result of internal discord, lethargy, or involvement in the Boulangist movement. On the other hand, the political forces of socialism were to emerge from the parliamentary elections of 1893 with their first significant success: twelve members of the POF and eleven representatives of the three other major organizations were elected to the Chamber, where they were joined by seventeen deputies who belonged to no national organization but who called themselves socialists. These Independents, as they came to be called, included several men with evident leadership potential: Jaurès, Millerand, René Viviani, Gustave Rouanet. When the Chamber met, most of the socialist deputies joined in an informal association to coordinate their activities and their votes. This *ad hoc* grouping, growing out of the political necessities of a small minority, was the first step toward the creation of a unified socialist party.

The experiences of the socialists in the 1893 legislature taught them the advantage of acting together while it revealed the weaknesses of their highly informal coordination. They felt the importance of more disciplined action not only because of their minority position but also because of their claim to be an ideological movement. As an ideological movement, socialism was handicapped (or at least it was thought to be) by excessive doctrinal diversity. Organizers complained that the great number of competing groups made recruiting difficult. Moreover, the socialist group in the Chamber was hampered by problems resulting from the lack of a generally accepted definition by which socialists could be separated from other left-wing politicians. The desirability of greater unity was appreciated all the more as socialist electoral success continued.

These, and even stronger, pressures were needed if unity was to be achieved and the obstacles of ideological disagreement overcome, but no compromise would be viable if any group was estranged by its terms. Fortunately for the movement, the most doctrinally rigid group, the Marxists, appeared to grow more flexible with political experience and success and it was willing to admit that a measure of political compromise might not be contrary to Marxist principles. The euphoria in the socialist ranks as a result of their unprecedented victories in the municipal elections of 1896 set the stage for the acceptance of a new minimum program that would be acceptable to all groups. This program was offered by Alexandre Millerand in a speech at the victory celebration and became known as the St. Mandé program. When Blum joined the Groupe d'Unité Socialiste, this program was the unofficial but generally accepted minimum definition of socialism.

There were three basic parts to Millerand's statement: a person was a socialist if he believed in (1) the intervention of the state "to convert from capitalist into national property the different categories of the means of production and exchange in proportion as they become ripe for social appropriation," (2) the conquest of all levels of governmental power through the workings of universal suffrage, (3) creation of an "international entente" of workers.[42] Because of its vagueness and generality, the St. Mandé program left many questions, especially tactical questions, unanswered, but this was necessary if there was to be unity between, say, Paul Lafargue and Paul Brousse, Jules Guesde and Aristide Briand. In the first two years after St. Mandé, it seemed that a unified party might be constructed on that foundation, but by the time Blum's group had formed, a new and unforeseen obstacle had arisen in the person of Millerand himself.

This curious turn of events was one of the by-products of the Dreyfus affair. The affair—like previous crises under the Republic— had varied, even contradictory, impacts on the socialists. Its first impact was divisive, with socialists unable to agree on what line of action to pursue, but ultimately it was to contribute to their unification.[43] The rise of an ultra-reactionary, anti-republican movement caused them to reassess the situation and, if not agree to defend the Republic under all circumstances, at least agree to oppose a rightist coup, even if this meant the continuation of the bourgeois republic. To prepare for such an eventuality, the Comité de Vigilance was formed in October 1898 with representatives of all the major factions. The committee quickly discovered that there was widespread sentiment for greater unity than was implied in this *ad hoc* organization, and its functions were expanded to include preliminary negotiations on unification. In December 1898 its name was changed to Comité d'Entente Socialiste. Its first important action was organization of the May Day celebration for 1899. Jaurès and others then called for the Comité d'Entente to organize a national unity congress of all socialist groups. But no sooner had preparations been undertaken than the affair rebounded to complicate matters.

The socialists had played a part in the fall of the Dupuy ministry, but they were astonished when Alexandre Millerand became Minister of Commerce in the new Waldeck-Rousseau government. Socialist opinion, until that moment moving toward unity, was immediately divided by this development.[44] For some, like Edouard Vaillant, hatred for the Minister of War overrode all other considerations: for a socialist to be associated in any way with the marquis de Galliffet, conqueror of the Commune, was unpardonable treason. Others, like Guesde, whose reaction was less emotional, were no less violently opposed to Millerand's action on the grounds that it was contrary to the requirements of the class struggle. Jaurès's immediate reaction was enthusiastic:

The Republic is in peril. If a ministry has the courage to strike these gold-braided rebels in order to save it, what instruments they use are of little importance to us. We need action. . . . For my part I approve Millerand's acceptance of a post in this "ministry of combat." It is a great fact, an historic date, that the bourgeois Republic, at the hour when it is struggling against the militarist conspiracy that envelops it, proclaims that it has need of socialist energy. An audacious, conquering party ought not, in my opinion, to neglect these offerings of destiny, these overtures of history.[45]

Blum sided with Jaurès, even going so far as to describe Millerand's action as truly revolutionary.[46]

While differences of opinion became increasingly bitter, the momentum already generated carried the unity movement forward. Each group was apparently willing to let the forthcoming congress decide what the socialist attitude toward Millerand and ministerial participation should be.

Blum's Groupe d'Unité Socialiste was formed by New Society members just in time to take part in the congress, which was held at Paris in the Salle Japy in December 1899. Indeed, the group was probably formed with the intent of helping promote unity on

Jaurès's terms, as the various socialist groups engaged in considerable preliminary jockeying for numerical advantage among the delegates at the congress. The group provided Blum an entrée, which enabled him to attend his first socialist congress.[47] He found it an exciting and inspiring experience, and he wrote a glowing account which appeared in *La Revue blanche*.[48] The New Society published a stenographic *compte rendu* with official sanction and was to be the publisher for the reports of subsequent congresses.

Blum's interpretation of the congress, at least for public consumption, was dominated by his desire to believe that durable unity had been achieved and to forward that achievement by a conciliatory interpretation of the events that had led up to it. He pointed to the areas of undisputed unity: the agreement to exclude anarchists and other non-socialists by the imposition of a doctrinal statement patterned on that of St. Mandé—and the general agreement that unity was necessary. Certainly Blum was justified in stressing that a central committee had been formed which seemed to satisfy everyone, but this had been made easier by the experiences of the Comité d'Entente. On the other hand, in referring to the agreement not to destroy the autonomous organizations in unification, Blum had to ignore the degree to which that "agreement" was a sign of disagreement and mutual suspicion. He played this down, as well as incidents in the congress that indicated how close to the surface that mistrust was.

The optimism in Blum's treatment of the congress was most conspicuous in his handling of the *cas Millerand*, which occupied the greater part of the congress debates. The issue was placed at the head of the agenda under the title "The Class Struggle and the Conquest of Positions of Public Power." Blum went to the other extreme by treating the often acrid debate as if it were little more than a conflict of personalities. Personalities indeed played a part in socialist politics, but the ideological conflict could not be glossed over so easily. The disagreement between those who argued that socialist participation in a bourgeois government was by definition a violation of the principle of the class struggle, and hence not permissible, and those who felt that, under some circumstances, participation could be in the interest of the proletariat was, as Blum said, a difference over tactics. Yet it was not merely a tactical question for it resulted from fundamental disagreements over the very nature of socialism, disagreements which were to continue to divide the socialists.

At the Salle Japy the struggle came to a confrontation between the compromise resolution, supported by Jaurès and accepted 49 to 7 by the resolutions committee, and an intransigent amendment offered on the floor by Guesde. The debate had been fought in the context of a general agreement on the sacredness of the class struggle but with differences as to what constituted socialist heresy. With his usual tactical subtlety, Jaurès had worked out a resolution which condemned ministerial participation in general, but left the door open a small crack. His wording could be interpreted as a victory for everyone:

While admitting that exceptional circumstances can occur in which the party would have to examine the question of socialist participation in a bourgeois government, the socialist congress declares that in the present state of capitalist society and of socialism, both in France and elsewhere, all the forces of the party ought to be aimed at the conquest in the commune, department, and the state of elective positions only, since these positions depend on the proletariat organized as a class party, which by installing itself in these [elective] offices legally and peacefully begins the political expropriation of the capitalist class which will end in revolution.[49]

Guesde's POF supported this resolution in committee, but then, through a change of opinion or by ruse, offered a "clarifying" amendment to show that the POF had yielded nothing. Guesde said simply: "I ask the congress to give its opinion on the following question: Does the class struggle permit the entrance of a socialist into a bourgeois government?" After considerable tumult, Guesde's question was answered: no, 818; yes, 634. The Jaurès-backed resolution was then adopted 1140 to 240.

The bourgeois press naturally crowed that the socialists had settled their differences by adopting contradictory motions, but Blum was partly right in replying that they were complementary, for one could argue that the sense of the amendment was included in the resolution. This, however, ignored the real gulf that the subtly different words concealed. Blum's lack of a doctrinaire spirit may have prevented him from appreciating the seriousness of Guesde's hairsplitting, but his description of the outcome as a "sincere vote" was disingenuous since he also indicated (elsewhere) that Guesde had gained an "artificial majority" because of the voting procedures adopted at the congress.[50] The Millerand question had not been laid to rest.

Blum was right in observing that the forces for unification were strong, for they easily overrode these disagreements. The day after the votes on participation, or "ministerialism" as it was sometimes called, all other passions seemed to have dissolved in the euphoria of unification. The propositions of the resolutions committee were ratified with minimum debate and enthusiastic acclamation, and the spirited singing of the "Internationale" as the delegates marched from the hall was no mere formality. Nonetheless, what emerged from the Salle Japy was not the "durable and sincere" union which Blum proclaimed, although he would have been justified in saying the results were as much as could have been expected at that moment.

The new Parti Socialiste Français (PSF) was a cautious federation in which proportional representation on the general committee assured the maintenance of the existing distribution of power, and undoubtedly it was necessary to go through this stage before a more complete unity was possible. The sentiment for unity was probably strongest at the grass roots of the movement, whereas the leaders of the factions were more concerned with the defense of their doctrinal positions and their own power. Blum saw Jaurès as the chief architect of unity because, more than anyone else, Jaurès was prepared to achieve union through democracy in the movement; he was prepared to accept its verdict, as many others were not. Neither Jaurès nor Blum, however, intended to give up their viewpoints in the united party (its statutes explicitly guaranteed that right). Nor did they insist that acceptance of their views be the basis of unification.

This view of party democracy clashed with the attitude of the Guesdists and Blanquists, who together had a majority in the main executive body of the PSF (the general committee) and intended to impose their version of doctrinal orthodoxy and their authority. Party moderates (not including Jaurès) were quick to charge them with dictatorial methods. Neither side had abandoned its views on the Millerand case, and there were further disagreements over the degree of support to be given the Waldeck-Rousseau ministry. A considerable number of the socialist deputies were inclined to go further in this support than the consciences of Marxists would allow, and no doubt the temptation to support the ministry was even leading some moderates away from the party. On the other hand, the doctrinal purists ignored some of the advantages to be gained by playing the parliamentary game. These disagreements within the party could be considered differences of degree only, since even the most intransigent socialist deputies on occasion defended a ministry against overthrow on some minor issue where their natural position would have been opposition. The disagreements were nonetheless acute.[51] Jaurès, who was not a deputy at this time, continued his moderating effort to keep the movement both parliamentary and socialist.

The long tenure of the "government of republican defense" served to keep the issue of ministerialism vital, and when the congress of the Second International was held at Paris in early September 1900, the issues which grew out of the Millerand case were hotly debated at that rather solemn assembly. Most of the sessions consisted of the unanimous ratification of the resolutions presented by the various committees; the only sharp divisions were on the questions of the general strike and ministerial participation. This specifically French issue also preoccupied the delegates from the other countries, who recognized that the union of 1899 was no union at all.

Jaurès presided over the first session, and in his welcoming address called for the complete unification of French socialism. He was followed by representatives of each national delegation, who also called on the French to unite. However, the results of the congress only exacerbated French dissension. In an attempt to conciliate the French factions, the congress adopted a resolution on ministerialism that was drawn up by the dean of orthodox theoreticians, Karl Kautsky. While in general condemning participation, the Kautsky resolution left the door open for the national parties (i.e., France) to decide for themselves: "Whether in a particular case the political situation requires this dangerous experiment is a question of tactics and not of principle: the international congress does not have to pronounce on this point."[52] Guesde and Enrico Ferri (of Italy) offered a countermotion condemning participation under any circumstances (which at least had the merit of being unequivocal), and Guesde announced that he and his followers would not accept the vote of the congress as binding and final. This made it clear that the national congress in December would see a repetition of this battle.

It is not certain that Blum was at the international congress, but at the Salle Wagram in December he witnessed the "violent and impassioned spectacle" of the undoing of the previous year's agreement, although his reactions to that unhappy gathering are concealed in the dry account in his *Congrès ouvriers* (1901). Only his final remark showed that his optimism was unquenched. A less firm conviction than his might not have withstood the impression of profound disunity which the congress gave from the start. There was a struggle over the verification of mandates, on which control of the congress hinged. Dominant on the general committee, Guesde and his allies saw their power threatened by a general validation of contested mandates and raised the procedural question of how the voting on validation should be conducted. Defeated on this issue, they thereafter refused to recognize the congress as legally constituted, remaining in the hall but refusing to participate in subsequent votes. This gave the floor to the right wing of the party, which seized the opportunity. Gustave Rouanet gave an able defense of the socialist deputies whose resistance to control by the general committee had been a major source of antagonism, and Aristide Briand attacked the general committee and engaged in violent exchanges with Paul Lafargue. One of these exchanges was interrupted by the "stabbing" of a Guesdist delegate, which proved the signal for a walkout by the POF.

The departure of the largest group in the congress, though perhaps premeditated, was clearly a blow to unity, but it was welcomed by many as a chance to unite on terms that were not dictated by Guesde. The Blanquist Parti Socialiste Révolutionnaire (PSR) remained at the Salle Wagram, hoping to serve as intermediary for the reintegration of the POF and to prevent a complete right-wing takeover. The congress voted to proceed with the steps for converting the federation of 1899 into a fully unified party. The POF, meeting separately, insisted on the organic unity of all socialists who were firmly committed to the class struggle (which obviously did not, in their opinion, include all the socialists at the Salle Wagram).

But Blum was not discouraged when he remarked (through "Goethe") that

Henceforth everything that people believe is being done against unity can only hasten it even more. You see that Guesde, in his dissident congress, has declared before anyone else that the old organizations ought to disappear. His very opposition has thus constrained him to outbid others in his advocacy of unity. You cannot fight against the necessities of history.[53]

This was apparently sufficient sustenance for Blum's optimism, for he concluded that "in spite of the faults, the rancors, the violence, socialist unity was on the march."[54]

Whether or not the spirit of unity was advancing, the practice of it was on the retreat. The next year saw the completion of the scission of French socialism into two competing groups. The Lyon congress of the PSF, which Blum attended but did not report on, saw the departure of the PSR and its allies, who left to join the POF when the congress refused to expel Millerand from the party. Jaurès, by this time somewhat disenchanted with Millerand's behavior, nonetheless fought against the expulsion attempt because it was repugnant to his conception of diversity within the party. Blum, who much later was to show a similar reluctance to deal harshly with those who had betrayed the party, probably supported Jaurès's stand, although he was beginning to see Millerand as an intermediary between the socialists and the Radicals rather than as the revolutionary he had at first hailed.[55] In spite of the widening scission, Blum perhaps drew encouragement from the decision of the POF and the PSR to form a single organization, the Parti Socialiste de France (PSDF), because the number of major socialist organizations had at least been reduced from five in 1899 to two in 1901. But might not two factions be more difficult to fuse than several?

After the scission at Lyon, Blum stayed with the PSF of Jaurès, which remained committed to unification. Blum proclaimed that unity was not far off, and indeed he seems to have been so convinced of this that his socialist activity in this period largely ignored the problems of achieving it. This impression may be in part a distortion, because of our ignorance of much of his activities, but it is nonetheless the impression conveyed by his socialist journalism.

We have seen that during the Dreyfus affair Blum added other types of writing to his accustomed literary criticism, even abandoning the latter in 1900. And even before his direct interest in the affair had slackened, he tried his hand at other areas of political journalism. His first efforts appeared in late 1898 in the review *Volonté*, which had just been established by a young Radical, Franklin-Bouillon, with support from Ernest Lavisse, Lucien Herr, and others.[56] The review was apparently short lived and not very satisfactory. Even more ephemeral was Herr's idea of founding a weekly, *Semaine*. Herr was lining up an editorial staff, to be composed of himself, Charles Seignobos, Félix Mathieu, Blum, Simiand, and Charles Andler, but his financial difficulties with the New Society cut short this project.[57]

Established periodicals offered a more effective if perhaps less exciting outlet, and *La Revue blanche*, more politically oriented by the affair, published two of Blum's earliest political efforts, in addition to his article on the Zola trial. The former, on the press and education laws, show that Blum's political position was still basically that of the Radical republicans; there was nothing particularly socialist in his forceful rhetoric. In the fall of 1898 he wrote a stinging attack on the press laws of 12 and 18 December 1893 and 28 July 1894, as well as their authors.[58] These laws were known to the left as the *lois scélérates* (as the Ferry education laws were known as the *lois scélérates* to the clerical right) for they had been adopted for the repression of anarchist and socialist propaganda. Blum's attack, however, was not so much socialist as republican and juridical. The article was signed simply "un juriste," and his legal training and concern were very evident. For example, Blum charged the laws with violating the traditions of French public law in denying "crimes of opinion" the right to jury trial and in defining "accomplice" and "accessory" to such crimes in dangerously broad terms.[59]

The severity of the penalties disturbed him both as a jurist and as a republican. As a republican, he believed freedom of the press is a vital part of the system of government, and he saw that these laws provided the government with powers as destructive of that freedom as any exercised by the monarchical regimes of the nineteenth century. These powers were held largely in reserve, but this did not justify their existence, and Blum warned that if some turn in the affair brought a clerical or military government to power, the Republic would have prepared for its enemies "as murderous and a surer arm than the laws of General Security or the Law of Prairial of the Year II"—with which they could destroy the Republic.[60] He did not consider such a development likely, but it was a possibility, and he wanted to show that the blame lay with the opportunist politicians who governed the country (in the midst of the affair): Charles Dupuy, Casimir-Périer, Gabriel Hanotaux, Raymond Poincaré, Louis Barthou, Félix Faure, Paul Deschanel, and Georges Leygues, whom he called authoritarians, militarists, and reactionaries.[61] Blum, in effect, was issuing a call for the liberal republicans to take over the Republic, while exposing the failures of the conservative republican leadership through an intensive analysis of the parliamentary debates and votes on the *lois scélérates*. The failures of those from whom he expected better were his special targets, with Léon Bourgeois, "a too-distinguished statesman," receiving the sharpest arrows. But Blum also observed the ironic fact that both Jaurès and Guesde had voted to support the Bourgeois ministry when it was challenged on its refusal to repeal or amend these anti-socialist laws; nor did he attempt to excuse his fellow socialists.

Blum's last political article for *La Revue blanche* was a product of the same inspiration as his study of the *lois scélérates:* the desire to expose the weakness of the moderate republican leadership.[62] The affair had stimulated in him, as in so many other Dreyfusards, concern for clerical influence in education and had led him to believe, rightly or wrongly, that there was a resurgence of clerical education. The vices of clerical education could be justly blamed for the anti-Dreyfusard mentality, Blum wrote, and the church schools had been "foyers" of anti-republicanism long before the affair. Blum assumed that his audience agreed that some state control of church-run education was necessary, and he devoted his article to the argument that nothing less than complete prohibition of teaching by the technically illegal but tolerated congregations (e.g., Jesuits, Dominicans, Oratorians) would be effective. Such a measure had been introduced years before, by Jules Ferry, and had nearly passed, which enabled Blum to call for revival of Ferry's famous Article Seven.

Blum defended Ferry's article on juridical grounds, showing its compatibility with the basic structure of French educational law and the French legal tradition in general. And as he had done in his treatment of the *lois scélérates*, he turned from legal analysis to the political side of the question through analysis of the original parliamentary debates. He was thus able to attack not only the late Jules Simon, the leader in the defeat of Article Seven, but, more importantly, the moderate republican leadership which had originally supported Ferry but which by 1900 had drifted further to the right.

These two articles show that Blum was with Jaurès in hoping to exploit the Dreyfusard victory to weaken the political grip of the republican old guard. It would be a mistake, however, to say simply that Blum was thus one of those whom Péguy condemned for subverting the *mystique* of the Dreyfus affair in favor of its *politique*. Certainly Blum was more political than Péguy, but he did not believe that politics necessarily meant the death of principle, and he saw the anti-clerical struggle as logically connected with the Dreyfusard struggle. Throughout the nineteenth century, French socialists and republicans had been forced into a rather anomalous position: their defense of secular, state-controlled education in a society where clerical education had long been dominant enabled the Catholics to claim to be defending freedom of education. Blum could scarcely be opposed to the principle of freedom of education, but where it meant freedom for the Church to erect a bulwark against social change, he could only adopt Louis Blanc's argument that clerical education hindered the development of a free society and, therefore, could not be tolerated until democratic ideals had been sufficiently rooted through state education. Blum was so sensitive to the dangers of creating an educational monopoly that he opposed such measures for the Université de France, and he hoped that merely banning the Jesuits and other orders from teaching would suffice. Jaurès had opposed a state's education monopoly even in a socialist society and Blum could not do less in a capitalist one, even though the emotions of the affair led him rather far in that direction.[63]

Despite his confession that, even before the affair, the *lois scélérates* had caused him to hate certain politicians, as well as certain policies, Blum wrote both of these articles with dispassionate clarity and revealed a real talent for objective political analysis. In the years following 1898, he was to be a frequent visitor to the Chamber of Deputies, and, as these articles showed, he acquired familiarity with back volumes of the *Journal officiel*. These were among the important sources for his grasp of political realities and his expertise in the workings of parliamentary politics, which he was to apply in only an advisory capacity before 1919 but which he turned to personal account after the death of Jaurès deprived him of his parliamentary leader. Thus as early as 1898, Blum revealed something of the talent that was to make his emergence as a parliamentary leader possible. Even more clearly, he demonstrated the qualities that would mark the future political director of *Le Populaire*. It was a natural development that Blum became a political leader in large measure through the path of journalism.

Preoccupied with the affairs of the New Society, and perhaps disappointed (though he would never admit it) with the lack of socialist unification, Blum published only one article in 1901, the last of his "Nouvelles conversations avec Eckermann" and his last contribution to *La Revue blanche*. It contained his reflections on Judaism, especially on Judaism and socialism.[64] This article was followed by a gap of over a year, when he worked on a play, which was to have been called *Anger* but which he never finished to his satisfaction. This "publication gap" was closed in December 1902, when he began a series of articles in *La Petite république*, the principal organ of the independent socialists.[65] This series, "Les monopoles," is of special interest in that it is our earliest evidence of Blum's ability to deal with economic questions in practical terms. As we have seen, his socialism was more moral than economic in its origins, and he was inclined to leave the question of the validity of Marx's economic analyses to others. But even a brief experience in the socialist movement showed him the importance of economic understanding, and his experience on the Conseil d'Etat pointed in a similar direction.

In undertaking to write on monopolies, Blum was venturing on well-worn ground, in part defending the legislative measures already proposed to the Chamber by Jaurès. Although lacking in originality, these articles are nonetheless important for showing a side of Blum's thought that is little revealed elsewhere in his early career. Over-all, the articles are a detailed application of the equation: reforms are necessary; reforms cost money; money must be found. Blum discarded the idea that the budget is merely a fiscal matter:

For us the budget of a democratic nation is not a great blackboard on which the figures must ultimately be found in balance, whatever the cost. For us the budget is a living and concrete reality through which the will of the nation is expressed and which ought to clearly express the direction of its collective action. If that will changes, if that action is pointed in a new direction, the budget ought to bear the traces of this change. In the life of a nation there is no act which is not expressed as an expenditure in the budget.[66]

This rather modern viewpoint did not mean that Blum was unconcerned about balancing the budget; on the contrary, he was as sure as any finance minister of the necessity of raising as much money as you spend: it was a "moral necessity" for the state as much as for the individual.[67] Where the socialists differed from the liberals was in calling for an expanding budget in which needs would determine revenues rather than vice versa. Blum advocated fiscal reforms aimed at building a budget surplus before the social reforms that were to absorb it were enacted.

The measures which Blum defended for creating this surplus were definitely socialist in inspiration, but of French rather than Marxist origin. He rejected the standard bourgeois formula of greater economy on the grounds that it was an inadequate means of providing the needed sums. Only one area of the budget even theoretically offered the necessary resources—the military—and Blum was realistic enough to see that while the drastic curtailment of military expenditures was part of the socialist program for the long run, it was not a short-term possibility. Even the anticipated reduction of the term of military service from three to two years was not likely to save money. Also, suppression of state support for the established churches, which he though imminent, would not be nearly enough. Blum was careful, however, to establish that he was in favor of economy in governmental operation even if he did not think it a remedy for current problems.

He likewise considered as inadequate the reform taken up by the Radicals with little success: the income tax. Blum and most other socialists favored an income tax—a mildly progressive tax by later standards—to replace the jumble of direct and indirect taxes which was a legacy of the Directory, but he considered this replacement a matter of equity and did not believe that an income tax should be used to increase the total tax revenue of the state. He believed, mistakenly, that an income tax would be enacted by 1904.

By this process of elimination, Blum arrived at what he considered the only solution under the circumstances: state monopolies over certain profitable economic activities, the *régie*.[68] He argued that the state was going to need so much new revenue for pressing obligations in primary education, professional education, and retirement programs (among others) that even non-socialists would have to accept it. He even suggested that the Radical party would have to take up this campaign or find itself without a *raison d'être*.

Blum's concern, however, was not to analyze the political situation but to argue that these reforms were both practicable and desirable. His argument was based on the idea of *services publics*— the idea that certain economic functions are public by nature and should not be operated for private benefit. This theory had been given particular development in France by the somewhat eclectic socialist Benoît Malon and the possibilist leader Paul Brousse, but it was not strongly endorsed by orthodox Marxists, who suspected it of petty bourgeois reformism. It was, however, a widely diffused idea and one that had a certain foundation in French legal tradition.[69]

Blum discerned three types of natural monopoly in which the responsibility of the state was intrinsically engaged: *services publics* which had been (1) turned over to private exploitation by the state to raise money during a moment of need, (2) casually or freely abandoned to private effort, or (3) discovered to be *services publics* only after they had been pioneered by private enterprise. He proposed immediate state action in the first and third categories. In the first category were the *offices ministériels*, that is, the positions of *greffier*, *huissier*, and *notaire*.[70] These were the principal survivors of the venality of office under the Old Regime; in theory presidential appointments, they were in fact passed from hand to hand like the private property of their holders. To Blum, this was offensive because it increased the financial burdens of legal action on private citizens while it cheated the state out of revenue properly its own. He believed that even with reasonable compensation for present officeholders, their replacement by a civil service corps would be financially profitable to the state.

In the third category Blum placed insurance, fire and life insurance being his main examples. He argued that insurance had proved to be a kind of *service public* because it was not really the insurance companies which protected their policyholders but rather the other policyholders. This being so, the natural unit of this mutual protection (under present circumstances) was the nation and the state was the natural intermediary among the insured. Once again Blum argued that state monopoly would be both an advantage to citizens, assuring them fairer treatment and security from fraud or failure, and a source of revenue for the state, since the monopolized industry would have lower costs of operation. The program of reforms which this revenue was to support would also be benefited through the state's improved facilities for organizing and managing a retirement and pension program. In both of these proposals for state monopolies Blum took pains not only to show the benefits he believed would result but also how the transition could be carried out, without drastic social readjustment or harm to the individuals involved. His proposed compensations would surely not have pleased all those expropriated, but they were based on a concern for fairness which would have seemed bourgeois weakness to a Guesde. Blum's socialism did not imply vendettas against the bourgeoisie.

Although starting with the idea of *services publics*, Blum did not limit himself to considering monopolies of this juridical type but went on to examine some monopolies or proposed monopolies that were more economic in origin. The workings of the capitalist economy had led to certain *de facto* monopolies, as French socialists had observed before Marx, and even the bourgeois economists generally held these to be evil. Thus Blum felt free to argue that even non-socialists could support the transfer of these monopolies to the state since the market economy would not be altered. Socialists had been concerned with the oil-refining and beet-sugar monopolies, and Jaurès had introduced a bill (in 1897) for the nationalization of the sugar manufacturing and refining industries (which were separate in France), but it was defeated 80 to 421.[71] Blum dealt with this proposal at length, analyzing, with clarity and succinctness, the state and evolution of the sugar industry and showing the dangers to consumers and sugar-beet growers from the failure of prompt action. This interest in the "little man" as the victim of monopoly power was joined, as usual, to a concern for state finances. Sugar was heavily taxed, but the industry received various subsidies, and Blum could argue that state ownership would result in considerable savings for the treasury. In concluding, he quoted the czarist minister Serge Witte to justify compensation only for past investment and not for hypothetical future profit.

The other monopoly which Blum proposed was of a different character, dealing with a situation which was in some respects peculiarly French: the purification of alcohol. International socialism had joined the campaign against the growing menace of alcoholism, but while Blum agreed that it was a problem, he saw little chance for state action. He did not raise the question of "legislating morality" but simply saw that there could be no effective legal means of reducing consumption. What the state could do, he believed, was strike at the health menace presented by the fact that 90 percent of French alcohol production was imperfectly purified. Legislative investigations had on three occasions proposed some sort of state control of purity, and Blum argued that only complete state monopoly of purification would be effective. His argument showed considerable sophistication about the difficulties of enforcement in this touchy field. Enforcement, of course, was also a fiscal question, and revenue from the alcohol tax had been declining in spite of increases in the tax rate, or perhaps because of them. This financial loss to the state resulted largely from the opportunities for fraud provided by the legal privileges of the hundreds of thousands (possibly millions) of *bouilleurs de cru* (still the most redoubtable pressure group in French politics).

Blum did not propose to attack the *bouilleurs de cru,* a practical impossibility, but he thought that the tax revenue could be more than doubled through the compulsory use of state purification facilities. He defended such a monopoly as more easily established and enforced than Vaillant's proposal of a state monopoly on liquor sales. Blum not only advanced the interest of increasing state revenue without raising taxes or borrowing but chose proposals which could be argued without reference (at least direct reference) to socialist theory, except to the very moderate theory of *services publics.* This was typical of the gradualist approach he thought could be—indeed should be—used to bring about the transformation of capitalist society.

Taken as a whole, Blum's articles on the nationalization of various monopolies and his articles for *La Revue blanche* displayed a side that was otherwise little revealed during this period of his life. They showed that he could turn his quick, analytical mind to social and economic questions with results that were models of argument in their forceful generalization and well-chosen illustrative detail. These articles had the kind of clarity which comes from the writer's full understanding of his subject, based on careful research. Not particularly original in inspiration, they were excellent journalism. The same was true of his one lengthy political article, an analysis of the impending election of 1902, which was intended for *La Revue de Paris* but which, unfortunately, never appeared.[72]

Blum's approach to politics was intellectual, but was not dogmatic or doctrinaire. More interested in the workings of the parliamentary mechanism than in the electoral process, he undertook to learn all the workings of the Chamber, the behavior of its members—how legislation was made, how and why specific individuals had voted.[73] In the process, he acquired not only considerable knowledge of the current scene but some general ideas which were to serve him well.

Most important was his ability to accept the shortcomings of parliamentary politics without adopting the cynicism toward politics so often generated in intellectuals. Politics and politicians deal with the "present and the possible," and he saw in this fact no reason to despair of the democratic regime.[74] This article on the 1902 election displayed the blend of optimism and realism that was characteristic of Blum.

In his analysis of the electoral struggle, Blum was dominated by the desire to comprehend—writing was always, for him, a kind of self-clarification. This election had a special attraction in that it presented, or so he thought, an uncommon clarity. Certainly, though he did not mention it, the 1898 election had been a model of confusion, and the long duration of the Waldeck-Rousseau ministry had helped clarify opinion. Because of his involvement in Jaurès's policy of support for the "Ministère de défense républicaine," Blum had come to see the political struggle in the 1898–1902 legislature as centering on support for, or opposition to, the ministry *as a whole*, with lesser issues put aside. The assumption that this basic dichotomy would carry over into the election of 1902 was the basis of his analysis of the positions of the confronting forces and the possible results of the balloting. Rather than predict the results, he suggested that there were only two (or perhaps three) serious possibilities, and he devoted the bulk of his article to examining the potential consequences in each case.

Quite expectedly, he saw victory for the conservative right as the least likely possibility, but rather than hold that such a victory would be a national disaster, Blum argued that it would bring relatively little change. He believed that most of the right had come to accept the inevitability of the Republic and that they could offer, as an alternative, only a conservative republic.[75] This analysis was in the spirit of his earlier dismissal of the dangers of the anti-Semitic movement, but it was not the product of blind optimism, for on the whole it is safe to say that before World War I the French right was still predominantly traditionalist and hesitant to venture into the unknown. Blum, characteristically, found corroboration of his estimate of the right in a new novel by Barrès.

While not expecting a major swing to the right, Blum realized that there was a good chance of a move in that direction, a half-step backward that would bring back the "cabinets of concentration" of the center. This result, he thought, was "perhaps the most probable " outcome.[76] And certainly the Third Republic had exhibited a marked tendency to seek its equilibrium in the center, although the precise location of the center had changed. Blum had little to say about a centrist combination, which he found a more distasteful possibility than the victory of the right. Everything that could be said of the centrist cabinets had been said a thousand times already, he remarked; and he had made his opinion clear in earlier articles. But while prudence dictated awareness of the possibility of another such government, Blum was looking for a continuation of the Waldeck-Rousseau combination.

Thus, alongside the disinterested analyst, the political partisan in Blum made its discreet appearance. In listing reasons why the conservatives disliked the Waldeck-Rousseau government, he was listing, with greater accuracy, his own reasons for favoring it: its aggressive republicanism, which precluded the conciliatory attitude toward former enemies of the regime that was characteristic of the centrist ministries; the law on associations, which was more than a chastisement of the congregations for their intervention in the Dreyfus affair as it was also a start for a vigorous anti-clerical program; the beginning of fiscal reform, leading at least to an income tax; and the activities of Millerand, in establishing or proposing social reforms.[77] Blum placed very great stress on the importance of Millerand, arguing that his membership in the ministry prevented Waldeck-Rousseau from following his own inclination to exchange socialist support for equivalent votes from the center. The center could not tolerate Millerand, thus blocking such a move. Seen from this point of view, even Millerand's aggressiveness in introducing himself into the governmental combination brought some benefits to the socialists.

There was as much validity in this view as in the conventional Marxist view held by Guesde and Lafargue, that Millerand was merely a hostage in the hands of the bourgeoisie, preventing the socialists from voting against the ministry. Blum also differed with the Marxists in assessing the value of Millerand's reforms:

Finally a socialist minister has either caused the Parliament to pass, or posed before public opinion, or realized on his own authority, a series of measures which consecrate the policy of state intervention between capital and labor with an obviousness which disturbs the conservatives and liberals: the law on hours of work, bills on strikes, on syndicats, on retirement and on employment offices; decrees on working conditions and on "labor councils," daily circulars and decisions. The personal action of M. Millerand, his very presence in a republican cabinet, while it has accelerated [the growth of] workers' demands, has also alarmed industry, large commerce, and all the forms of capital.[78]

To the Marxists, Millerand's presence in the government, and even his reform measures, could only arouse unfulfillable hopes in the workers and thus serve to discredit socialism.[79] Reforms granted by a bourgeois government were of no use to the Marxists unless they were "extorted" by the direct pressure of the organized proletariat. To Blum, on the other hand, amelioration in the conditions of the working class was valuable even if it came from the bourgeoisie. He too believed that the complete liberation of the working class could take place only with the establishment of a socialist regime, but he did not view this establishment as an apocalyptic process. To reach the goal, it was necessary to go through preliminary stages, which however unsatisfactory were nevertheless essential. Blum thought that a vital step in preparing society to accept the necessity of socialism was the creation of general acceptance of government intervention in the conflict between capital and labor—on the side of labor. This would ease the transition toward a government of, by, and for labor—the dictatorship of the proletariat.[80]

Despite his basic approval of the Millerand experiment, by 1902 Blum had apparently come to doubt that it was worth the price of the bitter division in socialist ranks. But in giving up the socialist presence in government, he consoled himself with the idea that the same type of transitional reform could be accomplished without it. Even in the event of a victory for the forces supporting the Waldeck-Rousseau ministry, there would be, Blum thought, a reshuffling which would perhaps exclude Millerand and his allies. In any case, there would be no authorized representative of socialism, for even the PSF (at its national congress at Tours, in March 1902) had decided against the experiment under the present circumstances. But the socialists would continue their support of the Radical government, either directly, if their numbers were needed, or covertly, if the Radicals were capable of standing alone. The Radicals would not be abandoned to the right, and thus distinctions among the bourgeois parties would continue to be observed in spite of Guesde's theoretical opposition.

Thus Blum supported Jaurès's policy of coalition with bourgeois parties for specific ends, which, in spite of the criticism at the international congress of 1900, would be reinforced after the 1902 election by the formation of the Bloc des Gauches in support of the new ministry of Emile Combes. Blum accepted this political tactic until Jaurès abandoned it under pressure from the International at the end of 1904. Later, Blum was to devote much of his political career to the search for a viable alternative—one which would avoid the risks of too close collaboration with the bourgeois parties while escaping the doctrinaire opposition-for-opposition's-sake which seemed to be the limit of Marxist tactical ideas. For the present, he was content to leave the problems in the more experienced hands of Jaurès.

Blum saw that there was no possibility of a socialist victory in 1902, or even in the immediate future, and that socialists must therefore try to understand the existing structure of politics. He was encouraged by discovering that most other European governments also were dominated by rather heterogeneous coalitions that were as disparate as the ministerial coalition in France.[81] This observation led him to suggest that the rate of change in economic life, international relations, and social problems was so great as to prevent the formation of homogeneous majority parties in any parliamentary state. Even in England, he observed astutely, two-party government was an illusion which covered constant change in the makeup of those parties. As for France, the ministerial coalition was solid, but it would certainly dissolve and be replaced by something else as circumstances changed. Such political change was necessary if the problems of national life were to be squarely faced, and the advantage of Jaurès's position was that it had the flexibility to face changing circumstances. Blum insisted that "the future cannot be confined within any program."

Having a program was neither unnecessary nor undesirable, but programs must be realistic and open-ended. In 1901 Blum had spoken of the socialists' minimum program (presumably referring to Marseille and not St. Mandé) as a distant objective—the sum total of the reforms which would be possible under the regime of private property.[82] He did not commit himself to the necessity of accomplishing all these reforms before the socialist revolution would be possible, but his idea of evolutionary revolution clearly lent itself to such a conclusion. Blum predicted that the period following the election of 1902 would be one in which a "democratic," but not socialist, majority would carry out a certain number of those minimum reforms with the aid of the socialists. His foresight vis-à-vis the political measures that would be taken proved to be superior to his prognostications of how much social reform the Radical party was committed to—or could be driven to: "From the political point of view the democrats will demand a whole-hearted republican purity from functionaries of all ranks."[83] On the other hand, Blum was right in his expectations of action on the church-state question:

They [the democrats] will execute the law on the Associations with the utmost rigor, and one can foresee that legislative authorization will not be liberally dispensed to the requesting congregations. They will prepare the way for and perhaps carry out the separation of Church and State. The laws on secular education will be applied; doubtless an atttempt will be made to exclude the congregations from primary education by the withdrawal of ancient charters; in any case the facilities which those regular clergy devoted to secondary education enjoy under the Falloux law will be withdrawn.[84]

What Blum did not foresee was that the fanaticism of *le père* Combes would prevent the government's going beyond the religious question, that it would help provoke a reaction which would lead subsequent governments considerably to the right, stalemating the cause of reform.

The reform program which Blum laid down for the Radicals in the next legislature was, in any case, more ambitious than he realized. Much of it won support only from the socialists: limitation of the workday, retirement programs financed by management and the state, health and unemployment insurance, old-age assistance, recognition and formal organization of the right to strike, compulsory arbitration (much opposed by the syndicats), collective bargaining, and labor's participation in the enforcement of labor legislation.[85] Blum returned to the suggestions in his articles on monopolies when discussing ways to pay for these programs; he spoke of the "probability" of the nationalization of insurance and sugar and oil refining. He also predicted the gradual conversion of all *services publics* into *services d'Etat*, especially through municipal acquisition of local transportation, water, and lighting services. Clearly, he underestimated the forces of resistance to change, even

153

the sheer inertia of French society, in thinking that the need for reforms was sufficient to ensure their adoption. In spite of the affair, he tended to see the opposition as men of reason, vulnerable to rational argument. His work as a socialist journalist was rooted in this premise.

Blum's period as a socialist journalist was extremely short lived, and in March 1903 he resumed his career of literary criticism, this time for *Gil Blas*, and began to write drama criticism for *La Renaissance latine*. Blum returned to political journalism only in 1917–18, when he published (anonymously) his "Lettres sur la réforme gouvernementale" in *La Revue de Paris*. He had never intended to pursue a career in political journalism, and his few articles were basically part of his self-testing and self-clarification, prompted by his involvement in the affair and in the socialist unity movement. In the process, he expanded his knowledge of society and acquired an understanding that would prove of great value to him many years later. Though ceasing for over a decade to write political articles, Blum remained interested in the socialist press, and played a role in the founding of Jaurès's *L'Humanité*.

About the time of his brief collaboration on *La Petite république*, Blum became convinced of the need for a more fully socialist-controlled organ in the daily press. *La Petite république* was owned largely by non-socialist bourgeois and directed by members of the right wing of the socialist movement: Millerand had been its editor, but the post was currently held by Gérault-Richard. Jaurès had made the paper his major Parisian outlet, comparable to his non-socialist outlet in his native south, *La Dépêche de Toulouse*, but the evolution of the unity movement made it important that he have an independent outlet. He did not intend to separate from his colleagues of *La Petite république*, but he needed to be less dependent on them.

Blum and Lucien Herr were among those who tried to persuade Jaurès to take the lead in establishing a socialist daily.[86] At first they thought of buying *La Petite république*, but this proved impracticable.[87] Serious consideration of founding a new journal became possible only when Jaurès was assured of support from other leaders of the PSF and the major independents. Whatever Blum's influence, the experienced professional politicians naturally had the decisive word at the organizing meeting, held at the home of Jaurès.[88] After much debate, the assembly yielded to Jaurès's desire that his journal be called *L'Humanité*.[89]

More important than the choice of a name was the distribution of editorial power, especially as *L'Humanité* was not to be the official organ of the PSF and the independents were to play a considerable role. Jaurès, of course, was its political director, with absolute power over the choice of personnel. His second-in-command was Gustave Rouanet and the other political editors were Jean Allemane, Aristide Briand, Eugène Fournière, Francis de Pressensé, Louis Revelin, and René Viviani.[90] The influence of Blum and Herr was apparent among the lesser staff members, among whom were several collaborators of the New Society: Charles Andler, who joined Herr on the foreign affairs staff; Etienne Burnet, on medical news; Marcel Mauss, on cooperatives; Edgar Milhaud, on economic questions; and Albert Thomas, on the labor movement. Other correspondents were the distinguished Prof. Gustave Lanson and, from the circle of *Cahiers de la Quinzaine*, Daniel Halévy.

This recruitment of intellectuals for the socialist movement was evidently of interest to Blum. His principal contribution at this point, however, seems to have been in assembling the literary staff.[91] For the few regular, paying positions, his problem was selecting from among the applicants, who were very numerous because of the difficulties writers had in earning a living by practicing their craft. This selection was an ungrateful task, which naturally earned Blum more enemies than friends. He reserved for himself the post of literary critic, and an old friend from *La Revue blanche*, Alfred Athis [Natanson], became the drama critic. In addition, Blum succeeded in bringing together an impressive group of "literary collaborators," headed by Anatole France and Jules Renard and including Octave Mirbeau, Abel Hermant, Gustave Geffroy, Tristan Bernard, Georges Lecomte, Jean Ajalbert, Michel Zevacco, and others. After the paper was launched, Blum was only a literary contributor and did not participate in the making of editorial policy.[92]

Opening day in the editorial offices of *L'Humanité* was a day of great enthusiasm. Many of the literary staff were present, including France and Mirbeau. Jules Renard, who felt he had never received a friendlier reception, found Blum especially excited—"active, feverish, resembling the nymph Egeria."[93] Jaurès, too, was optimistic about the venture, having received reassurance of its soundness from professional newspaper circles.[94] This optimism, however, proved to be premature, for only after many years and difficulties was the paper soundly established.

155

Circulation was the main problem. The early *Humanité* was of high quality, but it did not address itself to the proletariat, whose interests it sought to serve. It was moving directly against the current trends in popular journalism, which had been carrying the *journal d'information* to supremacy over the *journal d'opinion.* Rather than concede that workers should read papers like *Le Matin*, in which socialism was regularly vilified, Jaurès and his aides finally decided to meet the competition by publishing more "news." Doctrinal exposition was cut to a minimum, and so were the cultural departments.[95] (A hostile critic had already suggested that its name should have been *Les Humanités.*) Blum's literary column, which had often appeared on the front page, disappeared altogether, having lasted just a year.

No longer a direct participant, Blum continued to be a financial supporter of the paper. At its founding, he had helped secure the necessary financial backing, probably working with Herr in those academic circles which had supported the New Society. Jaurès also received considerable aid from middle-class Jewish circles, in part because of the affair, but it is not clear whether Blum helped recruit this support.[96] Blum was one of the original stockholders, investing the not inconsiderable sum of 1,000 francs.[97] When Jaurès announced, in an editorial in October 1906, that a financial crisis threatened the continuation of the paper, Blum took the lead in proposing a subscription to which contributors would promise a fixed sum each month until the crisis was over. He offered to launch it with 100 francs a month, and soon there was a long list of supporters.[98] Another crisis in 1907 forced yet another refinancing and reorganization, but after that the paper was stabilized.[99] In addition to his financial support of the paper, Blum frequently contributed to the various charitable and electoral causes for which *L'Humanité* organized collections.[100] Altogether, his financial contribution to the success of *L'Humanité* was large in proportion to his modest bourgeois resources.

During the early months of *L'Humanité* the question of socialist unity rebounded to the forefront, both for the movement in general and for Blum in particular. After the scissions of 1900 and 1901 the political fortune of the PSF had seemed to continue on the rise. In the 1902 election it sent thirty-two deputies to the Chamber, while the rival PSDF sent only twelve. But this apparent differential was deceptive. The membership of the solidly united Guesdists was growing steadily while the PSF continued to suffer the effects of its attempt at a compromise stand on the issue of ministerial participation. The electoral success of the PSF was in large part a result of its greater identification with the anti-clerical spirit that emerged from the affair, its more supple electoral tactics, and the political strength of some of its leaders. But instead of becoming more united, it suffered a continual splitting away on both left and right over the ministerial issue.

Jaurès's effort to steer a middle path between the condemnation of all participation and the overenthusiastic seeking out of every occasion for it became more difficult. Finally forced to withdraw his conditional support of Millerand, Jaurès did not give up his belief that socialism could benefit from some forms of cooperation with the bourgeois parties of the left. In committing himself to the anti-clerical program of the Bloc des Gauches, he was perhaps trying too hard to demonstrate the validity of his position and thus exaggerated the clerical menace. Blum, who doubted the power of clerical reaction, nonetheless favored disestablishment and the severe limitation of clerical education, thus accepting Jaurès's leadership. Both hoped that the success of their political program would be the basis for a resumption of socialist unification.

The attempt at unification was soon to take place, but not in the way Blum had hoped. He had not expected miracles from Jaurès's policy, but the lack of benefits for the working class from the government supported by the Bloc des Gauches was interpreted by their opponents as evidence of the doctrinal errors of the PSF. The rigid opponents of all collaboration thus found their position strengthened within the French movement. They also discovered increasing support in the International, as more member parties now had to deal with similar questions than had been the case in 1900. As usual, the main source of orthodox strength was the German SPD, and the Guesdists sought to appropriate this strength by adopting, at their Reims congress of September 1903, the anti-ministerialist resolution of the SPD's Dresden congress earlier that year. Then, in language designed to imply the abandonment of socialism by the PSF, the Guesdists (who had added "Union socialiste révolutionnaire" to their party name) appealed to the International's congress at Amsterdam (in August 1904) to give its sanction to their position.

Amsterdam was thus to see a renewal of the debate of 1900, with the same antagonists and the same arguments. This time, however, it was Guesde, rather than Jaurès, who went to the floor to defend a resolution from Germany, and Guesde who was victorious. Unlike Guesde in 1900, Jaurès in 1904 agreed to accept the verdict of the International. Blum was not present to watch Jaurès's last-ditch stand, but he was familiar with the terms. The Dresden resolution was more forceful in its rejection of all forms of nonelective participation than the Kautsky resolution of 1900 had been, leaving only the loophole of a reference to that earlier action: "Social democracy cannot accept any participation in the government in bourgeois society, in accord with the Kautsky order of the day adopted at the international congress of Paris in 1900."[101] This loophole was too small for the out-and-out ministerialists in Jaurès's PSF, and after the resolutions committee had given overwhelming support to the Dresden measure, he carried the fight to the floor in the form of a less-insulting version offered by Adler (Austria) and Vandervelde (Belgium). Jaurès's eloquence obtained no more than a tie vote, which defeated the conciliatory move. The Dresden resolution was adopted 25 to 5, with twelve abstentions, and the congress then issued a call for the French to accept its verdict and unify their forces.

Back in France, Jaurès hesitated about a month before deciding to proceed with unity negotiations. In November 1904 the leaders of the two factions came together and set up a Commission for Unification, which was responsible for drafting the Pact of Union. Jaurès had to face opposition within the PSF from those who were unwilling to give up the Bloc des Gauches, but ultimately an overwhelming majority followed his lead. Blum was especially anxious for the acceptance of unification, so much so that he stepped from his usual behind-the-scenes role to be a delegate to the final congress of the PSF at Rouen (26–28 March 1905). There he made his first, brief speech to urge acceptance of the pact.[102] Outside the formal debate, he tried to convince the hesitant that Jaurès was right in deciding that the period of useful collaboration with the bourgeois ministry was over.[103] The withdrawal of those who refused to yield removed the last obstacle to unification within the ranks of the PSF.

The national organizations having separately ratified the Pact of Union, the unity congress in the Salle du Globe at Paris was little more than a formality. In recognition of his support for unification, Blum was named a delegate of the PSF, representing the department of the Tarn alongside Jaurès.[104] Once again he made a brief speech for unity, which was not completely uncritical of the terms of the pact.[105] The Salle du Globe congress was not a great occasion for speech-making, although for many socialists the mystique of unity made it an emotionally moving occasion. Blum was certainly touched by that mystique and convinced that unity was worth a price, though by no means an exorbitant price.[106] Unity seemed to be a political necessity for the advancement of socialism in the face of strong, continued bourgeois resistance;[107] and as a political measure, its price could be assessed politically.

Blum undoubtedly shared Jaurès's belief that it would be possible to carry on the struggle for his policies within the united party.[108] He remained convinced that Jaurès's assessment of the situation had been right, and he repeatedly spoke of Jaurès as the "architect of unity."[109] At first glance, it may seem that Blum was carried away by hero worship, but despite the defeat at Amsterdam the unified party was to bear the imprint of Jaurès's brand of socialism. The Pact of Union represented a compromise for both of the contending factions; otherwise, neither would have felt secure enough to abandon its organization to fusion.[110] The Guesdists doubtless felt that their "scientific" orthodoxy had triumphed, but Guesde's victory was possible only because of the slow transformation of that orthodoxy. Even in the realm of doctrine, the Guesdists had become more supple, for the doctrinal preface to the Pact of Union bore a strong resemblance to the St. Mandé program:

The Socialist party is founded on the following principles: international understanding and action of the workers; political and economic organization of the proletariat into a class party for the conquest of power and the socialization of the means of production and exchange, that is, the transformation of the capitalist society into a collectivist or communist society.[111]

The unification of 1905 did not impose tighter ideological bonds on Blum than he had accepted in 1899.

The new party took the name Parti Socialiste (Section Française de l'Internationale Ouvrière) and was generally known as the SFIO.[112] The old organizations were completely dissolved and a new structure of departmental federations was created. These federations were to be represented at the national congresses in proportion to their membership. The national congresses, in turn, chose the party leadership: a large Conseil National and a smaller Commission Administrative Permanente. The party structure was thus a centralized democracy, not authoritarian, and the departmental federations exercised considerable autonomy. The political dividends which Blum had expected from unity were not long in coming. Some six months after unification, a party census counted 46,380 card-carrying members in good standing, as opposed to the total of 28,000 claimed by the separate groups. This total rose steadily to 72,765 in 1914.

Defections at first reduced the number of deputies, with such long-time socialists as Victor Augagneur, Briand, Gabriel Deville, Gérault-Richard, Pascal Grousset, Clovis Hugues, and Alexandre Zévaès declining to join the SFIO and eventually forming their own loose socialist federation in the Chamber.[113] Outside the Chamber, such important figures as Viviani and Millerand remained aloof.[114] The SFIO made up the loss of these able politicians with a steady increase in the number of candidates it sent to the Chamber after each election: fifty-one in 1906, seventy-four in 1910, one hundred and two in 1914. With the unity he had modestly helped forward thus completed at the Salle du Globe, Blum felt he was no longer needed in the public arena, and although he remained a dues-paying member, his relationship to the socialist movement entered a new and apparently dormant phase.

Although his role as a public militant was long interrupted, it would be inexact to say that Blum's socialist activity ceased. He had no ambition for a career as a socialist politician, and did not believe that his socialist commitment imposed such an obligation. With party unity achieved, the principal obstacle to socialism's advance was removed, and with Jaurès there to ensure a humanistic direction to that advance, Blum felt justified in yielding to the attractions of the literary life that he had temporarily abandoned. His year as literary critic for *L'Humanité* had shown that he could combine the socialist with the man of letters, and he saw no reason why this combination could not continue. Furthermore, there were certain aspects of his direct contribution to the socialist movement which he was able to continue—his behind-the-scenes services, such as those he had rendered to Jaurès during the Dreyfus affair.

Even during the phase of his most militant action, Blum had had little contact with the rank and file of socialism; he had served as an aide to the leadership, and he maintained many of his contacts with it after 1905. He was motivated by the desire to remain *au courant* with the movement and expand his socialist education—to learn more about the ideas and the men involved—as well as by the desire to be of service. Thus he attended, more or less regularly, the sessions of the fourteenth section of the Fédération de la Seine, the party organization in his home district, in the company of a friend and sometime deputy, Bracke (pseudonym of the classical scholar A.-M. Desrousseaux). Blum, content to remain an observer, seldom spoke at these local meetings.[115] Perhaps he also supported Bracke's electoral campaigns and went to hear Guesde and Jaurès when they appeared together at Montparnasse political rallies.[116] But his contacts with Jaurès and others at home or in salons were more important.

From the time of the affair, Blum had served as a party technician whose specialized competences helped implement the details of the party's program.[117] His aid to Jaurès during the affair was perhaps not direct aid to socialism but it was the prototype of the service he later rendered. During the first years of his socialist activity, Blum had become aware of the need for party specialists. Although very active in the movement for unity because it was essential to the political success of socialism, he saw that political victories and the support of the united proletariat were not enough to run a great nation, let alone remodel it. So important did he consider this discovery that in 1901, through "Goethe," he again observed:

A political party can live and prosper only so far as it has formed *specialists*. Often it can even survive on that alone when it has already been abandoned by all living ideals and all popular confidence. The history of the Third Republic entirely confirms this elementary truth. The opportunists outlived themselves for a decade because they included men capable of reading a finance law, of establishing a tariff schedule, of drawing up a penal text. The absolute dearth of specialists has condemned and will condemn the so-called Radical party to the most regrettable impotence in spite of its electoral successes. Perhaps one day the popular victories of socialism will run up against a similar difficulty. From now on it will be necessary to organize the division of labor. In the last Chamber one too easily relied on Jaurès's strong general culture and his incredible ability of assimilation.[118]

Blum was confident that the Socialist party would find the specialists it needed as long as others, like himself, recognized that need.[119] His experience on the Conseil d'Etat had first revealed this need to him by showing, in detail, the immense complexity of the life of the nation, as well as the critical role played by the national administration. This contact with everyday realities helped immunize him against the oversimplifications inherent in the political rhetoric of socialism, as in that of all other political movements. Furthermore, it helped him see the kind of role that he could play in the movement.

Blum's intimate knowledge of the parliamentary scene did not make him desire to sit in the Palais Bourbon. Jules Renard has recounted a conversation with Blum in the visitor's gallery at the Chamber in 1903:

> "You're very anxious to know if it's difficult to do what they are doing," Léon Blum said to me.
> "Yes. I'm afraid I've wasted my life."
> "Don't worry about that."
> "But, after all, are those men superior to artists?"
> "There's no comparison! The artist and the intelligent man can only meet on the heights, but I believe that it's easy to equal most of those men just as in art it's not a rare thing to have more talent than de Nion or Maizeroy." [120]

The year before, Jaurès had tried to persuade Blum to be a candidate for the Chamber, and he repeated this suggestion before the election of 1906, but Blum felt that his inclinations and abilities better fitted him for a place among the specialists.[121] Throughout the prewar period, Blum continued his personal service to the party leader, later describing himself as one of those "who have lived modestly, obscurely in his shadow."[122] During the sessions of the legislature, Jaurès often lunched with Blum, whose apartment was much closer than his own to the Palais Bourbon.[123] Blum offered him not only the hospitality of his table but information on legal and financial matters and a place to work.[124] Jules Renard arrived one day in 1907 to find Jaurès preparing what was to be a celebrated attack on the opening of the Paris market to the latest Russian loan.[125] There were less serious occasions, too: Joseph Paul-Boncour recalled being present the day that Jaurès's son, Louis, passed his baccalaureate.[126]

In addition to putting his talents at the disposal of Jaurès, Blum sought to use his social connections to enlist the expertise of others in the service of socialism. On occasion, as the following incident recounted by Georges Suarez indicates, he was able to find the right man for a given job. When Briand was chosen parliamentary reporter for the proposed legislation on the separation of church and state, he asked Jaurès to suggest someone to help him with the vast technical detail of the project. Jaurès referred him to Blum, who recommended his friend Paul Grunebaum-Ballin. Grunebaum-Ballin left the Conseil d'Etat to undertake this task, and remained Briand's close personal assistant throughout most of the future diplomat's career.[127]

The wide contacts made early in his life and his ability to persuade specialists to serve a cause were later to be a great benefit to Blum himself; they enabled the Popular Front government to make use of such talents as the brilliant physicists Jean Perrin and Paul Langevin, whom Blum had met at the New Society.[128] He had always been solicitous of his friends, even to the extent of occasionally offending the more sensitive, as Gide has testified, by being too protective, too profuse with recommendations that were not always solicited—a fencing-master for this person, a lawyer for that.[129] Gide's resistance was in part the self-defense of a much more inwardly oriented spirit, and most of Blum's many friends realized that his expansiveness was the product of a genuine concern for others and not a disguised self-aggrandizement. Blum's self-knowledge enabled him to put this trait of his personality at the service of his socialist conviction. His activities as a finder of specialists and a source of information were the result of a conscious attempt to find the role he was best qualified to play in the movement.

In his provocative *La République des professeurs*, Albert Thibaudet referred to Blum as the representative of the University *"in partibus Parisiorum."*[130] One could with perhaps greater accuracy use that felicitous expression to describe Blum's position in the socialist movement during the period 1905 to 1914. Although he maintained contact with the socialist leadership, especially with Jaurès and Herr, this was only a small part of his activity. Blum was just reaching the height of his career on the Conseil d'Etat, becoming *maître des requêtes* in 1907 and *commissaire du gouvernement* in 1910.[131] At the same time that his reputation as a jurist was beginning to spread, he was repeating his success as a literary critic and becoming, as we shall see, one of the most important Parisian drama critics.

Typically, he combined extensive professional activity with an extremely active social life. He and his wife entertained as much as their resources permitted, and his promotion in 1907 enabled them to seek more ample quarters. In 1908 they contracted for a comfortable apartment in a building under construction on the boulevard Montparnasse, and moved there in 1909.[132] The Blum salon on the boulevard Montparnasse brought a wide variety of personalities together: socialist militants, jurists and businessmen, artists and musicians—and especially representatives of the worlds of literature and the theater. Blum was concerned not only that socialism expand its efforts to attract specialized competence but also that the bourgeoisie see that socialists were not wild-eyed dreamers but men capable of managing the affairs of a great nation.

Blum believed that unification would solve the main problems of the relationship of the Socialist party to the proletariat, and in any case he did not feel especially qualified for that work. He could more easily represent socialism to the bourgeoisie, whose attitude, he thought, was important to the future of socialism. It is possible that he saw himself playing a role analogous to that of Herr at the Ecole Normale. He certainly did not imagine that bourgeois society, because of its sins, would be suddenly wiped out, like Sodom and Gomorrah. Rather, it would go through an evolutionary transformation of indeterminate duration, during which the socialists would take the initiative in implementing a growing number of reforms, until the minimum program had been carried out. The socialists, however, would not be strong enough to effect these reforms without the aid of part of the bourgeoisie.

Blum certainly believed that even in these years of nonmilitancy he was helping prepare the bourgeoisie for its part in these transformations. At one point he had hoped that the Radical party would play a key part in the socioeconomic reform of French society. When he became disappointed with the Radicals, Blum found hope in the increasing number of politicians of bourgeois origin who, though they did not join the socialists, at least not permanently, escaped the blindness to socioeconomic problems that afflicted the Radicals. This buffer group would help make the peaceful transition to socialism possible.[133] Unlike many others, Blum was not especially disturbed by the "treason" to the movement by the Briands and the Vivianis. He remarked to Jules Renard: "At bottom, they are skeptics, almost cynics, but they have passed through socialism, and something of it will always remain in them. They are worth more than Radicals."[134]

Blum carefully distinguished this group from the evolutionary socialists, like himself and Jaurès, who remained committed to the ultimate goal of collectivist economic organization. These socialists would work with the men of the bourgeois left when the situation called for it and even defend a Millerand against what seemed to be the too harsh strictures of their own would-be revolutionary wing, but they intended to go beyond the limits of bourgeois reform. Blum's "Goethe" once remarked that the true significance of the *universités populaires* was that they "revealed and propagated [among the bourgeoisie, not the workers] the state of mind of the young men who directed them" and that they were thus creating "hostages" whose commitment to liberty and reason would not permit them to resist the triumph of socialism.[135] Perhaps Blum considered himself, with his emphasis on socialism as the current embodiment of universal morality, as a "hostage-taker" among the bourgeoisie.

Blum later explained the irregularity of his early militancy in terms of his concern for party unity: he was active during the unification and he returned to activity when that unity was threatened.[136] That threat arose during the Great War from the defeatist movement associated with the Zimmerwald and Kienthal "congresses" and lies outside our period, but the pressing issues were already felt in the socialist world as the threat of war loomed larger. Blum did not take an active part in the public debate which divided the socialists on the issue of war, but he followed it with close interest. The lines were drawn as early as the Limoges congress of the SFIO in 1906. The socialists, because of their anti-colonialism, had been critical of the government during the Moroccan crisis of the previous year, and like many others they had realized that its apparent solution had not ended the threat of a European war. Thus the socialists were compelled to consider their position with respect to this threat.

At the time of the Dreyfus affair they had been virtually unanimous in denouncing the dangers of militarism, but this did not guarantee agreement in the face of war. Indeed, there were three basic positions within the party. On the right wing was the position of Jules Guesde, which was usually considered the orthodox Marxist position. Guesde held that wars were an inseparable part of the capitalist system, and he denounced pacifism as bourgeois senti- mentality. The doctrine of the Communist Manifesto, that workers have no country, was perhaps correct for 1848, but it no longer applied in a democratic republic. Proletarian internationalism was a necessary counterweight to capitalist internationalism, but it could not prevent war. Guesde denounced the idea that socialists should take revolutionary action in case of war, because to do so would inevitably lead to the defeat of socialism in the advanced countries by the armed might of the most backward countries. The other extreme position was incarnated (until 1912) in Gustave Hervé, who urged civil and military revolt against any kind of war. Hervé's anti-patriotic rhetoric, which found a more receptive audience in the CGT than in the SFIO, was so violent as to cause many socialists public embarrassment, and there were repeated efforts to expel him from the party.

Most French socialists held a position between these extremes, a position most eloquently represented by Vaillant, the ex-*Communard*, and by Jaurès. This position attempted to reconcile the patriotism which they shared with Guesde with the belief that international socialism should and could do something to prevent war. Jaurès asserted that the proletariat would certainly fight in defense of *la patrie* but would resist being led into aggressive conflict; and he tried to show that these two types of war could be distinguished. The proposals for military reorganization which were offered in his famous *Armée nouvelle* were designed to create a military instru- ment that would be a more effective defense force but useless for aggression. The sum total of military reform enacted with socialist support was, however, the two-year service law of 1905. Later, they vainly resisted the return to three years, demanded by the growing threat of war.

As the danger increased, Jaurès and his followers put increasing faith in the possibility that the threat of concerted international action by the proletariat would deter governments from making war. Jaurès tried repeatedly to get the International to declare itself in favor of meeting war with a general strike, but German opposi- tion constantly prevented such a move. Realizing that only inter- national solidarity could work, Jaurès did not intend that the French go it alone, but, finding no alternative course, he merely redoubled his efforts in support of this vain proposal.

With somewhat less hopefulness, Blum had followed Jaurès. Like most of his generation, Blum had been brought up in the atmosphere of *revanche*, and as a child had marched to the martial verses of Déroulède.[137] Subsequently, his patriotism had taken a more intellectual bent, becoming identified with the mission of revolutionary France to bring the ideas and example of *liberté*, *égalité*, *fraternité* to the rest of the world.[138] The glory of France's military past had little attraction for him, and during the Dreyfus affair he argued that the Dreyfusards were the true patriots, defending France's position as the most civilized nation in the world. Blum had great distaste for the military life (which he escaped because of poor eyesight), and found its authoritarianism a danger to the Republic, but he also realized that the military could not be dispensed with in the foreseeable future. He was a staunch defender of the two-year law. It was, again, the synthetic genius of Jaurès which reconciled the Frenchman's love for *la patrie* and the internationalism of the socialist movement.[139] As Blum wrote later:

Solidarity among the nations is a fact; it is engendered by the very necessity of things and not conceived by a caprice of the spirit. Thus, as Jaurès proclaimed a long time ago, true patriotism and true internationalism are blended. When we ask that the notion of solidarity serve as the first rule for the conduct of international affairs we are serving the true interest of the French nation, its material and almost egoistic interest as well as its moral interest.[140]

Even the universal triumph of socialism (and socialism in one country was scarcely possible) would not lead to the suppression of national identity and independence. Blum and Jaurès were too "French" even to contemplate such a long-range possibility.

On the other hand, they could not adopt a jingoistic outlook, and French socialists constantly faced the charge of being pro-German. They refused to admit that French foreign policy had been entirely innocent and defensive, and Jaurès had long denounced the dangers inherent in the Russian alliance (which proved to be the lightning rod which attracted German attack rather than deterring it). Blum, for his part, tended to attribute international tension to the policies of the British government.[141] Even though, like other socialists, he did not hesitate to rally to the government when the war came, he remained convinced that France had contributed to the atmosphere that led to war and never accepted the idea of Germany's unilateral guilt.[142] In the period before the war, however, he followed Jaurès in the hope that the mighty German SPD could check the aggressive ambitions of the monarchy. In the face of mounting evidence to the contrary, Jaurès clung desperately to that hope, until it cost him his life.

Earlier, Blum had begun to abandon hope that war could be averted, but could not wholly discount the possibility that Jaurès would somehow bring about the miracle. When Blum moved to the boulevard Montparnasse, a close neighbor was his old acquaintance Philippe Berthelot, who had risen to a high post in the foreign ministry. The conservative diplomat and the socialist had quarreled at the time of the affair but had since been reconciled, and as the war neared they frequently discussed France's prospects. Blum undoubtedly defended Jaurès's position, but Berthelot's informed pessimism was not without effect. Blum followed Jaurès's efforts closely, and although he saw the dangers intimated in the conflict between Jaurès and Bebel at the extraordinary congress of the International at Basel in 1912, he still sided with Jaurès against Charles Andler, who denounced Bebel and the German socialists as militaristic and chauvinist.[143] Jaurès, rather than Andler, was in the right insofar as the Germans, like the French, were victims of circumstances which made them feel they were fighting in self-defense. But this, unfortunately, did not help the cause of peace, and Andler was right in insisting that it was futile to expect the SPD to save the peace.

Repeated efforts had failed to find a stand on which all members of the Socialist International could agree, and the last effort was made at a hastily called meeting of the Bureau of the International in Brussels on 29–30 July 1914. Around 5 P.M. on 29 July, Blum met Jaurès at his *Humanité* office and accompanied him to the Gare du Nord, where Marcel Sembat, Guesde, and Vaillant were also preparing to leave for the Belgian capital.[144] It was the last time Blum saw his friend and mentor alive. The assassination of Jaurès by a nationalist fanatic two days later was not only Blum's most profound personal loss but the beginning of a revolution in his life. His personal preoccupations were swept away in the tumult of French mobilization, which followed only two days later. Soon, Blum was *chef de cabinet* to Sembat, who, like Guesde, had accepted a post in the first war ministry of the erstwhile socialist René Viviani. In 1917, Blum was swept back into the internal politics of the SFIO, which was racked by the defeatist schism. The tranquil life into which he had settled after 1905 was shattered and its pieces irrevocably scattered by the war.

The war and its sequel were to alter very little of the socialist conviction Blum had formed "in the shadow" of Jaurès, but his life as a socialist was never again the same. Before 1914, he could pursue his literary life secure in the knowledge of Jaurès's leadership. When that security was brutally removed, Blum discovered that he would have to fight for what Jaurès had represented. He had little inkling of where that decision would lead him, and—as his friend Bracke has said—had he known he might have refused to make it.[145]

CHAPTER SIX

THE CRITIC AND THE SOCIALIST

BLUM'S EXPERIENCES in the Dreyfus affair and in the socialist unity movement had a stimulating effect on the development of his thought. They not only shook him out of the routine of his literary career but had an imprint on his writing when that career was resumed. Their impact was emotional as well as intellectual, even moving Blum in 1902, the same year that he published his study on monopolies, to make his last and most ambitious attempt at creative literature—writing a play (or at least part of one) called *Anger*. He progressed far enough to show it to a few friends, whose reactions were not encouraging. What they said to Blum is unknown, but in January 1902, André Gide wrote in his journal, after listening to Blum read his first act: "Today Molière is revenged for Blum's preference for Marivaux."[1] By June he had gotten as far as act 3, but with no more success, as Romain Coolus remarked to Jules Renard: "His hero doesn't talk like an angry man."[2] Soon afterward Blum abandoned the project, and without having read the manuscript one can only surmise that the difficulty lay in converting his analytic understanding into an artistic synthesis.[3] His vocation as critic was thus reaffirmed; the impact of his socialist experience had not turned him into a creative artist. But it is in his literary criticism that the influence of this experience can be traced.

Blum's intellectual commitment to socialism antedated the years when he was critic for *La Revue blanche* (1896–1900), but it was not clearly reflected in his reviews until the last few months of that period, when he had become a militant through the New Society. Then the influence of socialism became slightly more visible in his criticism of the social philosophy of certain authors. For example, he criticized the anarchism of Max Stirner's *The Ego and Its Own* from a socialist viewpoint, as he did the Christian social philosophy of Tolstoy's *Resurrection*.[4] But the impact of Blum's recent experience in the affair and among the socialists was more evident when he revived an earlier inspiration to cast some broad reflections in the form of dialogues, under the title "Nouvelles conversations avec Eckermann." These appeared a few months after Blum had handed over his post as regular critic of novels to André Gide.[5]

The first of these anonymous essays was a lament on the excessive specialization of modern learning and on the failure of intellectuals to take a general view of the universe, a view which the leaders of society must have. He was particularly critical of modern science for losing the universality it had possessed from Aristotle to Leibniz and Descartes. Unable to form a total view of the universe, man could no longer understand his place in creation; science was unable to supply what religion had ceased to be able to provide. No individual could aspire to omniscience, and even the aspiration to preserve a universal curiosity was dangerous for one's intellectual or artistic accomplishment. Even Blum's "Goethe" affirmed himself primarily a poet whose other activities were subordinate to this vocation.

Because Blum conceived of the generalist as socially necessary, he could not concede that some sort of universal man was impossible. "Meyer," one of "Goethe's" interlocutors, argued:

There have existed . . . there still exist, men who without devoting themselves to a personal work, without attaching themselves exactly to any research, have precisely given themselves the task of penetrating each special science up to the point where its results can serve the general knowledge of the universe. They are a living encyclopedia, but a rationalized, unified—filtered, if I may say so—encyclopedia, harmoniously disposed in a single understanding. They represented the reflective conscience of the Universe at a determined moment of its existence. We have both known men of this sort. It seems to me that Herder, for example, was the finished type.[6]

"Eckermann" responded that such men should be called "critiques," and "Goethe" concluded that while they were only critics today, they would tomorrow be the "politiques"—the far-seeing leaders of society. Socialism offered Blum a universal standpoint from which he could understand society and man's fate; and Jaurès was the ideal type of the new universal man. Unlike some men of letters—Balzac and Zola, for example—Blum did not aspire to be one of these "men of the race of Herder," but he wanted to raise his vocation as literary critic to a level of greater social utility.[7]

It never occurred to Blum to attempt to construct a socialist theory of literary criticism—or indeed, for that matter, any kind of theory of literary criticism—since criticism was for him an art, not a science. But on the other hand, since he always attempted to see life as a totality, his socialist commitment could not help but have an impact on his criticism. Its principal influence was to orient him toward a greater social awareness and hence toward a greater interest in social problems and social ideas as he found them presented in literature. Blum may even have been tempted to give his criticism a more didactic purpose than formerly, but he did not see himself as one of the great critics to whom "it belongs to preach with a prophetic faith, and to show us for the first time, a world conquered, no longer by Force or by Miracle, but by Justice and Reason."[8] Such a large ambition would have run counter to his literary impressionism and to his habit of using writing as a means to self-understanding. Indeed, this second phase in his career as a critic shows Blum in the process of assimilating the ideas and experiences gained through his Dreyfusard and socialist activity.

After leaving *La Revue blanche,* Blum did not take another post as a regular reviewer until 1903, when he joined as book critic the daily *Gil Blas,* which had the reputation of the "*demimondain* newspaper *par excellence,*" and also became drama critic for *La Renaissance latine.*[9] He held the latter post until the end of 1903, when he was fired for refusing to give unqualified praise to a play by one of the editors, Paul Hervieu. He remained with *Gil Blas* until he joined the staff of *L'Humanité* in 1904.[10] During the first year of its existence, *L'Humanité* devoted considerable space to the arts, and Blum's column, "La vie littéraire," appeared almost weekly, and often on the first page. Although *L'Humanité* had a regular drama critic, Blum sometimes ventured into that field.[11]

Later he published two volumes of selections from his work of this period: *En lisant* and *Au théâtre* (the latter became a four-volume series).[12] *En lisant* received wide recognition, including a long notice by Emile Faguet in *La Revue latine*.[13] Blum's status as one of the leading critics of the day had become generally acknowledged by friend and foe alike. Jules Renard was prompted to write to Blum: "You now possess your mastery."[14] The *Au théâtre* volumes later confirmed Blum's position among the foremost drama critics of his time.

Blum's reviews for *Gil Blas* and *L'Humanité* unquestionably revealed new departures from his work for *La Revue blanche*, but these changes were not drastic; they represented a natural evolution. Blum's literary values remained essentially unchanged in this second phase of his literary career, but he placed more emphasis than before on the ideas embodied in novels—at the expense of more purely literary considerations. Not only was there increased concern for ideas, especially social ideas, but there was increasingly explicit evidence that the critic was a socialist. This trend, quite naturally, became more important when Blum moved to *L'Humanité*, but the change was largely in the degree of explicitness rather than in the orientation itself.

His socialist orientation at *Gil Blas* appeared in several ways, the most common of which was the simple interjection of his political opinions when the subject matter of the work under review touched on some aspect of the socialist movement. For example, Blum revealed his orientation implicitly in criticizing Paul and Victor Margueritte (*La Commune*) for giving a history of the Commune of 1871 which did not place it in the context of the growth of the socialist and labor movements.[15] In another case he took the author of a novel on the *universités populaires* to task for not sharing his own opinion of why they had not proved viable. Blum also inserted the standard socialist critique of cooperatives of production, while self-consciously admitting that his criticisms were political rather than literary.[16] His position within the socialist movement was revealed when he criticized Adolphe Brisson for basing his book on socialism entirely on interviews with Jules Guesde and anarchist Jean Grave, whom Blum did not consider sufficiently representative.[17] He also reviewed Jaurès's *Histoire socialiste de la Révolution française*, but this article was more an expression for his admiration for Jaurès than of Blum's socialism. Most of Blum's regular column for *Gil Blas* was devoted to novels, few of which offered an opportunity to express his socialist convictions.

The column Blum wrote for *L'Humanité* was equally devoted to novels, which, when available, were more frequently than in *Gil Blas* chosen to give scope for his socialist views. But Blum might handle a book which would seem ideal for socialist treatment, such as Paul Ginisty's *Paris intime en révolution* or Louis-Xavier de Ricard's *Histoire mondaine du Second Empire*, in a way that did not reveal that the critic was a socialist.[18] On the other hand, he occasionally went out of his way to find a socialist angle in his discussion, as in his efforts to find socialist sympathies in Maurice Maeterlinck's *Le double jardin*.[19] As a rule, though, he tempered his approach to fit the character of the work being reviewed. In an article titled "Diverses manières de voyager," he was sharply critical of Jules Huret's social commentary on the United States for neglecting to treat slums and labor unions, while he accepted Pierre Loti's emotional chronicles of his travels as a valid literary effort.[20]

Blum's most flagrant abuse of his literary column for political purposes was a review of Anatole France's *Crainquebille*, which he devoted largely to arguing that the France who was now a socialist sympathizer was the same man who embodied classical taste and universal skepticism. It is doubtful that France felt a need for this justification, and it was in part Blum's self-apology, since his admiration for France antedated the novelist's socialism, and perhaps even his own. Such a concern for continuity was not incompatible with Blum's oft-proclaimed disdain for internal consistency, either in authors or in himself. The only thing in which he demanded consistency was sincerity, and consistent sincerity could mean respecting the changes in one's sentiments. But ideas, if well founded in the first place, were less subject to change than sentiments, and it was important to Blum to be able to believe that in his own political evolution, he (like France) had remained true to himself. The considerable continuity in his reviews for *La Revue blanche* and *L'Humanité* shows that his basic concerns were unchanged though his emphases might differ.

Blum displayed particular interest in novelists who had ideas about society or about sexual psychology, or whose poetic style captivated him, independently of the content of their work. If a work did not have unusual stylistic importance, his inclination was to concentrate on the writer's ideas, and many of Blum's reviews were long discussions of an author's thesis or the ideas he found implicit in the work. The length of these discussions was dictated by his interest in the ideas, not by whether or not he agreed with them. He frequently devoted more space to those he disagreed with, as was the case with a novelist like Barrès, whose literary skill he admired, or even one like Bourget, whose work he deplored on artistic as well as intellectual grounds.

Blum continued to make effective use of his analytic intelligence to demolish the social theories of those few novelists of the right whose work merited refutation. Barrès, whom in 1905 in the pages of *L'Humanité* he could still call "perhaps the most original and striking of contemporary writers," stimulated Blum to his greatest efforts.[21] Blum was reluctant to recognize the continuity between the novelist of the *culte du moi*, whom he had admired in his youth, and the novelist of provincialism and ultra-nationalism. He therefore tried to deprecate Barrès's influence among young intellectuals and literary men, insisting on the novelist's originality only in order to isolate him. He seemed to feel that Barrès's nationalism was an intellectual error which could be remedied by intellectual criticism, and from this point of view Blum's critique was effective. In analyzing Barrès's *Au service de l'Allemagne*, Blum exposed more than one error in his argument, and even showed that his conclusions were at variance with his premises—that if Barrès's theories about the preeminent influence of blood and birthplace were true, the hero would have behaved in a diametrically opposite fashion. To reach this ironic conclusion, Blum did not have to push his argument much further than logic allowed, but in arguing that Barrès's hero could be explained in terms of Blum's cultural nationalism, rather than Barrès's racial nationalism, Blum showed that he did not realize the extent to which irrational ideologies are impervious to logical criticism.

The irrational, often hysterical chauvinism which Blum had encountered in the anti-Dreyfusards was a frequent object of his criticism. Because Barrès's later novels were written to promote nationalism, they provided suitable targets, but even an incidental display of sympathy for extreme nationalism could spoil another author's otherwise interesting book for Blum.[22] He did not hesitate to affront the cultural parochialism of his compatriots by insisting that the philosophers who had the greatest influence in France in the nineteenth century were Kant, Nietzsche, and Schopenhauer, or that the greatest contemporary novelists were Tolstoy, D'Annunzio, and Thomas Hardy.[23] Yet anyone but a fanatic can recognize Blum as an excellent example of French "high culture," and he justly maintained that his position was not anti-national.

His patriotism was not unemotional, even though he preferred to cast it in an intellectual mold and to insist that a nation "is not a homogeneous ethnic formation, but an abstract compound of ideas, political notions, and moral conceptions."[24] Blum did not adequately realize that the nation was far from homogeneous on these grounds and that the France with which he identified himself was only one-half of that schizophrenic nation.

To Blum, the true tradition of France was the defense of universal, not parochial, values. He shared the tradition of left-wing nationalism—the nationalism of the Convention, of the opponents of the July Monarchy, of Quinet and Michelet—which proclaimed a French mission to lead the struggle for social progress throughout the world. It was not simply as a socialist that he applauded the Russian uprising in 1905, appealed for the release of Maxim Gorki, or criticized the response of the French nationalist right to this appeal, but as a French nationalist—who wrote on learning that czarist prisoners in Siberia had celebrated the centenary of the French Revolution: "Every fortress destroyed is a Bastille, every revolution born in the world continues our Revolution, and that, at least, is a good subject for nationalistic pride."[25] If Blum's view of French tradition was partial, it was no more so than that of his critics, who even before 1914 insisted that he failed to understand French sentiment because he was Jewish. If, in fact, he failed to understand their version, it was because he was too intelligent, too imbued with the French tradition of rationalism.

Another aspect of the French conservative tradition came in for acid criticism in Blum's literary columns, and this was Catholicism. He gave his endorsement to anti-clerical works, from the novels of Anatole France to Georges Ancey's *Ces messieurs*, while generally ignoring the host of Catholic novelists, from the academician René Bazin on down. The single exception was Paul Bourget, whose reputation in *bien-pensant* circles as a casuist apparently irritated Blum. Thus he proceeded with ease, but at great length, to demolish the thesis of Bourget's *Un divorce*, showing that its logic was invalid even if one accepted its premises. The misfortunes Bourget rained on his heroine as judgments of God for the sin of divorce could have happened just as easily to a widow, who presumably was free from the wrath of the Catholic novelist's God.[26] Even Faguet, who taxed Blum with inability to understand the psychology of Catholicism and hence with inability to judge Catholic characters in fiction, had to admit that he made his case against Bourget.[27] Doubtless, Blum's reaction to such works would have been different if he had been more sympathetic to traditional religion, but even so his analytic intelligence would not have compromised its demands. In any case, he felt no need to put on the mask of impartiality when dealing with unsympathetic views, preferring to be conscious of his opinions and sincere in his expression of them in his criticism.

Even in those reviews that were most dominated by the analysis of ideas, Blum's aesthetic interests were seldom altogether absent. His aesthetic values had remained essentially constant from the time of his earliest writing. He demanded that an author do his best, whatever his style and he continued to insist that grammatical correctness was the minimal standard, accessible to almost anyone. Indeed, correctness was the only virtue he found in the marquis de Vogüé; and even this was lacking in Gabriel Hanotaux. Both, of course, were political opponents, but that was no bar to Blum's appreciation of style, as the cases of Barrès and Pierre Louys illustrate. Blum continued to admire the style he called classical, and perhaps used even more frequently, as his term of highest praise, "the prose of a poet." Evidently this meant that a writer had lavished the care in his choice of words and structuring of expressions that is typical of the poet. Blum also continued to be interested in poetry itself, publishing an article in *L'Humanité* on contemporary efforts at verse theater and another on young poets of promise. His preference was for practitioners of a kind of neo-romanticism, such as his friend Fernand Gregh or the aristocratic poetess of the commonplace, Anna, comtesse de Noailles. Blum was one of her most enthusiastic admirers, and he later devoted a lengthy article in *La Revue de Paris* to her verse.[28] In his literary taste, Blum remained faithful to his generation.

He was also interested in the novels of Mme. de Noailles, devoting many lines to her on the front page of *L'Humanité*, which must have puzzled most of its proletarian readers.[29] But while he gave extended consideration to the beauty of her style, he did not limit himself, even here, to questions of art. He considered her work in connection with that of several other woman novelists, on whom he wrote collective articles in *Gil Blas* and *L'Humanité*.

As one would expect from Blum's early interest in the new insights each generation of novelists should bring to their work, he was curious to see whether women's novels presented a significantly different psychology. His conclusions were probably no surprise to the authors concerned: he praised them as capable of revealing, in their heroines, nuances of female psychology which would escape the most astute male observer, while finding them—congenitally, so to speak—incapable of presenting convincing male heroes (George Eliot, for whom he had the greatest admiration, came closest with Adam Bede). This was a handicap he doubted they would overcome, and in general he seems to have felt that the novel, by its very nature, was a masculine genre.

This attitude was reinforced by, or perhaps was a cause of, the position Blum took when he turned from psychological to sociological consideration of female novelists. Projecting from their increased numbers, and from the declining interest of male writers in the genre, he forecast that the novel would become, for a time, a feminine domain.[30] He attributed this trend primarily to the greater number of female readers of novels, but he also sought a deeper reason, and thought he had found one in the changing place of women in society, where they were being emancipated from dependence but had not yet discovered their true vocations or achieved the equality they were coming to desire. "When women don't know what to do," he concluded, "they write novels."[31]

As a typical product of a certain period of social transition, he compared Mme. de Noailles's *La nouvelle espérance* to *Werther*.[32] Blum thought that, in the coming socialist society, literature should cease to be a profession and become an avocation, and that under those circumstances more men than women would be attracted to it. His estimate of the feminine character also led him to suggest that women would find outlets for their abilities and predispositions in the bureaucratic and statistical functions of government and industry and in teaching.[33] This position was typical of the socialist who sought equality of rights and equality of opportunity while recognizing that there were differences among individuals which would give them different positions in any society.[34] Because he was writing at the beginning of a change in woman's social position, he underestimated the potential variety of their accomplishments, but as a critic he did not hesitate to affront contemporary male prejudice by displaying a generous appreciation of the accomplishments of many female writers.

From his consideration of the sociology of the female novel, Blum turned to the general relationships between the novel and society, and in particular to the question of how the novel ought to be related to society. The "social novel," as it was called then, was widely debated among writers and critics, and it was one of these debates—an "inquiry" conducted by Eugène Monfort in his review *Les marges*—which stimulated Blum to present his views in *L'Humanité*. Knowing that as a socialist he might be suspected of wanting the novel to follow an ideological line or serve a propagandistic purpose, he was careful to dissociate himself from such views. He insisted that the social novel was not one with a social message—whether of left, right, or center—on the grounds that a work with a deliberate message would cease to be a work of art. The social novel must remain a work of art, "social art" to be sure, but art nonetheless.

He called the novel with a message a *roman à thèse:*

There is then a chance that a "roman à thèse" or "à prêche" would be a bad novel, without real artistic value. If it is always attempting to prove a point, how can the imagination preserve that noble and inspired liberty whose very deviations and fantasies move us? How can it resist the temptation to choose, from among the natural and logical consequences of the subject, those which confirm the thesis, setting aside those which are repugnant to it? These arguments are unanswerable, but they only weigh against the "roman à thèse" and not against the "social novel" because—and this is the confusion that I want above all to dissipate—I see no equivalence between the one and the other terms. There is a thesis from the time that the author ceases to be impartial toward his impressions or his ideas, from the time he reflects on his subject, whatever it may be, on the creation of his personages, whoever they may be, in order to express by all means a premeditated conclusion. The "thesis" or the "tendency" is therefore not a characteristic which belongs to the "social novel," but a danger and a vice of execution common to all forms of the dramatic and novelistic art.[35]

This was the kind of flaw he found, for example, in the novels of Paul Bourget.[36] Blum insisted that the success of a work of art is not determined by the intention of the author or the nature of his subject matter but by the work's interior perfection, its just adaptation of ends to means.[37]

By no means, however, was Blum indifferent to intention or content in the novels he reviewed. Even before becoming a socialist, he had rejected *l'art pour l'art* in favor of an art more intimately connected with life, and socialism helped direct that concern toward social life. Art should not be subservient to a social purpose, but neither should it be independent of social life. He praised Bernard Lazare's criticism for its insistence that the artist be conscious of his social role and utility but at the same time not bend to any purpose external to his art.[38] For Blum, such consciousness meant a close interest in the evolution of contemporary society in its many and varied aspects. The subject matter of a social novel had to be French society, and he even excluded from this category a novel that explored the evils of life in a major French colony on the grounds that they were only of "superficial and passing" interest to the French because their lives were not affected: "[They are] 'social novels' for the people down there, no doubt, but not for us."[39] Like most French socialists of that time, he had little interest in the problems of colonialism, nor was he aware of its influence on life in France.

As a critic, Blum was partial to social novels whose views were sympathetic to his socialism. He seldom reviewed works by conservative novelists, such as the popular (though mediocre) Gyp or Henry Bordeaux or René Bazin.[40] When Bazin was welcomed into the Académie Française by the conservative critic Brunetière, Blum remarked: "The novels of M. René Bazin are 'social novels' in the same measure as M. Ferdinand Brunetière is a socialist."[41] For Blum, then, the social novel was not just any work which portrayed the contemporary social milieu—since Bazin did this—but one which approached these subjects from a point of view which, if not socialist, was at least predisposed to question traditional values. Blum called for writers to pay more attention to peasant and proletarian milieus, as well as the more familiar scenes of bourgeois life, but their attitude toward the milieu mattered more than the milieu itself.[42] He thought this standard of judgment was legitimate because he thought socialism had become the most viable movement of ideas in France at that moment, as well as the most significant new political force. If literature was obliged to keep in touch with the evolution of society, it could not ignore socialism, the forces that helped create it, or its impact. Zola's novels were social novels when they were written, Blum remarked, and only the subsequent development of socialism separated them from the social novels of the prewar decade.[43]

Blum expected that the ferment in society created by socialism would lead writers to the social novel:

It is in this sense that the socialist movement [changed to "social ideas" in *En lisant*] has exercised on the art of the novel, and will exercise with a steadily growing power, a salutary attraction. It has brusquely uncovered before art a whole world of obscure or veiled realities. It has drawn out and formulated a certain number of new truths that the artist of good faith, even if he does not draw the necessary consequences from them, ought not, cannot any longer ignore. The attention of the artist has been directed toward certain new and ignored facets of life. And from then on, in the choice of his subject—even if he [is not a socialist, even if he] knows no more of socialism than the state of curiosity and general emotion that its propaganda has created—the artist is pointed toward other milieus, other conflicts, other problems, whose description or study will make of his novel a *social* work.[44]

This position is certainly a long way from *littérature engagée,* and still further from the "socialist realism" of the Russian Bolsheviks.

Blum would not have shared the opinion of the one-time Soviet arbiter of the arts, Andrei Zhdanov, who measured the worth of a work of art by its effectiveness "as a means of bringing about social reform."[45] Nor does Blum appear to have shared the opinion of French socialist writers Marius and Ary Leblond, that the power of literature to convey sentiments made it a powerful tool for reaching the masses.[46] Blum was never quite settled on the question of whether literature might have some effect at least on the bourgeoisie. The Marxist concept of ideology suggests that it could not, yet Marxists, and perhaps even Marx himself, did not consistently draw this conclusion. As a rule, Blum said that the novel had no influence, though it was much influenced by society.[47] But there were occasions when he at least wished that it had such influence; he even suggested that the social novel had helped prepare the way for reform in early nineteenth-century England.[48]

He frequently said that there were such things as "useful" novels, even among works that were not "social" novels.[49] This concept was always vague, and on the whole he was more concerned that socialism exercise an influence on literature, especially on the development of the social novel. He was optimistic about this possibility: "Fifty years from now, it will perhaps be as difficult to write a book which will not be, in some measure, a social book, as it would have been in the Middle Ages to create a work which was not part of Christian art."[50] The critic thought that the development of literary art would benefit from the rise of socialism even more than it had from the Christian inspiration because socialism was more closely adapted to the realities of this world.

While Blum was interested in the impact of socialism on literature and in the presentation of social ideas and description in literature, he did not develop what might be called a socialist theory of literary criticism. Blum had originally adopted an impressionist position because he disliked systematizing in criticism, and this dislike was not changed by his becoming a socialist. The influence of his socialism on his criticism was in accord with the nondogmatic nature of that socialism. Because Marxism was only one of several components of his socialism, Blum did not feel that compulsion to form a Marxist critique which was to weigh with such disastrous results on those who considered Marxism the key to everything. Blum's literary criticism was thus, through its gradual and minor changes— its development as well as its general character—an important index to the character of the socialist commitment he was to carry the rest of his life.[51] In the period before 1914, he was not a socialist critic but, rather, a critic who was also a socialist.

Blum's literary work for *Gil Blas* and *L'Humanité* was prefigured by a kind of summation of his earlier work which he published anonymously in 1901 under the title *Nouvelles conversations de Goethe avec Eckermann*.[52] The inspiration for this book obviously came from his "Nouvelles conversations avec Eckermann" articles, and the concept of the Goethe-Eckermann dialogues was expanded to form the framework for an elegant and ingenious pastiche of material from the original articles, book reviews from *La Revue blanche*, and some new material written for the occasion. Blum's authorship was no secret—the review material would have given it away—but he could not bring himself to avow it until the book was reissued in 1907.[53] In any case, as Jules Renard told Blum, his audacity was not in acknowledging authorship but in having had the idea of using the great German poet as his spokesman.[54]

No doubt Blum was tempted by the cleverness of his idea, which was certain to attract attention. He appreciated both the humor and the seriousness of his concept, and put something of both into his reply to another acquaintance who asked how he dared deliver his opinions through the mouth of a Goethe: "I had only to place myself at a superior viewpoint."[55] Blum made no pretense of trying to determine what Goethe might have thought if he had returned to life at the end of the nineteenth century: "Goethe" was frankly a spokesman for himself. To be more exact, both "Goethe" and "Eckermann" were spokesmen, and Blum's opinions emerged from their dialogue as well as from "Goethe's" monologues.

Blum incorporated all of the original "nouvelles conversations" into the book but only selections from his many critical columns. His selections, of course, are very important since they reveal something of Blum's appraisal of his early work, and especially his ability to take a detached view of it. The selections are not simply his best work, though they include most of it, they are representative of his work for *La Revue blanche* as a whole and give an accurate picture of his interests, values, and approach to criticism. For this reason, little can be added to the discussion of his criticism in chapter 2 from new insights from this book. The parts which pertain to the development of his socialism were also examined earlier.

Yet, in spite of these considerations, *Nouvelles conversations* deserves, even demands, additional attention because it is the most characteristic work of his career to 1914. Not all of Blum is in it, as later chapters will show, but there is no better introduction to his thought and personality. It remained Blum's favorite, at least until World War II, perhaps because it demonstrated the continuity between the preoccupations of his later political career and the attitudes and outlook of his very different early careers.[56] Among those who knew Blum well, his son Robert regards it as the *livre-clé* to understanding Blum's thought, and the Société des Amis de Léon Blum has published a pamphlet which demonstrates the links between *Nouvelles conversations* and *A l'échelle humaine*, the mature reflection of his later years.[57] These links have led some to speak of Blum's last years as those of "Goethe at Weimar," but the parallel is not exact.[58] Blum never thought of comparing himself to Goethe as a literary figure, and Goethe's political career was never so important as Blum's became.

Nouvelles conversations is especially valuable for the picture it gives of the integration of Blum's various concerns, in particular his socialism and his literary concerns. Both "Goethe" and "Eckermann" were portrayed as socialists of the Jaurès tendency, but this was more than a mechanical device to enable Blum to combine his socialist and literary concerns. The device is never forced, and the resulting *mélange* is a surprisingly harmonious whole that is tied together by Blum's personality, which gave unity to the character of "Goethe."[59] Its unity is not rigid; it is shaped by the harmony he managed to achieve among a variety of conflicting impulses. He was aware that socialists and *littérateurs* alike might find in him a lack of seriousness or commitment, but he did not think that the various aspects of human life and thought should, or could, be tightly compartmentalized. A socialism which decried art risked becoming a sterile materialism; an art which withdrew from the world's problems risked becoming a sterile narcissism.

The highly developed individualism which was one of the starting points of Blum's concern for the masses and his commitment to socialism is clearly revealed in *Nouvelles conversations*. This apparent, but only apparent, contradiction was paralleled by that between the tone of Olympian detachment associated with "Goethe" and Blum's very obvious commitment not only to socialism but to the literary activities and aspirations of his contemporaries. *Nouvelles conversations*, like the rest of his work and life, is permeated by Blum's uncompromising rationalism, but this rationalism avoids mechanical sterility by his vitalist assertion of the need to love life and labor and by his love of poetry—a striving for beauty.

Even poetry is linked with Blum's socialism, for "Goethe" exclaims: "From the socialist movement we will see a new lyricism born: Justice and happiness!"[60] In poetry, moreover, Blum found a constant renewal of the optimism that man needs to sustain the struggle for a better life. Yet he did not make the mistake of many in his day who "confused Goethe's cosmic optimism with belief in unbridled technical progress."[61] Blum conceded that the dual advance of science and the spirit of rational inquiry it promoted were necessary building blocks for a new society, but he saw that a better society requires the advance of the whole complex of activities that make man:

Read then the great lyricists. We must repeat that men do not have two souls, one to sing, the other to act. We must fortify ourselves in the thought that if the poets have known how to fulfill their task, the savants, the philosophers, the political leaders will little by little complete theirs too. That same mankind which has known how to create or to understand the most beautiful forms of lyric inspiration is worthy to achieve, through the effort of its reflective activity, science, justice, and the common happiness.[62]

Nouvelles conversations concluded with Blum's dialogue on the critic as universal man, which was reprinted from *La Revue blanche*. It was a fitting summation of his commitment to the defense of humanism in an age of science and specialization. "Goethe's" suggestion that the "critiques" would become the "politiques" reflects Blum's commitment to social action, which he had demonstrated through his participation in the Dreyfus affair and in such socialist activities as the first unity congresses and the New Society, and which he was also to demonstrate in the future. The position which Blum took in this dialogue was broad enough to encompass a variety of possibilities; his commitment was permanent, but it was not yet cast into a permanent mold, and it would not be until after World War I.

Changing literary trends were, in part, to bring about a change in Blum's literary career. While his work for *Gil Blas* and *L'Humanité* showed a growing concern for the "social novel" and an attempt to urge writers toward it, as well as a prediction of its wider popularity, the results had been disappointing. Despite the influence of the naturist movement and the hypothetical influence of the growing socialist movement, the prewar epoch did not produce much in the way of outstanding social novels. In fact, the novel was entering a period of stagnation, which finally depleted Blum's optimism. The lack of sufficiently inspiring material to review undoubtedly influenced his decision (after 1907) to devote almost all his critical work, with a few important exceptions, to the theater.

It was not that Blum lost interest in social life but that his interest found a different line of expression, one which gave greater emphasis to the moralizing strain in his literary activity. His critiques of ideas and *moeurs* took a narrower focus with the publication of *Du mariage* and his subsequent drama criticism, for the stage is much less suitable than the novel for the presentation of broad social issues. As a result, the influence of Blum's socialist commitment was less apparent in the remainder of his literary career than in the middle phase (covered in this chapter), just as it was less apparent in what we know of his public activity during the period 1905–14. His commitment was not any less, but changed circumstances led to different expressions of the social and intellectual concerns which had led Blum to socialism.

CHAPTER SEVEN

THE CRITIC OF
MORALS: *DU MARIAGE*

AFTER HIS COLLABORATION at *L'Humanité* ended in July 1905, Blum did not have a regular position as a critic until he joined *La Grande revue* in December 1907. This year and a half was not a period of idleness in his literary career but rather one of adjustment. For his legal career, it was a period of progress along already established lines. In November 1907 he was promoted to *maître des requêtes* on the Conseil d'Etat. For the first time he enjoyed a comfortable income, as well as a position of prestige in his profession. If there was ever a point in his career when Blum might easily have settled into a bourgeois routine and given up the effort to maintain his dual careers, this would have been the time. At thirty-five, he could have joined those whose youthful ambition and idealism give way before the realities of everyday existence. Nothing, however, was further from Blum's intentions; his literary career merely entered a new phase.

In this phase the moralist, who had long cohabited with the literary critic, came to play a larger role. This was the form Blum's intellectual maturation followed, as if from some inner necessity. It was from an inner necessity, too, that the moralist chose the subject of his next work. In May 1907 he published *Du mariage*, a long and critical essay on the sexual *moeurs* of contemporary

France, with some proposals for their reform.[1] The boldness of his proposals, the acuteness of his analysis, and the polish of his style brought this essay a fame—or notoriety—which was revived by republication thirty years later and which persists even today. It is perhaps Blum's best-known book, and it still receives serious attention. But even had it not been read, *Du mariage* would have acquired immortality through a well-known reference in Anatole France's *Penguin Island.*[2] Blum made it clear that, however respectable his legal career, he had no intention of sacrificing the independence of his literary career. At the moment when his socialist involvement entered a dormant phase, he took a public stand on sexual *moeurs* which was, if anything, more offensive to bourgeois prejudices than his socialism. Blum was not trying simply to *épater les bourgeois*, though he certainly did not regret that effect.[3] Rather, he was concerned about a moral evil, to the point where he felt the need to express his views.

Within the literary milieu in which Blum had moved for several years, sexual *moeurs* were a favorite topic of conversation and, increasingly, a subject for writing. It was an area in which the *literati* traditionally tried to divorce themselves from bourgeois conventionality, and there was a tradition of verbal offense to bourgeois sensitivities. Unconventional lives were perhaps less common than unconventional language, though the reverse was no doubt true among the middle class as a whole. Blum was also influenced by the tradition of romantic introspection, which was at least as old as Rousseau. In the *nouvelles* Blum wrote for *Le Banquet* and *La Revue blanche* very early in his literary career there are reflections on the relations between the sexes which were undoubtedly prompted by the emotional experiences of his own adolescence. But his subsequent literary work did not follow this path; it turned, instead, to a more abstract consideration of these problems. Having come to an understanding of himself, Blum set out to test that understanding in the light of the wider experience of others. He began to collect observations from society and literature, to formulate and test various hypotheses. It was in this fashion that he progressed from the individual to the general, from the personal to the social point of view. His drama reviews for *La Renaissance latine* in 1903 and for *L'Humanité* in 1904 and 1905 clearly reveal a growing concern with the sexual *moeurs* of his society. *Du mariage* was the most concentrated expression of this concern. Even after its publication, this concern was to play, as he predicted, a major role in his subsequent literary work, especially in his drama criticism after 1908. Indeed, Gide called *Du mariage* "an able preface to all of today's Jewish theater," but it was more an afterword since Blum had drawn much of his material from the theater.[4]

The degree to which *Du mariage* was a book *of* its time has been emphasized—even exaggerated—by Vichniac.[5] It was certainly a book *for* its time, and even more for the future. Evolutions in the *moeurs* of any society are difficult to detect and measure, and the chance of error, of being deceived by untypical examples, is great. Yet there is fairly general agreement that among the middle classes in pre–World War I France the established moral code was breaking down while no new code could be seen emerging to replace it—a phase of transition rather than decadence. Contrary to a widely held idea, respect for the code tended to break down among the bourgeoisie more rapidly than their society's outward respect for the conventional values. The changes in practice, however, encouraged writers to conduct a more public discussion of sex. Authors and publishers began to take new liberties with the verbal taboos, and more rapidly than the organized defense of the old order would tolerate, as many of them found out in court. But the conservatives, who were naturally aroused to the defense of the traditional *moeurs*, appeared increasingly ridiculous in these confrontations.

Both rebels and conservatives agreed that the institution of marriage was in crisis, however much they might disagree over the causes and cures.[6] Divorce was increasing, but only slightly, since the opposition of the Church was unrelenting and the anti-clerical Republic (though one of its first acts had been to legalize divorce) had not made it easy to terminate a marriage. It was a matter of general observation, but uncertain accuracy, that an increasing percentage of marriages was marred by adultery, at least among the bourgeoisie of the capital. Blum concurred in this observation. Given this problem, he began his search for a solution by postulating that people were neither more nor less predisposed to immorality than at any other time. If the fault was not in man, it had to be found in the institution of marriage as it was currently organized and practiced. Hence Blum's title was not "On Love" or "On Sex," but "On Marriage."

Blum saw the problem of marriage not simply in terms of

adultery or divorce but, more largely, in terms of happiness or the lack thereof. Unlike some of the more radical reformers, he did not believe that happiness was impossible in marriage and that the institution ought therefore to be abandoned. Rather, it was the current practice of marriage which he found faulty, and he believed that marriage could be redeemed by a greater understanding of its character, its values, and—perhaps especially—its limits. *Du mariage* was to lead toward such understanding.

Some contemporaries suggested that just as the aristocratic society of the eighteenth century had found adultery a remedy for the ills of marriage, the twentieth century might find a more adequate cure in the more liberal application of divorce. Both of these solutions were rejected by Blum at the outset. Adultery, obviously, did not make a marriage happier, though it might make an indissoluble union more tolerable. Divorce, of course, could terminate an unhappy marriage, and for this reason Blum recognized the right of divorce in its most thoroughgoing form—on the simple demand of either partner. The problem as he saw it, however, was not to terminate unhappy marriages but to increase the number of happy and therefore durable marriages.

There were values in marriage which Blum thought worth preserving, and marriage would be successful if both partners were in agreement in pursuing those values. For this reason, he did not accept *l'union libre* as a satisfactory substitute for marriage. As a moralist, he admired the effort to promote freedom and honesty that *union libre* required, the moral nobility of an engagement with no sanctions.[7] Ultimately, he accepted it as compatible with his system, as valid for some but inadequate for the satisfaction of the legitimate wants that marriage alone could satisfy.[8] Marriage, by his definition, was a stable and enduring relationship, capable of providing security and comfort as well as affection. It made possible the gratification of desires such as those associated with social life, the raising of children, one's career, the economic life of the household. It may be bourgeois, Blum admitted, but it is also wise to ask of one's future husband that he be honest, of stable character, and capable of supporting a family, or of one's future wife that she be provident, discreet, and capable of managing a household. A marriage should always be a *mariage de raison.*

The marriage of interests is more stable than the love match because interests are more durable than emotions, Blum insisted.

But he did not intend to rule emotion out of marriage. Aside from the fact that affection is necessary to make a prolonged common existence tolerable, satisfactory sexual relations are also necessary. What had to be avoided were emotions so strong that they led an individual to subordinate everything to their gratification. Such emotions were, from their very strength, short lived, tending to be destroyed by being gratified, and incapable of remaining satisfied with the same partner. Blum wished to defend the legitimacy of these overwhelming emotions while at the same time protecting marriage from their destructive effects. One should seek gratification of passion-love, but not marry for it. Thus the moral code which condemned the gratification of sexual desire outside of marriage was much to blame for the sorrows of those who sought in marriage something it could not give. Yet Blum refused to accept the traditional cynicism that love and marriage are totally incompatible.

Blum was convinced that the "first, most grave, most frequent" cause of marital discord was unsatisfactory sexual relations.[9] His essay concentrated almost exclusively on this problem, but it was not in any sense a manual of sex technique. Sex education could not be conveyed through books but only through experience, because the emotions are involved. Blum was convinced that in contemporary society the manner in which this experience was acquired was not merely faulty but in conflict with the basic character of man's sexual instinct and therefore doomed to frequent disaster. The gravest danger to a marriage came when the experience and education of the two partners were too widely at variance, and this was commonly the case in the bourgeois society of the time.

The typical bourgeois marriage, Blum thought, was the union of a sexually ignorant young female, a virgin, to a somewhat older and more experienced—but generally badly sexually educated—male. This husband, then, had to bear the full responsibility for the initiation and education of his virgin bride. But the social prejudice which attempted to assure the virginity of the female, to marry her in a state of ignorance, which can produce both exaggerated expectations and exaggerated fears, also helped assure that the education of the husband would be faulty, because the opportunities for acquiring sexual knowledge were narrowed by society almost entirely to relations with prostitutes. Whatever a young man might learn from prostitutes was directed at his own gratification, and thus he was helped to acquire a sexual egotism which would be a negative value when it came to educating his bride. A virgin instructed by such a husband might nonetheless, sooner or later, find her own sensual appetite awakened, but she would also find her husband ignorant of or indifferent to this development. Either adultery or unhappiness was thus the fate for most females under the present *moeurs*. This, in Blum's opinion, was the sad result of the prejudice of virginity. The moralist found it unjust that the psychosexual burdens of marriage should rest principally on the woman, and he wrote to defend her right to happiness both before and in marriage. It was the injustice and irrationality of society's denial of this right that moved Blum to write *Du mariage*.[10]

The prejudice of virginity seemed to Blum a survival from the ages of barbarism. It could not be explained simply as a masculine imposition because there was no advantage in it for the male. Blum avoided drawing special attention to the role of the Church in preserving this tradition, but he had made it clear elsewhere that he regarded the Christian dualism of body and soul as a morally pernicious and socially destructive doctrine. In *Du mariage* he concentrated on showing how marriage was damaged by prejudice, with some secondary attention to the trouble it caused to the unmarried.

Blum's argument was tightly organized around the basic postulate he felt was his contribution to understanding the relations of the sexes. He admitted that his postulate was undemonstrable, but he believed that it accorded with all his observations. This postulate was that the average person went through two inevitable phases in his emotional life: the first was polygamous, marked by an unstable passion-love; and the second was monogamous, marked by a stable marital love. He thought that this distinction was commonly recognized for the male in the popular belief that it was better for a young man to "sow his wild oats" before marriage if he was to be expected not to do so afterward. No matter how common this idea, many were shocked by Blum's assertion that women also went through a polygamous stage in their emotional development.

Reflecting on some observations of Balzac, Blum had concluded that if man were basically polygamous, an institution so contrary to his nature as monogamous marriage could not possibly work. If man had polygamous instincts and monogamous sentiments, both of which persisted throughout his life, he would find the conflict between his instincts and his sentiments unbearable, and "marriage, as Balzac said, would not be worth what it cost."[11] Balzac's conclusion, which Blum illustrated from his *Mémoires de deux jeunes mariées*, was that there are distinct polygamic and monogamic types. While Blum lauded Balzac's powers of observation, he found this conclusion too pessimistic because it closed too many possibilities of happiness for both of the presumed types. Moreover, he was convinced that although social convention might partially conceal it, the polygamous instinct was more widespread among women than Balzac had believed. If this were true, only Blum's postulate of successive stages held the possibility of happy marriage for most people.

Much of *Du mariage* was devoted to demonstrating that no matter how effective society's apparatus for teaching young girls the virtue of chastity, sooner or later instinct will demand its due, and the later this happens the more likely it is to have disruptive effects on the individual's life. Blum conceded the possibility that this instinct could be sublimated, even suggesting that much apparent fidelity resulted from sublimation of the polygamous instinct, but the permanence of such sublimation could not be guaranteed. Instead of seeing benefits in such sublimation, Blum saw considerable danger, such as encouraging young girls to exaggerate the importance of the "gift" of their bodies and making their first sexual experience (whether in marriage or not) an unnecessarily traumatic experience.

Sublimation implies a transference of object for instinctual forces, but there is another kind of transference which can be even more destructive. This is usually known as repression, and the transference may manifest itself as either physical or mental illness. Blum felt that something was evidently wrong: "Something today appears to be broken in the equilibrium of the feminine body, and a woman who is perfectly healthy, whose nervous system functions normally, without too much or too little sensitivity, is an exception worthy of note."[12] Blum asked those moralists who insisted on the evil of sexual relations outside of marriage to consider if there were not even greater danger in repression. He took delight in showing that Tolstoy, who thought that even married sex was sinful, portrayed the evils of repression all the more clearly because he did so unintentionally, in novels such as *Anna Karenina*.

The suppression of the sexual drive of unmarried young women was not only damaging to their future marriage and happiness, in

Blum's opinion, but was also a major cause of the vast dimensions which prostitution had assumed. Society could not contain the desires of unmarried males, but it could close off many sources of gratification. The demand for virgin brides led to the paradox that society had a large number of girls who would enjoy making love but were prevented by the *moeurs* from doing so while a much smaller number made a great deal of "love" without being able to enjoy it. Society, of course, did not care about the price paid by those who became prostitutes, even though it was aware of the misery of their existence. At the same time, society did not want to recognize that a price was also being paid by the "good" girls of "respectable" families. Blum did not have to stress the hypocrisy of the males from respectable families who supported prostitution, for it was well demonstrated in literature, but he had the harder task of demonstrating one of the reasons for it. Undoubtedly, he was not surprised to find himself the target of anti-Semitic attacks and charges that he wished to make prostitutes of all the respectable girls of France.[13]

Blum further offended conventional susceptibilities by detailing the sort of sexual experience he thought was necessary to escape the present evils. He not only insisted that girls, like boys, be free to have love affairs before marriage but that they should be free at an early age. If virginity was given up early (at fifteen on the average), it could not become a source of psychological constraint, as was commonly the case. Pursuing the logic of his position, Blum insisted that a girl's sexual initiation and subsequent education ought to be conducted by someone already experienced, not merely a man with a desire of his own, but a man with understanding and respect for female sensuality.[14] The attraction which adolescent girls find in mature men is well known, but Blum took a bolder step in pointing to the attraction which the *jeune fille* emerging from the *fillette* has for a mature man. Unfortunately, he did not have Nabokov's *Lolita* to demonstrate that a girl can emerge not only emotionally unscathed but morally strengthened.

Of course it was equally important that young men receive a proper sexual initiation and education. The problems they faced were different, but they too were serious. While Blum stressed the situation of the female because it was worse, he knew that young men learned about themselves in a defective manner, and came to learn about girls almost not at all. It was therefore desirable for a

193

young man to receive his education from a mature woman, one on the verge of entering the more stable, low-key years of marriage (age twenty-eight to forty). Such a woman could teach him one thing that could never be learned from a prostitute: there must be pleasure in sexual relations for both male and female. And because she would insist on her own pleasure, she would teach him not merely the necessary technique but respect for the strength and character of female sensuality. This experience would at least diminish the chance that the man would become that kind of husband whose egotism and ignorance made life miserable for his wife, and, ultimately, himself.

Blum thus postulated, for both sexes, a three-stage development: from lover through educator to spouse. Realistically, he did not expect his educators to act through altruism, but his theory compelled him to assume that there is a kind of natural and general desire to play the role of educator, though he could not demonstrate it convincingly. This was one point at which his logic outstripped his observation, but on the whole Blum was well aware of the difficulties of translating his moral insights into practice.

Blum did not mean that all relations during the polygamous period of one's life would be spent as either pupil or educator; the amount of variety would depend on the individual. From his point of view, it was especially important that passion, unmixed with more mundane concerns, would dominate these affairs. Not only was he opposed to early marriages, even so-called trial marriages, but also to the cohabitation of lovers. A temporary household would be both a heavy economic burden and a constraint on the freedom of the partners. More abstractly, it represented confusion between the polygamous and monogamous phases of life.

Defenders of the existing conventions seemed to believe that if it was not enforced and demanded at all stages of life, monogamy would become impossible. Either they felt monogamy was so unnatural that the full panoply of social pressure was needed to defend it or that polygamy was such a persuasive perversion that once entered into no one would abandon it.[15] There was little Blum's arguments could do to persuade those who held such attitudes. It was characteristic of a conservative, such as Emile Faguet, to be less frightened of adultery than of premarital sex.[16] Blum wanted to build enduring monogamous marriages and to protect marriage from the hypocrisy and falseness which adultery necessarily entails. He was convinced that most people outgrew the stage of polygamous passion through the process of indulging it. Women would not become life-long practitioners of polygamy but, instead, would reach a natural age of marriage—a psychological rather than a physical age.

The conservatives, of course, were also interested in the institution of the family, but so was Blum. There were aspects of the traditional French bourgeois family that repelled him—its authoritarianism and inequality, its preoccupation with money and status—but he accepted the family as a locus for certain social functions, among which was the rearing of children. He did not believe, however, that the family was a unique institution for providing this function, and he was inclined to give children emancipation as early as possible. Early sexual experience was one form of emancipation, and especially important to females. (Among other things, it would help prevent mother-in-law trouble after marriage.) Blum also thought that society had responsibility for children, which was manifested not only in providing public education but also in caring for children whose parents could not or would not do so. He occasionally admitted being attracted by the utopian commonalty of children, and he professed admiration for Rousseau's decision to make public wards of his children. But Blum's prime interest, as far as his own society was concerned, was to give unwed mothers an option that would be free of moral stigma. In general, he hoped that women would not want to have children during their polygamous period, for he feared that such children would be spoiled by excessive and misplaced affection. Of course the woman had to make this decision, since she had to bear the responsibilities.

He was frank in admitting that without modern contraceptive practices, the organization of life he was proposing would not be possible. Sexual desire was a primordial instinct, over which mankind had little control, but procreation was a social as well as a personal act, and one which would be ennobled by being freely willed rather than submitted to.[17] In recognizing what man could and could not control, Blum thought, man could extend the realm of freedom and morality. He accepted the bourgeois Malthusianism of restricted family size and thought that the individual and the family, as well as society, would benefit from it.

Inevitably, Blum's picture in *Du mariage* of the monogamous phase of sexual life tended to appear in largely negative terms, by way of contrast with the previous polygamous stage. His concept of a polygamous instinct which could be used up—exhausted—lent itself to a negative approach. Blum tried to avoid confusing this process with physical debility, even though he thought the age of marriage would ordinarily be later than the physical peak of youth. The two phases were psychological rather than physiological, and it did not matter, from his point of view, whether there was an underlying physiological explanation. Blum was familiar with the popular works of Elie Metchnikoff, the noted bacteriologist and professor of the Pasteur Institute who had recently put forward some views on the physiology of sex which were in accord with Blum's outlook, but his conclusions were not derived from the kind of data Metchnikoff and others sought in the laboratory.[18]

Blum's work fell in the realm of physiology only in the sense in which that term was used in the early nineteenth century. Had he lived then, he might have borrowed Balzac's title *Physiologie du mariage* for his own work.[19] Blum acknowledged a particular debt to Balzac for his point of departure, and indeed Blum's whole approach to psychology was in the tradition of Balzac and of amateur literary psychologizing.[20] But the roots of this approach went beyond Balzac, to the moralists of the seventeenth century, who, as we have seen, had influenced Blum's literary outlook.[21] Similarly, his attitude toward eighteenth-century thinking on life and sex was indicative of a literary rather than a scientific approach; his sympathies were all with Jean-Jacques Rousseau and Choderlos de Laclos, and not with Condillac and his followers. The materialist or sensationalist psychology of Locke and Condillac no doubt had attraction for Blum insofar as it attacked the traditional Christian metaphysics. But he thought that it, too, had proved inadequate in explaining the workings of human sentiments, and he was extremely critical of his literary idol, Stendhal, for following the sensationalists. He found Stendhal's attempt to systematize his outlook in *De l'amour* too narrow and mechanistic, unworthy of the psychological insight of *Le Rouge et le noir* and *La Chartreuse de Parme*, or even *Armance*.[22]

Having rejected the obviously unsuccessful attempts of the eighteenth century to found a scientific psychology, Blum apparently became skeptical of the power of science in this realm and did not give much attention to the work in progress in his own time. Like many of his contemporaries, he was inclined to feel that science had about reached its limits in the nineteenth century but had left certain areas, especially those having to do with man, largely untouched. There was no denying certain contributions, such as those of Pasteur and Metchnikoff in immunology, but Blum dismissed most practitioners of medicine as deficient in both science and humanity.[23] There is no indication that Blum knew of his Viennese contemporary, Sigmund Freud, whose most significant works had just been published.[24] Blum would have found much of Freud congenial, but the latter's approach to the problems of sex through his experience in clinical pathology gave him many insights that would have been foreign to Blum. Both owed part of their outlook to the somewhat similar bourgeois milieus of Paris and Vienna, but their paths did not converge.

Blum's approach to his subject came no closer to the natural sciences than a pair of references (only one explicit) to Metchnikoff's *La nature humaine.* Blum was equally uninfluenced by the emerging modern social sciences. In spite of his acquaintance with some of the leaders of modern sociology in France, among them François Simiand and Célestin Bouglé, he made no use of sociological techniques and was not concerned with their standards of evidence and demonstration.

Blum's techniques of argument and demonstration in *Du mariage* were drawn strictly from the literary tradition. His method was to start with a relatively simple proposition—that there are consecutive polygamous and monogamous phases in normal emotional life—and to proceed by deduction to unfold all its consequences. The bulk of the book was taken up by anecdotes designed to illustrate his thesis. These anecdotes were often excellent, and often made telling points, but they were nonetheless anecdotes; even if they had been true stories, there was no possibility of controlling their general validity.[25] These generalizations were products of a long and serious but highly individual study. Blum was a scrupulous observer, and not anxious to rush his conclusions into print, but while he would not have consciously falsified an observation, he may have tended, once his thesis began to take shape, to see only that which confirmed it. This failing is not the exclusive property of literary men; even the most dispassionate scientists have not been immune to it. Blum's conclusions could be attacked by other observers, but there was no way in which differences of opinion could be adjudicated. Blum was a literary moralist, writing within the framework of a venerable national tradition, a vein whose vitality is still unexhausted.

As a moralist, Blum was prompted to write *Du mariage* by his concern for happiness, a happiness he found lacking in the lives of so many of the married and the unmarried. He believed that the pursuit of happiness was both a moral activity and a human right. Blum, who had detected a puritan moralism in Gide's early writings, was doubtless not surprised that his friend considered the pursuit of happiness a highly immoral goal.[26] Blum's moral theory was not a simple hedonism; his concern for justice took precedence over his hedonism, but he shared Socrates' view that justice and happiness are inseparable. This outlook placed him in a tradition of Western thought which had encountered rough opposition between the rise of Christianity and the Enlightenment.[27]

Under Christianity, the right to happiness was opposed by the ideal of sacrifice. In many areas of life, resignation and sacrifice were, or had been, practical necessities. Calling these necessities moral virtues perhaps made them easier to bear, and Blum had no objection to making a virtue of necessity, but he saw that different ages call for different sacrifices. He thought that just as the progress of industry made it increasingly difficult to convince the poor that their poverty was necessary and was to be endured with resignation, it would become harder to convince women they should accept their inferior position in society and the double moral standard that went with it as more women came to feel it was not only unjust but unnecessary.[28] The increasing economic independence of women would also stimulate their desire for freedom. For Blum, "all forms of liberty are linked."[29]

He was aware that unhappiness cannot be completely banished from human life and that people will always have to be resigned to it, but he thought that it was a moral right—even an obligation—to seek to diminish it as far as humanly possible.[30] *Du mariage* was concerned with sexual happiness, particularly for women, but Blum did not think that sexual pleasure ensured happiness. He was, however, aware how intimately sexual and general happiness were related, and especially how an unsatisfactory sex life can cast a pall over every aspect of life.

Blum's concern with the pursuit of happiness was an important link between his sexual ethic and his socialism. This concern was in the mainstream of socialist thought, at least in France, for as Edouard Dolléans has justly pointed out: "Socialism, derived from the sensualist philosophy of the eighteenth century, rests on the right to happiness."[31] But while Marx's erratic son-in-law Paul Lafargue had maintained that the happiness of the masses is the sole aim of socialism, Blum and Jaurès saw that it was only part of the goal, necessary but not all-sufficient for the just society. The same concern for individual freedom and development that went into the making of Blum's socialism is also found in his moral treatise, but *Du mariage* had existence apart from his socialism.

Certainly *Du mariage* was not a party tract, not something written to forward the cause of socialism. Its intended audience was an elite, the ruling middle classes of France, but even if they had followed this advice they would not have been closer to accepting socialism. Blum offered the bourgeoisie an analysis of its own *moeurs*, and he admitted that some of his remedies were accessible only to those with abundant leisure time. He had not sought to observe the *moeurs* of the proletariat at equally close range, but he was probably right in suggesting that they had less need of his reforms.

Blum was aware that because of its focus on the bourgeoisie, some might consider *Du mariage* a curious book for a socialist to have written, and he attempted to forestall such criticism by insisting that while the book's ideas were not part of his socialism, they were not incompatible with it.[32] He argued that moral renovation could be accomplished without social revolution, even though moral and social life are intimately connected.[33] But why, as a socialist, should he have desired to reform the moral life of the bourgeoisie? To Marxists, the sins of the bourgeoisie were products of their character as a social class and would disappear only with their eventual elimination as a class. As a general proposition, Blum agreed with this analysis but, unlike more sanguine Marxists, he understood that the domination of the French bourgeoisie was not near its end; and because the bourgeoisie was dominant, he feared that the corruption of its *moeurs* would affect all of French life. The problem was urgent and its solution could not wait for the revolution. As a socialist, Blum was to take a similar position on the questions of war, which must be resisted even if it cannot yet be eliminated, and social reforms, which must be sought and accepted even within the context of bourgeois society.

199

Blum's concern with the condition of women was within a well-established socialist tradition. French socialists, with the principal exception of Proudhon, have been advocates of the emancipation of women, a development they considered an important measure of the progress of liberty within a society. Like many of them, Blum sought the emancipation of the individual—male or female—from all kinds of servitude, not just economic. He freely admitted his debt to one of the most sensitive and creative socialists to deal with the problems of sex, Charles Fourier.[34] Blum remarked, only half jokingly, that if Balzac had read Fourier's *Théorie des quatre mouvements*, the writing of *Du mariage* would have been unnecessary.[35]

Fourier and Blum shared a deep belief in the rights of the passions and the idea that the *moeurs* should be adjusted to fit the nature of the passions, rather than the passions repressed in the service of religious or economic ideas. There is even, in Blum's outlook, something of Fourier's naïveté about the benevolence of the passions, and in Blum's proposals an occasional hint of Fourier's fantasizing in dealing with sexual reforms. Fortunately, Blum's writing has a stylistic grace and self-consciousness that is almost totally lacking in Fourier.

The gradualism of Blum's socialism and his concern that methods be compatible with goals—that methods do not cause more harm than they yield in benefits—were also reflected in his moral treatise. He recognized that though the existing *moeurs* caused much unhappiness, the individual who went against them was likely to find unhappiness in the way society punished nonconformers. He knew that change requires risks, but he was aware and embarrassed that the risks would fall, not on his own generation, but on the young, and he even exhorted parents to help their children gain the independence they needed to mature emotionally. Blum's appeal was not a naïve hope so much as a recognition of the obstacles to any change in *moeurs*:

Envision all the conflicts which today leave our good faith so hesitant: conflicts between the precaution of the parents and the often rash passion of the young, between moral conscience and desire, between pride and tenderness, between the rights of the individual and the respect for contracted obligations, between the freedom of love and the stability of the family. On both sides the arguments are so strong, the interests so certain and so grave, that our reason is divided, and in this confusion the boldest spirits have sometimes rallied—as one has seen recently—to the narrowest solutions.[36]

Blum feared the possible consequences of an immediate and widespread application of his ideas, just as he feared the too sudden rise to power of the socialists before either they or society at large were prepared for the resulting transformations. At the end of *Du mariage* he made an explicit statement that he was not calling for the immediate implementation of his ideas. Whatever the present-day controversy over his book, it is not over the extent of its influence but over the extent to which it forecasted the changes which have taken place since 1907.[37]

Du mariage still has admirers and detractors in France, for the fame of the author and its literary style, as well as its content, have given it longer life than is usual for works of this kind.[38] But there can be little doubt that it was a work of its time, reflecting the milieu and the moment of the class which formed its subject and to which its author belonged.[39] For example, there is masculine bias in Blum's work, in spite of his interest in feminine emancipation. There is considerable truth in Viola Klein's observation that "at the beginning of the twentieth century it would have been not only scandalous to admit the existence of a strong sex urge in women, but it would have been contrary to all observation."[40] This comment, however, applies more to Blum's critics than to *Du mariage*.

Blum did not doubt that female sexuality is as strong as that of males, but (like Freud) he believed that male sexuality is primarily active whereas female sexuality is passive, and on this assumption he based a kind of double standard in the definition of adultery.[41] Thus Blum did not escape, or fully realize, the cultural conditioning of his thought, but his social orientation, and perhaps his exposure to Marxism, made him less vulnerable to feminist attack than Freud has been.[42]

The development of moral philosophy since *Du mariage* has doubtless seen the growth of the influence of those disciplines with which Blum was little concerned: sociology, clinical psychology, and even the study of nonhuman behavior. But Blum's outlook remains modern in its recognition of the infinite complexity of moral life, where "everything is linked, everything is interconnected; there is no provisional solution which does not involve an infinity of other problems," and in its determination to face the harsh reality that there are no all-embracing solutions, for "life is not such that one can keep all of its advantages at the same time," which led the moralist to conclude: "I have often thought that morality perhaps consists solely in the courage to choose."[43]

As a moralist as well as a man, Blum had that courage.

CHAPTER EIGHT

LÉON BLUM AU THÉÂTRE

AFTER THE PUBLICATION of *Du Mariage*, Blum became increasingly immersed in the contemporary theater. Although he continued to write a few scattered articles of literary criticism (including some of his best), the last seven years of his literary career were devoted mainly to drama criticism. During those years he gained a respected position among Parisian critics. Jacques Copeau, who was to become one of the leading movers of the modern French stage and whose approach to the theater was much different from Blum's, described Blum in 1912 as "the most distinguished, perhaps the most important, and certainly the most prominently in view of current drama critics."[1] Blum's reputation as a drama critic has been the most enduring aspect of his reputation as a man of letters.[2]

Léon Blum's transition from literary critic to theatrical critic was gradual. He had made his debut in the latter capacity while still at *La Revue blanche*, with an article on the production of *L'Enfant malade*, an early play by his friend and colleague Romain Coolus, but Blum did not hold his first regular post as a drama critic until he joined *La Renaissance latine* in 1903.[3] He published, however, only six articles there, and devoted most of his time that year to reviewing novels for *Gil Blas*. His first drama post came to an abrupt end when he was dismissed by *La Renaissance latine*'s editor, Paul

Hervieu, because he declined to praise his employer's *La dédale* effusively enough.[4] In a period when the independence and honesty of many critics was open to question, Blum had given a clear indication that he was his own man.

His next drama reviews appeared in *L'Humanité*, where on rare occasions he substituted for the regular critic, Alfred Athis, or more frequently used his own column, "La vie littéraire," to discuss a play that particularly interested him.[5] After his collaboration at *L'Humanité* came to an end, Blum brought out, under the title *Au théâtre: réflexions critiques*, a volume of his articles from *L'Humanité* and *La Renaissance latine*. It was the first of four volumes, which would do much to establish his importance as a theatrical critic.[6] During much of 1906 and 1907 he concentrated on writing *Du mariage*, and at the end of 1907 he began a literary column for *La Grande revue*, where he remained about a year.[7] At *La Grande revue*, then edited by Jacques Rouché, who was to have considerable impact on the theater as a director, Blum had a free hand and could range over topics which ran from novels to plays to general commentary on the *moeurs* of the day. Usually, though, it was a play which furnished the starting point for his comments.[8]

Writing for *La Grande revue*, Blum was able to work at the same pace as he had at *La Revue blanche*, as both appeared twice monthly. He abandoned this relaxed pace, however, and threw himself more deeply into the theatrical world when, in 1908, he joined the staff of the recently founded theatrical daily *Comoedia* as its chief critic.[9] *Comoedia*, founded and directed by the talented humorist Gaston de Palewski, was evolving into a journal of all the arts, but the theater continued to occupy the prime place. Blum's appointment thus put him in a spotlight he had never before enjoyed, and it soon became clear that he was ready for it. Many prominent figures from the theaters of the *Boulevard* were associated with *Comoedia*—Jean Richepin, Octave Mirbeau, Tristan Bernard, Alfred Capus, Georges Courteline, Pierre Veber, Eugène Brieux, Jules Renard, Lucien Descaves—and thus his position provided Blum with more than just a free seat at the *répétitions générales*: it gave him entry to the heart of the theatrical world.[10] Blum had already touched the fringes of this world through his many acquaintances (one of them, Octave Mirbeau, was a critic for *Comoedia* when it opened and may have been instrumental in Blum's entry).[11]

With apparently unflagging zeal, Blum remained at his new post until the end of 1911, when he became the critic for a mass-circulation daily, *Le Matin*, then edited by Stéphane Lauzanne and published by Maurice Bunau-Varilla. At *Le Matin*, Blum succeeded an intimate friend, playwright Georges de Porto-Riche, who had found criticism less congenial than creation.[12] Since the format of *Le Matin* offered little scope for his general reflections, Blum also wrote a series of articles on various theatrical topics for the daily *Excelsior* in 1912 and 1913. He was also tempted by the possibility of succeeding Emile Faguet at the weekly *Journal des débats*, but he remained at *Le Matin* until the outbreak of World War I.[13] In any case, the real measure of his critical ability had been given during his nearly four years on *Comoedia*.

The principal reason for Blum's abandonment of literary criticism in favor of drama criticism is to be found in the action of the creative writers, especially the younger ones, who were moving toward the theater.[14] Anyone who was interested in the movement of French literature had to recognize not only that dramatic production "has often held and still holds a preponderant place" in that literature, but also that it was on the ascendant.[15] Looking backward in 1912 on this general movement, Blum assessed the situation as accurately as anyone has done since.[16] At the turn of the century, he observed, the publishing industry was in the throes of an economic crisis, which reached its worst point around 1905. The theater, which had been at its nadir some fifteen years earlier, was by then in full revival, and an author who wanted to make a living from his writing had a choice of journalism or the theater. The theater offered a chance at the "big success," where the author's share (carefully protected by the Société des Auteurs Dramatiques) could make him rich; and even when the heights were missed, there were more rewards for the relatively unsuccessful than in any other literary endeavor. Furthermore, reputations could be made more quickly, if less securely, in the theater. Blum attributed the crisis of the book trade and the corresponding rush toward the theater to the "acceleration of the pace of life."

From sixty-odd years later, that acceleration seems quite moderate and life *circa* 1905 rather leisurely, but Blum was right in observing that the theater is especially sensitive to social change, even if its reactions are not always predictable or subject to precise formulation. Having heard the theater pronounced dead by one writer (Barrès), Blum preferred to attribute its revival to literary influences, to the work of men like Henri Becque, Ibsen, Porto-Riche, and François de Curel, and he seemed to treat his own sociological analysis as an interesting experiment in "historical materialism," as a *jeu d'esprit*.

Historians of the theater, as distinguished from literary historians, have been more inclined to attribute its revival to the pioneering work of a few directors, especially André Antoine, whose measured daring in his Théâtre-Libre (1887–94) had done much to revive interest in the theater as an art form.[17] Antoine had introduced an extreme realism, which served as a therapeutic shock to the French stage, but which, as he realized, quickly reached its limits.[18] Within a few years the avant-garde found new paths, often based on an aesthetic explicitly hostile to that of the Théâtre-Libre (such as the poetic symbolism of Paul Fort's short-lived Théâtre d'Art), but such experiments were possible because Antoine had cleared the air and made possible a return of sentiment and imagination and idealism free from the sentimentality of the late nineteenth century.[19] A fruitful synthesis of realism and poetic sensitivity was attained in the best work of Antoine's later career, as in that of other director-actors, such as Firmin Gémier and Lugné-Poë, and in the Théâtre des Arts of Jacques Rouché.[20] Blum was aware of the impact of Antoine, and usually praised his later work, but he was more impressed with the claims of the innovating authors. For Blum, the revival of the theater was primarily a literary movement.

Although attracted by the renewed literary and artistic vitality of the theater, Blum had a certain detachment from that vitality which was to shape his work as a critic. It seemed to him that the theater, more than any other literary form, needed periodic renewal because of two inherent weaknesses: the mediocrity of public taste and its indifference to artistic development, and the tendency of the usual run of works to dilute and debase every original movement.[21] The theater, he thought, always renewed itself against the resistance of public taste through the efforts of authors like Becque and producers like Antoine, who refused to bow to that taste and eventually compelled acceptance on their own terms. But success led to imitation, to debasement, and then to sterility, and the process had to be started over again. Seeing the inevitability of this cycle, Blum felt the futility of struggling against it.

Thus his criticism never espoused a movement of theatrical reform or expressed a yearning for some previous golden age. He came to theatrical criticism too late to participate in the battle for realism, which had already been won (insofar as such battles are won), and because he did not feel that realism's possibilities had been exhausted, he could not join those who were prepared to discard it altogether. While he believed that the theater should reflect reality, Blum was not doctrinaire about the manner in which it should do this. In any case, the cyclical development of the theater, as he described it, was not subject to the influence of the critics but, rather, had the inevitability of the succession of generations.

In his practice as a critic, Blum naturally took the position of an observer on the watch for the new and original, rather than that of an advocate. He lacked neither opinions nor taste, but both were developed within the observer's framework. For anyone who attends the theater frequently, the sense of *déjà vu* is familiar, and there were times when it weighed heavily on Blum, but he was able, at least for several years, to overcome this oppression because of his avid desire for the new and his unflagging energy, combined with subtlety of analysis, in his search for the new. Most plays, he thought, were of negligible importance, and the function of the critic was to detect the exceptions: "To catch in their flight, to put in their rank, to situate in the evolution of literature, those works which reveal a true talent or which mark a new state of the dramatic art."[22] The critic's prime obligation in this assessment was sincerity rather than consistency, and Blum, with his detachment from any particular literary school, had to re-examine his opinions vis-à-vis each new author or work.[23] The critic's historical relativism, his feeling for the dialectic of literary history, thus kept him "au-dessus de la mêlée."[24] This combination of acute observation and detachment in Blum's criticism was frustrating to his successor at *La Grande revue*, Jacques Copeau. Copeau admired Blum's intelligence and sensitivity while deploring his lack of engagement: "Monsieur Blum does not love the theater. He goes there with the other spectators. He speaks about it with taste and without passion."[25] Blum liked the theater, but he could not love it with the single-minded devotion of a reformer like Copeau.

The conditions under which Blum had to work, especially during the years with *Comoedia*, also militated against the development of any engagement on his part. His position at *Comoedia*, and to a lesser degree at *Le Matin*, required him to comment on virtually every new work, and these came with such frequency in some seasons that the task must have been physically wearying.[26] The theater audience, Tristan Bernard has observed, has "abnormal" demands because it is "composed of people who go to the theater too often."[27] This intellectual strain was all the more severe for Blum because he was under an obligation to his readers to deal interestingly with the greatest variety of works. Forced to deal constantly with mediocrity, the newspaper critic must eventually come to some accommodation with it. Blum soon became aware of this compulsion, and he tried valiantly to deal with it.[28]

There were entire genres—the *vaudeville*, the revue, the *grand-guignol*—for which he had little taste, but which were very popular. Realizing the futility of trying to convert the public to his point of view, he had a choice of giving up his job, taking refuge in sarcasm, or trying to handle these trivia in their own terms. Blum chose the last alternative, which tested his detachment and required an understanding of the dramatic *métier*. He found the *vaudeville*, for example, a "boring genre" which regularly lacked imagination and which degraded the spectator by treating him as if he were easy to entertain.[29] While he sometimes took refuge in merely reporting how much the public was amused (making it clear that he was not), he was capable of distinguishing between the masters of the genre (a Courteline or a Feydeau) and the failures. There was nothing, he remarked, so sad as a *vaudeville manqué*, and he sometimes took the trouble to show where one had failed conspicuously.[30] He accorded similar treatment to the melodrama, which was equally bound by its stereotypes and emotional shock effects, which were repugnant to his taste; and he expounded the conventions of the detective story to make palatable his review of *Nick Carter* or *Arsène Lupin*.[31]

Blum was aware that he might be regarded as indulgent toward these trivial entertainments and that his readers would not always understand that when he said something was "good for its kind" he did not mean that it was good in any absolute sense. Yet constant repetition of his reservations about a genre would first bore his readers and then be overlooked; so there was nothing to do but risk misunderstanding. Blum let his feelings show through frequently enough to make it clear that he had preserved his taste from corruption by too much contact with the trivial and that he was never fully reconciled to that contact. He was able, moreover, to make something of a virtue of this necessity by using his reviews to sharpen his eye for theatrical mechanics and the "laws of the genre." The trivial genres were precisely those which were most dependent on the "formula"—a kind of tacit contract with their special audience—and Blum was quick to decipher the formulas and report on the authors' success or failure in meeting them, regardless of his own lack of pleasure.[32]

Practice in this type of observation was by no means useless when he turned to more serious matters, for even in plays with intellectual pretensions, the construction and the author's grasp of his *métier* were important. The genre Blum disliked the most was the one that offered no room for this intellectual exercise and therefore lacked any redeeming virtue: the revue, of which there were "too many," and which relied too much on vulgarity, obscenity, and personalities for its effects.[33]

All of the genres Blum found offensive appealed to the mediocre author because they offered a good chance of public success for even the least imaginative application of certain well-worn principles and proven "effects."[34] Overemphasis on technique had had distressing results in the late nineteenth century, even in the work of authors who claimed to be serious artists, such as Dumas *fils*. Blum was aware that the *métier*, even if abused, was a necessity, but it is somewhat surprising to find him defending the literary qualities of an author who is generally considered a mere technician, Victorien Sardou.[35] This defense was perhaps more a rebuke to the would-be serious dramatists who tended to flaunt their lack of *métier* as a means of distinguishing themselves from the mere amusers. Both the lack of theatrical technique and overreliance on it were failings he believed a good writer could avoid. There were types of comedy less artificial than the *vaudeville* in which originality and individual style were possible and for which Blum sometimes framed "laws" to suit his critique or tried to fit into a recognized type by offering his own definition.[36] Perhaps the best example of this latter was his recognition of the *marivaudage*, a type he admired because of its emphasis on character rather than plot, which brought comedy into closer relationship to drama.[37] The comic writers he admired most were those who combined their understanding of stagecraft with a personal understanding of human nature and the ability to portray its comic aspects—the mature Tristan Bernard, and especially Jules Renard.[38]

Blum's technical criticism (whether applied to farce or to drama) —his analysis from the point of view of genre, plot, construction, etc.—illustrated his recognition that a play must be treated differently from a novel. On the other hand, he often found that the criteria he had applied to novels were also valid in the theater. Because he brought the same concerns to his confrontation with both media, he naturally asked many of the same questions of the literary and dramatic works he was examining. He found no reason, for example, to give up his penchant for locating an author or a work in the general history of literature, or in the history of a genre, or in the corpus of the author's work. In the theater, as in dealing with novels, Blum was confident, perhaps too confident, that he could trace the intellectual or artistic parentage of a work or define the nature of an author's talent.[39] He also continued, in his drama criticism, to be concerned with the literary-stylistic qualities of the writing, whether by a stylist he admired (like Octave Mirbeau) or by one who irritated him (like Henry Bataille). He used the same expression to describe Mirbeau's plays that he had applied to his other writings— "the prose of a poet."[40] Blum's stylistic criteria, worked out during his *Revue blanche* years, are all to be found in his drama criticism: naturalness and sincerity; classical clarity; individuality and origi- nality, within the limits of conventional syntax; and appropriateness to the subject. Likewise, the ex-poet in him could not always resist technical criticism of versification, imagery, and vocabulary in treating a new verse drama.

Occasionally, Blum carried his literary emphasis to the point of treating a play as if it were something he had read rather than seen performed. When he succumbed to this temptation, Blum was usually conscious of it. He sometimes admitted having read a work before seeing it (not always possible with new plays) and, less frequently, having received different impressions from the reading and the seeing.[41] The resultant problems of judgment presented themselves most acutely in the case of novels adapted for the stage. Such adaptations were popular with the general public and lazy playwrights, but Blum rarely found them successful. On the other hand, he was not especially concerned about the possible debasement of great novels by inferior adaptors. When his brother René proposed a law for the protection of literary masterpieces, Blum saw too many objections and thought it enough if the law would prevent adaptors from reaping financial profits at the expense of authors' heirs.[42] These problems were of course avoided when an author adapted his own work, but the artistic problems were nevertheless great. Blum seldom favored the play version over the novel, and he noted that many authors failed to make all the necessary adaptations in their work.[43] There were times, too, when Blum was not wholly successful in adapting himself, as when he praised Jules Renard's transformation of his *Ecornifleur* into *M. Vernet* but discussed the play in almost wholly literary, rather than dramatic, terms.[44]

There was a different but not wholly unrelated question of adaptation in which Blum's position was based on both literary and theatrical considerations. This was the question of whether foreign theatrical works should be "adapted, so to speak, to the French taste" in order to ease their acceptance or whether they should be presented in faithful translation.[45] During the nineteenth century, adaptation had been the rule, until Antoine's Théâtre-Libre—in deciding for a production of Ibsen's *Ghosts* in 1889/90 that would be faithful to the original—had opened the way for the partisans of translation.[46] Blum strongly supported translation and had the pleasure of seeing the first integral production of Shakespeare in France. In spite of his literary orientation, he realized that a play must be based on a dramatic idea, not merely a literary idea, and he held that the dramatic concepts of foreign literature deserved consideration in their own right, even from Frenchmen justly proud of their own dramatic tradition.

Although sensitive to dramatic ideas, Blum often seemed annoyed that the theatrical production had to come between him and the author's work. If he liked a work which was not well received by the rest of the audience, he could be quick to blame the actors for not doing justice to the play. And yet, as a good observer, he sometimes had to admit what many authors knew: a fine actor can rescue an inferior play or make a good one seem even better.[47] For the most part, his reviews gave slight attention to the actors or staging, unless they were exceptionally good or bad. His enjoyment of his years at *Comoedia* was probably augmented by the paper's policy of employing separate critics to report on the acting and the *mise en scène;* however, there were a few actors for whom Blum expressed appreciation (most of all Lucien Guitry, a mature romantic lead who was noted for his naturalness and realism), but the fame of actors seemed somehow unfair to him. Unlike an author, an actor who was not appreciated by his contemporaries was forever lost, and an overrated actor was forever safe from criticism. This sentiment led him to attempt to prove that the fame of Rachel, an early nineteenth-century actress, was the result of a cabal of enemies of romanticism who "puffed her up" in order to draw attention to the classical repertoire in which she appeared.[48]

Although his effort at debunking, based on argument rather than evidence, betrayed an overeagerness to revenge literature upon the theater, Blum's position as critic led him to develop greater concern for the art of acting. He was called upon by the editors of both *Comoedia* and *Le Matin* to report on the annual prize competitions of the Conservatoire National de Déclamation, and every year his reports expressed dissatisfaction both with the competitions themselves and with the products of the Conservatoire. Blum favored the realistic or naturalistic style, which would become dominant, but in spite of the pioneering efforts of Antoine and others had not yet spread from the theaters to the Conservatoire.[49] It was not entirely the fault of the system, he quipped, because "the lack of naturalness is one of the characteristics of youth."[50] By 1911 he was sufficiently interested in the problem of training actors to propose reforms in the competitions which he thought would make them more equitable, and in 1912 he suggested that the judges be actors and actresses rather than dramatists and critics.[51] Indeed, in 1912, after tracing the origins and rationale of the state-supported Conservatoire, he called for its abolition.

It was easier for Blum to sympathize with aspiring young playwrights than with novice actors; and as we have seen, he had himself tried to turn dramatic author. He began a drama in 1902, but after showing the first acts to several friends he again had to accept the fact that his proper vocation was criticism. The experience sharpened Blum's awareness of the difficulties faced by young authors, and he frequently tried to use his criticism to help or encourage them. He usually informed his readers when the object of his critique was the work of a beginner, and he urged them to take this into account in forming their opinions, as he did in forming his. Even when the generation that was entering the theater was no longer his own, Blum tried to maintain contact with its aspirations. Jean-Jacques Bernard, son of Blum's good friend Tristan Bernard (and destined to rival his father's fame as a comic playwright), has recounted the encouragement and assistance he received from Blum at the beginning of his career. Blum would have been flattered to know that he was one of the few members of the older generation who seemed both approachable and capable of understanding the problems of youth.[52]

Blum's gentility toward novice authors caused him to be accused of exhibiting, as a drama critic, the same excessive indulgence many had found in his literary criticism. His indulgence, whether or not one considers it excessive, stemmed from the same sources in both fields, but its expression was shaped by the different conditions under which his drama criticism was produced. The critic for *Comoedia* or *Le Matin* could not, unlike the critic for *La Revue blanche*, ignore the things which did not interest him, and his compulsion to review everything led to a relativism which could be taken for indulgence. Furthermore, it was more difficult for the drama critic than for the literary critic to feel that he had the perspective to render definitive verdicts. There were, to be sure, occasions when Blum was willing to risk anticipating the verdict of history, but usually this was out of enthusiasm rather than distaste. In the long run, the critic's mistakes would not make a success of a poor play or a failure of a good one, and Blum preferred to remain alert for the good one, which the critic could, "by a preliminary selection, send on to literary history, whose decrees are unknown and mysterious."[53]

Of the many attitudes Blum brought to the theater from his literary criticism, the most important was a greater concern for content than for form.[54] He explicitly rejected the critical theory of Francisque "*Mon Oncle*" Sarcey and his generation, who held that a playwright should be granted his premises and judged only on whether his plot and personages conformed to them.[55] In Blum's view, the internal logic of a work must indeed be coherent, but the work must also be grounded on true premises. When a play seemed to merit the effort, he would conduct a minute analysis of the characters of the principal personnae and their relationship to the actions the author put them through.[56] If the logic of those relationships seemed faulty, he would not only explain why but would on occasion offer his own version of what should have happened, sometimes convincing the reader that his version was more true to life than the playwright's. To his concern for the verisimilitude of a plot, Blum added even greater concern for the verisimilitude of character, holding that the "working" of a play depended on the solidity of the characters and that the dénouement would seem weak and artificial if the characters were not clearly drawn and convincingly human.[57] Blum preferred dramas where the author built around a conception of certain human characters, through which nuances of the human personality could be explored, to plays that were inspired by ideas

213

for dramatic situations.[58] This preference was one reason why he was not fond of certain genres, especially among the comic ones. The genre in which action unfolded most inexorably from the character of the personages was tragedy, and it was this aspect of classical tragedy which he liked to find in modern drama.[59]

While Blum loosed his critical barbs at authors whose personages did not seem real, he did not claim a monopoly on the knowledge of human character. He had some definite ideas, as *Du mariage* showed, but he did not want dramatists simply to repeat the types with which he was familiar. Rather, the playwright should seek out the new and present it convincingly. Unless he was an observer of the evolution of *moeurs*, the dramatist had little chance of being original:

Every change in the *moeurs* and in society makes possible and brings to light a new psychological detail. The art of the dramatic author is not only to discover and explain it, but also to make clear its relationship with the fundamental types and permanent forces of the human character.[60]

Blum was willing to concede that an author might be a better observer than himself, and the minuteness of his critical analyses was an aspect of his search for the new, which might be found only in some subtle nuance. The new in human psychology could not exist in isolation from the ongoing traits of man's nature, and thus change and continuity were inseparable. Blum's literary classicism, which insisted on maintaining a similar continuity in language, was thus related to his view of social reality. He could therefore maintain that there was no antithesis between the classical and the modern: "There is scarcely any classical work which has not been modern in its own time."[61] Blum found that his search for the classical qualities in modern works, as well as for the new, provided intellectual excitement which made the theater more than a mere diversion.

Blum's advocacy of social observation did not make him a partisan of any of the aesthetic schools associated with realism in the theater —and certainly not of naturalism, for he ridiculed the chief work of the Goncourt brothers as a "false masterpiece."[62] Nor did he think that staging needed to be confined to the path Antoine had set it upon. While he was sharply critical of some anti-realist experiments, like the short-lived Théâtre Impressif, he welcomed the innovative efforts of Jacques Rouché's Théâtre des Arts.[63] He had cooled toward the work of the naturists, and was even less impressed by their work in the theater than he had been by their novels. While he still liked their idea of blending romanticism and realism, Blum felt that their works were too forced and that the blend was better realized, independently of manifestos and schools, by talents such as Jules Renard.[64]

The examination of contemporary reality which Blum sought in serious dramatists, whatever their mode of expression, had been largely absent in the productions of the preceding generation, which were dominated by romantic sentimentalism and facile technique. By the time Blum became a drama critic, a "realist revolution" against the theater of Dumas *fils*, Emile Augier, and their colleagues had already taken place. The realist aesthetic first made its power apparent in the novels and criticism of Emile Zola, but Zola, like his followers, had been unable to transform his critical ideas into successful theater.[65] The first dramatist to conquer the artistic difficulties of this mode was Henri Becque, but the novelty of his work had been too great to find acceptance and the fame of the author of *Les Corbeaux* and *La Parisienne* was posthumous. It took the combined talents of actor, organizer, *metteur en scène*, and apostle possessed by André Antoine to produce with the Théâtre-Libre a force capable of creating an audience for the new realism.[66] While Becque had attacked the stereotypes of theatrical personages in search of a truer representation of reality, Antoine added the scenic realism that would give new dramatic impact to such works. Antoine's scenic realism was sometimes cumbersomely and crudely literal, but nothing less than strong medicine could have put life back into the French theater.[67] It raised the hope, Blum later observed, that the theater might become a vehicle for the expression of contemporary concerns.[68] When he became a drama critic, Blum had the opportunity to observe how much, and how little, that promise was being fulfilled.

As the plays of Becque had revealed, a theater which tried to take a fresh look at society would inevitably challenge the conventional pieties (not merely the theatrical conventions) and shock the audience, which was accustomed to going to the theater to have its self-esteem bolstered.[69] Blum, who was committed to an intellectual position highly critical of contemporary society, was naturally much attracted by the emerging theater of social ideas. The *théâtre d'idées* was at least as old as the eighteenth century, but it had been rejuvenated as a result of its contact with the realist movement, and

Antoine had once again played an essential role in drawing on domestic and foreign resources. He brought to the French stage, for the first time, the severe intellect of François de Curel and the greater genius of the Norwegian dramatist Henrik Ibsen.[70] The impact of realism tended to take the *théâtre d'idées* from the realm of abstract speculation and to engage it more fully in the problems of contemporary society.

Blum was happiest, of course, when he had occasion to deal with an "idea play" which criticized the cruelties and hypocrisies of bourgeois society from the point of view of the aspirations of the political left and which at the same time had strong literary and dramatic qualities—plays like Anatole France's adaptation of his *Crainquebille* or *Le Foyer* by Octave Mirbeau and Thadée Natanson.[71] *Le Foyer*, which stirred considerable controversy because it held a member of the Académie Française up to ridicule and attacked the abuses of certain private "philanthropies," was typical of the work Blum esteemed. The play was not an ideological or theoretical critique but a concrete portrayal of real abuses, which drew its effectiveness from the contrast between the ideals and the reality of hypocritical philanthropy. Blum made a personal visit to the director of the Comédie Française to urge its production, but Jules Claretie, who feared a scandal, refused to honor his original agreement until the authors compelled him with a court order.[72] As critic, Blum could content himself with describing the theme and its development, while underlining what seemed to him the truth of *Le Foyer*'s message.

On other occasions, when a play did not say all that he thought was needed, or when he wanted to add his affirmation to its message, Blum's exposition of his own opinions might play a prominent part in his reviews. For example, he revealed his strong hostility to Catholicism—the conflicts of the Dreyfus affair were still not forgotten—when treating works of anti-clerical intent. If his praise of Jules Renard's *La bigote* could be partly explained by his long-standing admiration for the author, the same could not be said of his great enthusiasm for Georges Ancey's *Ces messieurs*.[73] Ancey, whose play was long withheld by the censor, based his work on the idea that the religion of most women is no more than sublimated lust for the priest. Blum found this idea so convincing that he regretted that Ancey's priest was an unbeliever, since the point would have been sharper otherwise, and with the production of this

play in 1910 he elevated the author to the first rank of the contemporary theater.[74] Later, Blum showed that his feelings did not
prevent him from appreciating the constructive historical role of
Christianity, or even from dealing with a play about the problems
of contemporary Christianity on its own terms instead of forcing it
into his own framework.[75] In cases like these, Blum tended to
substitute the discussion of ideas, or even the exposition of his
personal views, for the criticism of the play ostensibly in question,
but he did this with full awareness of what he was doing.

Blum's powers of argument were brought more fully into action
when he opposed the social ideas expressed in a drama. His favorite
target was once again the conservative moralist Paul Bourget, who
like so many others was tempted by the propaganda possibilities of
the stage.[76] In both 1910 and 1911 Bourget brought out pointedly
anti-socialist dramas which were successful with the largely conservative theater public. Blum conceded that Bourget's success was
justified in artistic terms in the case of *Le Tribun* but not in that of
La Barricade.[77] Undoubtedly stimulated by a desire to undermine
Bourget's success, Blum not only pointed out several instances of
improbability but showed that in *La Barricade* the author failed to
be consistent with his own theses. Blum's demolition was in the
finest tradition of the French literary polemic. He could, on the
other hand, praise a work on a socialist theme written by a non-
socialist when the writer made a greater effort at objectivity than
Bourget had done.[78]

Blum did not limit his critical severity to ideas from the political
right, though he was less likely to use heavy sarcasm on the others.
Thus he devoted an article to analyzing the moral system propounded in Henry Bataille's *Les flambeaux*, showing that its
apparent libertarian appeal was based on a subtle egotism which led
to an elitist morality.[79] Blum, certainly a member of a cultural elite,
believed that humanity took precedence over genius and saw the
dangers inherent in any elitist morality, however well intentioned.[80]
His opposition to Bataille's Nietzscheanism rested on the same
foundation as his later opposition to fascism and communism.

The sharp criticism Blum brought to bear on antipathetic social
ideas did not prevent him from also being critical of a number of
works whose views were relatively sympathetic to his own but
showed faults of thought or a lack of dramatic art.[81] The pretentious
and awkward verbalism of Paul Hervieu largely nullified for Blum,

as for most critics, whatever interest the author's ideas might have had. On the other hand, Blum was sufficiently moved by the earnestness of Eugène Brieux's timid attacks on bourgeois morals and prejudices to moderate his critique of Brieux's generally acknowledged ineptitude as a dramatist.[82] Brieux was seldom, if ever, bold enough in drawing the consequences of his ideas to suit Blum, but Blum did not agree with those who classified Brieux in the same category as Dumas *fils*, as a purveyor of *mélodrames d'idées* that quieted, rather than disturbed, the conscience of the audience.[83] Blum was really harsh only immediately after Brieux had beaten Porto-Riche (Blum's candidate) for election to the Académie.[84]

Blum's awareness that noble intentions do not necessarily lead to effective theater did not discourage him from hoping to discover plays that were socially useful, but he realized that the drama took precedence over usefulness. The message had value in elevating a work, but it was necessarily a subordinate value.[85] Eventually, he wondered whether it was possible to write a successful play if one began with a nontheatrical idea: "The theater of ideas is decidedly a very perilous genre, which perhaps demands too many contradictory qualities, and in which it is quite difficult to avoid, on the one hand, having the idea harm the drama, and, on the other hand, . . . having the drama harm the idea."[86] Thus the same danger he had found in the social novel also applied to the *théâtre d'idées:* people did not go to the theater for intellectual stimulation, and the slightest hint of sermonizing would arouse their resistance.[87] Yet Blum would not agree with those who said that "to attach the social question to the tragedy is to throw an overcoat over a rosebush," and he believed that a skillful dramatist could cause people to think about some topic or become aware of some abuse without their becoming overly conscious of his intention.[88] He admitted that this would be difficult but denied that the ideas would have to be so denatured that the bourgeoisie could find the *théâtre d'idées* a substitute for serious thought and social concern.[89]

One thing the theater could do was enlarge the range of its subject matter to include wider sections of society and more diverse types of humanity. The virtues of a theater which attempted this could outweigh its artistic defects:

In place of expressing the artistic tastes and intellectual habits of a generation, the theater can express the needs, the sufferings, the passions of a society. It would be then a weightier, more grave art, and one which could, if need be, do without all the ornaments of the spirit.[90]

The greatest influence of Blum's socialism on his drama criticism can be seen in his desire that working-class milieus and sentiments be presented realistically on the stage. But while he praised Gustave Geffroy's *L'Apprentie* and Hermann Sudermann's *Parmi les pierres* (he did not have the chance to review the most famous work of this genre, Gerhardt Hauptmann's *The Weavers*), Blum was by no means uncritical in his reception of such works.[91] While he was vaguely sympathetic to the idea of bringing the theater to "the people," he was not sure that they wanted or needed it. His affection for the popular cause was not the product of illusions about the artistic or intellectual interests of the masses.[92] What he apparently envisioned was the possibility that the theater-going bourgeoisie might learn something about the lower strata of society which would help change their callousness and indifference to the fate of others.

This kind of social art would have a certain nobility even in failure, and Blum had to admit that no enduring masterpiece had yet appeared. Such nobility, however, was totally lacking in another kind of *théâtre d'idées*, which he strongly condemned: the "work of circumstance or of speculation" which attempted to capitalize on a currently fashionable idea or sentiment. Thus he attacked the exploitation of patriotism in 1913, while arguing that the patriotic efforts of Paul Déroulède's writings a generation earlier were justified by the low ebb of national feeling which followed the defeat of 1871.[93] A play like Henri Kistemaeckers's *Flambée*, on the other hand, was merely a profitable manipulation of sentiments that had been aroused earlier the same year by the Moroccan crisis.[94] An author, Blum argued, should be above suspicion in such a matter if he was not to damage the idea he had set out to exploit. As a critic, Blum often defended the purity of ideas against exploitation.

Blum's involvement in the theater stemmed in part from reasons that were "social" in a sense that was different from, and sometimes contrary to, the nature of his concern with social ideas. For the French middle classes and for the intelligentsia, the theater was not merely an art form, but had long been an important social institution whose affairs were treated with considerable seriousness. A typical attitude of the circles which Blum had begun to enter during his lycée days was that of Mme. de Caillavet, *grande amie* of Anatole

France, who would not miss an important opening night even if it meant a long trip for no other purpose. Her daughter grew up thinking that the opening of *Chantecler* (by Edmond Rostand) was as memorable as the battle of Austerlitz.[95] (It is true that Mme. de Caillavet's son was a popular author of *vaudevilles*, but she was scarcely an extreme case in her devotion to the theater.) The theater was thus almost an inescapable social necessity in Blum's world. The members of his milieu were involved in the theater on both sides of the curtain, and many of his friends had preceded him in becoming active participants, mostly as authors. During his years as a drama critic, Blum's friends included such playwrights as Tristan Bernard, Jules Renard, Edmond Sée, Romain Coolus, Edmond Rostand, and (his most intimate friend) Georges de Porto-Riche.[96]

While these were some of his closest friends, Blum was well aware that there was danger in the most innocent association of authors and critics and that the friendliness of authors was not always disinterested.[97] One may doubt, however, that friendship was a cause of much partiality in his criticism; his indulgence also extended to authors outside his circle of acquaintance.[98] The charge that he was systematically or even unconsciously partial to his Jewish friends is not supported by a study of his criticism.[99] There is, in any case, no reason to suppose that a critic who was resolutely isolated from the social world of the theater would be a better or even a more impartial critic.

Blum was able, for the most part, to avoid the love-hate tension which characterized much of the relationship between authors and critics in that, and indeed any, era. Some writers, such as Bataille and Bernstein, had a hair-trigger sensitivity that led them regularly to the field of combat, seeking revenge for critical insults. (A sense of the cash value of the resulting publicity may have sharpened their sensitivity.) Blum's efforts to steer clear of this kind of conflict failed only once, when he was assaulted by Pierre Veber, an erstwhile friend from his *Revue blanche* days but subsequently a nationalist. Blum, seconded by his editor Stéphane Lauzanne and by Porto-Riche, met his adversary behind the board fences of the Parc des Princes (but in front of *Comoedia*'s camera), and at the third reprise, "sur un double de seconde, par un coup de fouet," drew blood with a touch on a rib "a few centimeters from the liver," which ended the encounter. The victorious critic's hand was refused.[100] Blum certainly did not enjoy the experience, and the fact that it was his only venture *sur le pré* is perhaps more a testimony to the respect that playwrights held for the sincerity of his criticism than to their respect for his excellent swordsmanship. His duel emphasizes, by way of contrast, the tranquillity which generally characterized his involvement in the social world of the theater.

Blum would no doubt have gone to the theater for social reasons alone, but he would scarcely have become a critic had the theater not also provided an intellectual and emotional experience. The Parisian theater was largely Right Bank in its location and social orientation, but Blum, who lived on the Left Bank, was experienced in combining Right Bank worldliness with Left Bank intellectualism: *La Revue blanche* had been as much Right Bank as *Comoedia*, which was located over a café–concert hall on the boulevard Montmartre.[101] The branch of the contemporary theater on which Blum's social, intellectual, and emotional interests converged most strikingly was the *théâtre d'amour*, to which he devoted a major part of his efforts as a drama critic.

The *théâtre d'amour* was more artistically successful than the *théâtre d'idées* or the social drama because theatrical expression is better adapted to the realistic examination of intimate groups, such as the amorous couple or triangle, than to the treatment of abstract ideas or broad social classes or issues. Surprisingly, however, love themes had a minor place in most of the French theater of the nineteenth century, and in the age of Dumas *fils* the love of money supplied the motivation of the central personages. The theater had become, as Maurice Descotes has said, a place for the public worship of the golden calf.[102] The *drame bourgeois*, as we have seen, came under attack from the new realism, but its popularity was even more threatened by the competition of the *théâtre d'amour*.

From an early date, Blum campaigned for acceptance of his conviction that this new movement began in 1891 with the presentation of *Amoureuse* by Porto-Riche. *Amoureuse* had not only been immediately popular but had come to exercise profound influence on other playwrights, and the seminal influence Blum ascribed to it has been widely recognized (although interest in Porto-Riche is currently at a low ebb).[103] Porto-Riche presented himself as a psychological analyst who demonstrated that the power of sexual passion is supreme in the lives of men and women. He disregarded bourgeois conventions and spoke with a frankness rarely (if ever) used before on the stage—but which has subsequently become so commonplace (not to say surpassed) as to make it difficult to realize his originality. Although his dialogue could be direct and even brutal, it was not realistic but strove for a "theatrical" brilliance which has not aged so well as Blum thought it would.[104] On the other hand, the realism of Porto-Riche's psychology attained a timeless generality which gives it survival potential despite his current eclipse.

Blum's admiration for Porto-Riche was not only for the psychologist but also for the dramatic artist, whose rapid-fire dialogue he found moving as well as penetrating. As a critic, he did not find comparable skill in any other exponent of the *théâtre d'amour*.[105] But this art was effective primarily because it evoked a convincing view of reality, and Blum believed this reality was quite different from the social conventions which minimized the impact of sexuality on personality and behavior. It is difficult to tell how much the concurrence of views between Blum and Porto-Riche resulted from their long friendship, or how much their friendship was the product of a discovered empathy, but there can be little doubt that the dramatist, through his plays and his person, influenced the author of *Du mariage.*

The *théâtre d'amour* was only one aspect of the growing public discussion of love, which was a reaction against the hypocritical prudery of the nineteenth century. Romance was a serious avocation among the bourgeoisie of the *Belle Epoque,* more of whom than ever before enjoyed considerable leisure for amorous pursuits. Its reflection of these leisured lives makes the *théâtre d'amour* seem dated, and one may doubt that in this more "liberated" age the psychology of love is a more important object of social conversation than it was then. Alfred Fabre-Luce has recalled of Blum's wife that she "scarcely spoke of anything except love," and even if this is somewhat exaggerated, Blum's drama criticism reflects much practice in the constant "turning and re-turning of all the problems of the couple and the trio."[106]

Even the least sympathetic critics have recognized that Porto-Riche opened a rich vein of theatrical material, and the *théâtre d'amour* accounted for a major share of the work of many of the most prominent dramatists of the prewar years, among them Henry Bernstein, Henry Bataille, Maurice Donnay, and Edmond Sée. Blum, who was perhaps unwilling to admit how delicate a subject literary influence can be and how sensitive authors are about their originality, tended to see the influence of Porto-Riche everywhere.

But all the adepts of the *théâtre d'amour* were not of this progeny. On the other hand, Blum was in good company in believing that Porto-Riche's three greatest successes—*Amoureuse*, *Le Passé*, and *Le Vieil homme*—were the best of the genre. No less a person than the sober literary historian Gustave Lanson remarked, after seeing *Le Vieil homme* (1911), that "one must henceforth say Racine, Marivaux, and Porto-Riche."[107] However, Blum's enthusiasm for Porto-Riche did not prevent his paying close attention to other practitioners of the *théâtre d'amour*.

Although Blum was never as uniformly enthusiastic for the art of any other playwright, he came closest, perhaps, in his regard for the work of two other acquaintances, Coolus and Sée, whom he thought had the right combination of style and insight. (Both, however, would now rank as distinctly minor authors behind Bernstein and Bataille.) Blum treated the two Henrys as serious artists, but found Bernstein short on psychology and Bataille short on dramatic art. Bataille was a first-rate talent, gone wrong with a florid, byzantine verbal style which offended Blum with its artificiality. Though Bataille's themes pleased the critic for their attack on bourgeois conventionality, they seldom escaped unscathed from the minute analyses he devoted to them (he once chastised Bataille for misunderstanding one of his own personages, thinking she was in love when she really was not!). It was not until *La Vierge folle* (1910) that Blum allowed himself to be carried away by Bataille's success, and even to revise his opinion of some of his earlier works.[108]

Blum's criticism of serious writers of *théâtre d'amour* often used the plays as a take-off point for an examination of the *moeurs* or for the application of the ideas he had formulated in *Du mariage*, and he admitted that he sometimes substituted the role of moralist for that of drama critic.[109] It was perhaps because the theater offered so many opportunities for the moralist in Blum that it was able to engage his attention for so long. If an author was short on dramatic talent, Blum might devote his entire review to the subject or thesis, examining the author's views and defending the message while wishing it had been more boldly expressed, or finding it bold enough but inadequately expressed, or—more rarely—defending an idea for its unconventionality while not sharing it.[110] Defenders of the traditional moral order ventured their theses on the stage less frequently than the reformers, but even the best of these conservatives was no match for Blum's critique. When Paul Bourget adapted his *Un divorce*, Blum welcomed it as artistically superior to the novel, and then proceeded to the same detailed demolition he had given the original work.[111] This moralistic preoccupation may have detracted from his effectiveness as a theater critic, and it certainly helped preclude that devotion to improving dramatic art which Jacques Copeau thought essential in a critic, but it has also served to give Blum's criticism more enduring interest than most of the plays of his time.

Blum's principal interest in the *théâtre d'amour* was not so much in the presentation of theses or the entanglement of plots as in the representation of character types, and particularly female characters. The highest praise he gave Henry Bernstein was for bringing to the stage, in *Le Bercail*, a new type of modern woman "in whom neither passion nor intelligence yield anything to the other."[112] Blum saw Bernstein's heroine as a confirmation of his idea that contemporary women were passing through a transitional stage in which they were achieving the negative goal of emancipation without acquiring a positive direction or purpose. The blend of passion and intelligence was also prominent in the heroines of Porto-Riche, but their intelligence could do no more than leave them self-conscious victims of the irresistible force of their passions. This gave them a kind of tragic dignity, and indeed Blum defined a tragedy as a play in which the action depends on the passions.[113] It was this fatality of the passions which caused Porto-Riche to be compared to Racine, but it was also a fatality which could contain more modern implications. Porto-Riche himself did not draw these implications, and as Francis Pruner has argued, a more relentless logic could follow them (by way of Strindberg's *Miss Julie*) to a Nietzschean amoralism which Blum would have found abhorrent.[114]

While praising Porto-Riche for restoring the passions to their just importance, Blum was no more ready than the playwright to advocate amoralism. Blum never gave an explicit sign of having detected philosophic dangers in his friend's plays, but it is suggestive that his greatest enthusiasm was for a play by another author with a slightly different philosophy. This play, *Les affranchis*, was the first work of the young Mlle. Marie Lenéru.[115] Along with the power of passions, presented so ably by Porto-Riche, Mlle. Lenéru found another, even more powerful fatality: that of the milieu. *Les affranchis* was meant to demonstrate—and Blum heartily concurred in the moral—that "one does not do what one thinks or feels; one does what one can." It was toward this conclusion, which he associated with his Jewish heritage by calling it "Spinozist," that Blum's relativism, even his skepticism and detachment had long been pointing. *Les affranchis* touched the heart of his humanism, and his fondness for this play bears witness that the moralist had not been altogether mistaken in his youthful self-rapprochement with Goethe.

The *théâtre d'amour* seldom carried much philosophical weight, but it offered many opportunities for the moralistic critic. Even when an author did not aim much above mere entertainment, Blum found it easy to turn from the study of stage personages to that of contemporary society. He believed that the theater was not a precursor of evolutions in *moeurs* so much as a follower or a mirror.[116] It was therefore a convenient sourcebook from which the moralist could draw examples to illustrate his views; for example, his belief that human character changes little though *moeurs* vary widely. On occasion, Blum's reviews became little essays on the history of social attitudes as reflected in the theater.[117]

During the flourishing of the *théâtre d'amour* the French theater acquired an international reputation (partly justified) for immorality and obscenity (state censorship had been in effect at the turn of the century but it was abandoned shortly thereafter). Many theaters had adopted a kind of self-censorship under pressure from private groups, such as the League against Licence in the Streets, led by the prudish Senator Béranger.[118] The result was that many authors seemed to be stimulated by this constraint to perfect the art of the double-entendre and a dissimulating obscenity whose aim was pornographic—the exploitation of sex for profit. Although he considered such productions the necessary price of freedom, Blum did not hesitate to express his distaste for it with a frequency that caused him to be called a prude by a colleague at *Excelsior* (this colleague, who called himself Rip, was an author of "naughty" revues).[119] While denying the charge, Blum defended the public modesty of society, and, repeating an observation that men are more moral in a crowd than as individuals, argued that, although this is hypocrisy, it is necessary for society.[120] In defending hypocrisy against "direct brutality," Blum did not abandon his critique of contemporary *moeurs* and conventionality but, rather, reaffirmed his assertion of the power of sexual instinct, whose strength required care in its public manifestation. Sexuality in the theater could be handled without going to the extreme of obscenity or to the other pole of sexlessness, which Blum found disturbing in the Paris productions of Arthur Pinero and Bernard Shaw.[121] Blum's seriousness was not sanctimoniousness, and he must have enjoyed the friendly parody in the April Fools' Day edition of *Comoedia* (1910) which presented him as the new director of the Conservatoire, planning to reform the sex lives of the young *comédiennes* according to the principles laid down in *Du mariage*.

The question of immorality on the stage provided a new occasion for the anti-Semitic forces, which had been temporarily vanquished in the Dreyfus affair, to manifest themselves again. A substantial number of the leading playwrights of the *théâtre d'amour* were Jewish (among them Porto-Riche, Bernstein, Sée, and Coolus), and those who were gentiles were denounced as corrupted fellow travelers. The prominence of Jewish writers, together with several Jewish critics, including some who could also be charged with changing their names to conceal their ancestry (e.g., Nozière, *né* Weyl), was all the anti-Semites needed to invent yet another "Jewish plot" against the moral fiber of Christian society. The anti-Semitic campaign was waged on the stage by such works as Maurice Donnay's *Le retour de Jérusalem*, but more commonly the struggle was waged in the press, either in lavish praise for works that supposedly presented a "French" view of love, such as Jules Lemaître's *Massière* and Donnay's *Amants*, or in attacks on Jewish playwrights and critics. The climax of this anti-Semitic outburst was the riots which rocked the Place du Théâtre-Français in 1911, leading the management of the Comédie Française to suspend Bernstein's *Après moi*. Blum, by this time a prominent critic, came in for his share of abuse, most frequently from the virulent and unscrupulous polemicist Gustave Téry, whose gentlest epithet for Blum was "chief of the claque of the twelve tribes."[122] While Téry abandoned his prey when the emotions of the *affaire Bernstein* slackened, the charge was taken up in 1912 and 1913 by Paul Léautaud, the critic for the respectable *Mercure de France*, under the pseudonym Maurice Boissard.[123] While not indulging in the coarse vulgarity of Téry, Léautaud represented an equally vicious racism which denied Blum any capacity for judging French plays because he was not of "French blood." Many otherwise moderate writers revealed a latent racism by professing to see in the *théâtre d'amour* a specifically Jewish sensuality.[124]

Blum did not bother to reply to his attackers, although some of

Téry's remarks were probably libelous even under the lax French law. Blum did not even sign the list of protesters against the suspension of Bernstein's play, although it was signed by his brother René and published in *Comoedia*.[125] As a critic, Blum maintained his sang-froid in the face of Donnay's *Retour de Jérusalem*, while exposing the author's misconceptions and refuting his claim of impartiality. Blum exposed the flaws of that ethnic determinism which had also marred the later novels of Barrès, and he took the occasion to defend his own French patriotism, for nationalism and racism were as closely linked in the clash over the Jewish theater as they had been in the Dreyfus affair.[126]

Blum's patriotism was not the irrational love of *quelque coin de terre*, exalted by the racists, but rather the belief in France as a leader in bringing the ideals of liberty, equality, and fraternity to the world. Ideas know no national boundaries, and Blum was always eager to see foreign works produced on the French stage.[127] The reception he gave them was not uncritical—indeed, he was nowhere more vitriolic than in his denunciation of a work by the Italian futurist F. T. Marinetti—but the nationalists could not forgive him for putting Shakespeare above Corneille and Racine or recognizing Ibsen as the greatest contemporary dramatist.[128] Blum's breadth of taste, the product of his open and curious mind rather than extensive knowledge of the foreign theater, was perhaps unusual for a Frenchman of his time, but those who called it anti-French had a narrow and petty conception of their *patrie*.

Of the foreign dramatists whose work he reviewed, Blum was most enthusiastic about Gabriele d'Annunzio (who was not yet posing as the savior of Italy), much of whose work was produced in France (indeed, he wrote *Martyr de Saint-Sébastien* in French).[129] Blum's enthusiasm, which led him to clash with Jules Renard, is the most difficult part of his taste to understand in retrospect.[130] He attacked the resistance of other critics to d'Annunzio as narrow literary nationalism, but certainly he was not merely using d'Annunzio as a pretext for upbraiding the parochialism of much of French taste.[131] Only genuine enthusiasm could have led him to acclaim the Italian as the creator of the greatest heroine since Racine (equaled only by Porto-Riche), but somehow Blum's analyses of d'Annunzio's sensual personages and ideas are less convincing than those he devoted to Porto-Riche and others.

What was different about d'Annunzio was that he was a poet and his plays were in verse, and Blum had a definite weakness for attempts to revive the grandeur of verse drama. Blum praised d'Annunzio as a rare union of poetic and dramatic talent, but he seems to have been more impressed with the latter—to the point of feeling compelled to defend the "charms" of verse in translation.[132] Almost all of the French poets who were writing for the theater at that time were ineffective dramatists, whether Blum found them talented as poets (André Rivoire) or not (Albert du Bois).[133]

The one great popular success was something of an enigma— Edmond Rostand. Blum, like everyone else, had been carried away by the phenomenal success of *Cyrano*, and in 1913 he still considered it an enduring masterpiece, having in the meantime found *Chantecler* even better.[134] Yet Blum had to admit that Rostand was not a great poet, though certainly he was "something great."[135] Blum, who became a welcome visitor to the poet's retreat in south-western France, concluded that Rostand's genius derived from a unique combination of a diverse number of otherwise very ordinary talents.[136]

A greater poetic talent, but one who was little known before 1914, had been detected by Blum and a few others, but Blum had only rare occasions to tell his readers about Paul Claudel.[137] In the theater at least, Blum's appreciation of poetic genius took precedence over ideological considerations, and however much he deplored the social and intellectual influence of Catholicism, he saw it as a legitimate source of poetic inspiration in a Claudel or a Francis Jammes.[138]

In spite of his receptivity to any hint of something new in the theater, Blum grew impatient with its failure to provide the intellectual nourishment he sought. Even the most avid curiosity could stave off boredom only so long. Blum believed that the theater inevitably went through a series of ups and downs, and he had become a reviewer when he thought it was on the upswing. A genuine interest in the theater kept him at his post even after it had become clear that the trend was once more downward, and his articles continued to appear until the week preceding the beginning of war in 1914. The impact of the war on France was to turn him from the theater and literature for good, but there had been signs that he might not have continued as a drama critic in any event.

At the end of 1912 he was frankly confessing his disappointment: "When the exodus toward the theater as the dominant literary mode began some twenty years ago, one hoped that like the novel it would become the expression of the concerns of the day;—it has disappointed this hope as much as possible."[139] Some waning of his interest had already appeared in his decision to leave *Comoedia* for *Le Matin* in 1911. *Le Matin* could not have been very attractive, for it was one of the most violently anti-socialist and chauvinist of the bourgeois newspapers. Furthermore, drama criticism occupied an insignificant place in it, and Blum had only a fraction of the space *Comoedia* had afforded him, only a half dozen column-inches.

Until mid-1914 he wrote under the pseudonym Guy Launay, a name which had been used before and was still used occasionally by other members of *Le Matin*'s staff.[140] Blum had once remarked that the only sincere criticism was anonymous criticism, but it was an open secret that he was *Le Matin*'s reviewer. In making that remark, he had been thinking of the pressure on a critic because of his friendships and acquaintances among authors, but it was in part friendship which brought him to *Le Matin* for he replaced Porto-Riche, who had found reviewing uncongenial.

Certainly Blum did not use his "anonymity" to significantly alter any of the opinions about authors and works that he had previously expressed. Indeed, the brevity of his reviews for *Le Matin* makes it impossible to learn much about him from them; nor did he consider them interesting or important, for he ceased to collect them for republication in his *Au théâtre*. While he perhaps did not think of ceasing his attendance at the theater, it no longer commanded the best of his intellectual effort. Some hint of the path he might have followed had the war not intervened can be seen in his return to literature with "La prochaine génération littéraire" in *La Revue de Paris* in February 1913, and even more in his first work of extensive literary history, *Stendhal et le beylisme*, which appeared early in 1914.

In his concern for contemporary literature, Blum had always been close to his generation, but his critical intelligence had enabled him to take a somewhat detached position. Perhaps he was beginning to feel, at the age of forty-two, that a new literary generation was displacing his own and that the time was coming to retreat into the more sedate realm of literary history that he had spurned in his youth.[141] Certainly he did not anticipate the very different fate that was awaiting him.

CHAPTER NINE

LÉON BLUM AT FORTY

IF BLUM felt a touch of melancholy when he realized he no longer belonged to the young literary generation, he did his best not to let it show. He was never one to look back with regret—seldom one to look back at all—and when he could no longer identify himself with the young, he did not resent their intrusion on the literary scene. Early in his literary career, Blum had been conscious of the natural succession of generations and had self-consciously cast his lot with the aspirations of his contemporaries. He believed that without a commitment to the present no lasting achievement was possible, and he was determined to accomplish something worthwhile. At the same time, he recognized that each generation tends to exaggerate its own significance and originality, and this helped prepare him for the emergence of the next generation, which would inevitably be critical of his own generation and confident in itself. He remained true to this relativism—or historical perspective—when, at the age of forty, he turned to examine the "prochaine génération littéraire."

There were many things in this coming generation which were antipathetic to Blum, but he saw their movement as promising on the whole and he chose to emphasize that promise. Maturity had certainly not dimmed any of the optimism with which he habitually faced life. This optimism led him to underestimate the strength of the resurgence of anti-intellectualism, Catholicism, and nationalism in the new generation. On the other hand, Blum was justified in resisting the claims the spokesmen for those positions made to exclusive possession of the wave of the future. Instead of directly opposing them, he framed an interpretation of the age which incorporated their activities and aims as part of a larger and more diffuse movement—a twentieth-century version of romanticism. It was a romanticism like others in the past, characterized by "an infinite need to believe and to act, a total confidence in the intrinsic value of belief and of action."[1] Blum recognized in this need and this confidence the emotional force needed to raise French literature from the doldrums into which it had fallen. Even the narrowness of zealots might bear literary fruit. The important things were the optimism and energy, which he hoped would be channeled toward the needs of the present and the future rather than toward the past.

Blum's optimism was not the product of idle wishful thinking but of an informed view of France's literary history. Like many others, he saw this history as an alternation of phases: each century began with its romantic movement, which through a variety of changing reasons inevitably decayed into a period of formalism, analysis, and diversion under external influences. Romanticism was not simply a nineteenth-century phenomenon but an approach to literature that was common to all times in which love of life and respect for its indeterminacy and variety were dominant in literature.[2] The romantic movement of the nineteenth century had been long lived— Blum had been born early enough to meet its grandest figure, Victor Hugo—but it too had died out, and Blum did not believe that it was simply from old age. He thought that the rise of natural science had created, early in the second half of the century, a pernicious temptation to which literature had succumbed. This temptation was exemplified by Renan's excessive confidence in the universal beneficence of science and Taine's mistaken attempt to apply methods derived from the sciences to literature. They and others, he thought, had led literature toward a bloodless rationalism.

The false positions into which writers had been led ranged from the art-for-art's sake of Théophile Gautier and the Parnassians to the scientific pretensions of Zola's naturalism. Blum came to admire Zola as a social novelist only after the writer's heroic stand during the Dreyfus affair, and he tempered his position by admitting that there could be great art in spite of the artist's mistaken ideas. It was a concession he had to make in order to justify his admiration for Flaubert's *Education sentimentale*. Nonetheless, he believed that art and science are incompatible because science is the domain of exactitude, certainty, and quantitative measurement while art can flourish only in the atmosphere of the uncertain, the unfinished, the unmeasurable:

Art does not satisfy any of the conditions of scientific work since it is not susceptible to continuation or progress, since it does not prolong itself from generation to generation, but on the contrary begins again and so to speak risks itself anew with each new man and each new work, since its objective is neither stable nor even defined, and its processes are neither fixed nor uniform nor transmissible by teaching or example, since it admits neither predictions nor explanation in the scientific sense of the word, nor certitude or generality of any kind.[3]

He did not charge the scientists with intellectual imperialism but the writers and artists with losing faith in (or touch with) the true roots of their art.

The process of clearing away the pseudo-scientific debris which encumbered literature began in the generation before Blum's own, in the work of a few men. In criticism, the skepticism of Jules Lemaître, and even the anti-scientific dogmatism of Brunetière, had had a beneficial impact. Of those writers who contributed to this process, Blum felt he had been most influenced by Barrès, though he also accorded an important role to Anatole France and, surprisingly, even Bourget. He had long thought that the impact of these precursors would stimulate his own generation to bring about the great romantic revival. But as early as 1905 he began to feel that his generation would be only transitional: the sorry state of the novel was evidence that the spark for a new period of literary greatness was lacking.

Poetry, with the principal exception of the Parnassians, had fared better than the novel in escaping the influence of science, though it had tended to come under the less harmful influence of music. Blum was not very enthusiastic about the symbolists, but he found poets who had preserved the values of their art—from Verlaine through Mallarmé, to Marcel Schwob, Maeterlinck, Anna de Noailles, and Fernand Gregh. Music, "the most immaterial of all the arts," had helped keep the way open for the influences he thought would revitalize literature—idealist philosophy and religiosity. Blum's own philosophy had long been marked by the neo-Kantian idealism he had learned in the lycées, and he had always insisted on the central importance of emotion in literature, but he had not previously been so willing to identify this emotion with religiosity, however vaguely defined.

Blum's view of the sources of the new idealist and religious impulse was hardly acceptable to those who were proclaiming the new generation as a "renaissance française." Where they looked to the native resources of Latin Catholicism, he spoke of the current from the North: Tolstoy, Dostoevski, Ibsen, Wagner. Both sides were partially right: French Catholicism had not shown any particular intellectual or artistic vitality in the later nineteenth century, and most of what it acquired in the twentieth century was brought in from the outside by zealous "converts" like Péguy and Jacques Maritain. On the other hand (contrary to Blum's expectations), much of the religiosity of the age went into the Church and stayed there. On one point, Blum and most of the young Catholics agreed: the influence of the philosopher Henri Bergson had colored the religious temper of the age.[4]

Blum credited Bergson with providing the disquiet of the age—its reaction against scientism and its religiosity—with a coherent philosophy which enabled it to accept the genuine accomplishments of science and avoid blind anti-intellectualism, while legitimizing its spiritual aspirations. Bergson accomplished this by reviving philosophic dualism and proclaiming that "the world of life and of the soul no longer depends in its essential and profound qualities on scientific knowledge but on a special knowledge which is properly philosophic or metaphysical knowledge."[5] The way to such knowledge was through intuition, and Blum was pleased with Bergson's insistence that intuition and intelligence are mutually necessary for he knew that either, if pursued alone, leads to barbarism. Blum did not see Bergson so much as an inspiration to spiritualism as the source of a rationalization which helped reconcile the conflicting demands of reason and emotion which Blum and so many of his contemporaries felt within themselves. Blum's synthesis of these conflicts was his own and he never became one of Bergson's disciples, though his interest in the philosopher was permanent. He told an interviewer from the Jesuit *Etudes*, some six weeks before his death, that he was in the process of rereading Bergson's works

233

"with the pleasure of admiring and of allowing one's self to be convinced."[6] Obviously, he was never fully convinced.

Bergson not only appealed to the religious right but also to those on the left who had not accepted a narrowly materialist version of Marxism. His appeal was strongest to the anti-intellectualist fringe, typified by Georges Sorel.[7] To those who believed that both science and Marxism were leading to a determinism which ignored the individual's sense of freedom and responsibility, Bergson offered, as Gerhard Masur has observed, the triumph of optimism over determinism.[8] This strengthened his appeal to the natural moralism of the young, whether of the left or the right, for both felt that contemporary bourgeois society was morally corrupt (though they often included each other in that condemnation). The new generation boasted of its optimism, of its lack of doubts, which it contrasted with the "morose pessimism" of the preceding generation.[9] Blum, of course, did not accept this view of his generation, whose optimism he had always proclaimed, but there was an important difference between his outlook and the outlook represented by the "jeunes gens d'aujourd'hui," whose attitudes had been approvingly reported by Agathon.

The optimism of the young right tended toward a voluntary naïveté and a willful archaism which were characteristic of their move toward Catholicism. Blum preferred to see in the religiosity of the new generation a greater realism, a greater awareness of limits, but to find a suitable example of this he had to turn to the young Jewish poet and critic Henri Franck, who died at the age of twenty-three. Franck, who also had admirers on the right, was quoted by Blum as saying that "more than our elders we have the sense of the thousand resistances which today limit each destiny."[10] While Blum agreed with the young conservatives that the role of science was to satisfy material needs and that it could not answer all of man's legitimate questions, he insisted that it nonetheless limited the field in which faith and intuition could operate:

Certain forms of energy or of faith are conditioned by certain forms of ignorance. It is vain to hope to escape from science, for scientific habits will persist whenever there is a question which calls for evaluating future results or controlling present ones. After this apprenticeship confidence remains possible, even lyric confidence, but not credulity.[11]

The Catholicizers, of course, found too much of the rationalist in

Blum's view, and he was willing to associate his view with a more specifically Jewish religiosity—"always distinguished by this mixture of eagerness and of aridity of faith and of disenchantment."[12]

In contrast to those who were looking toward the religious movement to restore the "moral unity" France had lost (in the sixteenth century, one supposes), Blum insisted that the new generation embodied a religiosity so diffuse that it could embrace everyone from Paul Claudel to André Gide to Henri Franck, and beyond. Blum's stress on this religiosity becomes more comprehensible when it is realized that he identified it with romanticism. Indeed, it was the parallel he drew with nineteenth-century romanticism which gave him confidence in his interpretation of the coming generation. Both movements, he thought, represented reactions against exactly comparable systems of exaggerated scientism: "Bergson, for example, is opposed to Taine as sharply as Chateaubriand to Voltaire."[13]

There were other parallels, however, on which Blum laid less stress. For example, early in the nineteenth century there had been a Catholic revival in reaction to the deism and atheism of the revolutionaries, but, in spite of an apparently brilliant start, it had not dominated the romantic movement for long. The "Catholic renaissance" of the twentieth century was not to be so brilliant or important as its advocates proclaimed, but it seemed more remarkable, perhaps because society as a whole (not merely intellectual society) had become more thoroughly secularized than had been true a century earlier. Nonetheless, a Catholic literature of enduring stature was to emerge from this period with Péguy, Claudel, and, later, François Mauriac.[14] Blum was capable of appreciating the best of them.

Surprisingly, Blum's emphasis on youth prevented him from seeing that his own generation, laggard though it seemed in 1912, would produce three of the dominant writers of the century: Gide, whom Blum admired greatly; Proust (who had as yet not shown that he was more than an interesting dilettante), and Valéry, who had temporarily ceased to write. Gide and Proust, at least, belonged to the romantic movement he was analyzing, and they can be better understood in terms of his analysis than through the more common emphasis on the presumed influence of Bergson.[15]

Outside of literature, the intellectual influence of the Catholic revival was more ephemeral, and if Catholic students at the

Sorbonne turned from Emile Durkheim and Lucien Lévy-Bruhl (both Jewish sociologists) toward Catholic philosophers like Victor Delbos, the long-run triumph has remained with the former.[16] Blum's position—indifferent to the Catholic philosophers and dubious of the pretensions of the sociologists—found its most effective intellectual synthesis not in literature, or the University, but in the political philosophy of Jaurès.

It comes as no surprise that Blum was hostile to, and tried to minimize, an important attribute of the new generation: its nationalism. On the right, the links between political conservatism, Catholicism, and nationalism had become closely knit and there was much debate over what was "truly French," especially among those who wished to emphasize France's uniqueness and who inclined to blood-and-soil versions of nationalism. These nationalists charged Blum with ignoring the revival of "truly French" literature because of his "cosmopolitanism."[17] No doubt Blum had always tended to overestimate the impact of foreign thought in France, except when some event forced him to take stock of his countrymen's powerful self-preoccupation. He did not pay much attention to the growing influence of the Action Française and Charles Maurras, perhaps because Maurras represented a retrograde literary aesthetic, the kind of sterile intellectualistic classicism which Blum's own critics have often unjustly ascribed to him. Maurras was certainly outside the literary mainstream, but his nationalist extremism had considerable influence in young literary circles. As an emotional force capable of influencing literature, nationalism was not so acceptable to Blum as religion, because while religiosity was felt in many parts of the political spectrum, nationalism had become too closely identified with the right, with militarism and the anti-Dreyfusards. He did not see any possibility of its having a beneficent influence on literature or society.

Unfortunately, the younger generation which Blum was writing about was taking its nationalist rhetoric more seriously than he imagined and often carried the cult of action and vitality to the point of exalting martial virtues and hoping for war.[18] Its members tended to look upon Blum's generation as unnational and pacifistic, as having lost faith in France because of the defeat of 1870; and there was some truth in the suggestion of Agathon that there was "something like a sly revenge of a humiliated patriotism at the bottom of that humanitarian internationalism which the 'intellectuals' of 1890 professed with pride."[19] Blum and the other "humanitarian internationalists" believed—and rightly, as events proved—that going to war to recover French territory and pride would be too high a price to pay, but they underestimated the strength of the feeling that war with Germany was not only possible but inevitable. The lack of this sense of impending conflict separated Blum and much of his generation from the youth that now confronted them.

Blum's reflections on the new literary generation show how many basic attitudes the intellectual left could share with the intellectual right, but the gap in generations, as well as the difference in political philosophies, brought rather different conclusions from those similar basic attitudes. The greatest differences between Blum and the youth of the succeeding generation stemmed from the former's continuing preoccupation with domestic matters, whereas the latter's attention was increasingly monopolized by the foreign menace, symbolized by the *coup de Tanger* of 1905.[20] France was in drastic need of social reforms, in which she trailed the other industrialized lands of Europe, but the middle classes seized on the international situation to justify their refusal to come to grips with domestic needs.

Fear of impending social change was undoubtedly a motivation (though often unconscious) for these young bourgeois intellectuals, as it had been for the anti-Dreyfusards. Thus the period was also a prefiguring of the more complex and grave crisis which Blum would face in the 1930s. The decade before 1914, which saw the vigorous growth of the intellectual right, also saw the rapid growth of the Socialist party and the trade union movement. The atmosphere of confrontation was growing more tense and the political stakes more crucial. More than he was aware, Blum was becoming estranged from the literary life in which he had been so long immersed, and despite his apparent inactivity in the socialist movement, the importance of his commitment was again growing. The coming of war, which he resisted with all his spirit, greatly accelerated this subterranean process of change.

The younger literary generation of 1912 did not appreciate Blum's tolerance of its positions; indeed, his moderation seemed to demonstrate the lack of faith and energy with which it taxed its elders. Still, it felt a need for predecessors, and studied earlier generations for "professeurs' d'énergie." Nietzsche, much admired by Blum's generation, was rejected because he was considered useful only for the weak constitutions of earlier generations. A French model was necessary for these chauvinists, and many thought they had found one in Stendhal.[21] Devotees of Stendhal had been numerous—for different reasons—in the generation preceding Blum's. He too had long held the romantic novelist in particular affection and thus was qualified to point out the errors in the nationalistic interpretations. And thus Stendhal became the subject of his first major literary work that was not devoted to his contemporaries.[22]

Blum's *Stendhal et le beylisme*, a set of essays which first appeared serially in *La Revue de Paris*, was his longest and most ambitious literary work.[23] A study both of Stendhal as a person and a writer and of the Stendhal cult, it has generally been recognized as Blum's finest work of literary criticism.[24] It also seemed to mark the beginning of a new phase in his literary career. It was, instead, the culmination of that career, which would give way to his political career during the war.

In Blum's effort to further his self-understanding and self-development through the study of literature, his *Stendhal* occupies a key position. And because Blum's literary career had reached some sort of turning point around 1912, it is not surprising that this work reveals something of his effort at adaptation. After examining the generation that succeeded his own and establishing his relationship to it—both of distance and affinity—he was led to further reflection on his relationship to more remote generations. At the age of forty, Blum had to consider not merely his relationship to his own generation but had to probe more deeply than ever before into his relationship with the whole of French literature.

It seems no accident that he turned to the study of Stendhal for help in understanding his new position; no other writer could have served him so well. Through his analysis of Stendhal, Blum was able to learn more about himself and we, in turn, can thereby better understand Blum's character. In particular, it is the key to understanding the duality of romantic and rationalist qualities in Blum and how the fusion of these apparent opposites produced this finely nuanced man of many careers. His *Stendhal* cannot be treated, as some have tried, as an unconscious "autobiography" of the critic.[25] Blum did indeed find certain parallels between his own character and that of Stendhal, but his picture of Stendhal—particularly of

Stendhal's social frustrations—was neither a conscious nor an unconscious autobiography. His picture of Stendhal's life should have
quickly laid this misconception to rest.

Blum showed how Henri Beyle, who adopted the pseudonym
Stendhal, had been raised without the companionship of people his
own age and without the love of his family (and without love for
them). Out of this youth Beyle formed an interior world of ambition,
ambition for success in love and "society." The continual frustration
of these ambitions was one of the main driving forces behind the
creation of Stendhal's heroes, and Blum showed that one could find
traces of Beyle in Julien Sorel and Fabrice del Dongo, in Lucien
Leuwen and even Lamiel. All these young heroes, Blum insisted,
represented the ideas of Beyle's youth, not of his later years, when
he actually wrote them (though a less friendly critic might have
called them the products of an abnormally prolonged adolescence).
Thus Stendhal's primary appeal was to the youth who felt his
ambitions and frustrations were similar to their own. For adults, this
appeal persists largely through recollection and depends on a continued romantic *sensibilité*. As for Blum, his own life was enormously
happier than Beyle's, and while, if only because he was a Jew, Blum
may have experienced frustration in French society, all the evidence
shows that he easily adapted himself to the realities of life and
refused to feel thwarted by anti-Semitic prejudice.[26] But Blum also
refused to become a complacent adult, insensitive to the vital sentiments of youth, and both his *Stendhal* and his essay "Prochaine
génération" showed his ability to mature without stagnating.

Blum found two deeply rooted but antithetical strains of thought
in Stendhal which helped explain his life and writings. The first of
these was a mechanistic rationalism which led Stendhal to adopt a
psychology based on Helvétius and Condillac; the second strain was a
romanticism, derived from Rousseau, which often carried volun-
tarism to violent lengths. Blum agreed with his fellow Stendhalian
René Boylesve that this "excessive sensitivity" was foreign to the
character of the *Belle Époque* in which they lived, although a
reaction against excessive rationalism had set in.[27] Stendhal has had
an enormous influence on modern novelists because of his ability to
show them "what contrary qualities could exist side by side."[28]
Blum was among the first critics to grasp the importance of this
dualism, perhaps because he also found a mixture of the rationalist
and the romantic within himself.[29] It was not the same mixture as

in Stendhal, and Blum did not make the mistake of assuming that it was, for he realized that the proportions and the ingredients were different.[30] The intervention of a century, moreover, had given a different meaning to both of those terms, and Blum's romanticism was derived from Victor Hugo (rather than Rousseau) and his rationalism was more sophisticated than eighteenth-century materialism.

The differences between the rationalism of Blum and that of Stendhal can be seen by comparing their respective works on the subject of love. Stendhal's *De l'amour*, in Blum's opinion, was the master's weakest book; it tried to outline the route to happiness but proposed only a mechanism of pleasure.[31] Blum did not neglect pleasure as an element in happiness, but his concern with happiness was characterized by his choice of marriage as a subject, rather than love. Blum was concerned not only with the individual but also with society. Stendhal's novels, of course, show much greater subtleness than his treatise, which falls back on the simplistic mechanisms of Helvétius and LaMettrie. Blum had little confidence that science could offer a solution, let alone a simple solution, to the riddles of the human personality. Blum's psychology was rationalistic in its method but it made considerable use of intuition, and his rationalism operated from a base of assumptions which were more vitalistic than mechanistic.

Blum was consciously impressed by the complexity of life. He liked the nuanced and variable, and for this reason he preferred art to science. He saw that both the rational and the emotional were essential parts of human nature and that to deny either of them was to diminish man's humanity. Being a man of reason, he was not immune to the temptation to pursue his thoughts toward one or the other of these extremes, but he was too sensitive to allow himself to be permanently engaged either way. He was not afraid to contradict himself, and Stendhal helped convince him that all true artists are mobile and self-contradictory. Blum sought always to be sincere, with himself as well as others, though he did not push his concern for sincerity to the extremes of his friend André Gide. Without sincerity, rational self-development was impossible. To maintain a balanced position between the competing attractions of reason and emotion is difficult, but Blum was exceptionally successful at it.

Indeed, Blum's balance was so successfully maintained that observers have had difficulty deciding whether he became a socialist because of his rationalism (although he was emotionally attracted to the bourgeois arts) or whether, on the other hand, his emotional sympathies led him to socialism while his rationalism prevented him from becoming a true revolutionary. His friend Jules Renard, who combined literature and politics to the point of being elected mayor of the commune where he spent his summers, once mused on his own socialism: "A socialist, it doesn't cost anything to be one from reason, but sentiment ruins one. The socialist from reason can have all the faults of the rich; the socialist from sentiment ought to have all the virtues of the poor."[32] Blum, however, cannot be understood in terms of any such either-or explanation; reason and emotion were blended in his socialism. He described his early preparation for socialism as a growing conviction of the injustice of bourgeois society, but this emotional position bore no immediate fruit other than the creation of a predisposition. He then became something (but not very much) of an anarchist out of a literary enthusiasm for the "cult of the self," which was nothing if not romantic, and therefore emotional.

Like Stendhal, Blum came to feel very early that the "happy few" cannot be happy when the many are not, and this prevented him from being content with the extreme individualism which had first attracted him.[33] In his own opinion, Blum's conversion to a modern form of socialism resulted from a conversation with Lucien Herr, and his conversion did not bring about an emotional change but the rational acceptance of a particular outlook as the most likely cure for an evil he had learned to dislike. His rationalism may in part account for his nominal acceptance of Marxism, but rather than being attracted by its scientific pretensions, he was more impressed by its pragmatic potential. Marxism appeared to be the only system of ideas capable of leading to a profound alteration of society, but insofar as it sought to be a closed intellectual system, it could not comprehend the whole of life. Blum would never believe that Marxism (or any other system) could adequately encompass the human condition. It was not that he could not be seduced by ideas, he was simply incapable of believing wholeheartedly in *systems* of ideas. His participation in the socialist movement before 1914 bore the marks of this compound, rational-and-emotional origin of his socialist conviction.

His participation in the socialists' efforts to save Dreyfus was largely, but not exclusively, dominated by his emotional hatred of injustice, rather than by an intellectual concept of the proper structure of society. Colette Audry has found it a great error that he made a sort of "religion of justice," and he would have accepted the term while rejecting her attempt to impute to it any significant affinity with a transcendental religion. Blum sometimes traced his passion for justice to Hebraic roots, but his religious sentiments usually took the form of a vague pantheism which owed more to Spinoza than to Jewish tradition. Blum's concern for justice stood on its own, without need for a systematic underpinning, and was one of the fundamental tenets of his socialism. His participation in the socialist unity movement after the Dreyfus affair, on the other hand, was more marked by his rationalist strain; it was a political gesture which he reasoned would promote the socialist cause. The ease with which Blum ceased to be an active party militant after unity was accomplished in 1905 revealed that it was basically a rational calculation, rather than an emotional need, which had drawn him into the unity movement. He joined it for a specific purpose and then withdrew—at least to a different level of activity—when it was accomplished. Socialism, he wrote in 1904, "is the result of a purely rational conception of society."[34]

The distinction between the rational and emotional elements in Blum's socialist conviction should not be stressed too strongly. The two strains were usually fused, and both of them always played their part in the development of his action and thought. One must especially avoid the simplistic version of certain right-wing critics who, selecting a few points to suit their polemic purpose, have attempted to portray a dualistic Blum divided between a decadent aesthete (which he never was) and a messianic prophet (which he never was either).[35] Blum believed that strong men contain strong contradictions within themselves, whose synthesis is their originality. An important part of Jaurès's appeal for Blum was his ability to synthesize respect for the real and aspiration toward the ideal.[36] The two strains in Blum's socialism remained fused even when he decided to rejoin the socialist movement after the death of Jaurès in 1914. Rational and emotional factors also led him to reassess his relationship to the movement during the course of World War I and to begin a totally new career. This change was compatible with what had gone before, as is evidenced by the stability of the content of his socialist conviction, which remained largely as it had been formed in the pre-1914 era.

Much of the character of Blum's literary criticism also can be explained in terms of this dualism between the romantic and the rationalist. His reviews exhibited a pronounced taste for the romantic, the unfinished, the variable, the emotional, and he insisted on "life" rather than adherence to aesthetic codes. He even explained his love for many writers of the seventeenth century by claiming that theirs was not an age of cold rationalism but, on the contrary, an age of passion. Yet there can be little doubt that the impressionism in Blum's reviews reveals a man of reason who by no means abandoned himself to the play of his emotions. He exhibited an intense desire to understand what he read—a rational rather than an emotional goal—but he saw that the emotional reaction a book caused (or triggered) was also part of its meaning. His analyses of the workings of emotion in his theatrical criticism and in *Du mariage* explicitly emphasize his rational comprehension of the role of the emotions in life. Thus the same synthesis of opposites dominated Blum's literary career and his early socialist career. The same could probably be said of his simultaneous judicial career, but the bare official documents which are virtually our only access to that career do not permit certainty. The wholeness of Blum's personality makes it unlikely that any aspect of his life would have escaped this dualist or synthetic formation.

An important by-product of the complexity of Blum's understanding of the human condition was surely his skepticism. He was not in any systematic sense a skeptic, any more than he was systematically anything else, and he would certainly have described himself as a realist, if such labeling were inescapable. Realism was not a simple thing for him either; it was not a closed system. Rather, it was the highest form of idealism for him, just as idealism was the highest form of realism. In this context, his skepticism might be defined as the refusal to be taken in by the absolutist claims of either idealism or realism. Skepticism or realism—whichever one prefers—means thinking on the scale of man rather than that of God. In other words, it is humanism in the best sense of that term, the sense that realizes both man's grandeur and his limitations. In literature, it enabled Blum to share the aspirations of his generation without losing sight of the smallness of what they could bring to the sum of man's accomplishments in the arts. This same realism prevented him from believing that his political and social ideals could be realized overnight. At the same time, his idealism, his insistence on keeping the goals in sight, prevented him from becoming the kind of cynical politician who, seeing that immediate victory for his cause cannot be won, decides to get what he can for himself.

Finally, it might be said that the very dualism of Blum's early career marked the fusion of romantic and rationalist. The rationalist was represented by the steadily advancing member of the Conseil d'Etat, the romantic by the young essayist and then by the mature critic pursuing a literary career. This dualism, like the particular aspects we have examined, was not the dualism of a split personality; on the contrary, the two strains were blended in Blum into a distinct personality. Blum's contentment with his dual career, the serenity of his life in the decade 1905 to 1914, attested to that balance.[37] Beneath the somewhat deceiving exterior of the *Belle Epoque* man of letters there lived, in harmony, the acute intellect, romantic sensitivity, and moral strength whose fusion produced a man whose strengths and potential for national leadership were formed in the decades before World War I.

EPILOGUE

More than one observer has seen the period between 1914 and 1919 as an interim, even a kind of no-man's land, between the first and the second phase of Léon Blum's life—or, as some seem to put it, between the period of literary dalliance and the discovery of his true career. Our consideration of Blum's dual literary and legal careers, one hopes, will put an end to such undervaluation of the seriousness and importance of his early life. It is because I want to insist on the importance of this early life *in its own right*, not merely as a prelude to something else, that this study ends in 1914 and not in 1919 or 1920.

Nineteen-fourteen was an ending for Léon Blum: the end of his hopes for peace, the end of his reliance on Jaurès to carry forward the cause of democratic socialism, an end (almost) of his career on the Conseil d'Etat (he resumed it, briefly, from 1917 to 1919), and most of all the definitive end of his literary career. As we have seen, his literary career seemed to have entered a phase of transition and we cannot know where it might have led had not the war intervened, but certainly he was not on the verge of giving it up. His literary effort was not a pastime for idle hours but a professional engagement to which he gave the best of his talent and energy. There was no more radical break in his life than the one which ended his literary career.

The coming of the war also marked the beginning, however muted at first, of Blum's political career. When he entered the ministry of Marcel Sembat as *chef de cabinet,* Blum (whose near-sightedness had spared him from military service) was at first merely doing his part in the defense of *la patrie,* as were most other socialists. He could not have realized that it was also a step that would have great political consequences for his life. Not only did his experience in Sembat's office complete Blum's administrative education (and he had to learn fast in order to compensate for the deficiencies of his chief), it also furnished entrée into the socialist leadership that he had lost through the death of Jaurès.[38] Blum had no intention of becoming involved in the party leadership, but he soon found that he could not remain aloof from the issues that arose during the war and eventually realized that his beliefs needed not merely his support from the sidelines but his leadership.

With the breakdown of the *Union Sacrée* came the revival of political conflict. The coming of the war had dealt a crushing blow to the Second International and socialist internationalism, but the impact of these developments was delayed by the concentration of all effort on the national defense and in hatred of the invader.[39] When the war became a bloody stalemate, which would drain France's national energies for over a third of a century, the socialists were among the first to feel the consequences. The revival of their prewar pacifism and their doctrine of class struggle shattered the unity of their commitment to the national war.

A tiny minority at the time of the Zimmerwald and Kienthal conferences, the band of resisters to the continuation of the *Union Sacrée* was growing at the time of the abortive Stockholm conference. Enthusiasm for something other than the traditional concepts of military victory rose still higher with President Wilson's peace proposals. The outbreak of the Russian revolution, and especially the Bolshevik triumph in the fall of 1917, introduced a potent new force of division into the ranks of French socialism.

With the unity of the party threatened for the first time since 1905, Blum found himself at another socialist congress in 1917. From then on he was drawn more and more deeply into the effort to find a way by which French socialism could emerge united from the war without repudiating its commitment to the national cause so long as the war should last. From this crisis Blum would emerge a leader.

Having fully shared the party's prewar hopes for peace, Blum could readily sympathize with the revived force of pacifist sentiment. Having shared its hatred for the czarist autocracy, he could rejoice in the latter's destruction. But having identified his national and international commitments with one another, he insisted that the national cause must take precedence until peace was established. This, naturally, made him hostile to the Russian-formed Third International, and inclined him toward the effort to revive socialist internationalism on something closer to its prewar base.

With the establishment of peace, Blum tried to revitalize the party for the legislative elections of 1919, and it was in this electoral campaign that he emerged as one of the party's leaders. Believing that the party was on the threshold of a great victory if only it could remain united, he turned his efforts toward forging an electoral program. His quick mastery of the issues, his devotion to unity, and his status as a "new man" uncompromised by past quarrels enabled him to play a key role on the platform committee and to serve as its *rapporteur* to the national congress, at a time when he was unknown to the vast majority of militants. The program that emerged from the national congress was to have an important future for Blum and for the SFIO, and much of it would be reincarnated in the program of the Popular Front.

Blum's role in the internal affairs of the party, to this point, was in some sense a natural evolution of the role of specialist and adviser to Jaurès that he had played before the war. But a new element was added when he chose, for the first time, to become a candidate. Nothing marked his commitment to a new course in life more clearly than this decision to step into the public arena. Elected with some difficulty in the department of the Seine, Blum remained in the Chamber of Deputies (with one brief interruption) until the Chamber voted its own destruction in 1940. In the Chamber, Blum quickly won the respect of both his party (he was elected secretary of the parliamentary delegation) and his party's enemies on the other benches. From the inner struggle of the party, which revolved around adhesion to the Third International, he emerged as the leading spokesman of a small group that was determined to resist the apparently irresistible move toward adhesion.

Convinced that the kind of party he had joined before the war remained the only viable socialist party for France, Blum determined to do whatever he could to save that party, even at the price of a split in the socialist movement. The kind of unity that Jaurès had created, based on intraparty democracy as well as external commitment to the democratic republic, was the only kind that Blum could accept. It was also the only kind he thought compatible with the traditions and history of the French socialist movement. This stand would also be his basic position in the many difficult challenges Blum would have to face in later years as the leader of the SFIO. This stand, through his eloquent pleading at the Congress of Tours in 1920, would make him the leader of the struggle to save French socialism from the Bolshevik temptation.

In his celebrated speech at Tours, Blum laid bare, with the utmost clarity, the differences between French socialism and Russian bolshevism, and with almost prophetic insight saw (more clearly than his contemporaries) the future of Bolshevik rule.[40] This speech showed that Blum would bring to his new role of political leader both the qualities and the attitudes he had developed and displayed in his earlier careers. One finds not only his customary lucidity in analyzing the consequences of a situation but also the quality of self-understanding which enabled him to see that the nature of his commitment to socialism required him to resist the bolshevization of the French working-class movement.

He did not resist bolshevism because of distaste for revolution but because he realized that the revolution the Russians had made, however appropriate to their situation, was not the revolution envisioned by Marx or by Jaurès, or by the French socialist movement generally after it had freed itself from the influence of Blanquism. Blum remained true to his understanding of himself and of French socialism throughout his political career.[41]

NOTES

NOTES TO CHAPTER ONE

1. The author was inspired to undertake this study of the early careers of Léon Blum by the brilliant essay by James Joll in his *Three Intellectuals in Politics* (New York: Pantheon, 1960), which is the best brief introduction to the whole of Blum's life, although only the first fourteen pages are devoted to the period before 1914. The most important recent studies of Blum are Gilbert Ziebura's *Léon Blum: Theorie und Praxis einer sozialistischen Politik*, vol. 1: *1872 bis 1934* (Berlin: Walter de Gruyter, 1963) (French trans., *Léon Blum et le parti socialiste, 1872–1934* [Paris: Armand Colin, 1967]), which treats Blum's early life vis-à-vis his later career as a socialist leader, employing an analytical rather than biographical approach, and Joel Colton's *Léon Blum: Humanist in Politics* (New York: Knopf, 1966), which concentrates on Blum's political career and summarizes his early life in very brief compass. Both of these studies are scholarly works of high quality, which for the first time lift our knowledge of Blum's political career from the level of partisan polemic or journalism, but neither fills the need for a comparably thorough study of Blum's literary and judicial careers. The attempt of Louise Elliott Dalby in *Léon Blum: Evolution of a Socialist* (New York: Yoseloff, 1963) to give a well-rounded picture of his whole life is unfortunately marred by errors of fact and interpretation, although it has the virtue of taking his early careers seriously.

Three older biographies are also of some use: Geoffrey Fraser and Thadée Natanson's *Léon Blum, Man and Statesman* (Philadelphia: Lippincott, 1938) has a memoir quality for the early period, when Natanson was closely acquainted with Blum, but Natanson failed to verify many of his recollections. Richard L. Stokes's *Léon Blum: Poet to Premier* (New York: Coward-McCann, 1937) is the work of a conscientious journalist who, nevertheless, lacks the background for understanding French literary and political affairs. Marc Vichniac's *Léon Blum* (Paris: Flammarion, 1937) is an undocumented and popular account by a socialist militant, but it devotes considerable space to his early careers. For scholarly purposes, all three works have been superseded by the more recent works mentioned above.

2. Blum's recollection, quoted by André Blumel in *Léon Blum, juif et sioniste* (Paris: Editions de "La terre retrouvée," 1952), p. 3. See also Colton, p. 3; Ziebura, 1: 12; Dalby, pp. 25–26; Fraser and Natanson, p. 24; Stokes, pp. 6–8, 13; Vichniac, pp. 7, 9. Jean Jolly, ed., *Dictionnaire des parlementaires français . . . de 1889 à 1940* (Paris: Presses Universitaires de France, 1962), 2: 635, dates the family's move to Paris to 1868. This important reference work is extremely inaccurate about Blum's early life.

3. Blumel, pp. 3–4.

4. Fernand Gregh, in *L'âge d'airain: Souvenirs 1905–1925* (Paris: Bernard Grasset, 1951), speaks of Blum's father as "un vieil Alsacien savoureux" (p. 87).

5. Michel Roblin, *Les juifs de Paris: démographie-économie-culture* (Paris: Picard, 1952), p. 110. At that time over 90 percent of Parisian Jews were of Alsatian origin (ibid., pp. 136–37, 63).

6. Vichniac, pp. 8–9, 25; Fraser and Natanson, p. 39.

7. Fraser and Natanson, p. 33; Stokes, p. 8.

8. Interview with André Blumel, later Blum's *chef de cabinet*, 15 May 1962.

9. Interview with Marcel Blum, 25 May 1962. For the story of the care Blum devoted to a blind aunt, see Jules Renard, *Journal* (Paris: Gallimard, 1935), p. 360.

10. Recollections of Robert Blum, in a letter to the author, 25 June 1971.

11. [Jeanne Léon Blum], *Léon Blum, 9 avril 1872–30 mars 1950* ([Paris, 1951]), p. 48.

12. Recollections of Robert Blum.

13. Interview with Marcel Blum.

14. Fraser and Natanson, pp. 26–28.

15. There has been some uncertainty about the extent of her orthodoxy. Fraser and Natanson (pp. 25–26) and Vichniac (p. 10) say she was orthodox and kept a kosher home. Drawing on these sources, Colton (p. 5)

deduces too much. I am convinced by the recollections of Marcel Blum that the most one can say is that she was "religious in her fashion." The only religious traditions that Robert Blum recalls from his grandmother's home are the family dinner on Friday evenings and the use of unleavened bread during Passover.

16. Quoted by Louis Lévy in *Comment ils sont devenus socialistes* (Paris: Editions du *Populaire*, 1932), p. 18. Based on a series of interviews with party leaders, this useful work contains Blum's only extended account of his early socialist formation.

17. Ibid., pp. 17–18; see also Fraser and Natanson, p. 40.

18. Fraser and Natanson, p. 32; interview with Marcel Blum.

19. Fraser and Natanson, pp. 32, 39–40.

20. See ibid., p. 41. The verse is quoted in André Billy, *L'époque 1900* (*1885–1905*) (Paris: Jules Tallandier, 1951), p. 16.

21. Blum, quoted by Lévy, p. 18; Vichniac, p. 12. Stokes (p. 18) says that Blum attended a private elementary school, the Institution Roux, on rue d'Aboukir; Fraser and Natanson (p. 17) say that he was sent "to a local private school, the pension Roux." Blum attended the lycée Charlemagne from 1 October 1882 to 31 July 1888, according to an *attestation de scolarité* dated 25 September 1888 (item 14 in the Bibliothèque Nationale Exposition Léon Blum [1962]). Ziebura (1: 15) incorrectly dates his attendance from 1883.

22. Fraser and Natanson, p. 39.

23. See Alain Silvera, *Daniel Halévy and his Times: A Gentleman-Commoner in the Third Republic* (Ithaca: Cornell University Press, 1966), p. 54, and Maxime Leroy, *Les premiers amis français de Wagner* (Paris: Albin Michel, 1922).

24. Lucien Dintzer, *L'oeuvre littéraire de Léon Blum, ou Blum inconnu* (Lyon: Editions de l'Avenir socialiste, 1937), p. 7. (This book, it must be noted, is an inadequate and uncritical treatment of Blum's literary work.)

25. See the definitions given by Richard Hofstadter in his *Anti-Intellectualism in American Life* (New York: Knopf, 1964), pp. 26–27.

26. See Stokes (pp. 19–20) for a list of Blum's prizes.

27. Rollo Walter Brown, *How the French Boy Learns to Write: A Study in the Teaching of the Mother Tongue* (Cambridge: Harvard University Press, 1924), pp. 31, 33.

28. Ziebura (p. 16) and Colton (p. 8) wrongly date Blum's move to the lycée Henri IV as 1889. Stokes (p. 18) gives the correct year.

29. *L'idée de l'Etat: essai critique sur l'histoire des théories sociales et politiques en France depuis la Révolution* (Paris: Hachette, 1895).

30. "Diplôme de bachelier ès lettres," dated 19 July 1889 (item 16 in the Bibliothèque Nationale Exposition Léon Blum [1962]).

31. Colton, p. 8. The written examination for 1890 is reproduced as an appendix in Robert John Smith, "The Ecole Normale Supérieure in

the Third Republic: A Study of the Classes of 1890–1904" (Ph.D. dissertation, University of Pennsylvania, 1967), pp. 225–27.

32. Smith (p. 14) says that about one in ten was received.

33. This explanation was suggested by Vichniac (p. 15). Blum later reflected on this problem in an impersonal way in his *En lisant: réflexions critiques* (Paris: Ollendorff, 1906), p. 321: "Nothing is worse in the French bourgeoisie than this obstinate tendency of the father and mother to regulate in their thought and fabricate with their hands the happiness that they wish their child to have." Citations from Blum's writings are referred to *L'Oeuvre de Léon Blum* (Paris: Albin Michel, 1954–72) where possible, but all have been verified in the original sources.

34. See Stokes, pp. 22–23; Vichniac, p. 15; Fraser and Natanson, p. 45. Smith (p. 178) estimates that three-fourths of the *normaliens* of Blum's time pursued careers in public education.

35. Blum wrote simply on 28 July 1891: "Aujourd'hui j'ai été refusé à ma licence" ("Ebauche d'une nouvelle. Fragment autographe" [item 19 in Bibliothèque Nationale Exposition Léon Blum (1962)]). Maurice Le Ruel, in "Karl Marx ou Disraeli? Léon Blum vu par un de ses camarades d'études" (*Le Monde illustré*, 13 June 1936, p. 491), said that Blum failed both the examination in July and the *repêchage* in November because they stressed Greek and Latin whereas his strength was in history and philosophy. For other discussions, see Colton (pp. 8–9), Dalby (pp. 28–29), Fraser and Natanson (p. 47), Vichniac (p. 16), and Dintzer (p. 8).

36. Smith, p. 96.

37. The translation is by Fraser and Natanson (pp. 48–50), but I have not seen the original. If Blum indeed found the Ecole Normale too constricting for his literary interests, it is interesting that Durkheim, who attended the school a few years earlier, found it *too* literary and dilettantist (Harry Alpert, *Emile Durkheim and His Sociology* [New York: Columbia University Press, 1939], pp. 18–19).

38. I am not sure exactly when Blum received these degrees but it must have been by mid-1894 at the latest; Colton (p. 12) and Stokes (p. 24) say 1894, but Vichniac (p. 17), Fraser and Natanson (p. 59), and Gregh (p. 87) are vague on this point.

39. *Nouvelles conversations de Goethe avec Eckermann, 1897–1900* (Paris: Editions de la Revue blanche, 1901), pp. 15–16; *L'Oeuvre de Léon Blum*, 1: 203 (hereafter cited as *L'Oeuvre*).

40. *L'Oeuvre*, 1: 203.

41. Fraser and Natanson, pp. 37–38.

42. Interview with Marcel Blum; Romain Rolland, *Le cloître de la rue d'Ulm: journal de Romain Rolland à l'Ecole Normale, 1886–1889* (Paris: Albin Michel, 1952). Thus Blum was not a *condisciple* of Rolland at the Ecole Normale, as Annie Kriegel indicates.

43. According to Fraser and Natanson, Blum had a "genius for friendship" (p. 99).

44. Léon Blum, "Premiers paradoxes sur Renan," *Revue blanche*, 3 (1892): 249.

45. André Gide, *Journal, 1889–1939* (Paris: Nouvelle Revue Française, 1939), p. 397.

46. *L'âge d'airain*, p. 87.

47. Ibid., p. 89; for his reaction on the death of a close friend, see Edmond Sée, *Porto-Riche* (Paris: Firmin-Didot, 1932), pp. 236–37.

48. This is the view of Alfred Fabre-Luce in his *Journal, 1951* (Paris: Amiot-Dumont, 1951), pp. 68–69.

49. Interview with M. and Mme. Paul Grunebaum-Ballin, 4 April 1962. Nonetheless, Blum was not completely uncritical; see Jules Moch, *Rencontres avec . . . Léon Blum* (Paris: Plon, 1970), p. 90.

50. Stokes, pp. 22–23; Colette Audry, *Léon Blum ou la politique du juste: essai* (Paris: René Julliard, 1955), p. 195. The latter was a highly critical opponent within the Socialist party.

51. Fraser and Natanson, p. 101; Fabre-Luce, p. 67; see also Auguste Bréal, *Philippe Berthelot* (Paris: Gallimard, 1937), p. 109.

52. Fraser and Natanson, pp. 45–46; Vichniac, p. 16.

53. Fraser and Natanson, pp. 51–53.

54. Gregh, p. 87.

55. See Fraser and Natanson, p. 16.

56. Jean Schlumberger, *Madeleine et André Gide*, in his *Oeuvres*, vol. 7: (*1944–1961*) (Paris: Gallimard, 1961), p. 259.

57. *L'Oeuvre*, 1: 548 ("Sonnet," *Conque*, no. 3 [May 1891], p. 23):

> Les souvenirs du temps passé restent en nous.
> Nous avons beau prier et pleurer à genoux
> On n'exorcise pas leur mirage rebelle.
>
> Et cela reste en nous comme un parfum trop fort,
> Ou comme un vieux refrain boîteux que l'on épèle. . . .
> —Mon Dieu! Trouverons-nous le repos dans la mort?

58. *L'Oeuvre*, 1: 550 ("Vers: III," *Conque*, no. 9 [November 1891], p. 70):

> Nos espoirs sont ternis; nos désirs sont calmés,
> Mais laissez-moi, les yeux fermés, revoir en songe,
> Les jours enfuis, les rêves morts, les vieux mensonges
> Et croire que jadis nous nous sommes aimés.

59. Dalby's conclusion from an analysis of this poetry that "at the age of twenty, Blum had already formed one of the guiding tenets of his life: 'Cultivate the memory of happy days'" (p. 40), makes no sense. Blum always refused to live in the past.

60. *L'Oeuvre*, 1: 551 (*Banquet*, no. 6 [November 1892], p. 185):

C'est l'été de la Saint-Martin,
C'est la saison des chrysanthèmes.
Il faut taire nos anathèmes
Et sourire aux coups de destin.

Les éclairs du ciel incertain
Forment de bienveillants systèmes.
Si je suis triste, moi qui t'aime,
Des roses s'ouvrent au matin.

L'univers joyeux nous délaisse.
Le ciel rit à notre tristesse,
Le soleil insulte à nos pleurs.

Mais il faut se plier aux choses,
Il faut nous nier nos douleurs,
Puisque l'on voit encore des roses.

61. Fernand Gregh, *L'âge d'or: souvenirs d'enfance et de jeunesse* (Paris: Bernard Grasset, 1947), p. 151. Blum, apparently, had not intended to publish this sonnet, but it was brought to Gregh by a mutual friend and a short-lived quarrel resulted (ibid.). It is nonetheless representative of his published works.

62. Interview with Paul Grunebaum-Ballin.

63. Blum, "Fragment sur l'espérance," *Revue blanche*, 4 (1893): 341–55. Only an extract is reprinted in *L'Oeuvre* (1: 210–11).

64. George D. Painter, *Proust, the Early Years* (Boston: Little, Brown, 1959), pp. 172–73.

65. Both Louys and Régnier married Heredia's daughters.

66. Fraser and Natanson, p. 42. Blum was to be one of the three speakers at the funeral of Anatole France (André Billy, *L'époque contemporaine* [*1905–1930*] [Paris: Jules Tallandier, 1956], p. 223).

67. Fraser and Natanson, p. 56. For Anatole France and the Caillavet salon, see Carter Jefferson, *Anatole France: The Politics of Skepticism* (New Brunswick: Rutgers University Press, 1965), pp. 53–54. For the Caillavet salon, see also Emilien Carassus, *Le snobisme et les lettres françaises de Paul Bourget à Marcel Proust, 1884–1914* (Paris: Armand Colin, 1966), pp. 92–93.

68. Henri Mondor, *Précocité de Valéry* (Paris: Gallimard, 1957), pp. 159–60. Another *normalien* who would have an important political career was a reader of *La Conque*, Edouard Herriot (Michel Soulié, *La vie politique d'Edouard Herriot* [Paris: Armand Colin, 1962], p. 11). On p. 10, Soulié erroneously has Blum making his literary debut in *Ermitage*; Colton makes the correct reference to *La Conque* on p. 10, but on p. 8 he wrongly dates it 1889.

69. Dalby (p. 38) calls *La Conque* a failure because it published only eleven issues.

70. Gide, p. 397. Cf. Jacques Carat, "Léon Blum écrivain," *Paru*, no. 60 (May 1950), p. 56.

71. *L'Oeuvre*, 1: 295.

72. Ziebura (p. 22) is wrong in calling *La Conque* an exclusively symbolist review.

73. Gregh, *L'âge d'or*, pp. 7, 148; Léon Pierre-Quint, *Proust et la stratégie littéraire* (Paris: Corrêa, 1954), pp. 34–35; see also Silvera, pp. 43–45. Dalby (p. 38) confuses *La Conque* and *Le Banquet*. The account of Blum's literary career in Jolly, *Dictionnaire des parlementaires français*, vol. 2, is very unreliable.

74. Robert Dreyfus, *De Monsieur Thiers à Marcel Proust: histoire et souvenirs* (Paris: Plon, 1939), pp. 4, 16; Georges Cattaui, "L'homme [Proust] et l'oeuvre," *Nouvelles littéraires*, 25 July 1939, p. 3. For the salon of Mme. Strauss, see Carassus (pp. 86–87) and Silvera (pp. 45–47).

75. Dreyfus, p. 4.

76. Pierre-Quint, p. 35.

77. Gregh, *L'âge d'or*, p. 151.

78. See chapter 2 below. Contrary to Ziebura (p. 23), the Natansons did not found *La Revue blanche* but rather revived what had originally been a Franco-Belgian publication.

79. Although she says some sensible things about Blum's early prose work, Dalby's lack of comprehension is shown by her reference to them as "rather bizarre writings" (p. 44).

80. Gregh, *L'âge d'or*, p. 151.

81. *Banquet*, no. 4 (June 1892), p. 116.

82. See A[rthur] B[asil] Jackson, *La Revue blanche (1889–1903): origine, influence, bibliographie* (Paris: M. J. Minard, 1960), pp. 56–57.

83. *Revue blanche*, 7 (1894): 404–7.

84. *L'Oeuvre*, 1: 570–77, and *Revue blanche*, 5 (1893): 193–206.

85. *Revue blanche*, 4 (1893): 401–39.

86. Ibid., 5 (1893): 122–36.

87. Henri Peyre, *The Contemporary French Novel* (New York: Oxford University Press, 1955), p. 11.

88. Marcel Thiébaut (*En lisant M. Léon Blum* [Paris: Gallimard, 1937], pp. 36–37) observed this. See Blum's essays from this period: "Fragment sur la gloire," *L'Oeuvre*, 1: 556–62; "Fragment sur la prière," ibid., pp. 562–65; and "Fragment sur l'espérance," *Revue blanche*, 4 (1893): 341–55 (extracted in *L'Oeuvre*, 1: 210–11).

89. "Declamatio suasoria," *Revue blanche*, 3 (1892): 136–37.

90. *L'Oeuvre*, 1: 560–61.

91. Gide, p. 15.

92. Blum, "Declamatio suasoria," *Revue blanche*, 3 (1892): 144.

93. See Jackson, p. 112. For Fénéon, see also James Joll, *The Anarchists* (London: Eyre & Spottiswoode, 1964), pp. 168–69.

94. See Louis Faucon, "Léon Blum et Jules Renard ou les débuts d'une amitié qui fut parfois à sens unique," *Figaro littéraire*, 5 April 1952.

NOTES TO CHAPTER TWO

1. Blum's work as a literary critic has received very uneven attention. Of the two most thorough treatments, Thiébaut is unremittingly hostile and Dintzer is uncritically admiring. Neither is without value, but neither is sufficiently objective. Of the recent studies, Ziebura is interested only in how Blum's criticism helps us understand the later Socialist leader, and he does not adequately locate Blum in the literary milieu of the 1890s, whereas Dalby is evidently unfamiliar with the literary scene, fails to distinguish between Blum's literary and drama criticism, and relies too heavily on Blum's published collections of reviews, which do not adequately represent his early work. Colton deals only briefly with Blum's literary work.

2. *L'Oeuvre*, 1: 260.

3. Ibid., p. 330.

4. "Nouvelles conversations avec Eckermann," *Revue blanche*, 8 (1895): 355–56.

5. Ibid.

6. See Jackson (pp. 24–25) for some of the others. Jackson's is the most useful book on the *Revue blanche*.

7. Francis Jourdain, "Du côté de la *Revue blanche*," *Europe*, no. 112–13 (April–May 1955), p. 107.

8. Pierre Veber, "Jadis," *Nouvelles littéraires*, 21 March 1936, p. 3. Jean Schopfer wrote under the pen-name Claude Anet.

9. Misia Sert, *Misia* (Paris: Gallimard, 1952), p. 39. For the "snobbism" of the circle of *La Revue blanche*, see Carassus, p. 176.

10. See Jackson's chapter on Thadée Natanson and the art criticism of *La Revue blanche*. See also Fritz Herrmann, *Die "Revue blanche" und die "Nabis"* (2 vols.; Munich: Mikrokopie, 1959).

11. Fraser and Natanson, pp. 100–101; recollections of Robert Blum (which differ somewhat from those of Natanson). An obituary notice on Cortot in "Point du vue: Images du monde" (22 June 1962), a color supplement to *Maine libre* (Le Mans, 23 June 1962), credited Blum with having launched Cortot's career in France.

12. Renard, p. 437.

13. See the comments of Jackson (pp. 110–15 et passim) on the "esprit *Revue blanche*"; see also his chapter on the reasons for the end

of the journal. For a hostile commentary on this spirit, see Julien Benda, *La jeunesse d'un clerc* (Paris: Gallimard, 1936), pp. 208–9; for a comment on Benda's comment, see Billy, *L'époque 1900*, p. 120. Dalby (p. 38) calls *La Revue blanche* the "last major organ of Symbolism" and cites four non-symbolist prose writers as examples.

14. Address to the American Club of Paris on 15 May 1936, reprinted in Léon Blum, *L'exercice du pouvoir. Discours prononcés de mai 1936 à janvier 1937* (Paris: Gallimard, 1937), p. 125.

15. Alexandre, the oldest, had the business mind and supplied most of the financial support; Thadée, a complex character, was most deeply involved in the review; Louis-Alfred, who wrote under the pseudonym Alfred Athis, was the most talented and later was drama critic of *L'Humanité* for over a decade. See Jackson, pp. 28–32; Veber, *Nouvelles littéraires*, 21 March 1936, p. 3.

16. See Jackson, p. 6.

17. Most assimilated Parisian Jews were of Alsatian origin. Polish Jews who joined the ranks of the assimilated, such as the Natansons, were rare.

18. René Wellek, "Hippolyte Taine's Literary Theory and Criticism," *Criticism: A Quarterly for Literature and the Arts*, 1 (1959): 136.

19. Brunetière, "Après une visite au Vatican," *Revue des deux mondes*, 1 January 1895, pp. 97–118, cited by Victor Brombert in *The Intellectual Hero: Studies in the French Novel, 1880–1955* (Philadelphia: Lippincott, 1961), p. 26. See also Billy, *L'époque 1900*, pp. 142–44.

20. "La jeunesse," *Journal des débats*, 19 April 1890.

21. Lévy, p. 21.

22. Cf. the similar views of Henri Peyre in *The Failures of Criticism* (Ithaca: Cornell University Press, 1967), p. 20.

23. For a view of the criticism of the period, see ibid., pp. 118–19.

24. *L'Oeuvre*, 1: 8–9. See also Blum's remarks in ibid. (p. 4) and in *Revue blanche* (12 [1897]: 325–26, and 11 [1896]: 382). Cf. *L'Oeuvre*, 1: 29.

25. For a somewhat pedestrian study of these critics, see Alexandre Belis, *La critique française à la fin du XIXᵉ siècle: Ferdinand Brunetière —Emile Faguet—Jules Lemaître—Anatole France* (Paris: Librairie universitaire J. Gamber, 1926).

26. André Gide titled a volume of his literary criticism *Prétextes*.

27. "Nouvelles conversations avec Eckermann, I: sur la critique," *Revue blanche*, 6 (1894): 443.

28. Ibid., pp. 445–46.

29. Ibid., pp. 446–47.

30. *L'Oeuvre*, 1: 31.

31. See, for example, *Revue blanche*, 12 (1897): 101.

32. Peyre, *Failures of Criticism*, p. 191.

33. The just observation of Jules Bertaut, in Eugène Monfort, ed., *Vingt-cinq ans de littérature française* (Paris: Librairie de France, n.d.), 1: 246.

34. *L'Oeuvre*, 1: 247.

35. Ibid., p. 1.

36. See, for example, *Revue blanche*, 15 (1898): 69–70.

37. Blum later introduced important considerations of the author's life into his study of Stendhal (*Stendhal et le beylisme*, Paris: Ollendorff, 1914). See chapter 9 below.

38. Blum was ready to admit the wholly relativist position that the critic's work has no exterior efficacy or pedagogic value (*Revue blanche*, 6 [1894]: 444, 447).

39. The remark was made by his successor at *La Revue blanche*, André Gide; see ibid., 21 (1900): 232. See also Jackson, p. 79.

40. Blum would have agreed with Henri Peyre (*Failures of Criticism*, p. 2) that the critic should "strive for humility."

41. See the remarks of Paul Leclercq in "Memories of Léon Blum," *The Nineteenth Century and After*, 147 (1950): 379. See, for example, Blum, "Les livres," *Revue blanche*, 20 (1899): 553.

42. See, for example, Blum, "Les livres," *Revue blanche*, 19 (1899): 636–37.

43. Blum, "Jules Renard," *Mercure de France*, 15 (1895): 97.

44. "Un critique," *Comoedia*, 1 July 1910.

45. See, for example, *L'Oeuvre*, 1: 271.

46. See Jackson, p. 80. The age of many of these authors has been checked and the average age was approximately thirty-five; moreover, the average age of those Blum followed closely was lower than those to whom he gave only a casual look.

47. *L'Oeuvre*, 1: 16.

48. See Jackson, p. 60.

49. "Nouvelles conversations avec Eckermann, V: à l'Académie," *Revue blanche*, 9 (1895): 27.

50. Ibid., 6 (1894): 442–43. Abridged in *L'Oeuvre*, 1: 228.

51. *L'Oeuvre*, 1: 198.

52. The only exception seems to have been Romain Rolland, and Blum may have had personal reasons for not wanting to speak of him, since he certainly knew him.

53. Ibid.

54. Ibid. This partiality was not confined to contributors to *La Revue blanche*.

55. See the article "Naturisme" in *Oxford Companion to French Literature* (Oxford: Oxford University Press, 1959), p. 509.

56. *L'Oeuvre*, 1: 36–37. See Jackson, p. 83. Blum did not mention

that Bouhélier rejected his view of the value of foreign influences and called Jaurès a demagogue. See the manifesto of Saint-Georges de Bouhélier in Bonner Mitchell, *Les manifestes littéraires de la belle époque, 1886–1914: anthologie critique* (Paris: Seghers, 1966), pp. 51–61.

57. *L'Oeuvre*, 1: 37.

58. See Billy, *L'époque 1900*, pp. 206–14. For Gregh's manifesto, see Mitchell, pp. 65–74.

59. *L'Oeuvre*, 1: 37.

60. Ibid., p. 61; *Revue blanche*, 19 (1899): 76–77.

61. *L'Oeuvre*, 1: 37.

62. See chapter 6 below.

63. *L'Oeuvre*, 1: 303.

64. Ibid., pp. 21–23.

65. *Revue blanche*, 14 (1897): 155.

66. *L'Oeuvre*, 1: 277.

67. Ibid., pp. 41–42.

68. *Revue blanche*, 14 (1897): 230–31. The expression is Blum's.

69. *L'Oeuvre*, 1: 277.

70. Blum's first consideration of the "social novel" appeared in *La Revue blanche* (12 [1897]: 473–75), but it did not become a conscious preoccupation until he was writing for *L'Humanité* (1905). See chapter 6 below.

71. *Revue blanche*, 12 (1897): 146.

72. *L'Oeuvre*, 1: 69.

73. See Emile Henriot, *Maîtres d'hier et contemporains: courrier littéraire XIXe–XXe siècles*, vol. 3 (Paris: Albin Michel, 1955), p. 301.

74. See, for example, Gide, p. 228. This is also the opinion of Jackson (pp. 57, 80, 84–85, 87).

75. Renard seems to have been unable to make up his mind about Blum. In 1905, he told the latter that he was too intelligent to be a good judge of art (*Journal*, p. 647). In 1909, he counseled Blum to trust and follow his intelligence in his reviewing (Renard, *Correspondance* [Paris: Flammarion (1954)], p. 398). Renard was very sure of his own taste, but equally unsure of his intelligence; he may have been unconsciously projecting Blum as a sort of reverse image of himself, thus deprecating Blum's taste.

76. See, for example, Georges le Cardonnel, "Une renaissance française," *Mercure de France*, 104 (1913): 257–61, and Emile Faguet, "M. Léon Blum," *Revue latine*, 6 (1907): 65–78.

77. *Revue blanche*, 6 (1894): 445.

78. Ibid., 12 (1897): 188–89.

79. "Le goût classique," ibid., 6 (1894): 29–40.

80. Including Ziebura (pp. 25–26).

81. Thus Audry (p. 19) is quite wrong, having for ideological reasons read her own meaning into what Blum said.

82. *Journal*, p. 200.

83. Blum, *Revue blanche*, 6 (1894): 31.

84. Later, as a drama critic, he interested himself almost exclusively in new works, although he delivered lectures on Corneille and Shakespeare (*L'Oeuvre*, 2: 349–74).

85. *Revue blanche*, 6 (1894): 32; Blum even criticized a friend for sloppiness (ibid., 19 [1899]: 554).

86. Quoted by Alphonse Albalat in *Les ennemis de l'Art d'écrire* (Paris: Librairie Universelle, 1905), p. 203. Blum had criticized Albalat's method of teaching writing (through "correction" of the masters) as harmful to creativity. See ibid., pp. 195–200.

87. *Revue blanche*, 6 (1894): 32.

88. *L'Oeuvre*, 1: 233.

89. Ibid., pp. 310–13. For a criticism of Blum's viewpoint, see A. G. Lehmann, *The Symbolist Aesthetic in France, 1885–1895* (2d ed.; Oxford: Basil Blackwell, 1968), pp. 292–93.

90. *Revue blanche*, 11 (1896): 335 (abridged in *L'Oeuvre*, 1: 312). Blum praised intentional difficulty on the part of a writer who nonetheless meant to be understood (*L'Oeuvre*, 1: 248).

91. Blum was more generous to the symbolist poets. While they, too, tended to exalt obscurity, he praised Mallarmé for having preserved a certain simplicity even in his most *recherché* works (*Revue blanche*, 17 [1898]: 235).

92. At other times Blum also mentioned Henri de Régnier, who was perhaps less a symbolist in prose than he was in verse: "What is sure is that all conceptions of art have been able to inspire works of equal value, and no one will forget that for the most recent tendency of French art M. de Régnier has furnished in verse and in prose its most perfect expression" (*L'Oeuvre*, 1: 315). For a revival of interest in Schwob, see John A. Green's review of George Trembley's *Marcel Schwob: faussaire de la nature* (Geneva: Droz, 1969) in the *French Review*, 44 (1971): 613.

93. *Revue blanche*, 6 (1894): 31.

94. For the history of "sincerity" in literature, see the delightful and illuminating work of Henri Peyre, *Literature and Sincerity* (New Haven: Yale University Press, 1963).

95. *L'Oeuvre*, 1: 315.

96. *Revue blanche*, 6 (1894): 30–31. Blum's remark on France is in *L'Oeuvre*, 1: 9. Blum's emphasis on sincerity could even lead him to applaud a writer whose style did not appeal to him—Zola, for example. For Blum, a classical writer was a man who was in tune with his own time.

97. *L'Oeuvre*, 1: 18. Blum spoke of his philosophy as being close to

that of the Stoics and Epicureans. Pierre Louys's failing was to think of himself as a Greek when he was only an Alexandrian.

98. Ibid., pp. 293–94.

99. Ibid., p. 73. Peyre (*Failures of Criticism*, p. 123) overlooks Blum when he says all critics except Edmond Jaloux ignored Gide's *Nourritures terrestres.*

100. *L'Oeuvre*, 1: 321.

101. For related discussion, see *Revue blanche*, 19 (1899): 391.

102. See chapters 4 and 6 below.

103. "Nouvelles conversations avec Eckermann," ibid., 24 (1901): 358–63.

NOTES TO CHAPTER THREE

1. At that time about 10 percent of the *avocats* at the Paris bar were Jewish, and over half of these were of Alsatian background (Roblin, pp. 105–6; see also André Spire's essay "Les juifs au Conseil d'Etat" in his *Souvenirs à bâtons rompus* [Paris: Albin Michel, 1962]).

2. See Fraser and Natanson, pp. 60–61.

3. The best introduction is Charles E. Freedeman, *The Conseil d'Etat in Modern France* (New York: Columbia University Press, 1961). Also useful are the article "Conseil d'Etat" in the *Grande Encyclopédie* and *Le Conseil d'Etat: livre jubilaire publié pour commémorer son cent cinquantième anniversaire: 4 nivose an VIII–24 décembre 1949* (Paris: Recueil Sirey, 1952) (hereafter cited as *Livre jubilaire*).

4. See Georges Langrod, "The French Council of State: Its Role in the Formulation and Implementation of Administrative Law," *American Political Science Review*, 49 (1955): 677. See also Charles Seignobos, "La séparation des pouvoirs," *Revue de Paris*, 15 February 1895, pp. 718, 725.

5. "Conseil d'Etat," *Grande Encyclopédie*, 12: 481–82. For the organizational reforms of 1910, see René Brugère, *Le Conseil d'Etat, son personnel et ses formations: évolution—tendances* (Toulouse: Imprimerie Toulousaine, 1910), p. 132.

6. Law of 1 July 1887; *Recueil des lois et règlements concernant le Conseil d'Etat* (Paris: Imprimerie nationale, 1912), p. 61. These examinations were replaced in 1945 by courses at the Ecole Nationale d'Administration (Langrod, p. 679).

7. Fraser and Natanson, pp. 60–61.

8. For the difficulty of the competition, see Brugère, p. 79. The first elimination round was a six-hour written examination and a fifteen-

minute oral exposition. Those who passed this stage went on to another six-hour written examination and a final forty-five-minute public interrogation by the jury (*Recueil ... Conseil d'État* [1912], pp. 67–70). For the subject matter of the examinations, see ibid., pp. 66–67.

9. *Journal officiel de la République française*, 18 December 1895, p. 7079.

10. Fraser and Natanson (p. 59) say that Blum attended some classes there. For the école, see Freedeman, pp. 50–51.

11. For the undemocratic character of the low level of pay, see Brugère (pp. 78–81) and Freedeman (p. 38).

12. Fraser and Natanson, pp. 60–61.

13. Ibid., pp. 61–63, 93; Stokes, p. 11. Lise Blum died in 1931 and Blum married Thérèse Pereira in 1932; after her death in 1938, he married Jeanne Levilliers Humbert in 1943, who survives him. For Blum's marriages, see Dalby (pp. 30–33) and Colton (pp. 13–14).

14. Blum was married on 19 February 1896 (family record). Fraser and Natanson, p. 105; Vichniac, p. 65. See Jules Renard, *Correspondance*, p. 340, for a sidelight.

15. See *Grande Encyclopédie*, 12: 480.

16. See chapter 4 below.

17. For the salary, see *Grande Encyclopédie*, 12: 480. Blum was one of six who were named to newly created positions (*Journal officiel*, 10 May 1900, p. 2930).

18. For the duties of *auditeur de première classe*, see *Grande Encyclopédie*, 12: 480.

19. *Annuaire du Conseil d'État* (1903), pp. 16, 19. See Freedeman, pp. 39–40.

20. I think that Dalby (p. 60) and Nathaniel Greene, in *Crisis and Decline: The French Socialist Party in the Popular Front Era* (Ithaca: Cornell University Press, 1969 [p. 13]), exaggerate when they say that Blum was promoted rapidly.

21. As of 10 November 1907 (date given the author by the Bibliothécaire-archiviste of the Conseil d'Etat). The promotion again doubled Blum's salary, this time to 8,000 francs (*Grande Encyclopédie*, 12: 480). Jolly (1: 635) wrongly dates this promotion as 1910.

22. Date supplied by Bibliothécaire-archiviste of the Conseil d'Etat.

23. *Grande Encyclopédie*, 12: 490.

24. Ibid.

25. *Journal officiel*, 29 January 1910, p. 821.

26. *Grande Encyclopédie*, 12: 479; see also Brugère, pp. 75–78.

27. Georges Cahen-Salvador, "Un grand commissaire du gouvernement: Jean Romieu," in *Livre jubilaire*, p. 323.

28. Ibid.

29. René Worms, *La juridiction du Conseil d'Etat et ses tendances*

actuelles (Paris: Giard et Brière, 1906), pp. 4–5. The second suggestion is mentioned in Freedeman (p. 189).

30. See the comment by Georges Bonnet, quoted by Georges Lefranc in *Jaurès et le socialisme des intellectuels* (Paris: Aubier-Montaigne, 1968), p. 246, and by Colton (p. 13). Blum's conclusions in *Epoux Lemonnier* (26 August 1918) have been recently republished in M. Long, P. Weil, and G. Braibant, eds., *Les grands arrêts de la jurisprudence administrative* (5th ed.; Paris: Sirey, 1969), pp. 144–55.

31. Blum's contributions can be studied only in the text of his "conclusions," published either in *Recueil général des lois et des arrêts en matière civile, criminelle, administrative et de droit public* (Paris: Recueil Sirey, 1910–14) (which is known as the *Recueil Sirey*) or in *Recueil des arrêts du Conseil d'Etat statuant aux contentieux, des décisions du tribunal des conflits et de la cour des comptes* (Paris: Recueil Sirey, 1910–14) (which is known as the *Recueil Lebon*). The conclusions published in these annuals, while numerous, are only a small percentage of those Blum delivered. On the lack of private papers relating to his judicial career, see Pierre Juvigny, "Une grand commissaire du gouvernement: Léon Blum," in *Livre jubilaire* (p. 337); see also Cahen-Salvador (p. 324). Dalby (pp. 59, 294) betrays a complete lack of understanding of the workings of the Conseil d'Etat and Blum's functions within it.

32. See Worms (pp. 6, 24–25), who noted that this power was carefully limited to recourse against administrative acts, not acts of a political nature. See also Freedeman, pp. 116–17, 126–27.

33. Ziebura (p. 160) stresses this aspect of Blum's work.

34. According to Worms (p. 11), a Catholic spokesman expressed greater confidence in the impartiality of the Conseil than in that of the civil tribunals. See Freedeman, pp. 102–3. Blum's friend Paul Grunebaum-Ballin had been detached from the Conseil to aid Briand in formulating the legislation. See Joseph Barthélemy, *Essai sur le travail parlementaire* (Paris, 1934), p. 180 (cited in Freedeman, p. 78).

35. *Election d'Aïn-Berïda*, in *Recueil Lebon* (1910), pp. 145–46; *Abbé Bouchon; Abbé Hardel*, ibid. (1911), pp. 341–50. For the cases of military justice considered in the following paragraph, see *Sieur Desreumeaux*, ibid., pp. 507–25, and *Bergey*, ibid., pp. 1186–99.

36. For a good definition, see Freedeman (p. 134); see also Langrod (p. 678).

37. Langrod, p. 678. See the remarks of Maurice Hauriou in *Recueil Sirey* (1911), 3: 89–90.

38. This conclusion was reprinted in *L'Oeuvre*, 2: 593–99.

39. *Omer Decugis, Dubois et autres*, in *Recueil Lebon* (1911), pp. 797–807.

40. See Langrod, p. 678; but cf. Freedeman, pp. 152–53.

41. *Ministre des travaux publics c. Compagnie générale française des tramways*, in *Recueil Lebon* (1910), pp. 216–25.

42. Ibid.; see Juvigny, p. 338.

43. See Talcott Parsons, *The Structure of Social Action* (2d ed.; Glencoe, Ill.: Free Press, 1949), pp. 311–23.

44. *Recueil Sirey* (1911), 3: 1–2.

45. For the views of the opposition on municipal socialism, see Pierre Mimin, *Le socialisme municipal devant le Conseil d'Etat* (Paris: Recueil Sirey, 1911).

46. *Commune de Mesle-sur-Sarthe*, in *Recueil Lebon* (1911), pp. 137–40, 143.

47. See Freedeman, pp. 79, 106.

48. Roger Latournerie, "Essai sur les méthodes juridictionnelles du Conseil d'Etat," in *Livre jubilaire*, p. 257.

49. *Lacan et Lasserre*, in *Recueil Sirey* (1913), 3: 162–64. An anonymous commentator noted that Blum failed to find a precedent for his view. See also Blum's unsuccessful efforts to push the Conseil in *Aubry*, ibid. (1912), pp. 156–58.

50. Worms, p. 25.

51. *Sieurs Boussuge, Guépin et autres*, in *Recueil Lebon* (1912), pp. 1128–36. Hauriou (*Recueil Sirey* [1914], 2: 33–36) noted that Blum was thereby going against the trend of current jurisprudence.

52. See Juvigny, p. 339.

53. Quoted by Edouard Dolléans, *Histoire du mouvement ouvrier*, vol. 2: *1871–1936* (Paris: Armand Colin, 1939), p. 7.

54. See Juvigny, p. 337. Blum was also involved in an important case concerning the Conseil Supérieur du Travail (*Sieur Cotton*, in *Recueil Lebon* [1912], pp. 696–704).

55. *Sieur d'Azincourt et autres* and *Sieur Asselineau*, in *Recueil Lebon* (1913), pp. 678–90, and *Recueil Sirey* (1918–19), 3: 1–8.

56. Gustave Téry tried to make capital of the slowness of the Conseil in one of his anti-Semitic attacks on Blum: "Simple requête au maître des requêtes Léon Blum à seule fin d'être enfin jugé," *Oeuvre*, 16 March 1911, pp. 8–14.

57. In 1909, for example, there were 600 new pension cases and 1,160 *recours pour excès de pouvoirs*. Each of the eight *commissaires du gouvernement* would have had to handle 220 of these cases just to keep the backlog from growing. See n. 59 below.

58. Comments and recollections of Robert Blum.

59. Vichniac (p. 26) noted: "His function was all the more agreeable to him in that it did not demand a constant presence. He could prepare his work at home or at the library. He only had to attend the afternoon meetings and the sessions of the commissions where he had to read his reports."

The following table was compiled from the *Recueil Lebon:*

Year	Sessions per Year	No. of Conclusions Prepared by Blum
1910	14	152
1911	16	120
1912	17	141
1913	15	134
1914	12	115
Averages: 15		137

For the lightness of the workload, see Spire, p. 59, but see also p. 61, n. 2.

60. Dalby (p. 59) is certainly wrong in asserting that Blum's experience on the Conseil was important in directing him toward "a legalistic approach to political problems." If anything, that experience taught him something of the limitations of legal processes as a means to social reform. Curiously, Ziebura (pp. 157–60), who accurately notes some of the qualities and attitudes in Blum's legal work, does not appreciate the value of this practical experience, or see how it complemented—as well as paralleled—his literary work. Nor does he, I think, fully appreciate the vigor it took to pursue these dual careers. A more just appreciation is that of Pierre-Olivier Lapie in *De Léon Blum à de Gaulle: le caractère et le pouvoir* (Paris: Fayard, 1971), p. 13.

61. See Vichniac, p. 97. Blum's prominence was exaggerated by Alexandre Zévaès in "Léon Blum, écrivain," *Nouvelles littéraires*, 6 June 1936. Blum was named a *conseiller d'Etat honoraire* on 4 November 1932, when that designation was created (information supplied by the Bibliothécaire-archiviste of the Conseil d'Etat). For Blum's hat, see Fraser and Natanson (p. 96); Jacques Chastenet, *La Belle Epoque: la société sous M. Fallières* ([Paris]: Bibliothèque historique mondiale [1958]), p. 45; Léon Daudet, *Souvenirs des milieux littéraires, politiques, artistiques et medicaux*, vol. 2: *Au temps de Judas—Vers le roi—Alphonse Daudet* (Paris: Nouvelle librairie nationale, 1926), p. 72.

NOTES TO CHAPTER FOUR

1. Ziebura's treatment of Blum's early socialism is extensive but highly analytical; it stresses the content of his socialist thought but reveals less of the man than either Colton or Dalby. Dalby's chapter on this subject, though not completely accurate, is the best part of her treatment of Blum's early careers. Colton's compressed handling of these years is skillful; he stresses the impact of the Dreyfus affair more than that of

the unity movement. Ziebura is the best of the three in placing Blum in the context of the socialist movement.

2. Dalby, p. 21.

3. Quoted by Lévy, p. 17.

4. Ibid., p. 18; see chapter 1 above.

5. Annie Kriegel, in *Aux origines du communisme français, 1914–1920* (Paris: Mouton, 1964), 2: 797, rightly points out that this essential blend of charity and justice was typical of many Jewish families.

6. This incident is recounted by Vichniac (pp. 19–20). See also Fraser and Natanson, pp. 80, 94.

7. Interview with Marcel Blum.

8. Blum, *Pour être socialiste* (Paris: Librairie du Parti socialiste et de l'Humanité, 1919), p. 4.

9. Daniel Halévy, *Pays parisiens* (Paris: Bernard Grasset, 1932), p. 165.

10. "Isolated by my 'bourgeois'—very petit bourgeois—birth, and then by my education, from the spectacle of working-class life . . ." (Blum, "L'idéal socialiste," *Revue de Paris*, 1 May 1924, pp. 93–94).

11. Lévy, p. 18; cf. Stokes, p. 148.

12. Lévy, p. 18; Thiébaut, p. 52.

13. The quotation that follows is from Blum, *Revue de Paris*, 1 May 1924, pp. 92–93.

14. See, for example, Spire, p. 43.

15. Blum's parents liked to recount an incident in which he surprised them with a number of precocious questions about political matters (interview with Marcel Blum).

16. *L'âge d'airain*, p. 86.

17. According to Fraser and Natanson, p. 54.

18. "Les progrès de l'apolitique en France," *Revue blanche*, 3 (1892): 10–21. Kriegel (2: 798) and Colton (p. 16) exaggerate when they call this article an anarchist credo.

19. *Revue blanche*, 3 (1892): 20.

20. Lévy, p. 21.

21. See Jacques Chastenet, *Histoire de la troisième République*, vol. 3: *1893–1906* (Paris: Hachette, 1955), pp. 58–59.

22. For the trial, see ibid., p. 63; for Fénéon, see Jackson, pp. 95–100.

23. Lévy, pp. 18, 21.

24. *Revue blanche*, 3 (1892): 21.

25. "Les revues," ibid., 4 (1894): 191–97. Kriegel (2: 798) exaggerates the remnant of Blum's anarchist inclinations by quoting a favorable remark from his 1900 review of Max Stirner out of context. The review, as a whole, is a socialist-oriented critique of Stirner's ultra-individualism.

26. Lévy, p. 21. Daniel Ligou, in *Histoire du socialisme en France, 1871–1961* (Paris: Presses Universitaires de France, 1962), p. 99,

quotes C. E. Labrousse as saying that in the 1890s "in the eyes of France the extreme Left was not Jules Guesde, but Clemenceau."

27. The role of Herr in French socialism has been detailed, and his influence somewhat exaggerated, by his colleague, Professor Charles Andler, in *Vie de Lucien Herr (1864–1926)* (Paris: Rieder, 1932). For a less friendly but extremely biased view, see Hubert Bourgin, *De Jaurès à Léon Blum: L'Ecole normale et la politique* (Paris: Arthème Fayard, 1938). Smith (pp. 150–51) estimates that during the period 1890–1904 no more than one-fourth of the students became socialists.

28. Lévy, p. 21; Léon Blum, *Jean Jaurès, conférence donnée le 16 février 1933 au Théâtre des Ambassadeurs* (Paris: Librairie populaire, éditions du Parti socialiste, S.F.I.O., 1933), p. 28.

29. Fraser and Natanson (p. 46) claim that Blum was introduced to socialist ideas by Louis Revelin at the Ecole Normale and later through the Association des Etudiants Collectivistes. This group (affiliated with the Parti Ouvrier Français) was founded in 1892, while Blum was at the Sorbonne (Alexandre Zévaès, *Histoire du socialisme et du communisme en France de 1871 à 1947* [Paris: Editions France-Empire, 1947], p. 234). Zévaès—no admirer of Blum—does not mention him among the members in ibid. (p. 235) or in his *Notes et souvenirs d'un militant* (Paris: Marcel Rivière, 1915), p. 55. Colton (p. 9) cautiously asserts that Blum was "introduced to Marxist ideas by fellow students." Blum later denied having had any contact with socialism while he was in school (Lévy, p. 21). Elie Halévy (cited by Smith, pp. 149–50) indicated that he knew of no socialists at the Ecole Normale when he was there, from 1889 to 1892. Smith (pp. 72–77), in a good discussion of Herr and his influence, indicated that he had less impact on aesthetically inclined students than on the more academically oriented.

30. Lévy, p. 21. Andler also published two articles in *Revue blanche* (see Ernest Tonnelat, *Charles Andler, sa vie et son oeuvre* [Paris: Les Belles Lettres, n.d.], p. 54).

31. Lévy, p. 21.

32. *L'Oeuvre*, 1: 240–41.

33. Lévy, p. 22; Blum said of Herr that "with him conviction became evidence" (*L'Oeuvre*, 4–2: 521).

34. Blum, ibid.

35. Herr was at that time a member of the Allemanist group, according to Bracke (*Revue socialiste*, n.s., no. 38–39 [1950], p. 6); see also Lévy, p. 21.

36. Blum, in "Première et dernière rencontres avec Jaurès" (*Populaire*, 31 July 1937, and *L'Oeuvre*, 4–2: 479), said that they met in October 1897 but that he could not remember whether it was at Herr's or Jaurès's apartment. But earlier he told Lévy (p. 22) that the first meeting was in 1896. Cf. Fraser and Natanson, p. 64, and Marcel

Auclair, *La vie de Jean Jaurès, ou la France d'avant 1914* (Paris: Editions du Seuil, 1954), p. 311.

37. Blum, *Jean Jaurès . . .* , p. 10.

38. See Vichniac, p. 52. Kriegel (2: 798) rightly says that their relationships were never those of "maître à disciple." Blum's style of adherence was clearly his own; he did not have Jaurès's total commitment until after 1914. Bracke (in Blum, *L'Oeuvre*, 1: 341) also insists that Blum was never the pupil of Jaurès. Dalby (pp. 166–67) has drawn the conclusion from such testimony that Blum's influence on Jaurès may have been as great as that of Jaurès on Blum.

39. Blum, *Jean Jaurès . . .* , p. 9.

40. Blum's work was his *Souvenirs sur l'affaire* (Paris: Gallimard, 1935) (*L'Oeuvre*, 4–2: 513–78).

41. Vichniac, p. 32.

42. Of the many works that discuss the Dreyfus affair, Hannah Arendt's *The Origins of Totalitarianism* (2d ed.; New York: Meridian Books, 1958), has had the greatest influence on the author's interpretation. The most balanced general account of the affair is Douglas Johnson's *France and the Dreyfus Affair* (New York: Walker, 1967). Equally scholarly, but less convincing, is Guy Chapman's *The Dreyfus Case: A Reassessment* (London: Rupert Hart-Davis, 1955). For the Dreyfus affair and the situation of the Jews in France, see Robert F. Byrnes, *Antisemitism in Modern France*, vol. 1: *The Prologue to the Dreyfus Affair* (New Brunswick: Rutgers University Press, 1950) (the second volume has not appeared), and Michael R. Marrus, *The Politics of Assimilation: A Study of the French Jewish Community at the Time of the Dreyfus Affair* (Oxford: Oxford University Press, 1971). The popular work by Nicholas Halasz, *Captain Dreyfus: The Story of a Mass Hysteria* (New York: Simon & Schuster, 1955), does not distinguish adequately between fact and speculation. For further bibliography, see Johnson and Chapman.

43. See also Andler, p. 186.

44. See ibid., p. 116.

45. *L'Oeuvre*, 4–2: 545–46; both Louys and Valéry subscribed to the infamous Henry monument (Billy, *L'époque 1900*, p. 454).

46. See Chastenet, *Troisième République*, 3: 118.

47. Renard, *Journal*, p. 320.

48. Gregh, *L'âge d'or*, pp. 290–92. For the politics of Anatole France during the affair, see Jefferson, pp. 94–111.

49. Blum's observation (*L'Oeuvre*, 4–2: 544).

50. Un juriste, "Le procès," *Revue blanche*, 15 (1898): 401–14, and *L'Oeuvre*, 1: 343–58.

51. According to Zévaès (*Histoire du socialisme*, p. 264), the Zola trial finally convinced Jaurès to act.

52. Protest in *L'Aurore* in support of Zola (Billy, *L'époque 1900*, p. 449); petition in *Siècle* (ibid., p. 453).

53. See Dintzer, p. 21.

54. See Zévaès, *Nouvelles littéraires*, 6 June 1936.

55. Labori's commitment to the affair ruined *La Revue du Palais* through its subsequent loss of contributors and subscribers. It was rescued by Mathieu Dreyfus and Emile Strauss, who bought Labori's controlling interest and changed the name. *La Grande revue* had a long and success-ful career. See Marguerite-Fernand Labori, *Labori, ses notes manuscrites, sa vie* (Paris: Victor Attinger, 1947), pp. xxiv, 79, 81–82.

56. Some of Blum's friends have claimed that he was excessively modest in his assessment of his role, for example, Fraser and Natanson (p. 90). On the other hand, Mme. Labori (p. 356, n. 1) claimed that Blum exaggerated his importance. Blum's own version is the most plausible.

57. *L'Oeuvre*, 4–2: 568.

58. Déroulède, naturally, was acquitted by a Parisian jury.

59. See Zévaès, *Histoire du socialisme*, p. 274; Stokes, p. 69.

60. Blum ended the narrative of his *Souvenirs* with Henry's suicide and did not allude to the demonstration. He made a deposition for the parliamentary inquiry, according to Andler (p. 145).

61. Chapman (pp. 297–99) has tried to exculpate the judges.

62. Chapman systematically played down the role of anti-Semitism, but though he has shown that there were other forces at work, his over-all interpretation is not convincing.

63. Arendt, p. 95.

64. Byrnes (p. 98) argued that the decline of religion among Jews was a factor in this indifference, but the examples he cited were men who had left the faith but were ardent Dreyfusards. For the reaction of French Jews to the affair, see also Marrus (pp. 211–42).

65. Quoted by Arendt, p. 117.

66. See ibid., p. 106.

67. *L'Oeuvre*, 1: 259; but after their political paths diverged, Blum was more suspicious of Clemenceau's motivation in the affair (ibid., 4–2: 542–43).

68. See ibid., 1: 235–37, and Arendt, p. 91.

69. The anti-Semite thinks that, because he sees people only as Jews or gentiles, all Jews must do likewise (see, e.g., Georges Suarez, *Briand, sa vie, son oeuvre*, vol. 1: *Le révolté circonspect 1862–1904* [Paris: Plon, 1938], p. 321).

70. Thus Blumel (p. 7) exaggerated when he said that "one of the two motivations" that led Blum to socialism was his "reaction against anti-Semitism."

71. See Pierre Aubery, *Milieux juifs de la France contemporaine à travers leurs écrivains* (Paris: Plon, 1957), p. 131.

72. See Arendt, p. 118.

73. For Blum's reflections, see *L'Oeuvre*, 1: 263–64.

74. See Kurt Lewin, *Resolving Social Conflicts: Selected Papers on Group Dynamics* (New York: Harper, 1948), pp. 157, 159.

75. Ibid. Dalby (p. 92) rightly points out that Blum understood people in a social position similar to his own and that this, rather than any presumed "Jewish solidarity," accounts for the high proportion of Jews among his friends.

76. See Blumel, p. 7; Aubery, p. 308.

77. See ibid., p. 4, and Marrus, p. 163 et passim.

78. Quoted by Blumel (p. 13); Aubery (p. 325) rightly emphasized that this statement was made after Vichy and Buchenwald. Blumel (p. 11) admitted that Blum was not a Zionist until after World War I. It is doubtful that he was ever, properly speaking, a Zionist (interview with Grunebaum-Ballin).

79. A just observation of the hostile Thiébaut (p. 65).

80. According to Blumel (p. 5), after World War II Blum reached a definition of the Jew similar to that of Sartre: a Jew is a person whom other people hold to be one. Dalby (pp. 96–97) believed that Blum persisted in believing in racial characteristics. Marrus (pp. 10–27) shows that racial terminology was commonly accepted by French Jews at that time.

81. Etienne Weill-Raynal, in "Un livre de Colette Audry: Léon Blum ou la politique du juste" (*Revue socialiste*, n.s., no. 74 [November 1955], p. 409), rightly pointed out that this did not make Blum religious in a conventional sense. I would agree with Colton (p. 7) that, "a complete secularist, [Blum] found a rationalization of his beliefs in the faith of his fathers."

82. Fraser and Natanson (pp. 16–18) were guilty of a similar fallacy when they said that Blum became a socialist because of the "Jewish instinct to ride with the oppressed." In saying this they put themselves in the same class as Léon Daudet, who (p. 72) called Blum a "socialist by hereditary messianic deviation," and Bourgin (p. 398) and Thiébaut (p. 67), who asserted that Jews are behind all revolutionary movements. See also Anonymous, "M. Léon Blum," *Revue universelle*, 17 (1924): 648. One could go on at length with examples of such racist thinking. Even the more moderate assertion that Jews, because of their history rather than their race, are more sensitive than others to oppression, holds—if at all— only for small numbers of intellectuals.

83. See Jackson, pp. 58–59; Aubery, p. 363.

84. Roblin, p. 144; Marrus, pp. 131–33. There were some Yiddish-speaking socialist groups, such as the Bildungs-Gesellschaft of Charles Rappoport, but these were formed mostly of East European Jews who were new to Paris (Roblin, pp. 168–73). Dalby (pp. 102–3) does not note

the important distinction between established French Jews and recent immigrants.

85. Quoted by Vichniac, p. 10. The same view was held by other French Jews (Marrus, p. 106).

86. See Bracke, *Revue socialiste*, n.s., no. 38–39 (1950), p. 6.

87. The character of Guesde's Marxism is best explained by Claude Willard in *Le mouvement socialiste en France (1893–1905): les guesdistes* (Paris: Editions sociales, 1965). I cannot agree with the view of George Lichtheim in *Marxism in Modern France* (New York: Columbia University Press, 1966), pp. 9, 15–16, who insists that theoretical Marxism was not popularized in France until Georges Sorel took it up.

88. Lichtheim (p. 15) rightly stresses the importance of Malon and Brousse. The former neglect of Brousse has been rectified by the fine study by David Stafford, *From Anarchism to Reformism: A Study of the Political Activities of Paul Brousse within the First International and the French Socialist Movement, 1870–90* (London: Weidenfeld and Nicolson, 1971).

89. Stafford (p. 156) reminds us that there were other sources of collectivism besides Marxism.

90. For the complete text, see Paul Louis, *Histoire du socialisme en France, 1789–1945* (4th ed.; Paris: Marcel Rivière, 1946), pp. 247–49.

91. For the influence of Malon, see Blum's preface to François Simon, *Une belle figure du peuple: Benoît Malon, sa vie, son oeuvre* (Courbevoie: La Cootypographie, 1926).

92. As Audry (p. 25) has scornfully remarked. For the influence of the Ecole Normale, see Lichtheim, p. 30.

93. Jean Jaurès, *Idéalisme et matérialisme dans la conception de l'histoire. Conférence de Jean Jaurès et réponse de Paul Lafargue, février 1895* ([Paris]: Publication du groupe des étudiants collectivistes, [1895?]). Ligou (p. 191) says that Jaurès's synthesis was accepted by the vast majority of socialist militants.

94. "Léon Blum parle de Jean Jaurès, discours du 31 juillet 1917 au Palais des fêtes de la rue Saint-Martin," *Revue socialiste*, n.s., no. 37 (May 1950), p. 387 (hereafter cited as "Jaurès"). See also Blum's preface to Jean Feuillard, *Jaurès homme d'aujourd'hui* ([Périgueux]: Pierre Fanlac, 1948), pp. 13–14.

95. Lichtheim (p. 20) indicates that Jaurès's doctrine was not a "*revision* of Marxism, but an *adaptation* of Marx's doctrines to the traditions of French socialism, and indeed of French republicanism."

96. Blum, *Revue de Paris*, 1 May 1924, p. 103.

97. Blum, *Jean Jaurès . . .* , pp. 40–41.

98. Jaurès, *Idéalisme et matérialisme*, p. 13. Thus they avoided the pitfall of Bernstein's revisionism, which tended to substitute moral impetus for historical necessity (see Peter Gay, *The Dilemma of Demo-*

cratic Socialism: Eduard Bernstein's Challenge to Marx [New York: Columbia University Press, 1952], p. 82). They did, however, share Bernstein's view that science cannot prescribe ethical values; see ibid., p. 149.

99. Blum, *Revue de Paris*, 1 May 1924, p. 103.

100. André Philip, *Pour un socialisme humaniste* (Paris: Plon, 1960), p. 197.

101. See Weill-Raynal, *Revue socialiste*, n.s., no. 74 (1955), p. 409.

102. L[ucien] Lévy-Bruhl, *Jean Jaurès: esquisse biographique* (6th ed.; Paris: F. Rieder, 1924), p. 65.

103. Blum, on a later occasion, spoke of socialism as an economic rather than political doctrine, and as founded on the class struggle (*Pour être socialiste*, pp. 5–6). But even this pamphlet began by saying that socialism was born from a "sentiment of equality, with the sentiment of justice, with the sentiment of human solidarity" (p. 3).

104. "Every society which claims to assure liberty to men ought to begin by guaranteeing their existence" (*L'Oeuvre*, 1: 242).

105. Ibid., p. 13.

106. See Parsons, p. 340.

107. *L'Oeuvre*, 1: 243.

108. Ibid., p. 227. See Jaurès, *Origines du socialisme allemand* (p. 32), where he contrasts a "nihilistic individualism, 'each one living only for himself,' and a genuine freedom, 'when one lives for the good of all'" (quoted in Harvey Goldberg, *The Life of Jean Jaurès* [Madison: University of Wisconsin Press, 1962], p. 14).

109. *L'Oeuvre*, 1: 227.

110. The similar effects of these two extremes were examined at that time in Emile Durkheim's *Suicide* (1897).

111. "La vie littéraire," *Humanité*, 30 January 1905. Jaurès, too, was concerned with safeguarding individual liberty (Ligou, pp. 234–35).

112. For Jaurès, see the quotations in Lefranc (*Jaurès*, p. 65).

113. See Blum, *Revue de Paris*, 1 May 1924, pp. 94–96.

114. *L'Oeuvre*, 1: 256. Blum repeated this almost verbatim in *La Revue de Paris* (1 May 1924, p. 96), where he added: "Certainly the socialist does not deny the raw fact of natural inequality." Meanwhile, he had used almost the same language in *Pour être socialiste* (pp. 8–9, 11).

115. Albert Thibaudet, *La République des professeurs* (Paris: Bernard Grasset, 1927), pp. 128–29. See *L'Oeuvre*, 1: 315–20.

116. Quoted in Dintzer, p. 7.

117. *L'Oeuvre*, 1: 89.

118. See Renard, *Journal*, p. 645.

119. In *Du mariage*, he came close to advocating this, but not, I think, very seriously.

120. Blum, *Pour être socialiste*, p. 5.

121. Max Nomad, *Aspects of Revolt* (New York: Bookman Associates, 1959), p. 69.

122. Blum, in preface to James Burnham, *L'ère des organisateurs* [The Managerial Revolution] (Paris: C. Lévy, 1947), p. xxi. Cf. Nomad, p. 43.

123. Blum, "Jaurès," p. 396.

124. See ibid., pp. 387–89. For a view of the Radical party as elite intellects controlled by the "active citizens," see Thibaudet (pp. 237–38).

125. Blum, "Réflexions sur le congrès socialiste," *Revue blanche*, 21 (1900): 37.

126. Lévy-Bruhl, p. 99.

127. Blum, *Jean Jaurès. . .* , p. 35.

128. See Lévy-Bruhl, pp. 88–89.

129. *L'Oeuvre*, 1: 252.

130. Ibid.

131. Ibid.; Blum, *Revue de Paris*, 1 May 1924, pp. 108–9.

132. Blum, *Revue blanche*, 21 (1900): 40–41.

133. *L'Oeuvre*, 1: 244. See Fraser and Natanson, p. 67.

134. Benda, pp. 201–2. Aubery (pp. 203, 225) argued that Jews are rarely fanatic, being tempered by a "scepticisme désabusé." Blum would probably have agreed.

135. Blum, *Revue blanche*, 21 (1900): 47.

136. Paul-Boncour, *Recollections of the Third Republic*, trans. George Marion, Jr. (New York: Robert Speller, 1957), p. 69.

137. *L'Oeuvre*, 1: 253.

138. Blum, *Pour être socialiste*, pp. 4–5.

139. See *L'Oeuvre*, 1: 245, 254. See also Lévy-Bruhl, p. 64.

140. *L'Oeuvre*, 1: 12–15.

141. Ibid., pp. 210–11.

142. Ibid., p. 232.

NOTES TO CHAPTER FIVE

1. The story of the New Society has been told in some detail several times, but usually in defense of Herr or Péguy. For Herr's point of view, see Andler. Two friends of Péguy have written the least biased accounts: Felicien Challaye, *Péguy socialiste* (Paris: Amiot-Dumont, 1954), and Jules Isaac, *Expériences de ma vie*, vol. 1: *Péguy* (Paris: Calmann-Lévy, 1959). Blum's biographers have paid little attention to the episode; see Colton (p. 31), Dalby (p. 148); Ziebura (pp. 48–51, 82) is more aware of its importance.

2. Challaye (pp. 88–89) said 40,000 francs; Jérôme and Jean Tharaud, in *Pour les fidèles de Péguy* (Paris: Dumas, 1949), p. 155, said 30,000 francs.

3. See Jérôme and Jean Tharaud, pp. 15–16, and their *Notre cher Péguy* (Paris: Plon, 1926), p. 183; Bourgin, pp. 260–61; Challaye, pp. 96–97.

4. According to Isaac (p. 178), Péguy appealed for help. His training as a historian and his condition as a Jew, combined with his friendship for Péguy, gave Jules Isaac a particularly valuable point of view for judging the whole affair of the Librairie Bellais.

5. Quotation from Péguy's original appointment, dated 12 August 1899, and signed by Péguy and Herr (Archives Nationales, AQ 40 [1]). The records of the New Society were deposited in the Archives Nationales by Mario Roques (subsequent references will be abbreviated AN). Isaac is the only other author to have made extensive use of them. Challaye (p. 101) estimated Péguy's debts at 75,000 francs, which is much too high. A note in Romain Rolland's *Une amitié française: correspondance entre Charles Péguy et Romain Rolland* (Paris: Albin Michel, 1955 [p. 318]) gave the more reasonable figure of 6,438 francs. Shares in the New Society were valued at 100 francs; Péguy was given 200 shares and Bellais 50.

6. Notary's description of the organization of the New Society with capital of 50,000 francs in 500 shares of 100 francs each (document dated 9 August 1899, AN). A list of stockholders who were *normaliens*, with the date of their classes, is given by Smith (p. 147).

7. Herr told Simiand that Blum was supplying 20,000 francs (letter in AN, cited by Isaac, p. 178). Other records in AN show Blum's personal share was much smaller than this; did he, then, help recruit other stockholders?

8. "Procès-verbaux des assemblées générales de la Société Nouvelle de Librairie et d'Edition, 2me assemblée générale" (AN). Blum spoke of knowing Péguy's group in July (*Revue blanche*, 19 [1899]: 394).

9. *L'Oeuvre*, 4–2: 548. Isaac (p. 186) said that Simiand, Roques, and Bourgin did most of the work and Blum was little involved in the day-to-day operations.

10. Letter from Cl. E. Maître to Simiand, dated 20 August 1901; undated note by Simiand (AN).

11. There is no ground for Dalby's assertion (p. 148) that Blum under-took to proofread everything.

12. For the *Mouvement socialiste*, see Ziebura (pp. 82–83). I think Ziebura exaggerates the influence of Lagardelle's group on Blum. Their contact was short lived.

13. *Les congrès ouvriers et socialistes français*, vol. 1: *1879–1885*, vol. 2: *1886–1900* ("Bibliothèque socialiste," no. 6–7 [Paris: Société Nouvelle de Librairie et d'Edition, 1901]). In *L'Oeuvre*, 1: 391–491. The volumes

did not sell rapidly. The inventory of 15 May 1910 shows that 1,200 to 1,300 copies of each volume were left; the sales record for the period 1 May 1924 to 30 April 1928 shows that 165 copies were sold (AN).

14. Bourgin, p. 256.

15. *Revue d'histoire moderne et contemporaine: première table générale, 1899–1909* (Paris: Edouard Cornély, 1910), pp. v–vi.

16. Among the contributors listed on the cover of the December 1903 issue were Charles Andler, Camille Bloch, Georges and Hubert Bourgin, Emile Durkheim, Octave Festy, Arthur Fontaine, Herr, Emmanuel Lévy, Lucien Lévy-Bruhl, Marcel Mauss, Edgar Milhaud, M. Ostrogorski, Charles Rist, Philippe Sagnac, Charles Seignobos, Simiand, and Albert Thomas. Ziebura (p. 80, n. 9) found one review by Blum.

17. Tharaud, *Notre cher Péguy*, p. 184.

18. See Andler, pp. 151 ff. This should be balanced against Péguy's version, in "Pour moi," *Cahiers de la Quinzaine* (cahier 5, 2d ser. [1901], pp. 1–49).

19. For how Blum appeared to a member of Péguy's circle, see Isaac (pp. 185–86).

20. Thibaudet, p. 59.

21. Péguy's account is in his "Préface à *Jean Coste*," *Cahiers de la Quinzaine*, cahier 12, 2d ser. (1901), pp. 231–33. He did not mention Blum by name, but spoke only of a "rich administrator." The reference to Blum was confirmed by Challaye (p. 102) and Isaac (pp. 192–94). Isaac said that Blum denied making such a statement but that Péguy maintained his story.

22. See Isaac, p. 194.

23. According to Challaye, p. 103.

24. Péguy, *Cahiers de la Quinzaine*, cahier 5, 2d ser. (1901), p. 16. It has been recently suggested—with more ingenuity of argument than solid evidence—that Blum may have had a more crucial part in the quarrel between Péguy and the New Society than I have indicated here (Jacques Viard, "Une lettre inconnue de Charles Andler à Charles Péguy en 1913," *Revue d'histoire moderne et contemporaine*, 19 [1972], 498–509). The question can certainly be reopened, but more evidence will be needed.

25. Isaac, p. 254. For a picture of Péguy's subsequent moral decline (which most readers, but not this one, have found excessively severe), see Hans A. Schmitt, *Charles Péguy: The Decline of an Idealist* (Baton Rouge: Louisiana State University Press, 1967).

26. Andler (p. 155) thought that Péguy was incited by Georges Sorel. Isaac (pp. 214–15) refuted the explanation. Even the Tharauds, in *Pour les fidèles* (p. 156), thought that perhaps Péguy pushed his legal rights too far. For further details, see AN.

27. The Tharauds (*Pour les fidèles*, p. 156) were right about this.

28. Copy of the judgment of the Tribunal de Commerce, dated 10 January 1906. The struggle is reflected in a series of notes from the firm's lawyer in 1905 and 1906 (AN).

29. See also Andler, p. 163.

30. He was given a three-year contract on 12 August 1900 but the remainder was bought back for 850 francs on 25 January 1902. A letter to Simiand from Cl. E. Maître, dated 9 December 1901, commented on his continual unpunctuality (AN). During the summer that he was in charge for Simiand, Blum was apparently too lenient with their employee.

31. His contract began 1 February 1902. A new man was named to succeed him on 22 August 1904 (AN).

32. "Rapport du conseil d'administration à l'assemblée générale du 2.VIII.1900" (AN). Their best year was 1902/3, when they lost only 7,781.36 francs. When business was suspended in June 1905, total losses had reached 159,243.75 francs, exceeding the total capital, which by that time was 142,700 francs (AN).

33. A number of people gave Herr money with which to buy stock in his own name. At the liquidation, after his death, more than half of the shares were still in his name. According to a manuscript note in this dossier, some of the suppliers of additional funds were Blum, Mme. Ménard-Dorian, Lucien Lévy-Bruhl, and Salomon Reinach (AN).

34. Among the stockholders were Etienne Burnet, Pierre Caron, Felicien Challaye, André Créhange, Paul Grunebaum-Ballin, Maurice Halbwachs, H. Hubert, Marcel Mauss, Edgar Milhaud, Albert Monod, Jean Perrin, Eugène Petit, Mario Roques, Désiré Roustan, Philippe Sagnac, Simiand, André Spire, Albert Thomas, Ernest Tonnelat, Georges Weill, and Georges Weulersse (AN).

35. The stock of books was sold to another bookseller. The publishing operations were transferred to Edouard Cornély et Cie, 101 rue de Vaugirard (AN).

36. See Andler, p. 163; Suarez, 1: 225; Halévy, pp. 179–80.

37. Blum's recollection of his course is in *La méthode socialiste* (Paris: Editions de la liberté, 1945 [pp. 3–4]). Part of his lectures have been preserved in *Doctrines françaises contemporaines (Ecole Socialiste): leçon de Léon Blum*, 18 May 1901. Unpublished typescript in Bibliothèque de la Documentation Contemporaine Internationale, B 2912 (cited by Colton, p. 498). For further discussion, see Ziebura (pp. 107–8).

38. "La vie littéraire," *Humanité*, 30 January 1905.

39. See Lévy, p. 22; Bourgin, p. 115.

40. Bourgin, pp. 351–53.

41. The best study of the unity movement is Aaron Noland's *The Founding of the French Socialist Party, 1893–1905* (Cambridge: Harvard University Press, 1956). Among other works I have consulted for the following picture of the socialist movement are Louis, Ligou, Willard,

and Zévaès (previously cited), and Jean-Jacques Fiechter, *Le socialisme français: de l'affaire Dreyfus à la Grande Guerre* (Geneva: Droz, 1965), and Georges Lefranc, *Le mouvement socialiste sous la Troisième République (1875–1940)* (Paris: Payot, 1963).

42. Zévaès, *Histoire du socialisme*, p. 253.

43. See J[ules]-L[ouis] Breton, *L'unité socialiste*, vol. 3 of *Histoire des partis socialistes en France*, ed. Alexandre Zévaès (Paris: Marcel Rivière, 1912), p. 8.

44. See ibid., pp. 12–13.

45. In *Petite république*, 24 June 1899, quoted by Zévaès in *Histoire du socialisme*, pp. 283–84. Fiechter (p. 67) agreed that "the menace of a coup d'état was quite real."

46. Blum, "Réflexions sur le congrès socialiste," *Revue blanche*, 21 (1900): 40.

47. Jean Texcier, "Introduction," *L'Oeuvre*, 1: xxiv.

48. Cited in n. 46 above.

49. *Congrès général des organisations socialistes françaises, tenu à Paris du 3 au 8 décembre 1899. Compte rendu sténographique officiel* (Paris: Société Nouvelle de Librairie et d'Edition, 1900), p. 409.

50. Blum, *Revue blanche*, 21 (1900): 39, 43.

51. *L'Oeuvre*, 1: 372.

52. International Congress, Paris (1900), *Compte rendu sténographique*, p. 102.

53. *L'Oeuvre*, 1: 324.

54. Ibid., p. 489.

55. *Revue blanche*, 21 (1900): 42–43.

56. I was unable to locate a copy of this periodical. See Isaac, p. 140; Pierre Rimbert, "Léon Blum dans la lutte politique et sociale," *Revue socialiste*, n.s., no. 38–39 (1950), 141.

57. Andler, p. 136.

58. *L'Oeuvre*, 1: 359–74.

59. Ibid., p. 359.

60. Ibid., p. 371.

61. Ibid., pp. 372–73.

62. Un juriste, "L'article 7," *Revue blanche*, 21 (1900): 481–95, in *L'Oeuvre*, 1: 375–90.

63. See Aaron Noland, "Individualism in Jean Jaurès' Socialist Thought," *Journal of the History of Ideas*, 22 (1961): 63–80, reprinted in Philip P. Wiener and Aaron Noland, eds., *Ideas in Cultural Perspective* (New Brunswick: Rutgers University Press, 1962).

64. See chapter 4 above.

65. Reprinted in *L'Oeuvre*, 1: 509–36.

66. Ibid., p. 511.

67. Ibid., p. 509.

68. According to Lefranc, in *Mouvement socialiste* (p. 223), Blum expressed some reservations in 1919.

69. See chapter 3 above.

70. Roughly equivalent to clerk of the court, bailiff, and notary, but their functions do not exactly coincide with those of the Anglo-American legal system.

71. Zévaès, *Histoire du socialisme*, p. 248.

72. Published from the manuscript in *L'Oeuvre*, 1: 493–507.

73. See Renard, *Journal*, p. 506.

74. Blum, *L'Oeuvre*, 1: 498.

75. Ibid., pp. 498–500.

76. Ibid., p. 503.

77. Ibid., p. 494.

78. Ibid.

79. See Willard, p. 426.

80. See Ziebura's discussion (pp. 137–39), where he points to the paradoxes of a concept of democratic dictatorship. He rightly emphasizes the importance of this issue for Blum's later opposition to bolshevism.

81. Blum, *L'Oeuvre*, 1: 496–97.

82. Ibid., p. 509.

83. Ibid., p. 502.

84. Ibid.

85. Ibid., pp. 501–2.

86. Andler, p. 169.

87. Auclair, p. 449.

88. See Gregh, *L'âge d'or*, p. 11.

89. Blum, "Jaurès," p. 395.

90. Announced on p. 1 of the first issue, 18 April 1904.

91. Suarez, 1: 448–50.

92. See Fraser and Natanson, p. 121. Lefranc, in *Jaurès* (p. 133), errs in attributing an editorial role to Blum.

93. Renard, *Journal*, p. 609.

94. Ibid.

95. The paid staff was reduced to Jaurès, Herr, Briand, Viviani, Pressensé, Rouanet, and a few others (*brouillon* of the minutes of the Conseil d'Administration of *L'Humanité*, meeting of 5 August 1905, in the collection of the Institut Français d'Histoire Sociale, 87 rue Vieille-du-Temple, Paris). See Andler, p. 182. The place of literature in the press was declining markedly at that time (Billy, *L'époque 1900*, p. 368).

96. Our knowledge of the role of Blum, Herr, and Prof. Lévy-Bruhl in securing financial backing from Jewish circles comes mostly from the dubious source of Suarez (1: 431). It is likely that Jaurès's action during the affair opened some purses. The largest stockholder of *L'Humanité*, according to reports published in it, was A. Rosnoblet. It would be of

considerable interest to know something more concrete about the financing of the paper.

97. List of the original stockholders in *L'Humanité*, 8 January 1907.

98. Jaurès's article appeared on 5 October 1906, Blum's on 10 October.

99. See *Humanité*, 15 March 1907.

100. For example: for the benefit of victims of political oppression (24 January 1905), of natural catastrophe (15 March 1906); contribution to political campaign fund (27 April 1906).

101. *Congrès socialiste international d'Amsterdam des 14–20 août 1904: rapports et projets de résolutions sur les questions de l'ordre du jour*, by the Secrétariat Socialiste International (Brussels, 1904), p. 35.

102. Lévy, p. 23. Dalby (p. 149) refers to a Rouen congress of 1904, citing Blum's recollections to Janet Flanner. The 1904 congress of the PSF was at St.-Etienne, and unity was not the main issue.

103. See Paul-Boncour, pp. 147–48.

104. Parti Socialiste (Section Française de l'Internationale Ouvrière), *Premier Congrès national (Congrès d'Unité), tenu à Paris, les 23, 24 et 25 avril 1905, Salle du Globe. Compte rendu analytique* (Paris: Au siège du Conseil national [1905?]), p. 10. See Emmanuel Lévy's preface to Dintzer (p. 3).

105. Dintzer, p. 3; *L'Oeuvre*, 6: 65.

106. For Blum and the mystique of unity, see Lévy (p. 23) and Bracke (*Revue socialiste*, n.s., no. 38–39 [1950], p. 8).

107. See Fiechter, p. 91.

108. For Jaurès's view, see ibid., p. 93.

109. Blum, "Jaurès," pp. 398–99; *L'Oeuvre*, 4–2: 576. Cf. Breton, p. 51.

110. See Louis, p. 273.

111. SFIO congress (Paris, 1905), *Compte rendu analytique*, p. 23.

112. Sometimes referred to as the Parti Socialiste Unifié.

113. Parti Socialiste (Section Française de l'Internationale Ouvrière), *Deuxième Congrès national, tenu à Chalon-sur-Saône les 29, 30, 31 octobre et 1er novembre 1905. Compte rendu analytique* (Paris: Au siège du Conseil national [1905]), p. 58.

114. See Marcel Prélot, *Cours d'histoire des idées politiques* (Paris: Les cours de droit, 1959), p. 260.

115. Vichniac (pp. 110–11) and Fraser and Natanson (p. 109) said that Blum attended the local section regularly. André Blumel (interview of 15 May 1962) denied that he did. There seems to be no sure way of resolving this contradiction.

116. The fourteenth section was quite active but not very successful.

117. See Audry, pp. 15–16. From the time of the affair, Jaurès, too, had come to see the need for specialists (Lefranc, *Jaurès*, p. 43).

118. *L'Oeuvre*, 1: 232.

119. Blum, *Revue blanche*, 12 (1900): 46.
120. Renard, *Journal*, p. 546.
121. Lévy, p. 23.
122. Blum, "Jaurès," p. 399.
123. See Vichniac, p. 99.
124. Renard, *Journal*, p. 792.
125. Ibid., p. 750; Auclair, p. 516.
126. Interview with Paul-Boncour on 22 May 1962.
127. Suarez, 2: 23. See also Andler, p. 164. For a comment on Grunebaum-Ballin by Blum, see *Humanité*, 30 January 1905.
128. Blum, in preface to Jean Perrin, *La science et l'espérance* (Paris: Presses Universitaires de France, 1948), p. xxix. See Bourgin, p. 402.
129. Gide, *Journal*, p. 397.
130. Ibid., p. 14.
131. See chapter 3 above.
132. Fraser and Natanson, p. 100.
133. Blum, *Revue blanche*, 21 (1900): 42–43.
134. Renard, *Journal*, p. 748. After Viviani's death in 1925, Blum was a "membre fondateur" of the Société des Amis de René Viviani (*Le monument de René Viviani: Alger, le 4 mai 1930* [n.p.: Société des Amis de René Viviani (1930)], p. [50]).
135. See *L'Oeuvre*, 1: 269–70.
136. Lévy, p. 23; see also Blum's speech to the Congress of Tours in Annie Kriegel, ed., *Le congrès de Tours (décembre 1920), naissance du Parti communiste français* (Paris: Julliard, 1964), p. 134.
137. Fraser and Natanson, p. 43.
138. Cf. André Philip, p. 143.
139. Blum, "Jaurès," p. 392.
140. *Revue de Paris*, 1 May 1924, p. 106.
141. Fabre-Luce, p. 66; Blum displayed a certain anglophobia as early as 1898 (Renard, *Journal*, p. 345).
142. Blum later asserted that France and Russia could have saved the peace as late as 31 July 1914 (Lefranc, *Mouvement socialiste*, p. 194).
143. Fraser and Natanson, pp. 119–20.
144. Blum, *Jean Jaurès* . . . , pp. 8–9. See Auclair, p. 629.
145. *Revue socialiste*, n.s., no. 38–39 (1950), p. 4.

NOTES TO CHAPTER SIX

1. Gide, p. 116.
2. Renard, *Journal*, p. 517.
3. Blum preserved his manuscript, which is now in the possession of

his widow (item 45 in the Bibliothèque Nationale Exposition Léon Blum [1962]).

4. *L'Oeuvre*, 1: 73–74, 295–99.

5. Ibid., pp. 328–35, 262–67.

6. Ibid., p. 333.

7. For Balzac and Zola, see Brombert, p. 16.

8. *L'Oeuvre*, 1: 335.

9. The quotation is from Billy, *L'époque 1900*, p. 365.

10. Renard, *Journal*, p. 600.

11. But Lefranc, in *Mouvement socialiste* (p. 144), errs in calling him the dramatic critic of *L'Humanité*.

12. *En lisant: réflexions critiques* (Paris: Ollendorff, 1906); *Au théâtre: réflexions critiques* (Paris: Ollendorff, 1906, 1909, 1910, 1911).

13. "M. Léon Blum," *Revue latine*, 25 February 1907, pp. 65–78.

14. Renard, *Correspondance*, p. 340.

15. *L'Oeuvre*, 1: 168. Faguet, in *Revue latine* (25 February 1907, p. 71), was probably right in charging Blum with misreading the Marguerittes's dedication of the book to both victors and vanquished.

16. "Les livres," *Gil Blas*, 18 January 1904.

17. Ibid., 13 April 1903.

18. "La vie littéraire," *Humanité*, 16 August 1904, 1 November 1904.

19. *L'Oeuvre*, 1: 145.

20. Ibid., pp. 134–38.

21. *Humanité*, 15 May 1905. The quoted passage was omitted from the version of this review in *En lisant* (p. 16).

22. See, for example, *L'Oeuvre*, 1: 141.

23. See ibid., p. 94; "Les livres," *Gil Blas*, 21 September 1903.

24. *L'Oeuvre*, 1: 81.

25. "La vie littéraire: choses de Russie," *Humanité*, 13 February 1905; first list of protesters (ibid., 1 February 1905); "Au Figaro," ibid., 4 February 1905.

26. Ibid., 24 August 1904.

27. Faguet, *Revue latine*, 25 February 1907, p. 76. Ziebura (p. 110) is wrong in chiding Blum for ignoring or misunderstanding Léon Bloy, Paul Claudel, and Péguy. None of the three had published novels when Blum was reviewing novels, and Blum praised quite highly the Claudel dramas that he had the opportunity to review.

28. "L'oeuvre poétique de Madame de Noailles," *Revue de Paris*, 15 January 1908, pp. 225–47, in *L'Oeuvre*, 2: 407–24.

29. *L'Humanité* also published a front-page article by Octave Mirbeau, thanking Blum for having led him to overcome his prejudices and to read Mme. de Noailles ("À Léon Blum," 11 September 1904).

30. Much of Blum's assessment of their importance in that period is confirmed by Billy (*L'époque 1900*, pp. 214–33).

31. *L'Oeuvre*, 1: 103.

32. "Les livres," *Gil Blas*, 6 April 1903.

33. *L'Oeuvre*, 1: 102–3.

34. The legal status of women was still one of great inferiority in France. Blum had earlier been on a committee, set up by the New Society, to investigate the legal ramifications of allowing a woman to become a stockholder in the firm (AN). Such a measure, however, was by no means unprecedented.

35. *L'Oeuvre*, 1: 185–86.

36. Bourget himself condemned the *roman à thèse* in a speech to the Académie in 1907, but it may be doubted that he avoided it (Brombert, pp. 66–67).

37. "La vie littéraire," *Humanité*, 30 January 1905.

38. "Les livres," *Gil Blas*, 7 September 1903.

39. "La vie littéraire," *Humanité*, 5 June 1905.

40. For these authors, see Elizabeth M. Fraser, *Le renouveau religieux d'après le roman français de 1886 à 1914* (Paris: Les belles lettres, 1934), pp. 77–79 et passim.

41. A note on Bazin's reception, signed "L. B.", in *Humanité* (29 April 1904).

42. Ibid., 17 May 1904.

43. Ibid., 29 May 1905.

44. *L'Oeuvre*, 1: 185–86. The words in brackets were deleted in *En lisant* from the original *Humanité* article (6 December 1904).

45. Quoted by Alex Inkeles in "The Totalitarian Mystique: Some Impressions of the Dynamics of Totalitarian Society," in Carl J. Friedrich, ed., *Totalitarianism* (New York: Grosset & Dunlap, 1964), p. 104.

46. Marius-Ary Leblond, *La société française sous la Troisième République d'après les romanciers contemporains* (Paris: Félix Alcan, 1905), p. 297.

47. See, for example, *L'Oeuvre*, 1: 91.

48. "Les livres," *Gil Blas*, 1 February 1904.

49. See, for example, "La vie littéraire," *Humanité*, 10 April 1905.

50. *L'Oeuvre*, 1: 191; see also ibid., p. 187.

51. Of course, one has to know something about socialism in order to assess his position. After reading *En lisant*, Faguet thought that Blum was a Guesdist! (*Revue latine*, 25 February 1907, p. 67).

52. Paris: Editions de la Revue blanche, 1901; in *L'Oeuvre*, 1: 197–335.

53. By Ollendorff, who had become his regular publisher.

54. Renard, *Journal*, p. 437.

55. Gregh, *L'âge d'airain*, p. 87. There is a slightly different version of this story in his *L'âge d'or* (p. 190).

56. Vichniac, p. 74.

57. Interview with Robert Blum. Léon Blum, *Des Nouvelles conversations de Goethe avec Eckermann* (*1897–1900*): *A l'échelle humaine* (*1942*), ed. Olga Raffalovich (Paris: Albin Michel, 1957).

58. See, for example, Dalby's last chapter.

59. Observed also by Vichniac (p. 76).

60. *L'Oeuvre*, 1: 322.

61. Gerhard Masur, *Prophets of Yesterday: Studies in European Culture, 1890–1914* (New York: Macmillan, 1961), p. 46.

62. *L'Oeuvre*, 1: 254; see, for example, pp. 176–77.

NOTES TO CHAPTER SEVEN

1. Paris: Ollendorff, 1907; in *L'Oeuvre*, 2: 1–181.

2. See Dalby, pp. 119–20.

3. Emile Faguet, in "L'anarchie morale: deux livres contre le mariage" (*Revue latine*, 6 [1907]: 593), is thus wrong in comparing it to Diderot's *Supplément au voyage de Bougainville*.

4. Gide, *Journal*, p. 250; cf. Sée, *Porto-Riche*, p. 135.

5. Vichniac, p. 95.

6. See André Billy, "Les livres: Quand Léon Blum voulait réformer le mariage," *Figaro*, 28 February 1962, p. 20.

7. *L'Oeuvre*, 2: 6.

8. See Blum's preface to Paul Abram, *L'évolution du mariage* (Paris: E. Sansot, 1908), pp. xvi–xvii. Dalby generally presents the theses of *Du mariage* accurately, but she misconstrues Blum's intentions when she refers to his "frivolous views of marriage" (p. 115).

9. *L'Oeuvre*, 2: 26–27.

10. Dintzer (p. 18) justly stressed this point. Joll (p. 15) calls the book a "plea for honesty and reason in human relationships."

11. *L'Oeuvre*, 2: 177.

12. Ibid., p. 145.

13. Anonymous, *Vie de Monsieur Léon Blum* (Paris: Nouvelles éditions latines, 1936), p. 5. The most violent criticisms were touched off by the untimely re-publication of the work in 1937; see, for example, Jean d'Alsace [pseud. ?], *Mères françaises qu'en dites-vous? extraits du Mariage de Léon Blum* (Strasbourg: Nouvelle voix d'Alsace et de Lorraine, n.d.), which described *Du mariage* as part of a "judeo-masonic-bolshevik-laic" plot to destroy Christian society by undermining the family.

14. Dalby (p. 117) wrongly says that Blum objected to the "mating of an experienced man with a virginal female." He objected to this only *in marriage*, not before.

15. For example, Faguet, in *Revue latine*, 6 (1907): 601.

16. Ibid., pp. 602–3.

17. Viola Klein, in *The Feminine Character: History of an Ideology* (New York: International Universities Press, 1949 [p. 95]), noted how this increases equality between the sexes.

18. Blum, "Les livres," *Gil Blas*, 20 April 1903 (review of Metchnikoff's *Etudes sur la nature humaine: essai de philosophie optimiste*).

19. Billy, *Figaro*, 28 February 1962.

20. The descent of Blum's thought from that of Balzac and Rousseau is pointed out by Abram (p. 154).

21. See Carat, *Paru*, no. 60 (May 1950), p. 58.

22. See chapter 9 below.

23. *L'Oeuvre*, 2: 256–58.

24. Only in German, it is true, but some of Blum's scientific friends should have heard of Freud.

25. One of these anecdotes was published separately as a short story: "Elisabeth Masson," in *Les lettres*, 1 (1906): 87–103. Blum had apparently intended to be a regular contributor to this monthly, founded by Fernand Gregh, and had accepted the rubric "XIXe siècle," but he apparently found little time for it. *Les lettres* lasted only about a year, but it had a promising start with articles by Gregh, Anatole France, Jules Renard, Marcel Boulenger, and Henri Barbusse, and lesser contributions by G. Trarieux, Emile Chartier, Robert Dreyfus, and Louis Gillet. On Blum's anecdotes, see Faguet (*Revue latine*, 6 [1907]: 597). In 1907 Blum announced a novel, *Les raisons du coeur*, which he never completed, perhaps because *Du mariage* conveyed what he wanted to say (Julien Cain, introduction to vol. 2 of *L'Oeuvre*, p. xii).

26. Gide, pp. 248, 250. The "perplexity" to which Dalby confesses (p. 120) in attempting to understand Blum's motivation in writing *Du mariage* seems to stem from the fact that she shares Gide's misreading of it as simply the advocacy of sensual pleasure.

27. Blum thought Christianity had declined to the point where it was no longer necessary to consider its objections to premarital sex (*L'Oeuvre*, 2: 152).

28. See Klein, pp. 16, 177.

29. *L'Oeuvre*, 2: 77.

30. See ibid. (p. 92), where Blum borrows a socialist concept to make this point.

31. *Le caractère religieux du socialisme* (Paris: Librairie de la Société du recueil J. B. Sirey et du Journal du Palais, 1906), p. 8.

32. Blum's eulogist, Dintzer (p. 20), made the following remark: "A friend, a very expert art critic, insisted to me that *Du mariage* was a *bourgeois* work. But a bold study can never fall into the *bourgeois*, which is made of narrowness and meanness." Dalby (p. 125) rightly suggests

that Blum's socialism might have led him to stress the environmental factors in shaping the feminine character more than he does, but she fails to show how Blum's views in *Du mariage* did relate to his socialism. Ziebura (pp. 113–15) also fails to show the significance of *Du mariage* for Blum's socialism. He merely draws the conclusion that Blum's moral theory was based on extreme rationalism, as was his socialism. By not seeing *Du mariage* in terms of the larger tradition of French moralism, he does not see that Blum's rationalism was not mechanistic or simplistic.

33. In this he differed somewhat from Fourier (see *L'Oeuvre*, 2: 162).

34. Jaurès's "very bourgeois *sensibilité*" was shocked by Blum's proposals (interview with Grunebaum-Ballin).

35. *L'Oeuvre*, 2: 162.

36. Ibid., p. 177.

37. See Chastenet, *Belle époque*, pp. 51–52, 167–68; Billy, *Figaro*, 28 February 1962; Michel Puy, "Les essayistes," in Monfort, 1: 236.

38. See the mild treatment in the Jesuit *Etudes* (Etienne Borne, "Les dernières années de Léon Blum," *Etudes*, 265 [1950]: 265). For an uncritical view by a supporter, see Gilbert Sigaux, "Léon Blum était aussi un écrivain" (*Démocratie 62*, 22 February 1962, pp. 12–13).

39. See Vichniac, p. 95.

40. Klein, p. 85. For one critic, see Paul Escoube, "La femme et le sentiment de l'amour chez Rémy de Gourmont," *Mercure de France*, 159 (1922): 45–46.

41. Dalby (p. 123) rightly shows how Blum's views would be objectionable to feminists.

42. Especially if Freud asserted, as Klein (p. 72) reported: "Anatomy is destiny."

43. *L'Oeuvre*, 2: 21; see also p. 5.

NOTES TO CHAPTER EIGHT

1. Jacques Copeau, *Critiques d'un autre temps: études d'art dramatique* (Paris: Nouvelle Revue Française, 1923), pp. 214–15.

2. See René Peter, *Le théâtre et la vie sous la Troisième République* (Paris: Marchot, 1947), 2: 274. Sée, pp. 87–88. Chastenet, *Belle époque*, p. 101. Pierre Descaves, *Le théâtre* (Paris: Hachette, 1963), pp. 132–33.

3. *Revue blanche*, 12 (1897): 796–97; 13 (1897): 222–26. Cf. *L'Oeuvre*, 1: 218.

4. Renard, *Journal*, p. 600.

5. For example, when Athis's own play was produced (*Humanité*, 4 February 1905).

6. Léon Blum, *Au théâtre: réflexions critiques* (4 vols.; Paris: Ollendorff, 1906–11). Selections appear in *L'Oeuvre*, 2: 184–348.

7. From 25 December 1907 to 10 November 1908.

8. See Claude Barjac, "Léon Blum, chroniqueur et moraliste à la *Grande revue*," *Grande revue*, 150 (1936): 575–90.

9. See Billy, *L'époque contemporaine*, p. 10; Charles Ledré, *Histoire de la presse* (Paris: Arthème Fayard, 1958), p. 324 ("One of the most brilliant staffs"). See also André Warnod, "J'étais journaliste en 1909," *Figaro littéraire*, 10 February 1955, p. 6.

10. The names are taken from the first issue, 1 October 1907.

11. I have no direct evidence, but Mirbeau once proposed Blum for the Goncourt Academy (Renard, *Journal*, p. 777). Mirbeau, forgotten today, was a major figure in his time (see Martin Schwarz, *Octave Mirbeau: vie et oeuvre* [The Hague: Mouton, 1966]).

12. Sée, p. 90; see also Vichniac, p. 70.

13. Cain, *L'Oeuvre de Léon Blum*, 2: ix.

14. For Blum's motives, see ibid. For the ascendancy of the younger generation, see Peter, 2: 206.

15. *Humanité*, 24 November 1904.

16. *Excelsior*, 1 May 1912. See André Billy, "Autour de l'année cinq et des suivantes," *Figaro littéraire*, 30 April 1955; "Il y a cinquante ans: la littérature française en 1905," ibid., 8 January 1955; "La crise littéraire de 1905," ibid., 26 March 1955.

17. See Francis Pruner, *Les luttes d'Antoine: au Théâtre Libre*, vol. 1 (Paris: M. J. Minard, 1964).

18. André-Paul Antoine, *Antoine, père et fils: souvenirs du Paris littéraire et théâtral 1900–1939* (Paris: René Julliard, 1962), p. 99.

19. See Sylvain Dhomme, *La mise en scène contemporaine d'André Antoine à Bertolt Brecht* (Paris: F. Nathan, 1959), pp. 78–79.

20. See Chastenet, *Belle époque*, pp. 107–8; Antoine, pp. 114–15.

21. See *L'Oeuvre*, 2: 216–17; others have charged the public of pre–World War I days with exceptionally low taste (Peter, 2: 26–27); Jules Romains, quoted by Descaves (p. 159). Blum's principal complaint was that the public was too easily satisfied (*Comoedia*, 14 December 1910).

22. *Humanité*, 24 November 1904; adapted in *L'Oeuvre*, 2: 214.

23. *Au théâtre*, 2: vi–vii.

24. See *Comoedia*, 15 March 1910.

25. Copeau, p. 220.

26. Determined by inspecting the relevant issues of Edmond Stoullig, ed., *Annales du théâtre et de la musique* (19 vols.; Paris: Ollendorff, 1897–1916). In 1911, Blum had to attend six openings in one week (see his comment in *Comoedia*, 6 March 1911).

27. *Auteurs, acteurs, spectateurs* (Paris: Pierre Lafitte, 1909), p. 23.

28. See Blum's preface to the 1912 edition of Stoullig. See also Copeau (pp. 209–10).

29. *Comoedia*, 1 October 1911; 18 November 1909.

30. Ibid., 24 March 1911.

31. Ibid., 5 November 1909; 4 November 1910; 27 February 1910; *Grande revue*, 10 November 1908.

32. Definition given by Copeau (p. 184).

33. Blum was himself satirized in one revue, and he paid its authors back in his review (*Comoedia*, 25 November 1911).

34. See Copeau, pp. 145–46.

35. *Excelsior*, 30 May 1912.

36. See, for example, *Comoedia*, 23 March 1910.

37. See especially ibid., 10 October 1911.

38. See Blum's review of Bernard's *Théâtre complet* in *Grande revue* (10 September 1908) and his obituary notice on Renard (*L'Oeuvre*, 2: 284–86).

39. See his definition of the talent of Alfred Capus (*Comoedia*, 5 November 1910).

40. Ibid., 4 April 1909.

41. In ibid. (23 November 1909), he acknowledged the questionable nature of this practice. See also *Renaissance latine*, 15 May 1903, pp. 437–41.

42. *L'Oeuvre*, 2: 396–99.

43. *Comoedia*, 21 December 1909.

44. *L'Oeuvre*, 2: 201–4.

45. Francis Pruner, *Le Théâtre Libre d'Antoine*, vol. 1: *Le répertoire étranger* (Paris: Lettres modernes, 1958), p. 61.

46. Ibid.

47. See his praise of Lucien Guitry for contributing to the great success of Anatole France's *Crainquebille* (*Renaissance latine*, 15 April 1903, pp. 209–10). Copeau also disliked the prestige of actors, according to the actress Béatrix Dussane (*Dieux des planches* [Paris: Flammarion, 1964], p. 112).

48. "L'immortalité des comédiens," *Excelsior*, 19 April 1912.

49. Antoine, p. 82; Pruner, *Théâtre Libre*, p. 59.

50. *Matin*, 22 March 1912.

51. *Comoedia*, 8 July 1911; *Excelsior*, 13 July 1912.

52. Jean-Jacques Bernard, *Mon père Tristan Bernard* (Paris: Albin Michel, 1955), pp. 224–26.

53. *Matin*, 23 November 1913.

54. See Copeau, pp. 220–21; see also Thiébaut, pp. 127–29.

55. *Comoedia*, 26 November 1908; review intended for *Renaissance latine* but not published in it (*Au théâtre*, 1: 147–65).

56. Even hostile critics have admitted Blum's analytical skill; see, for example, Thiébaut, p. 123.

57. *Comoedia*, 10 December 1908.

58. Ibid., 17 February 1909.

59. For Blum's views on tragedy, see *Au théâtre* (2: 211–21 [a combination of reviews]).

60. *L'Oeuvre*, 2: 253.

61. Ibid.

62. *Renaissance latine*, 2 (1903): 697.

63. *Comoedia*, 2 February 1911; for the Théâtre des Arts, see ibid., 10 January 1909, 26 November 1910, 31 January 1911.

64. See ibid., 26 November 1910. For the naturists in the theater, see Maurice Edgar Coindreau, *La farce est jouée: vingt-cinq ans de théâtre français, 1900–1925* (New York: Editions de la Maison française, 1942), p. 174.

65. Dhomme, p. 30.

66. Ibid., p. 36; Peter, 2: 10.

67. See Pruner, *Théâtre Libre*, p. 31 et passim.

68. *Excelsior*, 4 December 1912.

69. See Maurice Descotes, *Le public de théâtre et son histoire* (Paris: Presses Universitaires de France, 1964), p. 344.

70. See Coindreau, p. 37; Antoine, pp. 42–43; Pruner's *Théâtre Libre*, pt. 2, ch. 1, is on the introduction of Ibsen in France.

71. *Renaissance latine*, 2 (1903): 209–11; *L'Oeuvre*, 2: 265–71.

72. Jules Claretie, "Journal: vingt-cinq ans au Théâtre-Français," *Revue des deux mondes*, 15 January 1951, p. 304.

73. *Comoedia*, 22 October 1909; *Humanité*, 12 June 1905.

74. *Comoedia*, 13 October 1910.

75. Ibid., 21 May 1911.

76. Bourget was generally regarded as less successful as a dramatist than as a novelist (see Coindreau, p. 35); Copeau (p. 42) called him an "author of melodramas."

77. *L'Oeuvre*, 2: 325–31, 290–97. For the social conservatism of the theater public, see Pruner, *Théâtre Libre* (p. 94) and Peter (2: 292).

78. See, for example, *Comoedia*, 13 March 1909.

79. *Excelsior*, 4 December 1912.

80. See *L'Oeuvre*, 2: 279–83.

81. See *Comoedia*, 20 February 1909, 3 June 1910, 11 April 1911.

82. See, for example, *Comoedia*, 29 September 1909; *Matin*, 22 December 1912.

83. But at least Brieux was sincere, avoiding the cheap theatricality of Dumas *fils*, who always "saved" the social conventions with an arbitrary dénouement (*Renaissance latine*, 2 [1903]: 437–41). See Copeau, pp. 136–37.

84. *Comoedia*, 29 September 1909. Blum urged the election of Porto-Riche over Brieux and Capus in ibid. (18 March 1909).

85. Ibid., 14 December 1911.

86. Ibid., 29 September 1909.

87. See his article "Le théâtre et les moeurs: L'influence des repas sur le théâtre," *Excelsior*, 27 February 1912.

88. Descaves, p. 31.

89. See Copeau's discussion of the problem of the *pièce à thèse* (pp. 228–29).

90. *L'Oeuvre*, 2: 217. Mere historical description did not interest him very much (see *Comoedia*, 19 September 1909, 29 October 1909), although he was angered by historical inaccuracy (ibid., 24 September 1909, 26 November 1909).

91. Among those he liked were Gustave Geffroy's *L'apprentie* (*Grande revue*, 25 January 1908, pp. 367–73) and Hermann Sudermann's *Parmi les pierres* (ibid., 25 October 1908); less explicable was René Wismer's *Les désarmés* (*Comoedia*, 27 February 1909). For unfavorable comments on social dramas of leftist orientation, see ibid. (14 June 1909, 4 April 1911, 9 November 1911, 14 December 1911).

92. *Humanité*, 16 January 1905, in *L'Oeuvre*, 2: 222–23.

93. "Le patriotisme au théâtre," *Excelsior*, 15 February 1913.

94. *Comoedia*, 8 December 1911.

95. Simone de Caillavet Maurois, in Coindreau (pp. 9–10).

96. See Paul Faure, *Vingt ans d'intimité avec Edmond Rostand* (Paris: Plon, 1928), pp. 202–4, and Sée, pp. 87–89, 210, 235–37.

97. Preface to the 1912 edition of Stoullig. See also Copeau, pp. 212–13.

98. See Copeau, pp. 221–22.

99. For anti-Semitic criticism, see Anonymous, "La Gazette du Ghetto," *Oeuvre*, 26 January 1911, pp. 30–33; Thiébaut, pp. 125–26.

100. The quotations are from *Comoedia* (15 October 1912), whose account seems more reliable than that in Fraser and Natanson (p. 106).

101. For the location, see Dussane (p. 151).

102. Descotes, p. 313.

103. See Antoine, pp. 59–60; Coindreau, p. 95; Peter, 2: 33–35; Bernard, in *Bernard* (pp. 130–33), gave a well-balanced appraisal of Porto-Riche.

104. See Antoine, p. 60.

105. See, for example, *L'Oeuvre*, 2: 218.

106. Fabre-Luce, p. 65. For the *moeurs*, see Dussane (pp. 95–96).

107. Cited by Blum in *Matin*, 21 November 1912.

108. See *L'Oeuvre*, 2: 214–18, 235–45; *Comoedia*, 31 March 1909, 26 February 1910, 28 February 1911, 26 March 1911.

109. Preface to *Au théâtre* (2:·[v]–vi).

110. Article intended for *Renaissance latine* but not published in it (ibid., 1: 141–45); *Humanité*, 10 May 1904; *Comoedia*, 19 December 1908; *Grande revue*, 10 November 1908, pp. 167–71.

111. *Grande revue*, 10 February 1908, pp. 566–77.

112. *Humanité*, 2 January 1905. He chided Bernstein, however, for not drawing the character to its logical limits, a failing made good by Porto-Riche in *Le Passé*.

113. *Renaissance latine*, 2 (1903): 454–59.

114. Pruner, *Théâtre Libre*, pp. 120–21.

115. *L'Oeuvre*, 2: 336–43.

116. "Le féminisme au théâtre," *Excelsior*, 29 January 1913.

117. *L'Oeuvre*, 2: 399–401; "L'âge de l'amour, à propos de *La patronne* de M. Maurice Donnay," *Grande revue*, 10 December 1908, pp. 537–44.

118. See Peter, 2: 57–58.

119. Rip, in "La rosière d'Excelsior" (*Excelsior*, 9 April 1912), included a sketch of Blum with a crown of roses and a veil. Blum had hit hard at a Rip revue in *Comoedia* (16 January 1909). See also ibid., 30 October, 24 November 1909, 17 December 1910. For other comments on the morality of crowds, see Descotes (p. 17) and Descaves (p. 164).

120. "Plaidoyer pour la vertu," *Excelsior*, 3 April 1912.

121. *Grande revue*, 10 October 1908, pp. 592–95.

122. "Les juifs au théâtre: le Vieil homme ou l'enfant précoce," *Oeuvre*, 26 January 1911. See also Téry, "Les juifs au Théâtre Français: le déserteur Bernstein" (ibid. 16 February 1911).

123. Pseudonym identified by Dhomme (p. 126). Boissard, "Les théâtres," *Mercure de France*, 106 (1913): 175; 98 (1912): 411.

124. For example, Peter, 2: 33–35.

125. *Comoedia*, 5 March 1911.

126. *Renaissance latine*, 2 (1903): 690–97.

127. See *Comoedia*, 27 January 1909.

128. For Marinetti, see ibid. (3 April 1909). Marinetti fought a duel with another French critic, Charles-Henry Hirsch, over the play; Blum served his friend and colleague as a second. For Shakespeare, see *L'Oeuvre* (2: 220–21).

129. See ibid., pp. 331–35.

130. Renard, *Journal*, pp. 646–47.

131. *L'Oeuvre*, 2: 212.

132. *Renaissance latine*, 2 (1903): 145–46.

133. *Humanité*, 18 April 1905; *Comoedia*, 8 October 1908; *Grande revue*, 25 October 1908, pp. 810–11. *Comoedia*, 29 December 1909, 12 October 1910.

134. *L'Oeuvre*, 2: 297–302; *Matin*, 15 March 1913. See Dussane, pp. 67–68.

135. *Gil Blas*, 8 June 1903.

136. Faure, p. 202.

137. *L'Oeuvre*, 2: 213–14.

138. *Matin*, 12 April 1913.

139. *Excelsior*, 4 December 1912.

140. The researchers of the Société des Amis de Léon Blum have determined, by consulting the records of *Le Matin*, which articles were by Blum (see *L'Oeuvre*, 2: 627–39).

141. Even so, he continued to seek out and welcome new talents (see, e.g., *Matin*, 26 October 1912, 14 March 1913).

NOTES TO CHAPTER NINE

1. "La prochaine génération littéraire," *Revue de Paris*, 1 February 1913, p. 534, in *L'Oeuvre*, 2: 437.

2. See chapter 2 above for Blum's definition of romanticism.

3. *L'Oeuvre*, 2: 427.

4. See Agathon [Henri Massis and Alfred de Tarde], *Les jeunes gens d'aujourd'hui: le goût de l'action, la foi patriotique, une renaissance catholique, le réalisme politique* (Paris: Plon, 1913), pp. 77–78, 284–86, et passim.

5. Bergson, quoted in ibid., p. 77.

6. Quoted by Borne in *Etudes* (265 [1950]: 353).

7. See Masur, p. 263.

8. Ibid., p. 260.

9. Agathon, pp. 16–17.

10. *L'Oeuvre*, 2: 437; see Agathon, p. 18.

11. *L'Oeuvre*, 2: 437.

12. Ibid., p. 436.

13. Ibid., p. 435.

14. See Peyre, *Contemporary French Novel*, pp. 116–17.

15. See ibid., p. 81, and Henri Peyre, *Le classicisme français* (New York: Editions de la Maison française, 1942), p. 68.

16. See Agathon, p. 71.

17. See, for example, Georges le Cardonnel, *Mercure de France*, 104 (1913): 261. For a friendly review, see Charles-Henry Hirsch, "Les revues" (ibid., 102 [1913]: 177–79).

18. See Agathon, p. 31.

19. Ibid., p. 23.

20. See Chastenet, *Histoire de la Troisième République*, vol. 4: *1906–1918*, pp. [7], 18–19.

21. See Agathon, p. 55.

22. With the minor exceptions of lectures on Corneille and Shakespeare and an occasional review.

23. Paris: Ollendorff, 1914. The serialized parts were as follows: "Stendhal, I: sa personne" (*Revue de Paris*, 1 February 1914, pp. 564–97), "Stendhal, II: ses personnages" (ibid., 15 February 1914, pp. 781–814), "Stendhal, III: esquisse du beylisme" (ibid., 1 May 1914, pp. 148–86), "Stendhal, IV: histoire du beylisme" (ibid., 15 May 1914, pp. 325–61). In *L'Oeuvre*, 2: 463–590.

24. See Gregh, *L'âge d'airain*, p. 88; Billy, *L'époque contemporaine*, p. 20; Billy's review of *L'Oeuvre* in *Figaro*, 28 February 1962. Peyre, in *Failures of Criticism* (p. 105), speaks of Blum's "brilliant mastery." See also Carlo Cordiè, *Interpretazioni di Stendhal dal Bourget ai nostri giorni* (Milan: Francesco Montuoro, 1947), pp. 21–22. Part of Blum's work is included in Victor Brombert, ed., *Stendhal: A Collection of Critical Essays* (Englewood Cliffs, N.J.: Prentice-Hall, 1962). Others have expressed the opinion that Blum could have had a distinguished career as a literary critic (Henriot, 3: 297; René Lalou, *Histoire de la littérature française contemporaine*, vol. 2 [Paris: Presses Universitaires de France, 1941], p. 527).

25. The error of treating Blum's *Stendhal* as autobiography was made by Carat (*Paru*, no. 60 [May 1950], p. 58) and Thiébaut (pp. 38–41). Thiébaut often did violence to the plain meaning of Blum's interpretation, but he understood that the study of Stendhal helped Blum understand himself. The objectivity of Blum's work was praised by René Boylesve in *Réflexions sur Stendhal* (Paris: Le Divan, 1929), p. 35.

26. The passages on the Jews and persecution in the *Nouvelles conversations* (cited in chapter 4) are evidence of this.

27. Boylesve, p. 41.

28. Somerset Maugham, quoted by Harry Levin in *The Gates of Horn: A Study of Five French Realists* (New York: Oxford University Press, 1963), p. 119.

29. For Blum's originality, see Boylesve (p. 78).

30. Albert Thibaudet wrote that, in writers after Renan, "emotion, intuition, and skepticism argued with reason, religion, and philosophy; those inner experiences argued with science, a system of external experience" (*Histoire de la littérature française* [Paris, 1936], p. 407), quoted by Goldberg (p. 246).

31. See also Boylesve, pp. 65–66.

32. *Journal*, p. 645.

33. For Stendhal, see Levin, pp. 127–28.

34. *L'Oeuvre*, 1: 89.

35. See, for example, *Revue universelle*, 17 (1924): 649.

36. Jean Texcier, "Léon Blum, écrivain et moraliste," *Preuves*, 5 (1955): 79.

37. Blum's contentment was testified to by Grunebaum-Ballin (interview). Fabre-Luce (p. 64) wrote: "Until I was forty-two, he [Blum] told me [in 1924], I was the most tranquil man in the world." See Maurice Delépine in *Revue socialiste*, n.s., no. 38–39 (1950), p. 9.

38. The best appreciation of the importance of Blum's experience in Sembat's office is that of Ziebura (pp. 164–65). See also Colton, pp. 37–38.

39. Most valuable for the history of this period of French socialism are Annie Kriegel's *Aux origines du communisme français* and Robert Wohl's *French Communism in the Making, 1914–1924* (Stanford: Stanford University Press, 1966).

40. The text of Blum's speech can most easily be found in Kriegel's edition of the report of the Tours congress (pp. 101–36).

41. See Joll, pp. x–xi, cf. Lefranc, *Jaurès*, pp. 140–48.

BIBLIOGRAPHY

PRIMARY SOURCES

WORKS OF LÉON BLUM

Special attention is called to *L'Oeuvre de Léon Blum* (Paris: Albin Michel, 1954–72), a multivolume selection of most (but unfortunately not all) of Blum's most important writings, published under the auspices of the Société des Amis de Léon Blum.

Vol. 1: *Critique littéraire. Nouvelles conversations de Goethe avec Eckermann. Premiers essais politiques. 1891–1905.* (1954).

    2: *Du mariage. Critique dramatique. Stendhal et le beylisme. 1905–1914.* (Bibliography 1891–1914) (1962).

    3–1: *L'Entrée dans la politique active. Le Congrès de Tours. De Poincaré au Cartel des Gauches. La Réforme gouvernementale. 1914–1928.* (1972).

    3–2: *Réparations et désarmement. Les problèmes de la paix. La montée des fascismes. 1928–1934.* (Bibliography 1914–1934) (1972).

    4–1: *Du 6 février 1934 au Front Populaire. Les lois sociales de 1936. La guerre d'Espagne. 1934–1937.* (1964).

    4–2: *La fin du Rassemblement Populaire. De Munich à la guerre. Souvenirs sur l'Affaire. 1934–1940.* (Bibliography 1934–1940) (1965).

    5: *Mémoires. La prison et le procès. A l'échelle humaine. 1940–1945.* (1955).

6–1: *Naissance de la IVᵉ République. La vie du partie et la doctrine socialiste. 1945–1947.* (1958).

6–2: *La fin des alliances. La troisième force. Politique européenne. Pour la justice. 1947–1950.* (Bibliography 1945–1950) (1963).

The following bibliography of Blum's literary works is based on the bibliography published in vol. 2 of *L'Oeuvre.* Cross-checking with the original sources has made it possible to make several additions and corrections to this valuable listing.

Articles: Literary

The following are abbreviations for the titles of periodicals.

B	— *Banquet*	H	— *Humanité*
C	— *Conque*	L	— *Les lettres*
CO	— *Comoedia*	M	— *Matin*
E	— *Excelsior*	RL	— *Renaissance latine*
GB	— *Gil Blas*	RB	— *Revue blanche*
GR	— *Grande revue*	RP	— *Revue de Paris*

[The literary articles are arranged in chronological order. Repetition of dates indicates a second article in the same issue. For the review articles, the works discussed by Blum are cited following the publishing information.]

1891

Mar. 15 "La nuit, l'eau calme des bassins . . . ," *C*, p. vii.

Apr. 1 "Des fleurs d'hiver sur vos cheveux . . . ," *C*, p. xii.

May 1 "Les souvenirs du temps passé . . . ," *C*, p. xxiii.

June 1 "Quand je me coucherai dans l'ombre . . . ," *C*, p. xxx.

July 1 "Vous avez murmuré, votre main dans ma main . . . ," *C*, p. xxxvii.

Aug. 1 "Les nuits d'été . . . ," "Votre robe . . . ," "Là bas? Où donc? . . . ," *C*, p. xlv.

Sept. 1 "Le vent glisse . . . ," "Pendant que tu te recueilles . . . ," "La pluie en tombant . . . ," *C*, pp. l–li.

Oct. 1 "Les arbres que le vent . . . ," *C*, p. lx.

Nov. 1 "Dans le jardin . . . ," "O! vous . . . ," "Nous viendrons nous asseoir . . . ," *C*, p. lxx.

Dec. 1 "Le mouvement lascif et brusque . . . ," *C*, p. lxxvi.

1892

June "Méditation sur le suicide d'un de mes amis," *B*, no. 4, pp. 115–16.

July "Fragment sur l'amitié," *B*, no. 5, pp. 149–53.

Aug./Sept. "Declamatio suasoria," *RB*, 3: 134–45.

Nov. "Stoïcisme d'automne," *B*, no. 6, pp. 185–87.

Nov. "Premiers paradoxes sur Renan," *RB*, 3: 235–50.

Dec. "Fragment sur la gloire," *RB*, 3: 318–27.

1893

Mar. 15   "Fragment sur la prière," *RB*, 4: 197–202.
Apr. 15   [Untitled: "Une soirée Verlaine"], *RB*, 4: 268.
May 25   "Fragment sur l'espérance," *RB*, 4: 341–55.
June 25   "Le livre de mes amies," *RB*, 4: 401–39.
Sept. 15   "Annie ou les fiançailles d'argent," *RB*, 4: 122–36.
Oct.   "Eliane ou le regret," *RB*, 5: 193–206.

1894

Jan.   "Le goût classique," *RB*, 6: 29–40.
Jan.   "Les revues," *RB*, 6: 91–92.
Feb.   "Les revues," *RB*, 6: 191–97.
Mar.   "Les revues: *La Revue des deux mondes* en 1893," *RB*, 6: 285–88.
May   "Nouvelles conversations avec Eckermann, I: sur la critique," *RB*, 6: 442–47.
May   "Les revues," *RB*, 6: 477–80.
July   "M. Paul Bourget," *RB*, 7: 10–15.
Aug.   "Nouvelles conversations avec Eckermann, II: sur les relations littéraires," *RB*, 7: 145–49.
Sept.   "La proie et l'ombre," *RB*, 7: 215–24.
Nov.   "A propos d'une anecdote sur la danse," *RB*, 7: 404–7.

1895

Feb. 15   "M. Anatole France," *RB*, 8: 168–71.
Apr. 15   "Nouvelles conversations avec Eckermann, III: les moeurs politiques," *RB*, 8: 353–56.
June 1   "Nouvelles conversations avec Eckermann, IV: essais critiques d'Eckermann," *RB*, 8: 497–501.
July 1   "Nouvelles conversations avec Eckermann, V: à l'Académie," *RB*, 9: 25–28.
July   "Jules Renard," *Mercure de France*, 15: 97–101.
July 15   "Ceci et cela," *RB*, 9: 71–80.
Sept. 15   "Nouvelles conversations avec Eckerman, VI: les étoiles," *RB*, 9: 257–60.

1896

Feb. 1   "Les livres," *RB*, 10: 139–43: reviewing Henry Michel, *L'idée de l'Etat*; Comtesse de Ségur, *Les deux nigauds*; Jules Verne, *L'Ile à Hélice*.
May 15   "Les livres," *RB*, 10: 470–73: reviewing Paul Adam, *La force du mal*; Paul Hervieu, *Le petit duc*; Jules Renard, *Histoires naturelles*; Léon Daudet, *Le voyage de Shakespere*; Pierre Louys, *Aphrodite*.
June 1   "Les livres," *RB*, 10: 510–12: reviewing Gustave Kahn, *Le roi fou*; Georges Lecomte, *Espagne*; Adolphe Boschot, *Pierre Rovert*; Georges Hugo, *Souvenirs d'un matelot*; Georges Clemenceau, *Le Grand Pan*.

June 15 "Les livres," *RB*, 10: 571–73: reviewing Emile Zola, *Rome.*

July 1 "Les livres," *RB*, 11: 44–48: reviewing Arthur Schnitzler, *Mourir*; Maurice Talmeyr, *Sur le banc*; Fernand Vandérem, *La patronne* and *Charlie*; Maurice Beaubourg, *La saison au bois de Bologne*; Victor Barrucand, *Le pain gratuit* and *La vie véritable du citoyen Jean Rossignol*; the Goncourts, *Journal*; Marcel Proust, *Les plaisirs et les jours*; Paul Bourget, *Une idylle tragique*; Ernest la Jeunesse, *Les nuits, les ennuis, et les âmes de nos plus notoires contemporains.*

Oct. 1 "Les livres," *RB*, 11: 333–36: reviewing Maurice Maeterlinck, *Le trésor des humbles*; Marcel Schwob, *La croisade des enfants* and *Les vies imaginaires.*

Oct. 15 "Les livres," *RB*, 11: 381–82: reviewing René Boylesve, *Le médecin des dames de Néans*; Henry Bauër, *De la vie et du rêve.*

Nov. 1 "Les livres," *RB*, 11: 431–32: reviewing Jules Claretie, *Brichanteau, comédien*; Albert Lantoine, *Elisçuah*; Saint-Auban, *La voix des choses*; Aurélien Scholl, *Tableaux vivants.*

Dec. 1 "Les livres," *RB*, 11: 520–23: reviewing the correspondence of Victor Hugo.

1897

Jan. 15 "Les livres," *RB*, 12: 99–103: reviewing Lucien Muhlfeld, *Le monde où l'on imprime*; Fernand Gregh, *La maison de l'enfance*; Guy de Passillé, *Histoire d'un gentilhomme de province.*

Feb. 1 "Les livres," *RB*, 12: 144–47: reviewing Gustave Geffroy, *L'enfermé*; Anatole France, *L'orme du mail.*

Feb. 15 "Les livres," *RB*, 12: 188–90: reviewing Ernest la Jeunesse, *L'imitation de Notre Maître Napoléon*; Paul Gavault, *Mon bon oncle*; Maurice Maeterlinck, *Douze chansons*; Eugène Demolder, *La légende d'Yperdamme.*

Mar. 1 "Les livres," *RB*, 12: 236–40: reviewing André Gide, *Le voyage d'Urien* and *Paludes*; Saint-Georges de Bouhélier, *L'hiver en méditation* and *La resurrection des dieux*; Maurice Leblond, *Essai sur le naturisme*; Eugène Monfort, *Sylvie*; Jules Huret, *Enquête sur la question sociale*; Alphonse Daudet, *La trésor d'Arlatan*; Charles Foley, *M. Belle-Humeur.*

Mar. 15 "Les livres," *RB*, 12: 325–26: reviewing Henry Bordeaux, *Sentiments et idées de ce temps*; Anon., *Amitié amoureuse.*

Apr. 1 "Les livres," *RB*, 12: 389–93: reviewing Paul Adam, *L'année de Clarisse*; Bernard Lazare, *Les porteurs des torches*; Emile Pouvillon, *L'image*; Alfred Poizat, *Avila des saints*; Martin Videau, *Les deux amours de Jean Séguin*; Jean de la Brète, *L'esprit souffle où il veut*; Mme. de Peyrebrune, *Les fiancées.*

Apr. 15 "Les livres," *RB*, 12: 473–77: reviewing Fernand Vandérem, *Les deux rives*; V. Bérard, *La politique du sultan*; C. Oudinot, *Noël Savare*; G. Sarrazin, *Le roi de la mer*; C. Vergniol, *L'enlisement*; Mlle. de Bovet, *Partie du pied gauche*; D. Lesueur, *Invincible charme.*

May 1 "Les livres," *RB*, 12: 551–54: reviewing Tristan Bernard, *Contes de Pantruche et d'ailleurs*; Paul Hervieu, *La bétise parisienne*; Eugène

Morel, *La rouille du sabre*; Georges Darien, *Biribi*; Jean Grave, *La grande famille.*

June 1 "Les livres," *RB*, 12: 720–24: reviewing Paul Adam, *La bataille d'Uhde*; Camille Mauclair, *L'orient vierge*; Robert Scheffer, *Le prince narcisse*; Mme. J. Marni, *Les enfants qu'elles ont*; Picard-Destelan, *Mon droit.*

June 15 "Notes dramatiques," *RB*, 12: 796–97: reviewing Romain Coolus, *L'enfant malade.*

July 1 "Les livres," *RB*, 13: 77–79: reviewing André Gide, *Les nourritures terrestres.*

July 15 "Les livres," *RB*, 13: 156–59: reviewing Jean de Tinan, *Penses-tu réussir?*; Rachilde, *Les hors-nature*; Hugues Rebell, *La Nichina*; Félicien Champsaur, *La glaneuse*; Pierre d'Alheim, *Sur les pointes*; André Bellessort, *La jeune Amérique.*

Aug. 1 "Les livres," *RB*, 13: 222–26: reviewing Romain Coolus, *L'enfant malade.*

Oct. 15 "Les livres," *RB*, 14: 153–57: reviewing Michel Bréal, *La sémantique*; Paul Adam, *Lettres de Malaisie*; Jacques Saint-Cère, *La noce sentimentale.*

Nov. 1 "Les livres," *RB*, 14: 230–33: reviewing Anatole France, *Le mannequin d'osier*; Peter Nansen, *Marie*; Henri Ouvré, *Sur les marches du temple*; Louis Dollivet, *Sale juif!*

Nov. 15 "Les livres," *RB*, 14: 292–97, 301–3: reviewing Maurice Barrès, *Les déracinés*; Henri de Régnier, *La canne de jaspe*; Alfred Jarry, *Les jours et les nuits*; Jean Viollis, *L'émoi*; Brada, *Lettres d'une amoureuse*; The Napoléon of Stendhal; Charles Andler, *Les origines du socialisme d'Etat en Allemagne.*

Dec. 1 "Les livres," *RB*, 14: 381–83: reviewing René Boylesve, *Sainte Marie des fleurs*; Rémy Saint-Maurice, *Temple d'amour.*

1898

Jan. 1 "Les romans," *RB*, 15: 68–70: reviewing Georges Lecomte, *Les valets*; Pol Neveux, *Golo*; Paul Leclercq, *L'étoile rouge*; Jean Psichari, *Le rêve de Yanniri.*

Feb. 15 "Les romans," *RB*, 15: 308–11: reviewing Paul and Victor Margueritte, *Le désastre*; Pierre Veber, *L'aventure.*

Apr. 1 "Les romans," *RB*, 15: 551–57: reviewing Emile Zola, *Paris*; Eugène Morel, *Terre promise*; "Une circassienne," *Dans l'ombre du harem*; Gustave Kahn, *Les petites âmes pressées*; Pierre Louys, *Chansons de Bilitis.*

Apr. 15 "Les livres," *RB*, 15: 628–31: reviewing Georges Clemenceau, *Les plus forts.*

May 1 "Les livres," *RB*, 16: 71–73: reviewing Maurice Maindron, *Saint-Cendre*; Paul Adam, *Les tentatives passionnées.*

May 15 "Les livres," *RB*, 16: 151–52: reviewing the correspondence of Ernest Renan and Marcelin Berthelot.

June 1 "Les livres," *RB*, 16: 233–35: reviewing Henry Bourgerel, *Les pierres qui pleurent*; Marcelle Tinayre, *Avant l'amour*; Henri Allais, *Histoires pénales*; Edouard Ducoté, *Aventures*; Mme. J. Marni, *Fiacres*; Michel Corday, *Les confessions d'un enfant du siège*; Anatole Le Braz, *Pâques d'Islande*; René Claparède, *Toynbee Hall*.

June 15   "Les livres," *RB*, 16: 313–15: reviewing Jules Renard, *Les bucoliques*; Jean Ajalbert, *Sous le sabre*; Léon Bloy, *Le mendiant ingrat*; Jean de Childra, *L'heure sexuelle*; Camille Pert, *Les florifères*; Maurice Montégut, *Rue des martyrs*.

July 15   "Les livres," *RB*, 16: 475–79: reviewing René Boylesve, *Le parfum des îles Borromées*; Jean de Tinan, *L'exemple de Ninon de Lenclos, amoureuse*; Camille Mauclair, *Le soleil des morts*; Paul Adam, *Le triomphe des médiocres*; François de Nion, *Les façades*.

Sept. 15   "Les livres," *RB*, 17: 155: reviewing Felicien Champsaur, *Régina Sandri*; Louis de Robert, *L'envers d'une courtisane*; J.-Joseph Renaud, *Le cinématographie du mariage*; Henry Bataille, *Ton sang* and *La lépreuse*.

Oct. 1   "Les livres," *RB*, 17: 232–35: reviewing Gustave Kahn, *Le conte de l'or et du silence*; Jean Ajalbert, *Celles qui passent*; Eugène Monfort, *Exposé du naturisme*; Raymond Aynard, *Ames recluses*; Marcel Batilliat, *Chair mystique*; François de Nion, *L'inutile vertu*.

Nov. 15   "Les livres," *RB*, 17: 476–80: reviewing Lucien Muhlfeld, *Le mauvais désir*; Eugène Rouart, *La villa sans maître*; Urbain Gohier, *L'armée contre la nation*.

Dec. 1   "Les livres," *RB*, 17: 556–58: reviewing Jean de Tinan (on the occasion of his death); Gustave Kahn, *Le cirque solaire*; Robert Scheffer, *Grève d'amour*; Paul Bosq, *Désillusion*.

Dec. 15   "Les livres," *RB*, 17: 633–34: reviewing Pierre Louys, *La femme et le pantin*; Jean de Ferrière, *Leur fille*; Tristan Bernard, *Sous toutes réserves*; Alphonse Allais, *Le bec en l'air*; Georges Auriol, *Ma chemise brûle*.

1899

Jan. 15   "Les livres," *RB*, 18: 143–47: reviewing Ernest la Jeunesse, *L'holocauste*; Marcel Boulenger, *La femme baroque*; Mathilde Serao, *Coeur malade*; Butti, *L'automate* and *L'âme*; Girolamo Rovetti, *L'illustre Matteo*; Fogazzaro, *Malombra*; Jean Ajalbert, *Les deux justices*.

Feb. 1   "Les livres," *RB*, 18: 233–35: reviewing Paul Adam, *La force*.

Mar. 1   "Les livres," *RB*, 18: 394–97: reviewing Jane Austen, *Catherine Morland* [Northanger Abbey]; Georges Clemenceau, *L'iniquité*; Marcel Lami, *La débandade*.

Mar. 15   "Les livres," *RB*, 18: 468–72: reviewing Anatole France, *L'anneau d'améthyste*; Jean Lorrain, *La dame turque*; Mme. J. Marni, *Celle qu'on ignore*; Charles Foley, *Zéphyrin Baudru*; Jean and Jérôme Tharaud, *Le coltineur débile*; Auguste Germain, *En fête*; Jeanne Schultz, *Le main de sainte Modestine*; Jean Bertheroy, *La danseuse de Pompeï*.

Apr. 1   "Les livres," *RB*, 18: 558–60: reviewing René Boylesve, *Mlle Cloque*.

Apr. 15 "Les livres," *RB*, 18: 634–35: reviewing Rudyard Kipling, *Le livre de la jungle.*

May 1 "Les livres," *RB*, 19: 72–77: reviewing Edouard Estaunié, *Le ferment*; Maurice Barrès, *Un amateur d'âmes*; Henri de Régnier, *Le trèfle blanc*; Paul Fort, *Le roman de Louis XI*; Henri Vignemal, *Vain effort*; Jean de Ferrières, *Les messieurs de Séryac*; Eugène Monfort, *Essai sur l'amour*; M. de Grandfort, *Les franches-fileuses*; Maurice Vaucaire, *Le demi-grand monde.*

May 15 "Les livres," *RB*, 19: 150–54: reviewing Charles Andler, *Le prince de Bismarck*; Tristan Bernard, *Mémoires d'un jeune homme rangé.*

June 15 "Les livres," *RB*, 19: 311–13: reviewing Les Rosny, *La fauve*; Marquis de Vogüé, *Les morts qui parlent.*

July 1 "Les livres: les romans," *RB*, 19: 391–93: reviewing Ernest la Jeunesse, *L'inimitable*; Georges Ohnet, *Au fond du gouffre*; Maurice Maindron, *Le tournoi de Vauplassans*; Albert Pinard, *Samuelle Servais*; Pierre Valdagne, *Une rencontre*; Jean Lorrain, *Poussière de Paris.*

July 1 "Les livres: états, sociétés, gouvernements," *RB*, 19: 393–95: reviewing Jean Jaurès, *Action socialiste.*

July 15 "Les livres," *RB*, 19: 475–78: reviewing Octave Mirbeau, *Le jardin des supplices*; François de Nion, *L'amoureuse de Mozart*; Joseph Reinach, *Le crépuscule des traîtres*; X., *Histoire des variations de l'Etat-major*; Stéphane Arnoulin, *L'affaire La Roncière.*

Aug. 1 "Les livres," *RB*, 19: 552–55: reviewing Jean Psichari, *La croyante*; Louis Bertrand, *Le sang des races*; Charles-Henry Hirsch, *La possession*; Maxime Formont, *Voluptés*; Jean Schopfer, *Voyage idéal en Italie*; Paul Hamelle, *Hommes et choses d'outre-mer* and *Les minutes parisiennes.*

Aug. 15 "Les livres," *RB*, 19: 635–37: reviewing Anatole France, *Pierre Nozière*; Jean de Tinan, *Aimienne*; Paul and Victor Margueritte, *Femmes nouvelles*; Rachilde, *La tour d'amour*; Paul Flat, *Les premiers vénitiens.*

Sept. 1 "Les livres," *RB*, 20: 77–80: reviewing André Gide, *Le Prométhée mal enchaîné* and *Philoctète.*

Nov. 15 "Les livres," *RB*, 20: 472–76: reviewing Marcel Boulenger, *Le page*; Dr. J.-C. Mardrus (trans.), *Le livre des mille et une nuits*; Hugues Rebell, *La câlineuse.*

Dec. 1 "Les livres," *RB*, 20: 552–55, 559–60: reviewing Eugène Vernon, *La demeure enchantée*; Anatole France, *Clio*; Paul Adam, *Basile et Sophia*; Urbain Gohier, *Les prétoriens de la congrégation*; Gaston Moch, *L'armée d'une démocratie.*

1900

Jan. 1 "Les livres," *RB*, 21: 75–78: reviewing Max Stirner, *L'unique et sa propriété*; Dr. J.-C. Mardrus (trans.), *Le livre des mille et une nuits*; Rémy de Gourmont, *Le songe d'une femme*; Jules Case, *Les sept visages*; Paul Lévy, *Fleurs d'oppression*; Marcel Rouff, *Les pèlerins*; Micislas Golberg, *Vers l'amour.*

Jan. 15 "Les livres," *RB*, 21: 153–57: reviewing Leo Tolstoy, *Résurrection*.
Nov. 1 "Nouvelles conversations avec Eckermann," *RB*, 23: 371–78.

1901

Mar. 1 "Nouvelles conversations avec Eckermann," *RB*, 24: 358–63.

1903

Mar. 9 "Les livres," *GB*: reviewing Joris-Karl Huysmans, *L'oblat*.
Mar. 15 "Les théâtres," *RL*, pp. 644–54: reviewing Alfred Capus, *Le beau jeune homme*; A. Janvier, *Les appeleurs*; Edmond Sée, *L'indiscret*.
Mar. 16 "Les livres," *GB*: reviewing Henri de Régnier, *Mariage de minuit*; Albert le Roy, *George Sand et ses amis*.
Mar. 23 "Les livres," *GB*: reviewing Maurice Barrès, *Amori et dolori sacrum*.
Mar. 30 "Les livres," *GB*: reviewing Gérard d'Houville, *L'inconstante*; René Bazin, *Donatienne*.
Apr. 6 "Les livres," *GB*: reviewing Anna de Noailles, *La nouvelle espérance*.
Apr. 13 "Les livres," *GB*: reviewing Adolphe Brisson, *Les prophètes*; H. Le Roux, *Chasses et gens d'Abyssinie*; Paul Léautaud, *Petit ami*; P. de Querlon, *Les joues d'Hélène*.
Apr. 15 "Les théâtres," *RL*, pp. 203–11: reviewing Emile Fabre, *La rabouilleuse*; Marcel Girette, *Sans lui*; Maurice Boniface, *Clarisse Arbois*; Anatole France, *Crainquebille*.
Apr. 20 "Les livres," *GB*: reviewing Elie Metchnikoff, *Etudes sur la nature humaine*.
Apr. 27 "Les livres," *GB*: reviewing Pierre Loti, *L'Inde*.
May 11 "Les livres," *GB*: reviewing Paul Adam, *Le temps et la vie*.
May 15 "Les théâtres," *RL*, 2: 437–50: reviewing Alexandre Dumas, *fils*, *La princesse Georges*; Octave Mirbeau, *Les affaires sont les affaires*; Berr de Turique, *Le supplice du silence*; A. de Lorde and Masson-Forestier, *L'attaque nocturne*; Jules Renard, *Monsieur Vernet*.
May 18 "Les livres," *GB*: reviewing Anatole France, *Histoire comique*.
May 25 "Les livres," *GB*: reviewing Georges Lecomte, *Le veau d'or*; Francisque Sarcey, *Journal de jeunesse*.
June 1 "Les livres," *GB*: reviewing Gabriel Hanotaux, *Histoire de la France contemporaine*; Willy[-Colette], *Claudine s'en va*; Max and Alex Fischer, *Pour s'amuser en ménage*.
June 8 "Les livres," *GB*: discussing Edmond Rostand [on the occasion of his reception by the Académie Française].
June 15 "Les livres," *GB*: reviewing Georges de Porto-Riche, *Bonheur manqué*; Abel Hermant, *Cinq discours*; Jules Bois, *Visions de l'Inde*.
June 29 "Les livres," *GB*: reviewing Claude Ferval, *Le plus fort*; Abel Hermant, *Confession d'un enfant d'hier*.
July 6 "Les livres," *GB*: reviewing Edouard Rod, *L'inutile effort*; Paul

Acker, *Un amant de coeur*; A. Maurel, *Mémoires d'un mari*; G. Chérau, *Monseigneur voyage*.

July 27 "Romans de femmes," *GB*.

Aug. 3 "Les livres," *GB*: reviewing Pierre Louys, *Sanguines*; Dr. J.-C. Mardrus (trans.), *Le livre des mille et une nuits*.

Aug. 10 "Les livres," *GB*: reviewing Paul Adam, *Le soleil de juillet*; Maxime Formont, *Les énervées*; H. Duvernois, *Le roseau de fer*; M. Morel, *Sappho de Lesbos*.

Aug. 24 "Les livres," *GB*: reviewing André Gide, *Prétextes* and *L'immoraliste*.

Aug. 31 "Les livres," *GB*: reviewing Charles-Louis Philippe, *Le père Perdrix*; A. Aderer, *Chez les rois*; A. Hallays, *A travers la France*.

Sept. 7 "Les livres," *GB*: reviewing Bernard Lazare (on the occasion of his death); Alphonse Albalat, *Le travail du style*; Rémy de Gourmont, *Le problème du style*.

Sept. 14 "Les livres," *GB*: reviewing Eugène Vernon, *Giselle Chevreuse*; Marius and Ary Leblond, *Le zézère*; J. A. Nau, *La force ennemie*; Henri Ghéon, *Le consolateur*.

Sept. 21 "Les livres," *GB*: reviewing Jacques Morland, *Enquête sur l'influence allemande*.

Oct. 5 "Les livres," *GB*: reviewing Barbey d'Aurevilly, *Lettres à Léon Bloy*; E. Blémont, *A quoi tient l'amour*; Paul Ginisty, *Heures difficiles*; Edouard Ducoté, *En ce monde ou dans l'autre*.

Oct. 12 "Les livres," *GB*: reviewing Abel Hermant, *Confession d'un homme d'aujourd'hui*.

Oct. 15 "Le théâtre de M. Gabriel D'Annunzio," *RL*, 2: 145–69.

Oct. 26 "Les livres," *GB*: reviewing Marcel Boulenger, *Couplées*; Marquis de Vogüé, *Le roi de la mer*.

Nov. 2 "Les livres," *GB*: reviewing Henri de Régnier, *Les vacances d'un jeune homme sage*; René Boylesve, *L'enfant à la balustrade*.

Nov. 15 "Les théâtres," *RL*, pp. 448–60: reviewing Romain Coolus, *Antoinette Sabrier*; Alfred Capus and Emmanuel Arène, *L'adversaire*; Pierre Soulaine, *L'héritier*; Robert de Flers and Gaston de Caillavet, *Les sentiers de la vertu*.

Nov. 16 "Généralités sur le roman contemporain," *GB*.

Dec. 7 "Les livres," *GB*: reviewing Jules Renard, *L'écornifleur*.

Dec. 14 "Les livres," *GB*: reviewing Maurice Barrès, *Les amitiés françaises*.

Dec. 15 "Les théâtres," *RL*, 2: 690–97: reviewing Maurice Donnay, *Le retour de Jérusalem*; the Goncourts, *Germinie Lacerteux*; Xanrof and Chancel, *Le prince consort*; Georges Courteline, *La paix chez soi*.

Dec. 26 "Les livres," *GB*: reviewing Jean Jaurès, *Histoire socialiste*.

1904

Jan. 18 "Les livres," *GB*: reviewing J. Vignaud, *Les amis du peuple*; "Réflexions sur le prix Goncourt."

Jan. 25 "Les livres," *GB*: reviewing Frédéric Masson, *Napoléon et son fils*.

Feb. 1 "Les livres," *GB*: reviewing Louis Cazamian, *Le roman social en Angleterre.*

Feb. 8 "Les livres," *GB*: reviewing Séverine, *Sac-à-tout.*

Feb. 29 "Les livres," *GB*: reviewing Gustave Geffroy, *L'apprentie.*

Apr. 5 "Les livres," *GB*: reviewing Paul and Victor Margueritte, *La commune.*

Apr. 29 [On the reception of René Bazin by the Académie Française], *H.*

May 10 "La vie littéraire," *H*: reviewing Marcel Prévost, *La plus faible.*

May 17 "La vie littéraire," *H*: "Romans de la terre."

May 24 "La vie littéraire," *H*: reviewing Anatole France, *Crainquebille*; *Putois*; *Riquet.*

June 1 "La vie littéraire," *H*: "Maurice Donnay et l'antisémitisme."

June 8 "La vie littéraire," *H*: reviewing Ernest Renan, *Mélanges religieux et historiques.*

June 15 "La vie littéraire," *H*: reviewing Pierre Loti, *Vers Ispahan*; Fernand Bernard, *A travers Sumatra*; Jules Huret, *De New-York à la Nouvelle-Orléans.*

June 30 "Carnet du liseur," *GB*: reviewing Anna de Noailles, *Le visage émerveillé.*

July 1 "A l'Académie," *H.*

July 4 "La vie littéraire," *H*: "A propos de quelques poètes" [Fernand Gregh, Louis le Cardonnel, Henry Bataille, François Porché].

July 16 "La vie littéraire," *H*: Continuation of the preceding.

Aug. 1 "La vie littéraire," *H*: reviewing George Sand, *Souvenirs et idées.*

Aug. 8 "La vie littéraire," *H*: reviewing Jean Aicard, *Le père Lebonnard.*

Aug. 16 "La vie littéraire," *H*: reviewing Paul Ginisty, *Paris intime en révolution.*

Aug. 24 "La vie littéraire," *H*: reviewing Paul Bourget, *Un divorce.*

Aug. 31 "La vie littéraire," *H*: "Le salaire de l'artiste."

Sept. 7 "La vie littéraire," *H*: reviewing Lafcadio Hearn, *Le Japon inconnu.*

Oct. 11 "La vie littéraire," *H*: reviewing Maurice Maeterlinck, *Le double jardin.*

Oct. 24 "La vie littéraire," *H*: reviewing Marcel Mielvaque, *La vertu du sol*; Marius-Ary Leblond, *Sarabande*; André Maurel, *Chevauchée.*

Nov. 1 "La vie littéraire," *H*: reviewing Louis-Xavier de Ricard, *Histoire mondaine du Second Empire.*

Nov. 24 "La vie littéraire," *H*: reviewing Henry Bataille, *Maman Colibri.*

Dec. 6 "La vie littéraire," *H*: "Le roman social."

Dec. 15 "La vie littéraire," *H*: Continuation of the preceding.

Dec. 26 "La vie littéraire," *H*: reviewing Gustave Geffroy, *La Bretagne.*

1905

Jan. 2 "La vie littéraire," *H*: reviewing Henry Bernstein, *Le bercail.*

Jan. 9 "La vie littéraire," *H*: "Autour de Victor Hugo."

Jan. 16 "La vie littéraire," *H*: reviewing Shakespeare, *Le roi Lear.*
Jan. 30 "La vie littéraire," *H*: reviewing Anatole France, *L'Eglise et la République*; M. Bouchor, *Chansons joyeuses*; G. Laurent, *Fondateurs de la morale laïque*; Célestin Bouglé, *Solidarisme et libéralisme.*
Feb. 4 "Les premières," *H*: reviewing Alfred Athis, *Les manigances*; Bénière, *Les experts*; Pierre Veber, *L'amourette.*
Feb. 13 "La vie littéraire," *H*: reviewing Hugo Ganz, *La débâcle russe*; Leo Deutsch, *Seize ans en Sibérie*; Melchine, *Dans le monde des réprouvés.*
Feb. 20 "La vie littéraire," *H*: reviewing Abel Hermant, *M. de Courpière marié.*
Feb. 27 "La vie littéraire," *H*: "G. d'Annunzio et la tragédie moderne."
Mar. 13 "La vie littéraire," *H*: "Marcel Schwob."
Mar. 21 "La vie littéraire," *H*: reviewing Paul Adam, *Le serpent noir.*
Apr. 3 "La vie littéraire," *H*: "Jules Verne."
Apr. 10 "La vie littéraire," *H*: reviewing Paul and Victor Margueritte, *Le prisme*; Tristan Bernard, *Amants et voleurs.*
Apr. 18 "La vie littéraire," *H*: reviewing Alfred de Vigny, *Le marchand de Venise*; André Rivoire, *Il était une bergère*; Catulle Mendès, *Scarron.*
Apr. 21 "Leur bonne foi," *H*: reviewing P. Maumus, *L'Eglise vengée.*
Apr. 29 [no heading], *H*: reviewing Eugène Fournière, *Ouvriers et patrons.*
May 1 "La vie littéraire," *H*: "Romans de femmes."
May 8 "La vie littéraire," *H*: reviewing Henri de Régnier, *Le passé vivant*; André Lichtenberger, *Les centaures*; Paul Reboux, *Maison de dames*; Jean-Antoine Nau, *Prêteur d'amour.*
May 15 "La vie littéraire," *H*: reviewing Maurice Barrès, *Au service de l'Allemagne.*
May 29 "La vie littéraire," *H*: "Romans sociaux."
June 5 "La vie littéraire," *H*: reviewing Jean Ajalbert, *Sao-Van-Di*; Marius-Ary Leblond, *Les sortilèges.*
June 12 "La vie littéraire," *H*: reviewing Georges Ancey, *Ces messieurs*; Henri Lavedan, *Le duel.*
July 3 "La vie littéraire," *H*: reviewing Marcelin Berthelot, *Science et libre pensée.*
July 17 "La vie littéraire," *H*: reviewing Anna de Noailles, *La domination.*

1906

Mar. 6 "Elisabeth Masson," *L*, pp. 87–103.

1907

Nov. 15 [Response to the inquiry: "Tolstoi ou Shakespeare?"], *L*, pp. 66–67.
Dec. 25 "A travers la quinzaine: l'aveu et le pardon au théâtre," *GR*, pp. 778–90: reviewing Mathilde Serao, *Après le pardon*; Paul and Victor Margueritte, *L'autre.*

1908

Jan. 15 "L'oeuvre poétique de Mme de Noailles," *RP*, pp. 225–47.

Jan. 25 "Les théâtres," *GR*, pp. 367–73: reviewing Gustave Geffroy, *L'apprentie.*

Feb. 10 "Impressions et commentaires," *GR*, pp. 566–77: "Paul Bourget et le divorce."

Feb. 25 "Impressions et commentaires," *GR*, pp. 787–98: "Autour du romantisme."

Mar. 10 "Impressions et commentaires," *GR*, pp. 156–67: reviewing Henry Bataille, *La femme nue.*

Apr. 10 "Impressions et commentaires," *GR*, pp. 578–88: reviewing Gérard d'Houville, *Le temps d'aimer*; René Boylesve, *Mon amour.*

May 10 "Impressions et commentaires," *GR*, pp. 156–68: "Les liaisons dangereuses."

June 10 "La vie théâtrale," *GR*, pp. 571–81: reviewing G. B. Shaw, *Candida*; Albert Samain, *Polyphème*; Maurice Magre, *La Velleda*; A. Picard, *Jeunesse.*

June 25 "La vie théâtrale," *GR*, pp. 776–84: reviewing Georges de Porto-Riche, *Amoureuse.*

June 30 "L'amant et l'amour," *GB.*

July 10 "La vie théâtrale," *GR*, pp. 179–86: reviewing Jules Lemaître, *La princesse de Clèves.*

Sept. 10 "La vie théâtrale," *GR*, pp. 186–93: "Le théâtre de M. Tristan Bernard."

[The drama reviews in *Comoedia*, which follow, were for the most part untitled, but the names of the plays and their authors have been supplied in order to give a more detailed picture of Blum's reviewing.]

Sept. 25 *CO*: reviewing R. Peter and R. Danceny, *L'or.*

Oct. 2 *CO*: reviewing Dartigues, *Répudiée*; Serge Basset, *L'auberge rouge.*

Oct. 8 *CO*: reviewing Andre Rivoire, *Le bon roi Dagobert.*

Oct. 10 "La vie théâtrale," *GR*, pp. 590–95: reviewing R. Peter and R. Danceny, *L'or*; F. Malefille, *Le coeur et la dot*; Raymonde and Sylvane, *Le petit fouchard* [?]; Serge Basset, *L'auberge rouge*; L. Dartigues, *Répudiée*; Arthur Pinero, *La maison en ordre.*

Oct. 11 *CO*: reviewing Hermann Sudermann, *Parmi les pierres.*

Oct. 15 *CO*: reviewing F. Nozière, *L'après-midi byzantine*; Fargue and Charron, *V'là le potin mondain*; Germain and Trébor, *La petite femme forte*; E.-G. Gluc, *Madame est de bois.*

Oct. 16 *CO*: reviewing H. Delorme, *Gros béguin*; A. Barde, *Suzy*; Carré and Barde, *La double r'vue.*

Oct. 25 "La vie théâtrale," *GR*, pp. 805–11: reviewing Paul Bourget, *L'émigré*; Henry Bernstein, *Israël*; Hermann Sudermann, *Parmi les pierres*; André Rivoire, *Le roi Dagobert.*

Nov. 10 "La vie théâtrale," *GR*, pp. 167–73: reviewing Franz Wedekind, *L'éveil du printemps*; F. de Croisset and Maurice Leblanc, *Arsène Lupin*; G. Thurner, *Le passe-partout.*

Nov. 21 *CO*: reviewing H. Cain and E. Adenis, *Les révoltés*.

Nov. 22 *CO*: reviewing A. Bassan, *Une présentation*; Léon Frapié, *La première mise*; Morsier, *Machin fils*; C. Torquet, *Cent lignes émues*; E.-M. Laumann and P. Olivier, *Nuit d'Illyrie*.

Nov. 25 *CO*: reviewing Paul Spaak, *Kaatje*.

Nov. 26 *CO*: reviewing Emile Fabre, *Les vainqueurs*.

Nov. 27 *CO*: reviewing J. Blanchard, *Au temps des fées*; Hugo von Hofmannsthal, *Elektra*; Tristan Bernard, *Le jeu de la morale et du hasard*.

Nov. 29 *CO*: reviewing M. Prax, *Héloïse*.

Dec. 3 *CO*: reviewing G. Maldague, *La boscotte*.

Dec. 4 *CO*: reviewing Tristan Bernard, *Le poulailler*; Sacha Guitry, *Après . . .* ; P. Mortier and A. Mycho, *Asseyez-vous*.

Dec. 5 *CO*: reviewing J. Bouchor, *Bienheureuse*; E. Guiraud, *Le poussin*; L. Legendre, *Pylade*.

Dec. 8 *CO*: reviewing Octave Mirbeau and Thadée Natanson, *Le Foyer*.

Dec. 9 *CO*: reviewing P. Rameil and F. Saisset, *Les vieux*; Paul Spaak, *La madone*.

Dec. 10 *CO*: reviewing Alfred Capus, *L'oiseau blessé*.

Dec. 10 "L'âge de l'amour," *GR*, pp. 537–44: reviewing Maurice Donnay, *La patronne*.

Dec. 16 *CO*: reviewing A. Bisson, *La femme X*.

Dec. 17 *CO*: reviewing M. Soulié and C. Darantière, *Jeanne qui rit*; Hermann Sudermann, *Fritzschen*.

Dec. 18 *CO*: reviewing M. de Faramond, *La dame qui n'est plus aux camélias*.

Dec. 19 *CO*: reviewing Pierre Wolff and Gaston Leroux, *Le lys*.

Dec. 24 *CO*: reviewing J. Mary and E. Rochard, *La beauté du diable*.

1909

Jan. 8 *CO*: reviewing Saint-Georges de Bouhélier, *La tragédie royale*; Alexandre Arnoux, *La mort de Pan*.

Jan. 10 *CO*: reviewing Gniéditch, *Les lettres brûlées*; Collijn, *La tour du silence*.

Jan. 16 *CO*: reviewing Rip, *O gué! L'an neuf!*; Laval and Van Ysen, *La 23-Z*; Michel Provins, *Le médecin du coeur*.

Jan. 18 *CO*: reviewing André Paysan, *Notre fille*; Régis-Lamotte, *Balsamine et le bon brigand*.

Jan. 22 *CO*: reviewing Maurice Hennequin and Pierre Veber, *Une grosse affaire*.

Jan. 22 *CO*: reviewing Gabriel Trarieux, *La dette*; Tristan Bernard, *Les jumeaux de Brighton*.

Jan. 23 *CO*: reviewing Colette, *En camarades*.

Jan. 27 *CO*: reviewing Pierre Veber and Serge Basset, *Les grands*.

Jan. 27 *CO*: reviewing Wildenbruck, *La fille des Rabenstein*; Miguel Zamacoïs, *Bohemos*.

Jan. 28 *CO*: reviewing Gaston Marot and Victor Darlay [music by Marius Baggers], *Les aventures de Gavroche*.

Jan. 28   "Le nouveau spectacle de la Comédie Royale," *CO*: reviewing Ardot and Laroche, *Revue*; Serge Basset, *Henriette ou les avantages de la lecture*; Berteyle, *L'édredon*; Mme. Sylviac, *Coiffeurs pour dames.*

Jan. 30   *CO*: reviewing Romain Coolus, *4 fois 7 = 28.*

Jan. 31   *CO*: [Reviewing works from the Théâtre du Grand Guignol] André de Lorde and Charles Foley, *Un concert chez les fous*; Léon Sazie and Alévy, *Chez Agathe*; Maurice Prax and Gabriel Tallet, *Justice est faite.*

Feb. 2   *CO*: reviewing Romain Coolus, *4 fois 7 = 28* [continued from 30 January].

Feb. 3   *CO*: reviewing Maurice Level and Jacques Monnier, *La chaîne*; J. Dortzal [music by Jules Massenet], *Perce-Neige et les sept gnomes.*

Feb. 17   *CO*: reviewing Abel Hermant, *Trains de luxe.*

Feb. 18   *CO*: reviewing Jules Bois, *La Furie.*

Feb. 18   *CO*: reviewing Robert d'Humières, *La Marquesita.*

Feb. 20   *CO*: reviewing Robert Reinert, *Guerre*; Léon Madard, *Le donataire*; Charles Esquier, *Lorsque l'enfant paraît.*

Feb. 27   *CO*: reviewing Lucy Achalme, *Notre fils*; René Wisner, *Les désarmés.*

Feb. 28   *CO*: reviewing Georges Courteline and Pierre Wolff, *J'en ai plein le dos de Margot!*; Erckmann-Chatrian, *Le juif polonais.*

Mar. 5   *CO*: reviewing Jean Richepin, *La route d'émeraude.*

Mar. 10   *CO*: reviewing René Fauchois, *Beethoven.*

Mar. 13   *CO*: reviewing Maurice Donnay and Lucien Descaves, *La clairière.*

Mar. 18   *CO*: reviewing Maurice Sergine, *Le greluchon* [and discussion of an election to the Académie Française].

Mar. 26   *CO*: reviewing G. Montignac, *La notion du mari*; René Fraudet, *F.Z.V.?*; Jean-Jacques Bernard, *Le voyage à deux.*

Mar. 28   *CO*: reviewing Paul Bilhaud and Maurice Hennequin, *La meilleure des femmes.*

Mar. 30   *CO*: reviewing Paul Hervieu, *Connais-toi.*

Mar. 31   *CO*: reviewing Henry Bataille, *Le scandale.*

Apr. 2   *CO*: reviewing André Sardou, *L'étau.*

Apr. 3   *CO*: reviewing F.-T. Marinetti, *Le roi Bombance.*

Apr. 4   *CO*: reviewing Catulle Mendès, *L'Impératrice.*

Apr. 6   *CO*: reviewing Robert de Montesquiou, *Mikhaïl.*

Apr. 8   *CO*: reviewing William Busnach and Octave Gastineau, *L'assommoir* [adapted from the novel by Emile Zola].

Apr. 15   *CO*: reviewing H.-R. Lenormand, *Les possédés*; P.-H. Raymond-Duval, *Demain* [adapted from Joseph Conrad].

Apr. 16   *CO*: reviewing C. Gevel, *La cloison*; A. Vély and L. Miral, *La paix des ménages*; H. Bocage and A. Livrat, *Le petit abbé*; C. Desfontaines, *M. de Saint-Christophe, professeur de chinois*; P. Franck, *La romanichelle.*

Apr. 17   *CO*: reviewing Gustave Guiches and François de Nion, *Lauzun.*

Apr. 18   *CO*: reviewing A. Vély and L. Miral, *Le petit terme*; Sacha Guitry, *Tell père, Tell fils*; Charles Méré, *Les ruffians*; Willy, *Jeux à la coq.*

Apr. 22　CO: reviewing Henri de Brisay and Marcel Lauras, *Master Bob* (*gagnant du Derby*).

Apr. 28　CO: reviewing Léon Gandillot, *L'ex*.

May 2　CO: reviewing Georges Darien, *Non, elle n'est pas coupable*.

May 7　CO: reviewing Dario Niccodemi, *Le refuge*.

May 8　CO: reviewing Alfred Mortier, *Oeuvre posthume*; Remon and Chalençon, *L'éventail de Lady Windemere* [adapted from Oscar Wilde].

May 13　CO: reviewing Jean Richepin, *La Glu*.

May 16　CO: reviewing Léon Xanrof and Fred Amy, *L'impasse*.

May 19　CO: reviewing Romain Coolus, *Effets d'optique*; Carré and Menier, *Le premier pas*; L. Mayrargue, *Nuit sicilienne*.

May 23　CO: reviewing J. Hérold, *Maisonseule*; G. Nigond, *Keroubinos*.

May 25　CO: reviewing M. Carré and A. Barde, *Pari-sport*; Michel Bourdonneau, *Y a une suite!*

May 30　CO: reviewing Valentine de Saint-Pol, *Le déchu*; Jacques Nayrat, *L'éclipse*; Jehan Bouvelet, *Aimée*.

June 9　CO: reviewing Pierre Veber and Guillaume Wolff, *La vierge du forum*; J. Mirande and H. Caen, *Un petit trou pas cher*; Genemas, *Les dessous indiscrets*; Savières and Roval, *Gontran déménage*; G. Delamare, *La solution élégante*.

June 14　CO: reviewing A. Clevers, *La grève* and *Une forte tête*.

June 16　CO: reviewing Louis Péricaud and Henri Desfontaines, *La pierre de lune* [adapted from the novel by Wilkie Collins].

June 18　CO: reviewing Pierre Berton, *La rencontre*.

June 21　CO: reviewing Th.-W. Robertson, *Caste*; Sosie, *Vicomte Parsanne, valet de chambre*.

June 30　CO: reviewing François de Nion and J. Buysieulx, *La veille du bonheur*; Max Maurey, *Le Stradivarius*.

July 7　CO: reviewing Fernand Nozière and André Fijan, *Les sabots de Vénus*.

July 8　"Les concours publics du Conservatoire," CO.

July 15　CO: reviewing Charles Méré and H. Fescourt, *Festin du roi*; Théodore de Bainville, *Le baiser*.

Aug. 2　CO: reviewing Achille Richard, *Hercule*.

Sept. 19　CO: reviewing A. Bernède and H. Cain, *La Révolution française*.

Sept. 24　CO: reviewing Pierre Decourcelle, *Le roy sans royaume*.

Sept. 29　CO: reviewing Eugène Brieux, *Suzette*.

Sept. 30　CO: reviewing Nancey and Armont, *Théodore et Cie*.

Oct. 2　CO: reviewing Louis Bénière, "*Papillon*" dit "*Lyonnais-le-Juste*"; G. Sorbets and A. Cahuet, *Le roi s'ennuie*.

Oct. 9　CO: reviewing Ferrier, *La cornette*; L. Forest, *Un mariage à Londres*.

Oct. 14　CO: reviewing M. and A. Fischer, *Tonton, ou les drames de l'amour*; J.-J. Frappa, *Madame Dagobert*; Fernand Nozière, *Les deux visages*; Gregnon and Segrestaa, *Ferdinand, vas-tu t'en aller?*

Oct. 15　CO: reviewing Georges Mitchell, *Philosophie* and *Le petit de la bonne*.

Oct. 20   *CO*: reviewing Henri de Rothschild, *La rampe.*

Oct. 22   *CO*: reviewing Jules Renard, *La bigote*; Charles-Henry Hirsch, *Les émigrants.*

Oct. 23   *CO*: reviewing Henry Bernstein, *La griffe.*

Oct. 24   *CO*: reviewing *La petite chocolatière.*

Oct. 25   *CO*: reviewing J. d'Orliac, *Pulcinella.*

Oct. 29   *CO*: reviewing V. Darlay and H. de Gorsse, *La petite caporale.*

Oct. 30   *CO*: reviewing Georges Feydeau and Francis de Croisset, *Le circuit.*

Oct. 31   *CO*: reviewing Maurice Donnay, *Lysistrata.*

Nov. 5   *CO*: reviewing A. Bisson and G. Livet, *Nick Carter.*

Nov. 6   *CO*: reviewing Gaston Devore, *Page blanche*; B. Reynold, *Les bagatelles de la porte.*

Nov. 14   *CO*: reviewing Fernand Nozière and C. Müller, *La maison de danses* [adapted from the novel by Paul Reboux].

Nov. 18   *CO*: reviewing Léon Hennique and Johannès Gravier, *Jarnac*; A. Mars and A. de Bei, *La revanche d'Eve.*

Nov. 21   *CO*: [Reviewing works from the Théâtre du Grand Guignol] P. Pointu, *Le testament*; François de Nion, *La halte*; F. Fauré and E. Helsey, *Le hangar de la rue Vicq-d'Azir*; H. Caen, *L'ami des deux*; A. de Lorde and A. Binet, *Horrible expérience*; Y. Mirande and M. Simon, *Madame Aurélie.*

Nov. 23   *CO*: reviewing Henri Lavedan, *Sire.*

Nov. 24   *CO*: reviewing C. Nanteuil and H. de Gorsse, *Ça fait la . . . R'vue Michel*; D. Bonnaud and V.-M. Hoerter, *Le 12 bis*; R. Spitzer, *Les deux pigeonnes*; M. Vaucaire and Y. Mirande, *L'affreux homme.*

Nov. 26   *CO*: reviewing Emile Moreau, *Le procès de Jeanne d'Arc.*

Nov. 28   *CO*: reviewing Romain Coolus, *Le risque.*

Nov. 30   *CO*: reviewing Georges Duval, *L'article 301.*

Dec. 2   *CO*: reviewing Giacosa, *Comme les feuilles*; C. Rial-Faber, *La moralité nouvelle d'un empereur.*

Dec. 5   *CO*: reviewing Mouézy-Eon and J. Durieux, *Le papa du régiment* and *Un joli cadeau.*

Dec. 10   *CO*: reviewing Gardel-Hervé, *Un mariage de gourdes.*

Dec. 15   *CO*: reviewing Alfred Capus, *Un ange.*

Dec. 21   *CO*: reviewing Marcel Prévost, *Pierre et Thérèse.*

Dec. 22   *CO*: reviewing Jules Lemaître, *La massière.*

Dec. 23   *CO*: reviewing Sarah Bernhardt, *Un coeur d'homme.*

Dec. 24   *CO*: reviewing Emile Moreau and Charles Clairville, *Madame Margot.*

Dec. 29   *CO*: reviewing Albert du Bois, *Nonotte et Patouillet.*

Dec. 30   *CO*: reviewing Tristan Bernard, *Le danseur inconnu.*

1910

Jan. 7   *CO*: reviewing Maurice Hennequin and Pierre Veber, *Noblesse oblige!*

Jan. 8   *CO*: reviewing Paul Bourget, *La barricade.*

Jan. 16   *CO*: reviewing Adolphe Brisson, *Le théâtre* [book review].

Jan. 18   *CO*: reviewing Lecomte du Nouy, *Le drame de Three Corner's Bar*; Maurice Maeterlinck, *L'intérieur*; H.-R. Lenormand, *Au désert*.

Jan. 19   *CO*: reviewing Edouard Bourdet, *Le Rubicon*; Serge Basset, *Petites femmes*; De Poncheville, *Le flagrant délit*.

Jan. 20   *CO*: reviewing André Picard, *L'ange gardien*; Jean Passier, *Le monsieur au camélia*.

Jan. 22   *CO*: reviewing H. Kéroul and A. Barré, *L'éprouvette*.

Jan. 23   *CO*: reviewing Fernand Nozière and A. Savoir, *La sonate à Kreutzer* [adapted from the story by Leo Tolstoy].

Feb. 5   *CO*: reviewing L. Forest, *L'homme à deux têtes*.

Feb. 8   *CO*: reviewing Edmond Rostand, *Chantecler*.

Feb. 11   "*Après Chantecler*," *CO*.

Feb. 12   *CO*: reviewing Thurner, *Gaby*; Landay and Valdier, *Son auteur*.

Feb. 13   *CO*: reviewing Chekri-Ganem [music by Rimsky-Korsakoff], *Antar*.

Feb. 16   *CO*: reviewing Ferri-Pisani, *La femme et le masque*; Octave Bernard, *Quand l'amour voyage*; J. Gilquin and S. Bernstamm, *Conséquence*.

Feb. 19   *CO*: reviewing M. Carré, *V'là la comète*; Maurice Hennequin and Serge Basset, *Une aventure impériale*; Maxime Vermont, *Le grand cerf*.

Feb. 20   *CO*: reviewing Etienne Garnier, *L'offensée*; René Fabre, *Chacun son tour*.

Feb. 22   *CO*: reviewing Georges Courteline, *Boubouroche*; Tristan Bernard *Le peintre exigeant*; Victor Margueritte, *L'imprévu*.

Feb. 26   *CO*: reviewing Henry Bataille, *La vierge folle*.

Feb. 26   *CO*: reviewing Romain Coolus, *Une femme passa*.

Feb. 27   *CO*: reviewing Emile Rochard, *Le péché de Marthe*.

Mar. 1   *CO*: reviewing Dario Niccodemi, *La flamme*; André Picard, *Le protecteur*.

Mar. 2   *CO*: reviewing Gabriel Nigond, *1812*.

Mar. 5   *CO*: reviewing Jean Richepin, *La beffa* [adapted from the play by Sam Benelli].

Mar. 6   *CO*: reviewing J. Oudot, *Passion secrète*; H. Caen, *Il pleut ... il neige*; C. Torquet, *Le mal au ventre et le pectoral*; E. Vigneux, *Le prête-nom*; M. Simon, *Je t'amène mon fils*.

Mar. 15   *CO*: reviewing Honoré de Balzac, *L'école des ménages*.

Mar. 18   *CO*: reviewing Jacques Richepin, *Xantho chez les courtisanes*; P. Mortier, *Le jeune homme candide*.

Mar. 23   *CO*: reviewing Gaston de Caillavet and Robert de Flers, *Le bois sacré*.

Apr. 13   *CO*: reviewing Valabrègue, *Le phénix*; Georges Feydeau, *On purge Bébé*.

Apr. 15   *CO*: reviewing Tristan Bernard and Alfred Athis, *Le costaud des épinettes*.

Apr. 22   *CO*: reviewing Shakespeare, *Coriolan*.

Apr. 23   *CO*: reviewing Pierre Berton, *Bridge*.

Apr. 27   *CO*: reviewing Henry Bataille, *Le songe d'un soir d'amour*.

Apr. 29   *CO*: reviewing André Barde [music by Cuvillier], *Les muscadines*; L. Hennevé, *Il est en bas dans la voiture*; B. Montès, *L'inondé.*
Apr. 30   *CO*: reviewing André Rivoire and Lucien Besnard, *Mon ami Teddy.*
May 6   *CO*: reviewing P. Bossuet and P. Léglise, *Le bien du mari*; L. Léon-Martin, *L'heure sincère*; M. Allou, *La leçon d'esprit ou les maris échangés.*
May 11   *CO*: reviewing Louis Leloir and Gabriel Nigond, *Mademoiselle Molière.*
May 11   *CO*: Sacha Guitry, *Nono*; Jean Ajalbert, *La fille Elisa* [adapted from the novel by Edmond de Goncourt].
May 16   *CO*: reviewing Emile Bergerat, *Vidocq, empereur des policiers.*
May 22   *CO*: reviewing Rip, *Bigre.*
May 23   "Ceux qui s'en vont: Jules Renard," *CO.*
May 24   *CO*: reviewing Miguel Zamacoïs, *La fleur merveilleuse.*
May 25   *CO*: reviewing Antoine Bibesco, *Jacques Abran.*
June 2   *CO*: reviewing R. Dieudonné, *Le crampon.*
June 3   *CO*: reviewing André de Lorde and Pierre Chaine, *Bagnes d'enfants.*
June 8   *CO*: reviewing F. Fonson and F. Wicheler, *Le mariage de Mlle Beulemans.*
July 5   *CO*: reviewing Paul Bourget and Serge Basset, *Un cas de conscience*; Leconte de Lisle, *Les Erinnyes.*
July 7   "Les concours publics du Conservatoire," *CO.*
July 10   *CO*: reviewing Fernand Nozière, *Joconde.*
Oct. 5   *CO*: reviewing P. Bilhaud and Maurice Hennequin, *M'amour.*
Oct. 8   *CO*: reviewing Emile Fabre, *César Birotteau* [adapted from the novel by Honoré de Balzac].
Oct. 9   *CO*: reviewing Louis Artus, *Le petit dieu.*
Oct. 12   *CO*: reviewing Albert du Bois, *La conquête d'Athènes.*
Oct. 13   *CO*: reviewing Georges Ancey, *Ces messieurs.*
Oct. 16   *CO*: reviewing Henry Kistemaeckers, *Le marchand de bonheur.*
Oct. 19   *CO*: reviewing Gabriel Trarieux, *Un soir*; G. Traversi, *Les plus beaux jours.*
Oct. 27   *CO*: reviewing Pierre Wolff, *Les marionettes.*
Oct. 29   *CO*: reviewing G. Berr and M. Guillemaud, *Le million*; V. Darlay and Henri de Gorsse, *Arsène Lupin contre Herlock Schlomès.*
Oct. 30   *CO*: reviewing Grenet-Dancourt and R. Dieudonné, *Chou Blanc.*
Nov. 4   *CO*: reviewing André de Lorde and Binet, *L'homme mystérieux*; André de Lorde and Masson-Forestier, *L'attaque nocturne.*
Nov. 5   *CO*: reviewing Alfred Capus, *L'aventurier.*
Nov. 9   *CO*: reviewing Francis de Croisset, *Le feu du voisin*; J.-J. Frappa, *A l'impossible*; Miguel Zamacoïs, *La dame du second.*
Nov. 19   *CO*: reviewing L. Marchès, *Le train de 8 h. 47* [adapted from the novel by Georges Courteline].
Nov. 20   *CO*: reviewing M. de Faramond, *Le mauvais grain*; R. d'Humières, *L'amour de Késa*; H. and J. Bouvelet, *Poupard.*
Nov. 25   *CO*: reviewing Pierre Frondaie, *Montmartre.*

Nov. 26 *CO*: reviewing Saint-Georges de Bouhélier, *Le carnaval des enfants*; Molière [music by Lully], *Le sicilien ou l'amour peintre*.
Nov. 27 *CO*: [Reviewing works from the Théâtre du Grand Guignol] E. Thurus, *Saturnin*; Urbain Gohier, *Un peu d'idéal*; C. Hellem, C. Valcros, P. d'Estoc, *Sabotage*; P. Arosa, *Condoléances*; André de Lorde and G. Montignac, *Figures de cire*; Max Maurey, *Le pharmacien*.
Dec. 4 *CO*: reviewing Armont and Nancey, *Le zèbre*.
Dec. 7 *CO*: reviewing Romain Coolus, *Les bleus de l'amour*.
Dec. 9 *CO*: reviewing Pierre Louys and Pierre Frondaie, *La femme et le pantin*; Anatole France, *Crainquebille*; Georges Clemenceau, *Le voile du bonheur*.
Dec. 10 *CO*: reviewing Marie Lenéru, *Les affranchis*.
Dec. 11 *CO*: reviewing Marie Lenéru, *Les affranchis*.
Dec. 12 *CO*: reviewing Marie Lenéru, *Les affranchis*.
Dec. 14 *CO*: reviewing André Picard, *La fugitive*.
Dec. 17 *CO*: reviewing Fernand Nozière and Y. Mirande, *Excelsior*.
Dec. 22 *CO*: reviewing E. and E. Adenis, *Les noces de Panurge*.
Dec. 23 *CO*: reviewing Shakespeare, *Roméo et Juliette*.

1911

Jan. 13 *CO*: reviewing Georges de Porto-Riche, *Le vieil homme*.
Jan. 14 *CO*: reviewing A. Mars and H. Lyon, *Madame l'Amirale*.
Jan. 23 *CO*: reviewing Jean Richard, *L'inquiète*.
Jan. 25 *CO*: reviewing L. Mayrargue, *Il y a une suite*; A. Gragnon, *Le vrai chemin*; Y. Mirande, *Un tout petit voyage*; Georges Courteline and E. Norès, *Le gendarme est sans pitié*.
Jan. 30 "Conférence à l'Odéon sur *Rodogune* de Corneille," *CO*.
Jan. 31 *CO*: reviewing Maurice Magre, *Le marchand de passions*; Maurice de Faramond, *Nabuchodonosor*.
Feb. 1 *CO*: reviewing Louis Artus, *Les midinettes*.
Feb. 2 *CO*: reviewing Fernand Crommelynck, *Le sculpteur de masques*.
Feb. 3 *CO*: reviewing Sacha Guitry, *Le veilleur de nuit*; Pierre Veber, *La femme et les pantins*; D. Riche, *Le complice*.
Feb. 9 *CO*: reviewing J. Nayral and H. Clerc, *Les camelots du 201e*.
Feb. 10 *CO*: reviewing Abel Hermant and Y. Mirande, *Le cadet de Coutras*.
Feb. 12 *CO*: reviewing Robert de Flers and Gaston de Caillavet, *Papa*.
Feb. 12 *CO*: reviewing Jean Martel, *La boulangère*; René Benjamin, *Le pacha*.
Feb. 19 *CO*: [Reviewing works from the Théâtre du Grand Guignol] F.-H. Michel, *Roméo*; E. de Bassan, *Les mines de Ganeffontein*; A. Massart and A. Vercourt, *Alcide Pépet*; P. Jeanniot, *La fugue de Mme Caramon*; Mouézy-Eon and G. Jubin, *Dichotomie*; Max Maurey, *Le chauffeur*.
Feb. 21 *CO*: reviewing Henry Bernstein, *Après moi*.
Feb. 28 *CO*: reviewing Henry Bataille, *L'enfant de l'amour*.
Mar. 3 *CO*: reviewing Mme. Dick-May, *Mère*; P. de Puyfontaine, *La cour d'amour de Romanin*; Lecomte du Nouy, *Maud*.

Mar. 3   *CO*: reviewing Maurice Maeterlinck, *L'oiseau bleu*.
Mar. 4   *CO*: reviewing Arthur Bernède, *Le roi soleil*.
Mar. 5   *CO*: reviewing Jules Romains, *L'armée dans la ville*.
Mar. 6   *CO*: reviewing Alfred de Musset, *Fantasio*; Léon Frapié, *Le dépensier*.
Mar. 11   *CO*: reviewing A. Valabrègue, *Mariages d'aujourd'hui*.
Mar. 12   *CO*: reviewing Mouézy-Eon, *L'amour en manoeuvres*.
Mar. 16   *CO*: reviewing Paul Bourget, *Le tribun*.
Mar. 19   *CO*: reviewing Euripides (trans. Silvain and Jaubert), *Hécube*.
Mar. 24   *CO*: reviewing Benjamin Rabier, *Et ma soeur!* . . . .
Mar. 25   *CO*: reviewing Pierre Veber and Henri de Gorsse, *La gamine*.
Mar. 26   *CO*: reviewing Henry Bataille, *Maman Colibri*.
Mar. 29   *CO*: reviewing René Fauchois, *Rivoli*.
Apr. 11   *CO*: reviewing Henri Lavedan, *Le goût du vice*.
Apr. 30   *CO*: reviewing Oscar Franck, *Coeur maternel*.
May 3   *CO*: reviewing G. Mitchell and Maurice Hennequin, *Aimé des femmes*.
May 4   *CO*: reviewing Paul-Hyacinthe Loyson, *L'apôtre*.
May 9   *CO*: reviewing Fernand Nozière, *Les oiseaux* [adapted from Aristophanes]; Henri Bordeaux and E. Denarié, *Un médecin de campagne*; G. Battanchon, *Sur le seuil*.
May 10   *CO*: [Reviewing works from the Théâtre du Grand Guignol] J. Gravier, *La fée déçue*; L. Descaves, *Atelier d'aveugles*; M. Level and E. Rey, *Sous la lumière rouge*; P. Valdagne, *Le devoir*; R. Berton, *Après vous, Capitaine!*
May 11   *CO*: reviewing Georges Feydeau, *Un fil à la patte*.
May 16   *CO*: reviewing Victor Hugo, *Le roi s'amuse*.
May 18   *CO*: reviewing Ossip Dymof, *Niou*; Jean-Louis Vaudoyer, *La nuit persane*.
May 20   *CO*: reviewing P. de Lancy, *Paysans et soldats*.
May 21   *CO*: reviewing Edouard Schneider, *Les mages sans étoiles*; E. Pataud and E. Garin, *Demain*; Romain Coolus, *Les bleus de l'amour*; Tristan Bernard, *L'incident du 7 avril*.
May 23   *CO*: reviewing Gabriele d'Annunzio, *Le martyr de Saint Sébastien*.
June 4   *CO*: reviewing Maurice de Faramond, *Diane de Poitiers*.
June 14   *CO*: reviewing Gabriel Nigond, *Monsieur de Preux*; J. Monnier and L. Michel, *La reconnaissance*.
June 20   *CO*: reviewing J. and H. Bouvelet, *La philanthrope, ou la maison des amours*.
June 23   *CO*: reviewing Henri Lavedan, *Le vieux marcheur*.
July 6   *CO*: reviewing Gabriel Faure, *Un jour de fête*.
July 8   "Les concours publics du Conservatoire," *CO*.
Sept. 22   *CO*: reviewing G. Duval and R. Charvay, *Monsieur Pickwick* [adapted from the novel by Charles Dickens].
Oct. 1   *CO*: reviewing Claude Roland, *Le canard jaune*.
Oct. 4   *CO*: reviewing H. R. Fellinger, *Le vagabond*; R. Dieudonné, *Perdreau*.

Oct. 5   *CO*: reviewing André de Lorde and Pierre Chaine, *La petite Roque* [adapted from the story by Guy de Maupassant]; R. Dieudonné and R. Aubry, *Messieurs les ronds-de-cuir* [adapted from the story by Georges Courteline].

Oct. 10   *CO*: reviewing Gaston de Caillavet and Robert de Flers, *Primrose*.

Oct. 11   *CO*: reviewing F. Duquesnel and A. Barde, *Sa fille*.

Oct. 13   *CO*: reviewing Tristan Bernard, *Le petit café*.

Oct. 18   *CO*: reviewing Sacha Guitry, *Un beau mariage*.

Oct. 18   *CO*: reviewing Jean-Jacques Bernard, *Voyage à deux*; Clevel and Erzog, *Article de Paris*; Francis de Croisset, *La bonne intention*.

Oct. 25   "La pornographie et l'art," *GB*.

Oct. 29   *CO*: reviewing A. Karcher and R. Jeanne, *Le tribut*.

Nov. 4   *CO*: reviewing A. Guinon, *Le bonheur*.

Nov. 8   *CO*: reviewing Pierre Wolff, *L'amour défendu*.

Nov. 9   *CO*: reviewing Max Maurey, *David Copperfield* [adapted from the novel by Charles Dickens].

Nov. 9   *CO*: reviewing Henri Ghéon, *Le pain*.

Nov. 10   *CO*: reviewing Pierre Veber and M. Provins, *Les berceuses*; Pierre Veber, *La cascade*; A. Auvard, *Le piège*.

Nov. 11   *CO*: reviewing M. de Marsan and G. Timmory, *La course aux dollars*.

Nov. 13   *CO*: reviewing E. Jodelle, *Cléopatre captive*; Scarron, *Jodelet*.

Nov. 19   *CO*: reviewing Gabriel Trarieux, *La brebis perdue*.

Nov. 23   *CO*: reviewing J. Vincent, *La plus heureuse des trois*.

Nov. 24   *CO*: reviewing André de Lorde, F. Funck-Brentano, and J. Marsèle, *L'amour en cage*.

Nov. 25   *CO*: reviewing XXX, *La revue des X*.

Nov. 26   *CO*: reviewing Tristan Bernard and Michel Corday, *L'accord parfait*; Georges Feydeau, *Mais n'te promène donc pas toute nue!*; Alfred Athis, *Grasse matinée*.

Nov. 26   *CO*: reviewing José Felin y Codina, *Aux jardins de Murcie*.

[Blum's reviews for *Le Matin* appeared over the pseudonym Guy Launay until 4 June 1914. Blum cannot be held responsible for the titles of these reviews, but they are included here in order to give further evidence of the scope of his reviewing.]

Nov. 30   "L'Ambigu redevient décidément l'Ambigu comique," *M*.

Dec. 1   *CO*: reviewing D. Bonnard, N. Blès, and L. Boyer, *La revue de l'Ambigu*.

Dec. 2   *CO*: reviewing Alfred Capus, *Les favorites*.

Dec. 6   "*Princesse Dollar* à la Scala," *M*.

Dec. 7   "A la Porte Saint-Martin, *La Flambée* d'H. Kistemaeckers s'achève sur un très gros succès," *M*.

Dec. 8   *CO*: reviewing Henri Kistemaeckers, *La flambée*.

Dec. 9   "On applaudit au Théâtre Antoine Dostoievsky et Chocolat," *M*.

Dec. 9   *CO*: reviewing A. Savoir and Fernand Nozière, *L'éternel mari* [adapted from the novel by Feodor Dostoevski]; E. Guiraud, *Moïse*.

Dec. 10   *CO*: reviewing A. Sylvane and Mouézy-Eon, *Le pavillon*; Georges Feydeau, *Léonie est en avance, ou le mal joli*; P. Montrel, *Bonne maison.*

Dec. 11   "La Comédie-Royale opère une heureuse réouverture," *M.*

Dec. 13   "M. Emile Fabre ouvre au Vaudeville un cours de politique coloniale," *M.*

Dec. 14   *CO*: reviewing Emile Fabre, *Les sauterelles.*

Dec. 17   *CO*: reviewing Rip and Bousquet, *La revue sans-gêne.*

Dec. 17   *CO*: reviewing Ch. Hell and A. Villeroy, *Les frères Lambertier.*

Dec. 17   "A l'Odéon, *Les frères Lambertier* de Ch. Hell et A. Villeroy," *M.*

Dec. 18   "Le diable apparaît au Grand-Guignol," *M.*

Dec. 18   "Le nouveau spectacle du Grand-Guignol," *CO*: reviewing Gaston Leroux, *L'homme qui a vu le diable*; Spitzer et Géraldy, *Le bon droit*; A. Mydro, *Une femme charmante*; R. Dieudonné, *La chambre à côté.*

Dec. 21   *CO*: reviewing P. Souchon and A. Avèze, *Gribouille.*

Dec. 21   "On joue au Théâtre-Français un *Gribouille* de P. Souchon et A. Avèze. Pourquoi?," *M.*

Dec. 22   "Au Gymnase, une pièce écrite pour les enfants est acclamée par les grandes personnes," *M.*

Dec. 23   *CO*: reviewing R. Gérard and M. Rostand, *Un bon petit diable* [adapted from the novel by Mme. de Ségur].

Dec. 23   "Les théâtres subventionnés fêtent l'anniversaire de Racine. L'Apollo joue *Les petites étoiles* de Veber, Xanrof et Hirchmann," *M.*

Dec. 28   "Pour bien achever l'année, le Théâtre Michel donne un spectacle d'une rare qualité littéraire," *M.*

Dec. 29   *CO*: reviewing Edmond Sée, *La brebis*; E. Rey, *Peau neuve.*

1912

Jan. 21   "L'Odéon donne *Le redoutable*, drame en 3 actes, de Marie Lenéru," *M.*

Jan. 26   "Aux Variétés, brillante réussite d'une comédie de P. Gavault," *M.*

Jan. 30   "A l'Oeuvre, il serait temps que M. Lugné-Poe nous offrît un spectacle intéressant," *M.*

Feb. 1   "A la Comédie-Royale," *M.*

Feb. 2   "H. Bernstein donne au Gymnase *L'assaut* et remporte un éclatant succès," *M.*

Feb. 8   "A l'Odéon, *Esther, princesse d'Israël*, d'A. Dumas et S.-C. Leconte; décors persans, musique russe et vers français," *M.*

Feb. 14   "A l'Ambigu, grâce à deux reporters, G. Leroux et Rouletabille, l'étonnant *Mystère de la chambre jaune* s'éclaircit à minuit dans les bravos," *M.*

Feb. 16   "Au Théâtre des Arts, une âpre satire sociale de B. Shaw. Au Théâtre Michel, une exquise fantaisie sentimentale de Colette Willy," *M.*

Feb. 17   "Au Théâtre Réjane, *L'aigrette*, de D. Niccodemi. Indiscrétions, communiqués. La revue de la Scala est amusante. La reprise des *Maris de Léontine*, aux Bouffes-Parisiens, est un succès," *M.*

Feb. 18   "La Porte Saint-Martin inaugure les 'Matinées Alfred de Musset,'" *M.*

Feb. 22   "Gros succès à l'Athénée pour une charmante comédie de F. de Croisset," *M.*

Feb. 22   "A l'Oeuvre," *M.*

Feb. 23   "F. Nozière a tiré, pour le Vaudeville, du *Bel-Ami* de Maupassant, une pièce habile et souvent émouvante," *M.*

Feb. 25   "Spectacles inédits de l'Odéon: *Près de lui* de Denys Amiel. Au Théâtre des Chefs-d'oeuvre," *M.*

Feb. 27   "Le théâtre et les moeurs: l'influence des repas sur le théâtre," *E.*

Mar. 3   "Matinées Musset à la Porte Saint-Martin: *Carmosine* et *Idylle*," *M.*

Mar. 9   "A la Comédie-Royale," *M.*

Mar. 10   "Au Théâtre-Français, *Le ménage de Molière* de M. Donnay est un à-propos en 5 actes," *M.*

Mar. 13   "A l'Apollo, gros succès pour la musique de F. Lehar et pour une divette inédite," *M.*

Mar. 14   "Au Théâtre Michel," *M*: reviewing E. Bourdet, *La cage ouverte.*

Mar. 17   "Matinées inédites à l'Odéon. Matinées Musset à la Porte Saint-Martin," *M.*

Mar. 17   "Le théâtre et les moeurs: la délimitation du chef-d'oeuvre," *E.*

Mar. 19   "A la Renaissance, *En garde!* d'A. Capus et P. Veber," *M.*

Mar. 22   "Matinées Shakespeare," *M.*

Mar. 25   "*Troïlus et Cressida* de Shakespeare. Spectacle nouveau au Grand-Guignol," *M.*

Mar. 27   "Au Théâtre François Coppée," *M.*

Mar. 28   "Aux Bouffes-Parisiens, *Agnès, dame galante*, d'H. Cain et L. Payen," *M.*

Apr. 2   "Un spectacle de 'vraie beauté' au Théâtre de l'Oeuvre," *M.*

Apr. 3   "Le théâtre et les moeurs: plaidoyer pour la vertu," *E.*

Apr. 5   "Au Vaudeville, répétition générale: P. Berton nous apitoie et T. Bernard nous juge," *M.*

Apr. 6   "Au Théâtre Réjane, *Les moulins qui chantent*, de Fonson et Wincheler, musique de Van Oost," *M.*

Apr. 11   "Théâtre Sarah-Bernhardt: *La reine Elisabeth*, d'E. Moreau," *M.*

Apr. 11   "Le Théâtre Fémina joue une amusante comédie-revue de Rip et Bousquet," *M.*

Apr. 18   "A l'Odéon, *L'honneur japonais*, de P. Anthelme. Le drame a de l'héroïsme et le spectacle de la magnificence. La Renaissance reprend *Divorçons* de V. Sardou et E. de Najac," *M.*

Apr. 19   "Le théâtre et les moeurs: l'immortalité des comédiens," *E.*

Apr. 24   "A l'Ambigu, *Le coquelicot*, de J. Joseph-Renaud," *M.*

Apr. 27 "Matinée Claudel et matinée Shakespeare," *M.*

May 1 "Le théâtre et les moeurs: les romanciers au théâtre," *E.*

May 3 "A la Porte Saint-Martin, *La crise*, de P. Bourget et A. Beaunier," *M.*

May 4 "Au Théâtre Antoine, *Gaspard de Besse*, de Sauvaire et Nus. *Les trois amoureuses*, opérette d'Ordonneau, musique de F. Lehar," *M.*

May 5 "*Hélène de Sparte* d'E. Verhaeren, au Châtelet," *M.*

May 5 "Au Théâtre-Français, une reprise inutile de *Sapho* [by Alphonse Daudet]," *M.*

May 7 "Aux Bouffes-Parisiens, *La cote d'amour*, de R. Coolus," *M.*

May 9 "Aux Théâtre Réjane, une pièce remarquable: *Ames sauvages* de S. Mars et Mme de Clermont," *M.*

May 12 "Aux Variétés, reprise d'*Orphée aux enfers*," *M.*

May 13 "A l'Oeuvre, *Dernière heure*, de J.-J. Frappa," *M.*

May 21 "A la Renaissance, *Le feu de la Saint-Jean*, de Fonson et Wicheler," *M.*

May 22 "Au Théâtre Sarah-Bernhardt, reprise de *Lorenzaccio* [by Alfred de Musset]," *M.*

May 23 "Au Théâtre-Français, *Poil-de-Carotte*, de J. Renard, et *Iphigénie*, de J. Moréas," *M.*

May 23 "A la Comédie-Royale," *M.*

May 24 "Au Théâtre des Arts, *Jeannine*, de P. Grasset," *M.*

May 25 "Au Vaudeville, la troupe allemande de M. Reinhardt joue une pantomime orientale," *M.*

May 25 "La *Foi*, pièce en 5 actes d'E. Brieux, musique de C. Saint-Saëns," *M.*

May 26 "A l'Oeuvre, *Morituri*, de M. Prozor. *Grégoire*, 1 acte d'H. Falk," *M.*

May 30 "Le théâtre et les moeurs: Sardou et le métier," *E.*

June 3 "Au Théâtre Sarah-Bernhardt," *M.*

June 8 "Au Théâtre Michel," *M.*

June 9 "Aux Escholiers," *M.*

June 13 "Au Châtelet, *Salomé*, d'O. Wilde," *M.*

June 15 "Au Théâtre-Français, *Comediante*, 1 acte en vers de M. Magre," *M.*

June 16 "Au Grand-Guignol," *M.*

June 18 "Le théâtre et les moeurs: il est périlleux pour un artiste de sortir de son emploi," *E.*

June 19 "Odéon, Ambigu, Vaudeville," *M.*

June 23 "Répétitions générales: *La cour mauresque*, chez M. de Clermont-Tonnerre. Aux Variétés et à l'Apollo," *M.*

June 28 "A la Comédie-Française, reprise d'*Antony*, de Dumas père," *M.*

June 30 "Indiscrétions. Communiqués. A la Renaissance, *Petite peste*, de R. Coolus," *M.*

July 3 "Le théâtre et les moeurs: le Conservatoire n'a pas besoin de concours publics," *E.*

July 3 "Conservatoire: concours de tragédie," *M.*

July 4   "Conservatoire: concours de comédie," *M.*
July 13   "Le théâtre et les moeurs: réformons le Conservatoire," *E.*
Aug. 24   "*Match de boxe* aux Variétés," *M.*
Sept. 21   "Inauguration du Théâtre-Impérial," *M.*
Sept. 28   "A la Porte Saint-Martin, reprise de *La robe rouge*, d'E. Brieux," *M.*
Oct. 2   "Encore une reprise: *Patachou*, de M. Hennequin et Duquesnel, à la Renaissance," *M.*
Oct. 4   "Gros succès pour une nouveauté: *La prise de Berg-op-zoom*, de S. Guitry au Vaudeville," *M.*
Oct. 6   "*Le malade imaginaire* [Molière] à l'Odéon," *M.*
Oct. 10   "Théâtre Michel et Théâtre Cluny: six pièces et une soirée," *M.*
Oct. 11   "Au Théâtre Fémina, *L'enjôleuse*, de X. Roux et M. Sergine," *M.*
Oct. 13   "Au Théâtre des Arts, *Marie d'Août*, 3 actes de L. Frapié. *Une loge pour Faust*, 1 acte de P. Veber," *M.*
Oct. 16   "Au Théâtre Antoine, *Une affaire d'or*, 3 actes de M. Gerbidon. Au Gymnase, très brillante reprise du *Détour*, d'H. Bernstein," *M.*
Oct. 23   "A l'Ambigu, *Coeur de française*, d'H. Bernède et A. Bruant," *M.*
Oct. 24   "Le théâtre et les moeurs: digression sur B. Shaw," *E.*
Oct. 26   "Matinées inédites de l'Odéon. *Dans l'ombre des statues*, de G. Duhamel," *M.*
Oct. 27   "A la Comédie-Française, *Bagatelle*, 3 actes de P. Hervieu," *M.*
Oct. 31   "A la Renaissance, la pièce de P. Gavault: *L'idée de Françoise* finit tard, mais finit bien," *M.*
Oct. 31   "Au Trianon-Lyrique, *Amour tzigane* [Franz Lehar]," *M.*
Nov. 2   "Matinée a l'Ambigu," *M.*
Nov. 6   "Au Théâtre Sarah-Bernhardt, *La maison de Temperley*, de Conan Doyle, adapté par E. Gugenheim," *M.*
Nov. 8   "Au Théâtre Apollo, *Le soldat de chocolat* [Oscar Strauss]," *M.*
Nov. 9   "Au Théâtre des Arts, *Le grand nom*, de L. et L. Feld, adaptation française de P. Veber," *M.*
Nov. 12   "Au Théâtre Réjane, *Un coup de téléphone*, de P. Gavault et G. Berr a fait rire," *M.*
Nov. 12   "Aux Bouffes-Parisiens, Mme Loïe Fuller et son école de danse," *M.*
Nov. 13   "Le théâtre et les moeurs: réflexions sur le succès," *E.*
Nov. 14   "Au Théâtre Antoine, une curieuse pièce de L. Benière: *Crédulités*," *M.*
Nov. 15   "A l'Athénée, *Le diable ermite*, de L. Besnard," *M.*
Nov. 15   "Au Théâtre des Arts, la *Marie-Madeleine* d'Hebbel," *M.*
Nov. 17   "Aux Variétés, *L'habit vert*, de R. de Flers et G. de Caillavet, connaîtra le succès du *Bois sacré* et peut-être du *Roi*," *M.*
Nov. 21   "Théâtre Fémina, gala G. de Porto-Riche," *M.*
Nov. 22   "Au Théâtre Fémina, *Le valet de coeur* et *La casquette blanche* de L. Gilbert sont un plaisant spectacle," *M.*
Nov. 22   "A l'Odéon, *Madame de Chatillon*, de P. Verola," *M.*

Nov. 23 "Au Châtelet, *Le roi de l'or*, 4 actes et 23 tableaux de V. Darlay et H. de Gorsse," *M*.

Nov. 23 "Aux Bouffes-Parisiens, *La bonne vieille coutume*, de Davis et Doermann, adapté par J. Benedict," *M*.

Nov. 25 "Au Théâtre Michel, *L'escapade*, de G. Trarieux. Reprise de *La cruche*, de G. Courteline et P. Wolff," *M*.

Nov. 26 "A la Porte Saint-Martin, H. Bataille remporte avec *Les flambeaux* la plus hardie et la plus haute victoire," *M*.

Nov. 27 "Au Palais-Royal, *Madame la Présidente*, de M. Hennequin et P. Veber. On a ri," *M*.

Dec. 2 "Matinées inédites à l'Odéon," *M*.

Dec. 4 "Le théâtre et les moeurs: H. Bataille et les morales nouvelles," *E*.

Dec. 5 "A la Comédie-Royale," *M*.

Dec. 13 "Au Grand-Guignol," *M*.

Dec. 15 "Aux Bouffes-Parisiens, *Le Noël de Pierrot*, mimodrame de F. Beissier," *M*.

Dec. 17 "Au Théâtre-Français," *M*.

Dec. 18 "Au Théâtre Sarah-Bernhardt, *Kismet*, d'E. Knoblauch, texte français de J. Lemaître," *M*.

Dec. 19 "Au Théâtre Gémier, succès net pour *L'homme qui assassina*, de Frondaie, d'après le roman de Cl. Farrère," *M*.

Dec. 21 "A l'Odéon, le *Faust* de Goethe, adapté par E. Vedel, est un surprenant spectacle," *M*.

Dec. 22 "Au Gymnase, *La femme libre*, de Brieux agite honnêtement les plus importants problèmes," *M*.

Dec. 23 "A l'Oeuvre, *L'annonce faite à Marie*, mystère de Paul Claudel," *M*.

Dec. 23 "Au Théâtre-Français," *M*.

Dec. 24 "Aux Bouffes-Parisiens, *La part du feu*, de Mouézy-Eon et Nancey," *M*.

Dec. 25 "Au Théâtre Michel," *M*.

1913

Jan. 5 "A la Porte Saint-Martin," *M*.

Jan. 8 "Le théâtre et les moeurs: la jeune fille au théâtre," *E*.

Jan. 9 "A l'Athénée, *La main mystérieuse* de Fred Amy et J. Marsèle," *M*.

Jan. 10 "Au Théâtre Réjane, G. Leroux et L. Camille font applaudir ardemment *Alsace*," *M*.

Jan. 15 "A la Renaissance, un peu incertaine au début, la jolie pièce de L. Besnard, *La folle enchère*, obtient au troisième acte un très réel succès," *M*.

Jan. 24 "Le Théâtre Apollo reprend *Monsieur de La Palisse*. L'oeuvre est fort agréable et la reprise brillante," *M*.

Jan. 25 "Au Théâtre Fémina, la comédie d'A. Picard et A. Savoir, *L'épate*, est une pièce d'une qualité très remarquable et qui mérite pleinement son succès," *M*.

Jan. 26   "*Les éclaireuses*, de M. Donnay, inaugurent avec le plus vif éclat le Théâtre Marigny," *M.*

Jan. 26   "Matinées inédites à l'Odéon: *Sylla*, d'A. Mortier," *M.*

Jan. 28   "Au Théâtre des Arts, *On ne peut jamais dire*, de B. Shaw, est une pièce absurde et d'ailleurs fort amusante," *M.*

Jan. 29   "Le théâtre et les moeurs: le féminisme au théâtre," *E.*

Jan. 30   "La reprise de *L'enchantement* [H. Bataille], à la Renaissance, a tout l'attrait et tout le succès d'une nouveauté," *M.*

Jan. 31   "A Cluny, on a joué de M. Emile Herbel, *La cocotte bleue*, vaudeville d'une certaine gaîté," *M.*

Feb. 1   "La prochaine génération littéraire," *RP.*, pp. 519–36.

Feb. 2   "Au Théâtre Molière, *Le Docteur Miracle*, de P. Sales et J. Mazel," *M.*

Feb. 8   "Au Théâtre Sarah-Bernhardt, on acclame la pièce d'H. Lavedan: *Servir*, qui est un drame d'intention cornélienne, et L. Guitry, qui est un comédien admirable," *M.*

Feb. 9   "Au Théâtre-Français, *L'embuscade*, d'H. Kistemaeckers, est un drame qui exercera sans doute sur le public un attrait considérable," *M.*

Feb. 13   "Au Gymnase, *La demoiselle de magasin*, de Fonson et Wicheler, est une soeur à peine cadette de *Mlle Beulemans*," *M.*

Feb. 14   "Au Châtelet, *Le champion de l'air*, est une pièce à grand spectacle selon la formule connue, mais adroitement coupée et très bien montée," *M.*

Feb. 15   "Le théâtre et les moeurs: le patriotisme au théâtre," *E.*

Feb. 16   "Matinées inédites de l'Odéon. Il faut retenir le nom d'A. Fernet, l'auteur de *La maison divisée*," *M.*

Feb. 21   "Avec *Manette*, de Beissier et Le Bel, musique d'A. Fijan, le Trianon-Lyrique fait un nouvel effort pour ranimer l'opérette française," *M.*

Feb. 22   "A l'Odéon, *La nuit florentine*, d'E. Bergerat, est l'adaptation, en vers banvillesques, de *La mandragore*, de Machiavel," *M.*

Mar. 6   "Le théâtre et les moeurs: le confort au théâtre," *E.*

Mar. 12   "Le nouveau spectacle du Grand-Guignol comprend un numéro excellent, *S. O. S.*, de C. Muller et M. Level," *M.*

Mar. 14   "Il y a dans *Hélène Ardouin*, d'A. Capus, de la peinture des moeurs, de la chronique, et même du drame. Et cependant ce n'est qu'un conte," *M.*

Mar. 14   "Au Théâtre des Arts, *Le combat*, de G. Duhamel, est l'oeuvre d'un auteur dramatique de grand avenir," *M.*

Mar. 15   "A la Porte Saint-Martin, *Cyrano de Bergerac*, est décidément un chef-d'oeuvre," *M.*

Mar. 20   "Au Théâtre de la Renaissance, *Le minaret*, de J. Richepin, est avant tout une surprenante exposition de costumes," *M.*

Mar. 21   "Aux Bouffes-Parisiens, *Le secret*, d'H. Bernstein recueille le plus beau succès d'attendrissement et d'émotion," *M.*

Apr. 4   "Une pièce d'H. Kistemaeckers, *L'exilée*, à la fois dramatique et romanesque inaugure la Comédie des Champs-Elysées," *M.*

Apr. 9 "Au Théâtre Antoine, *Le chevalier au masque*, d'Armont et Manoussi, est, dans un genre connu, une pièce réussie et amusante," *M*.

Apr. 10 "Au Conservatoire," *M*.

Apr. 11 "Au Théâtre des Arts, *Les deux versants*, de W. V. Moody, est un curieux mélange d'Ibsen et de . . . G. Aymard," *M*.

Apr. 12 "A l'Oeuvre, après P. Claudel, F. Jammes," *M*.

Apr. 17 "A l'Odéon, P. Decourcelle et Maurel nous remontrent que, *Rue du Sentier*, les belles-mères sont despotiques, les femmes incomprises et les maris amoureux," *M*.

Apr. 18 "Au Vaudeville, une pièce ingénieuse et gaie de M. Hennequin remporte, *Les honneurs de la guerre*," *M*.

Apr. 24 "Le Théâtre-Français joue *Riquet à la houppe*, l'adorable chef-d'oeuvre de T. de Banville, et *Venise*, une fine saynète de R. de Flers et G. de Caillavet," *M*.

May 1 "Au Théâtre Sarah-Bernhardt, reprise du *Bossu*, d'A. Bourgeois et P. Féval.—Le Théâtre Antoine joue avec succès une pièce habile de C. Esquier: *L'entraîneuse*," *M*.

May 7 "Mise en scène d'*Esther* [Racine] à l'Odéon," *M*.

May 9 "Au Théâtre Réjane, *La petite reine des roses*, de Leoncavallo, inaugure sans éclat la saison d'opérettes italiennes," *M*.

May 11 "La Comédie des Champs-Elysées joue une étude intéressante d'E. Fleg: *Le trouble-fête* et une pochade de T. Bernard: *La gloire ambulancière*, de l'humour le plus savoureux," *M*.

May 15 "A l'Ambigu, *Mon ami l'assassin*, de S. Basset et A. Yvan, est un mélo à gros effets et à grand spectacle, avec un 'clou' sensationnel," *M*.

May 17 "Reprise de *David Copperfield* à l'Odéon," *M*.

May 18 "A la Comédie-Française, la comédie de G. Guiches, *Vouloir*, est pleine de velléités engageantes, mais pèche par un curieux défaut de volonté," *M*.

May 21 "Spectacles inédits à l'Odéon," *M*.

May 28 "Au Châtelet, *Marie-Madeleine*, drame en 3 actes de M. Maeterlinck," *M*.

May 29 "Au Théâtre Apollo, l'opérette d'H. Verne et G. Faure: *La jeunesse dorée* est un spectacle élégant, que fait valoir une habile musique de M. Lattes," *M*.

May 31 "A l'Athénée, très vif succès pour la reprise du *Bourgeon*, de G. Feydeau," *M*.

June 1 "L'Oeuvre joue un grand drame d'E. Dujardin, *Marthe et Marie*, qui retarde un peu," *M*.

June 3 "Aux Variétés, *La dame de chez Maxim's* retrouve son inépuisable succès," *M*.

June 4 "Le Théâtre Cluny joue un mélo à grand spectacle, *Les loups noirs*, qui n'est pas indigne d'un si beau titre," *M*.

June 5 "La Comédie des Champs-Elysées reprend *Le poulailler*, qui est la pièce la plus brillante de T. Bernard. L'Ambigu reprend *Les Oberlé*, d'E. Haraucourt, qui sont une pièce noble et vraiment tragique," *M*.

June 6 "A la Comédie-Française," *M*.

June 7 "A l'Oeuvre, Escholiers et Nouveau Théâtre d'Art," *M*.

June 16 "Au Grand-Guignol," *M.*
June 18 "A Maisons-Laffitte," *M.*
June 20 "Au Théâtre-Français, *Les ombres*, de M. Allou," *M.*
July 3 "Au Conservatoire: tragédie," *M.*
July 4 "Concours du Conservatoire: comédie," *M.*
July 18 "A la Renaissance," *M.*
Sept. 7 "Reprises au Grand-Guignol et aux Variétés," *M.*
Sept. 25 "L'Athénée reprend le délicieux *Triplepatte* de T. Bernard et Godfernaux," *M.*
Sept. 26 "L'Odéon rouvre et Daltour débute," *M.*
Sept. 29 "Suite des débuts de l'Odéon," *M.*
Sept. 30 "A la Renaissance, le beau drame de R. Coolus, *Les roses rouges*, est le premier événement dramatique de la saison," *M.*
Oct. 1 "Au Théâtre Antoine, Suzanne Desprès dans *Hamlet*," *M.*
Oct. 2 "A l'Ambigu, *La saignée*, de L. Descaves et F. Nozière, est une pièce très hardie et très poignante," *M.*
Oct. 2 "Au Palais-Royal, reprise de *La Présidente*," *M.*
Oct. 4 "Au Théâtre Fémina, *Les travaux d'Hercule*, de G. de Caillavet, R. de Flers et C. Terrasse, retrouvent leur charmant succès d'autrefois," *M.*
Oct. 7 "Pourquoi la Comédie-Française a-t-elle monté la *Sophonisbe* d'A. Poizat?," *M.*
Oct. 8 "Au Gymnase, *Les requins*, de D. Niccodemi sont l'oeuvre déconcertante d'un homme de talent," *M.*
Oct. 11 "La Porte Saint-Martin reprend, avec éclat, l'admirable *Amoureuse* [Porto-Riche]," *M.*
Oct. 11 "Au Théâtre Cluny, *Monsieur le Juge*, de Nancey et J. Rioux provoque des rires abondants," *M.*
Oct. 16 "Au Théâtre Antoine, le drame d'H. Gorsse et L. Forest, *Le procureur Hallers*, fournit à Gémier l'occasion d'un beau succès," *M.*
Oct. 18 "A l'Odéon, D. Gold ouvre la série des *Manon*," *M.*
Oct. 20 "Les Bouffes-Parisiens reprennent, en grand gala, *Le secret*, d'H. Bernstein," *M.*
Oct. 22 "Au Vaudeville, *La Phalène*, d'H. Bataille, est une oeuvre dont l'audace et les beautés singulières soulèveront d'ardentes discussions," *M.*
Oct. 24 "Ouverture du Théâtre du Vieux-Colombier. *L'oiseau bleu* au Théâtre Réjane," *M.*
Oct. 28 "Le Théâtre Sarah-Bernhardt joue *La vivante image*, de J. Joseph-Renaud d'après le drame anglais d'E. Orcsy," *M.*
Nov. 1 "Au Théâtre des Arts," *M.*
Nov. 4 "A la Renaissance, *Occident*, d'Henri Kistemaeckers. La pièce est pittoresque, saisissante, un peu touffue. Le succès a été grand," *M.*
Nov. 7 Preface to Edmond Stoullig, ed., *Les annales du théâtre et de la musique* (*1912*). Paris: Ollendorff, 1913.
Nov. 8 "Au Châtelet, on applaudit M. Poincaré, un accident de chemin de fer, un paquebot grandeur nature . . . et même une pièce," *M.*
Nov. 12 "Au Théâtre Léon-Poirier, on applaudit franchement une satire très libre et très gaie, *Le veau d'or*, de L. Gleize," *M.*

321

Nov. 12 "A la Porte Saint-Martin, on accueille avec un vif agrément, *Le ruisseau*, de P. Wolff.—Le Théâtre du Vieux-Colombier donne une pièce fort remarquable de J. Schlumberger: *Les fils Louverné*," *M.*

Nov. 13 "Le Théâtre Réjane joue une oeuvre très attendue, *L'irrégulière*, d'E. Sée," *M.*

Nov. 13 "*Rafles* à l'Ambigu," *M.*

Nov. 18 "Le Gymnase reprend avec un plein succès, *Samson*, d'H. Bernstein," *M.*

Nov. 21 "Aux Variétés, *L'institut de beauté*, d'A. Capus, est une comédie élégante et un peu froide," *M.*

Nov. 21 "Au Théâtre Déjazet, *Les dégourdis de la 11ᵉ*, de Mouézy-Eon et C. Daveillans," *M.*

Nov. 22 "Le Théâtre Fémina donne une satire par trop massive, *Paragraphe 1ᵉʳ* et une comédie un peu légère, *Petite Madame*," *M.*

Nov. 23 "A l'Odéon, *Rachel*, de G. Grillet, est un fort curieux spectacle," *M.*

Nov. 23 "Au Théâtre-Français, *La marche nuptiale*, d'Henry Bataille, s'installe victorieusement au répertoire," *M.*

Nov. 30 "Au Théâtre Apollo, *Cocorico* est une opérette chantante et claire comme son titre," *M.*

Dec. 3 "Le Palais-Royal donne un charmant vaudeville, *Les deux canards*, de T. Bernard et A. Athis," *M.*

Dec. 13 "Aux Bouffes-Parisiens, *Mon bébé*, de M. Hennequin, est une clownerie innocente et folle," *M.*

Dec. 13 "A l'Oeuvre" *M*: reviewing J. M. Synge, *Playboy of the Western World* (in French).

Dec. 14 "A la Porte Saint-Martin, *Le chèvrefeuille*, de G. d'Annunzio, est accueilli avec un admirable respect," *M.*

Dec. 16 "Le drame de T. Bernard, *Jeanne Doré*, vaut un triomphe à Mme Sarah Bernhardt," *M.*

Dec. 19 "Au Théâtre Fémina, la pièce de G. Berr, *Un jeune homme qui se tue*, part fort bien et s'achève un peu languissamment," *M.*

Dec. 23 "Au Vaudeville, très gros succès pour *La belle aventure*, de G. de Caillavet, R. de Flers et E. Rey," *M.*

Dec. 24 "Nouveau spectacle au Grand-Guignol," *M.*

Dec. 27 "A la Gaîté-Lyrique, *Les contes de Perrault*, féerie lyrique en 4 actes d'A. Bernède et P. de Choudens. Musique de F. Fourdrain," *M.*

Dec. 30 "A l'Athénée, *Le tango*, de Mme et J. Richepin, est une bien étrange chose," *M.*

Dec. 30 "A la Renaissance, une comédie romanesque de P. Veber et Gerbidon, *Un fils d'Amérique*, réussit bien," *M.*

1914

Jan. 11 "Au Théâtre Antoine," *M.*

Jan. 15 "Aux Bouffes-Parisiens, *La pèlerine écossaise*, de S. Guitry a très agréablement réussi," *M.*

Jan. 17 "L'Ambigu reprend la comédie réaliste de P. Wolff, *Leurs filles*, et donne une oeuvre très rare de F. de Curel, *La danse devant le miroir*," *M.*

Jan. 20 "Au Théâtre Antoine, *Un grand bourgeois*, d'E. Fabre, est une oeuvre solide et généreuse," *M.*

Jan. 23 "Au Gymnase, *Les cinq messieurs de Francfort*, sont une pièce agréable, d'un agrément savoureux et décroissant," *M.*

Jan. 23 "Au Théâtre des Arts," *M.*

Jan. 24 "Aux Variétés, *Les merveilleuses* sont un spectacle plaisant et fastueux," *M.*

Jan. 24 "Au Vieux-Colombier," *M*: reviewing Paul Claudel, *L'échange*.

Jan. 28 "A la Comédie des Champs-Elysées, *La prétentaine*, de R. Peter," *M.*

Jan. 29 "Le *Philoctète* de Sophocle au Théâtre Réjane," *M.*

Feb. 1 "Stendhal, I: sa personne," *RP*, pp. 564–97.

Feb. 4 "A la Comédie-Royale," *M.*

Feb. 5 "A Marigny, *Le mannequin*, de P. Gavault, a joliment réussi," *M.*

Feb. 7 "Au Vieux-Colombier, *Le testament du père Leleu*, de R. Martin du Gard," *M.*

Feb. 8 "A la Renaissance, spectacle coupé où on pourrait couper encore," *M.*

Feb. 8 "*L'école des femmes* [Molière], au Théâtre Fémina," *M.*

Feb. 10 "A la Porte Saint-Martin, *Madame*, d'A. Hermant et A. Savoir, est une comédie d'un tour et d'une élégance rares," *M.*

Feb. 11 "A l'Odéon, la pièce d'E. Brieux, *Le bourgeois aux champs*, est simple et rustique comme son titre," *M.*

Feb. 12 "Au Châtelet, *Le diable à quatre*, de V. Darlay et H. de Gorsse, est une très amusante opérette de music-hall," *M.*

Feb. 15 "Stendhal, II: ses personnages," *RP*, pp. 781–814.

Feb. 18 "A l'Athénée, très vif succès pour *Je ne trompe pas mon mari* de G. Feydeau et R. Peter," *M.*

Feb. 18 "Trianon-Lyrique: *Le roi des montagnes*, opérette de Victor Léon et Ordonneau, musique de Lehar," *M.*

Feb. 22 "Au Théâtre Antoine, *La grande famille*, d'Arquillière, est une pièce fort remarquable," *M.*

Feb. 27 "Au Nouvel-Ambigu, très vif succès pour une pièce habile et attachante: *L'épervier*, de F. de Croisset," *M.*

Feb. 28 "Mme E. d'Alençon au Théâtre Réjane," *M.*

Mar. 4 "Au Théâtre Fémina, aimable reprise de *Madame Flirt*," *M.*

Mar. 5 "A la Comédie des Champs-Elysées, une comédie fine et même ténue de Vandérem et Franc-Nohain. Une fantaisie charmante de T. Bernard," *M.*

Mar. 8 "Au Théâtre-Français, Mlle Valpreux débute avec éclat dans une reprise de *Georgette Lemeunier* [Maurice Donnay]," *M.*

Mar. 12 "Au Théâtre Apollo, on applaudit une opérette espagnole et bien française," *M.*

Mar. 13 "Au Théâtre Cluny, *Bicard, dit le Bouif*, de G. de La Fouchardière et P. Héon," *M.*

323

Mar. 17 "Au Théâtre des Arts," *M.*

Mar. 18 "A la Renaissance, *Aphrodite* est un spectacle brillant, provocant, fatigant," *M.*

Mar. 20 "Aux Variétés, une pièce de P. Gavault, *Ma tante d'Honfleur*, plaît très vivement," *M.*

Mar. 24 "Nouveau spectacle au Grand-Guignol. Cinq pièces: deux drames, trois comédies," *M.*

Mar. 28 "Au Théâtre Antoine, *La force de mentir*, drame de T. Bernard et Morullier. *La tontine*, fantaisie d'Arnout et Gerbidon," *M.*

Mar. 29 "Au Théâtre-Français, deux heures neutres: *L'envolée*, de G. Devore; vingt jolies minutes: *Deux couverts*, de S. Guitry," *M.*

Apr. 1 "A l'Oeuvre, intéressante représentation," *M.*

Apr. 2 "Au Gymnase, *Pétard*, d'H. Lavedan, est une oeuvre séduisante, baroque, incertaine," *M.*

Apr. 2 "*Psyché*, à l'Odéon, fut un régal," *M.*

Apr. 5 "Au Théâtre Marigny, *Le talion*, 3 actes d'Henri de Rothschild," *M.*

Apr. 7 "Au Théâtre des Arts. Aux Escholiers," *M.*

Apr. 9 "A la Porte Saint-Martin, P. Hervieu, R. de Flers, G. de Caillavet. Belle affiche et grand succès," *M.*

Apr. 16 "Mme Sarah Bernhardt joue un drame romantique, *Tout à coup*, de P. et G. de Cassagnac," *M.*

Apr. 24 "Au Théâtre du Vieux-Colombier, *L'eau-de-vie*, d'H. Ghéon.— *Tartuffe*, à la Comédie des Champs-Elysées," *M.*

Apr. 26 "A l'Odéon," *M.*

Apr. 30 "Au Conservatoire," *M.*

May 1 "Stendhal, III: esquisse du beylisme," *RP*, pp. 148–86.

May 1 "Première de *Poussière* et de *L'honnête fille*, au Théâtre Antoine," *M.*

May 3 "L'Opéra-Comique reprend avec éclat *Le rêve*, d'A. Bruneau," *M.*

May 6 "A la Comédie-Française," *M*: reviewing Molière, *Les femmes savantes.*

May 9 "Au Palais-Royal, *J'ose pas*, de G. Berr, manque un peu d'audace," *M.*

May 15 "Stendhal, IV: histoire du beylisme," *RP*, pp. 325–61.

May 16 "A l'Apollo," *M.*

May 20 "Un aimable début, *Ce qu'il faut taire*, d'A. Meyer, aux Bouffes-Parisiens," *M.*

May 20 "A la Renaissance, un conte bleu—bleu et or—de J.-J. Frappa et Dupuy-Mazuel: *L'homme riche*," *M.*

May 22 "Au Vieux-Colombier, *La nuit des rois.*—Au Théâtre Sarah-Bernhardt, *La jeunesse des mousquetaires.*—Au Théâtre Antoine, *Le supplice de Tantale*, d'E.-R. Trémois," *M.*

May 30 "Un beau spectacle à la Comédie-Française, *Macbeth*, traduit par J. Richepin," *M.*

June 4 "Le gala Antoine.—Au Gymnase.—Au Grand-Guignol," *M.*

June 6 "La bataille de *L'Aiglon* [Edmond Rostand]," *M.*

June 7 "A l'Oeuvre, *L'otage*, de P. Claudel," *M.*

June 14 "Aux Escholiers," *M.*
June 19 "A l'Odéon," *M.*
June 26 "La Comédie-Française reprend une des oeuvres les plus hautes du théâtre contemporain: *La nouvelle idole,* de F. de Curel," *M.*
June 30 "Concours du Conservatoire: tragédie," *M.*
July 1 "Concours du Conservatoire: comédie," *M.*
July 12 "Le dernier sourire de la saison," *M*: reviewing T. Bernard, *Le prince charmant.*
July 16 "Au Conservatoire: après les concours," *M.*
July 17 "Au Conservatoire: après les concours," *M.*
July 18 "Au Conservatoire: après les concours," *M.*
July 19 "Au Conservatoire: après les concours," *M.*

Articles: Political and Social

"Au Figaro," *H,* 4 February 1905.
"L'article 7," *RB,* 21 (1900): 481–95.
"Leur bonne foi," *H,* 21 April 1905.
"Les lois scélérates," *RB,* 16 (1898): 338–52.
"Les monopoles," *Petite république,* 14, 17, 24, 28 December 1902; 4, 14 January 1903.
"Le procès," *RB,* 15 (1898): 410–14.
"Les progrès de l'apolitique en France," *RB,* 3 (1892): 10–21.
"Réflexions sur le congrès socialiste," *RB,* 21 (1900): 37–48.

Books: Literary

Au théâtre: réflexions critiques. 4 vols. Paris: Ollendorff, 1906–11.
Elisabeth Masson. Paris: Chaix, 1906. (A *nouvelle.*)
En lisant: réflexions critiques. Paris: Ollendorff, 1906.
Nouvelles conversations de Goethe avec Eckermann, 1897–1900. Paris: Editions de la Revue blanche, 1901.
Stendhal et le beylisme. Paris: Ollendorff, 1914.

Books and Pamphlets: Political and Social

L'article 7. Paris: Société Nouvelle de Librairie et d'Edition, 1900.
Les congrès ouvriers et socialistes français, vol. 1: *1876–1885*; vol. 2: *1886–1900.* ("Bibliothèque socialiste," no. 6–7.) Paris: Société Nouvelle de Librairie et d'Edition, 1901.
Du mariage. Paris: Ollendorff, 1907.
Preface to Paul Abram, *L'évolution du mariage.* Paris: Sansot, 1908.

Selected Works after 1914

A l'échelle humaine. Paris: Gallimard, 1945.
L'exercice du pouvoir. Discours prononcés de mai 1936 à janvier 1937. Ed. Robert Blum. Paris: Gallimard, 1937.
"L'idéal socialiste," *RP,* 1 May 1924, pp. 94–111.
Jean Jaurès (conférence donnée le 16 février 1933 au Théâtre des Ambassadeurs). Paris: Librairie Populaire, 1933.

"Léon Blum parle de Jean Jaurès, discours du 31 juillet 1917 au Palais des fêtes de la rue Saint-Martin," *Revue socialiste*, n.s., no. 37 (May 1950), pp. 385–406.

La méthode socialiste. Paris: Editions de la Liberté, 1945. [A speech originally delivered in 1931.]

Pour être socialiste. Paris: Librairie du Parti socialiste, 1919.

Preface to James Burnham, *L'ère des organisateurs* [The Managerial Revolution]. Paris: C. Lévy, 1947.

Preface to Jean Feuillard, *Jaurès homme d'aujourd'hui.* [Périgueux]: Pierre Fanlac, 1948.

Preface to Jean Perrin, *La science et l'espérance.* Paris: Presses Universitaires de France, 1948.

Preface to François Simon, *Une belle figure du peuple, Benoît Malon.* Courbevoie, 1926.

La réforme gouvernementale. Paris: Bernard Grasset, [1918].

Souvenirs sur l'affaire. Paris: Gallimard, 1935.

WORKS BY OTHER AUTHORS

Articles

Anon. "La gazette du Ghetto," *Oeuvre*, 30 March 1911, p. 26.

Bernard, Tristan. "La galérie des bustes: Léon Blum," *Excelsior*, 27 February 1912.

———. "Un critique," *Comoedia*, 1 July 1910.

Boissard, Maurice. "Les théâtres," *Mercure de France*, 98 (1912): 411–12.

———. "Les théâtres," *Mercure de France*, 106 (1913): 175.

Borne, Etienne. "Les dernières années de Léon Blum," *Etudes*, 265 (1950): 346–53.

Bourgin, Georges. "Léon Blum: de la rue Cujas à Jouy-en-Josas," *Revue politique et parlementaire*, October 1950, pp. 142–44.

Bracke. Preface to "Pages choisies de Léon Blum," *Revue socialiste*, n.s., no. 38–39 (1950), pp. 3–8.

Burckhardt, Carl J. "Un dîner avec Gide chez Léon Blum," *Figaro littéraire*, 19 December 1959, pp. 1, 5–6.

Le Cardonnel, Georges. "Une renaissance française," *Mercure de France*, 104 (1913): 257–61.

Claretie, Jules. "Journal: vingt-cinq ans au Théâtre-Français," *Revue des deux mondes*, 1 December 1950, pp. 485–500; 15 December 1950, pp. 690–705; 15 January 1951, pp. 301–19; 1 February 1951, pp. 489–503; 15 March 1951, pp. 298–312; 1 April 1951, pp. 486–501.

Faguet, Emile. "L'anarchie morale: deux livres contre le mariage," *Revue latine*, 6 (1907): 577–605.

———. "M. Léon Blum," *Revue latine*, 6 (1907): 65–78.

Gourmont, Jean de. "Les livres," *Mercure de France*, 62 (1906): 423.

Hirsch, Charles-Henry. "Les revues," *Mercure de France*, 102 (1913): 177–79.

Jourdain, Francis. "Du côté de la Revue blanche," *Europe*, 33 (1955): 154–69.

Lavisse, Ernest. "La jeunesse," *Journal des débats*, 16 April 1890.

Leclercq, Paul. "Memories of Léon Blum," *Nineteenth Century and After*, 147 (1950): 378–80.

Mauclair, Camille. "La critique française devant l'étranger," *La Revue de Genève*, 1 (1920): 186–99.

———. "L'état actuel de la critique littéraire française," *La Nouvelle revue*, 1 (1900): 349–62.

Mazel, Henri. "Les livres," *Mercure de France*, 69 (1907): 519–21.

Natanson, Thadée. "Rencontre de Léon Blum et de Jaurès," *La Nef*, no. 39 (February 1948), pp. 67–80.

Péguy, Charles. "Pour moi," *Cahiers de la Quinzaine*, cahier 5, ser. 2 (1901), pp. 1–49.

———. "Préface de l'éditeur [to *Jean Coste*]," *Cahiers de la Quinzaine*, cahier 12, ser. 2 (1901), pp. 3–5.

Le Ruel, Maurice. "Karl Marx ou Disraeli? Léon Blum vu par un de ses camarades d'études," *Le monde illustré*, 13 June 1936, p. 491.

Téry, Gustave. "Les juifs au Théâtre Français: le deserteur Bernstein," *Oeuvre*, 16 February 1911.

———. "Les juifs au théâtre: le 'Vieil homme' ou l'enfant précoce," *Oeuvre*, 26 January 1911.

Veber, Pierre. "Jadis," *Les nouvelles littéraires*, 21 March 1936.

Warnod, André. "J'étais journaliste en 1909," *Figaro littéraire*, 10 September 1955.

Books

Agathon [Henri Massis and Alfred de Tarde]. *Les jeunes gens d'aujourd'hui: le goût de l'action, la foi patriotique, une renaissance catholique, le réalisme politique.* Paris: Plon, 1913.

Albalat, Alphonse. *Les ennemis de l'Art d'écrire: Réponse aux objections de MM. F. Brunetière, Emile Faguet, Adolphe Brisson, Rémy de Gourmont, Ernest Charles, G. Lanson, G. Pélissier, Octave Uzanne, Léon Blum, H. Mazel, C. Vergniol, etc.* Paris: Librairie Universelle, 1905.

D'Alsace, Jean. *Mères françaises qu'en dites-vous? Extraits "du mariage" de Léon Blum.* Strasbourg: Nouvelle voix d'Alsace et de Lorraine, n.d.

Antoine, André-Paul. *Antoine, père et fils: souvenirs du Paris littéraire et théâtral, 1900–1939.* Paris: René Julliard, 1962.

Benda, Julien. *La jeunesse d'un clerc.* Paris: Gallimard, 1936.

Bernard, Jean-Jacques. *Mon père Tristan Bernard.* Paris: Albin Michel, 1955.

Bernard, Tristan. *Auteurs, acteurs, spectateurs.* Paris: Pierre Lafitte, 1909.

Daudet, Léon. *Souvenirs des milieux littéraires, politiques, artistiques et medicaux.* Vol. 2: *Au temps de Judas—vers le roi—Alphonse Daudet.* Paris: Nouvelle librairie nationale, 1926.

Dreyfus, Robert. *De Monsieur Thiers à Marcel Proust: histoire et souvenirs.* Paris: Plon, 1939.

Dussane, Béatrix. *Dieux des planches.* ("Collection '1900 vécu.'") Paris: Flammarion, 1964.

Fabre-Luce, Alfred. *Journal, 1951.* Paris: Amiot-Dumont, 1951.

Faure, Paul. *Vingt ans d'intimité avec Edmond Rostand.* Paris: Plon, 1928.

Gide, André. *Journal, 1889–1939.* ("Bibliothèque de la Pléiade.") Paris: Nouvelle Revue Française, 1939.

Gregh, Fernand. *L'âge d'airain: souvenirs 1905–1925.* Paris: Bernard Grasset, 1951.

————. *L'âge d'or: souvenirs d'enfance et de jeunesse.* Paris: Bernard Grasset, 1947.

Halévy, Daniel. *Pays parisiens.* Paris: Bernard Grasset, 1932.

Herriot, Edouard. *Jadis.* Vol. 1: *Avant la première guerre mondiale.* Paris: Flammarion, 1948.

Isaac, Jules. *Expériences de ma vie.* Vol. 1: *Péguy.* Paris: Calmann-Lévy, 1959.

Jaurès, Jean. *Les deux méthodes: Conférence par Jean Jaurès et Jules Guesde à l'Hippodrome Lillois.* ("Bibliothèque du Parti ouvrier français.") Lille: Imprimerie ouvrière, 1900.

————. *Idéalisme et matérialisme dans la conception de l'histoire: Conférence de Jean Jaurès et réponse de Paul Lafargue, février, 1895.* [Paris]: Publications du groupe des étudiants collectivistes (adhérant à l'agglomeration parisienne du Parti ouvrier) [1895?].

Lévy, Louis. *Comment ils sont devenus socialistes.* Paris: Editions du Populaire, 1932.

Moch, Jules. *Rencontres avec . . . Léon Blum.* Paris: Plon, 1970.

Nattier-Natanson, Evelyn. *Les amitiés de la "Revue blanche" et quelques autres.* Vincennes: Les éditions du donjon, 1959. Substantial parts of the passages on Blum are lifted bodily from the work of Mme. Jeanne-Léon Blum.

Paul-Boncour, Joseph. *Entre deux guerres. Souvenirs sur la IIIᵉ République.* Vol. 1: *Les luttes républicaines 1877–1918.* Paris: Plon, 1945. English trans., *Recollections of the Third Republic* (vol. 1). New York: Robert Speller and Sons, 1957.

Renard, Jules. *Correspondance.* Paris: Flammarion [1954].

————. *Journal.* Paris: Gallimard, 1935.

Rolland, Romain. *Le cloître de la rue d'Ulm: journal de Romain Rolland à l'Ecole Normale, 1886–1889.* Paris: Albin Michel, 1952.

————. *Une amitié française: correspondance entre Charles Péguy et Romain Rolland.* Ed. Alfred Saffrey. ("Cahiers Romain Rolland," no. 7.) Paris: Albin Michel, 1955.

Schlumberger, Jean. *Madeleine et André Gide.* Schlumberger, *Oeuvres,* vol. 7: *(1944–1961).* Paris: Gallimard, 1961.

Sée, Edmond. *Porto-Riche.* ("Visages contemporains.") Paris: Firmin-Didot, 1932.

Sert, Misia. *Misia.* [Paris]: Gallimard, 1952.

[Sorlot, Fernand]. *Vie de Monsieur Léon Blum. Suivie d'un portrait du Président du Conseil par Gustave Téry, directeur-fondateur de l'Oeuvre.* ("L'action publique," no. 2.) Paris: Nouvelles éditions latines, 1936. Often erroneously attributed to Téry.

Spire, André. *Souvenirs à bâtons rompus.* ("Présence du judaïsme.") Paris: Albin Michel, 1962.

Tharaud, Jérôme and Jean. *Mes années chez Barrès.* Paris: Plon, 1928.

————. *Notre cher Péguy.* Paris: Plon, 1926.

————. *Pour les fidèles de Péguy.* Paris: Editions Dumas, 1949.

[Viviani, René]. *Le monument de René Viviani: Alger, le 4 mai 1930.* N.p.: Edité par les soins de la Société des Amis de René Viviani, n.d.

Zévaès, Alexandre. *Notes et souvenirs d'un militant.* Paris: Marcel Rivière, 1913.

Other Documents

Congrès général des organisations socialistes françaises. Tenu à Paris du 3 au 8 décembre 1899. Compte rendu sténographique officiel. Paris: Société Nouvelle de Librairie et d'Edition, 1900.

Deuxième congrès général des organisations socialistes françaises. Tenu à Paris du 28 au 30 septembre 1900. Compte rendu sténographique officiel. Paris: Société Nouvelle de Librairie et d'Edition, 1901.

Troisième congrès général des organisations socialistes françaises. Tenu à Lyon du 26 au 28 mai 1901. Compte rendu sténographique officiel. Paris: Société Nouvelle de Librairie et d'Edition, 1901.

Congrès socialiste international d'Amsterdam des 14–20 août 1904: rapports et projets de résolutions sur les questions de l'ordre du jour. Par le Secrétariat socialiste international. Brussels, 1904.

Parti Socialiste (Section Française de l'Internationale Ouvrière). *Premier congrès national (Congrès d'Unité). Tenu à Paris, les 23, 24 et 25 avril 1905, Salle du Globe. Compte rendu analytique.* Paris: Au siège du Conseil national [1905?].

Annuaire du Conseil d'Etat. Paris: Imprimerie nationale.

Recueil des arrêts du Conseil d'Etat statuant aux contentieux, des décisions du tribunal des conflits et de la cour des comptes. Paris: Recueil Sirey. Known as the *Recueil Lebon.*

Recueil des lois et règlements concernant le Conseil d'Etat. Paris: Imprimerie nationale, 1912.

Recueil général des lois et des arrêts en matière civile, criminelle, administrative et de droit public. Paris: Recueil Sirey. Known as the *Recueil Sirey.*

SECONDARY SOURCES

Biographical Studies of Blum

Audry, Colette. *Léon Blum ou la politique du juste: essai.* ("Les Temps Modernes," gen. ed. Jean-Paul Sartre.) Paris: René Julliard, 1955.

[Blum, Mme Jeanne-Léon]. *Léon Blum, 9 avril 1872—30 mars 1950.* [Paris, 1951].

Blumel, André. *Léon Blum, juif et zioniste.* Paris: Editions de "La terre retrouvée," [1952?].

Colton, Joel. *Léon Blum: Humanist in Politics.* New York: Alfred A. Knopf, 1966.

Dalby, Louise Elliott. *Léon Blum: Evolution of a Socialist.* New York: Thomas Yoseloff, 1963.

Dictionnaire des parlementaires français: notices biographiques sur les ministres, sénateurs et députés français de 1889 à 1940. Ed. Jean Jolly. Paris: Presses Universitaires de France, 1960– .

Downs, Katherine Watson. "Léon Blum: The Evolution of His Socialist Doctrine." Unpublished master's thesis, Stanford University, 1956.

Fraser, Geoffrey, and Thadée Natanson. *Léon Blum, Man and Statesman.* Philadelphia: J. B. Lippincott, 1938.

Joll, James. *Three Intellectuals in Politics.* [New York]: Pantheon Books, 1960.

Lapie, Pierre-Olivier. *De Léon Blum à de Gaulle: le caractère et le pouvoir.* ("Les grandes études contemporaines.") [Paris]: Fayard, 1971.

Stokes, Richard L. *Léon Blum: Poet to Premier.* New York: Coward-McCann, 1937.

Vichniac, Marc. *Léon Blum.* [Paris]: Flammarion, 1937.

Ziebura, Gilbert. *Léon Blum: Theorie und Praxis einer sozialistischen Politik.* Vol. 1: *1872 bis 1934.* Berlin: Walter de Gruyter, 1963. French trans. *Léon Blum et le Parti socialiste (1872–1934).* Paris: Armand Colin, 1967.

Books and Articles on Blum's Literary Career

Anon. "Léon Blum critique littéraire," *Les nouvelles littéraires*, 25 May 1936.

Barjac, Claude. "Léon Blum, chroniqueur et moraliste à la 'Grande Revue'," *Grande revue*, 150 (1936): 575–90.

Billy, André. "Les livres: quand Léon Blum voulait réformer le mariage," *Figaro*, 28 February 1962, p. 20.

Carat, Jacques. "Léon Blum écrivain," *Paru*, no. 60 (May 1950), pp. 55–60.

Copeau, Jacques. *Critiques d'un autre temps: études d'art dramatique.* Paris: Nouvelle Revue Française, 1923.

Dintzer, Lucien. *L'oeuvre littéraire de Léon Blum, ou Blum inconnu.* Preface by Emmanuel Lévy. Lyon: Les éditions de l'Avenir socialiste, 1937.

Faucon, Louis. "Léon Blum et Jules Renard ou les débuts d'une amitié qui fut parfois à sens unique," *Figaro littéraire*, 5 April 1952.

Henriot, Emile. *Maîtres d'hier et contemporains: courrier littéraire, XIXe–XXe siècles.* [Vol. 3] Paris: Albin Michel, 1955.

Jackson, A[rthur] B[asil]. *La revue blanche (1889–1903): origine, influence, bibliographie.* ("Bibliothèque des lettres modernes," no. 2.) Paris: M. J. Minard, 1960.

Lévy, Louis. "La critique," *Les nouvelles littéraires*, 6 June 1936.

Monfort, Eugène, ed. *Vingt-cinq ans de littérature française.* Vol. 1; Paris: Librairie de France, n.d.

Pierre-Quint, Léon. "L'émancipation de la femme," *Revue de France*, 4 (1931): 321–45.

Roll, Maximin. "M. Léon Blum et le *Jules César* de Shakespeare: les conférences de l'Odéon," *Comoedia*, 28 May 1909.

Sigaux, Gilbert. "Léon Blum était aussi un écrivain," *Démocratie 62*, 22 February 1962.

Texcier, Jean. "Léon Blum, écrivain et moraliste," *Preuves*, 5 (1955): 79–82.

Thiébaut, Marcel. *En lisant M. Léon Blum*. Paris: Gallimard, 1937.

Zévaès, Alexandre. "Léon Blum, écrivain," *Les nouvelles littéraires*, 6 June 1936.

Studies of French Literature and the Theater

Belis, Alexandre. *La critique française à la fin du XIXᵉ siècle: Ferdinand Brunetière—Emile Faguet—Jules Lemaître—Anatole France*. Paris: Librairie universitaire J. Gamber, 1926.

Billy, André. "Autour de l'année cinq et des suivantes," *Figaro littéraire*, 30 April 1955.

———. "La crise littéraire de 1905," *Figaro littéraire*, 26 March 1955.

———. *L'époque contemporaine (1905–1930)*. ("Histoire de la vie littéraire," ed. André Billy.) Paris: Jules Tallandier, 1956.

———. *L'époque 1900 (1885–1905)*. ("Histoire de la vie littéraire," ed. André Billy.) Paris: Jules Tallandier, 1951.

———. "Il y a cinquante ans: la littérature française en 1905," *Figaro littéraire*, 8 January 1955.

Boylesve, René. *Réflexions sur Stendhal*. ("Notes Stendhaliennes," no. 5.) Paris: Le divan, 1929.

Brombert, Victor. *The Intellectual Hero: Studies in the French Novel, 1880–1955*. Philadelphia: J. B. Lippincott, 1961.

Brown, Rollo Walter. *How the French Boy Learns to Write: A Study in the Teaching of the Mother Tongue*. Cambridge: Harvard University Press, 1924.

Carassus, Emilien. *Le snobisme et les lettres françaises de Paul Bourget à Marcel Proust, 1884–1914*. Paris: Armand Colin, 1966.

Cattaui, Georges. "L'homme [Marcel Proust] et l'oeuvre," *Les nouvelles littéraires*, 25 July 1936.

Charles-Brun. *Le roman social en France au XIXᵉ siècle*. ("Etudes économiques et sociales publiées avec le concours du Collège libre des sciences sociales," no. 10.) Paris: Giard et Brière, 1910.

Coindreau, Maurice Edgar. *La farce est jouée: vingt-cinq ans de théâtre français, 1900–1925*. New York: Editions de la Maison française, 1942.

Cordiè, Carlo. *Interpretazioni di Stendhal dal Bourget ai nostri giorni*. ("Biblioteca di saggi e lezioni accademiche," no. 23.) Milan: Francesco Montuoro, 1947.

Descaves, Pierre. *Le théâtre*. ("Notes et maximes.") [Paris]: Hachette, 1963.

Descotes, Maurice. *Le public de théâtre et son histoire*. Paris: Presses Universitaires de France, 1964.

Dhomme, Sylvain. *La mise en scène contemporaine d'André Antoine à Bertolt Brecht.* ("L'activité contemporaine.") Paris: F. Nathan, 1959.

Escoube, Paul. "La femme et le sentiment de l'amour chez Rémy de Gourmont," *Mercure de France*, 159 (1922): 45–46.

Fraser, Elizabeth M. *Le renouveau religieux d'après le roman français de 1886 à 1914.* Paris: Société d'édition "Les belles lettres," 1934.

Hermann, Fritz. *Die "Revue Blanche" und "die Nabis."* 2 vols. Munich: Mikrokopie, 1959.

Lalou, René. *Histoire de la littérature française contemporaine.* Vol. 2. Paris: Presses Universitaires de France, 1941.

Leblond, Marius-Ary. *La société française sous la Troisième République d'après les romanciers contemporains: l'enfant—les officiers—les financiers—la noblesse—les anarchistes et les socialistes.* Paris: Félix Alcan, 1905.

Ledré, Charles. *Histoire de la presse.* ("Le temps et les destins.") Paris: Arthème Fayard, 1958.

Lehmann, A. G. *The Symbolist Aesthetic in France, 1885–1895.* 2d ed.; Oxford: Basil Blackwell, 1968.

Levin, Harry. *The Gates of Horn: A Study of Five French Realists.* New York: Oxford University Press, 1963.

Mitchell, Bonner. *Les manifestes littéraires de la belle époque, 1886–1914: anthologie critique.* Paris: Seghers, 1966.

Mondor, Henri. *Précocité de Valéry.* Paris: Gallimard, 1957.

Painter, George D. *Proust, the Early Years.* Boston: Little, Brown, 1959.

Peter, René. *Le théâtre et la vie sous la Troisième République.* Vol. 1; [Paris: Editions littéraires de France], 1945. Vol. 2; Paris: Marchot, 1947.

Peyre, Henri. *Le classicisme français.* New York: Editions de la Maison française, 1942.

———. *The Contemporary French Novel.* New York: Oxford University Press, 1955.

———. *The Failures of Criticism.* Ithaca: Cornell University Press, 1967. Emended edition of *Writers and Their Critics.*

———. *Literature and Sincerity.* ("Yale Romanic Studies, 2d series," no. 9.) New Haven: Yale University Press, 1963.

Pierre-Quint, Léon. *Proust et la stratégie littéraire, avec des lettres de Marcel Proust à René Blum, Bernard Grasset et Louis Brun.* Paris: Corrêa, 1954.

Pruner, Francis. *Les luttes d'Antoine: au Théâtre Libre.* Paris: M. J. Minard, 1964.

———. *Le Théâtre Libre d'Antoine.* Vol. 1: *Le répertoire étranger.* ("Aux sources de la dramaturgie moderne.") Paris: Lettres modernes, 1958.

Stoullig, Edmond, ed. *Les annales du théâtre et de la musique.* Paris: Ollendorff, 1897–1916.

Wellek, René. "Hippolyte Taine's Literary Theory and Criticism," *Criticism: A Quarterly for Literature and the Arts*, 1 (1959): 1–18, 123–38.

Studies of the Conseil d'Etat

Brugère, René. *Le Conseil d'Etat, son personnel et ses formations. Evolution—tendances.* Toulouse: Imprimerie Toulousaine, 1910.

Le Conseil d'Etat: livre jubilaire publié pour commémorer son cent cinquintième anniversaire: 4 nivôse an VIII—24 décembre 1949. Paris: Recueil Sirey, 1952.

Freedeman, Charles E. *The Conseil d'Etat in Modern France.* ("Columbia Studies in the Social Sciences," no. 603.) New York: Columbia University Press, 1961.

Langrod, Georges, "The French Council of State: Its Role in the Formation and Implementation of Administrative Law," *American Political Science Review*, 49 (1955): 673–92.

Worms, René. *La juridiction du Conseil d'Etat et ses tendances actuelles.* Paris: Giard et Brière, 1906.

Studies of Socialism and the Socialist Movement in France

Auclair, Marcelle. *La vie de Jean Jaurès, ou la France d'avant 1914.* Paris: Éditions du Seuil, 1954.

Bernstein, Samuel. *The Beginnings of Marxian Socialism in France.* New York, 1933.

Bourgin, Hubert. *De Jaurès à Léon Blum: l'Ecole normale et la politique.* Paris: Arthème Fayard, 1938.

Breton, J[ules]-L[ouis]. *L'unité socialiste.* (*Histoire des partis socialistes en France*, ed. Alexandre Zévaès, vol. 7.) Paris: Marcel Rivière, 1912.

Charnay, Maurice. *Les allemanistes.* (*Histoire des partis socialistes en France*, ed. Alexandre Zévaès, vol. 5.) Paris: Marcel Rivière, 1912.

Dolléans, Edouard. *Le caractère religieux du socialisme.* Paris: Librairie de la Société du recueil J.-B. Sirey et du Journal du Palais, 1906.

———. *Histoire du mouvement ouvrier.* Preface by Lucien Febvre. 2 vols. Paris: Armand Colin, 1936–39.

Fiechter, Jean-Jacques. *Le socialisme français: de l'affaire Dreyfus à la Grande Guerre.* Preface by Henri Guillemin. Geneva: Droz, 1965.

Gay, Peter. *The Dilemma of Democratic Socialism: Eduard Bernstein's Challenge to Marx.* New York: Columbia University Press, 1952.

Goldberg, Harvey. *The Life of Jean Jaurès.* Madison: University of Wisconsin Press, 1962.

Greene, Nathaniel. *Crisis and Decline: The French Socialist Party in the Popular Front Era.* Ithaca: Cornell University Press, 1969.

Humbert, Sylvain. *Les possibilistes.* (*Histoire des partis socialistes en France*, ed. Alexandre Zévaès, vol. 4.) Paris: Marcel Rivière, 1911.

Joll, James. *The Anarchists.* London: Eyre & Spottiswoode, 1964.

Kriegel, Annie. *Aux origines du communisme français, 1914–1920: contribution à l'histoire du mouvement ouvrier français.* (Ecole pratique des hautes études—Sorbonne, sixième section: sciences économiques et sociales. "Société, mouvements sociaux et idéologies," première série: études, VI.) 2 vols. Paris: Mouton, 1964.

————, ed. *Le congrès de Tours (décembre 1920), naissance du Parti communiste français.* Paris: Julliard, 1964.

Lefranc, Georges. *Jaurès et le socialisme des intellectuels.* Paris: Aubier–Montaigne, 1968.

————. *Le mouvement socialiste sous la Troisième République (1875–1940).* Paris: Payot, 1963.

Lévy-Bruhl, L[ucien]. *Jean Jaurès: esquisse biographique.* 2d ed. Paris: F. Rieder, 1924.

Lichtheim, George. *Marxism in Modern France.* New York: Columbia University Press, 1966.

Ligou, Daniel. *Histoire du socialisme en France, 1871–1961.* Paris: Presses Universitaires de France, 1962.

Louis, Paul. *Histoire du socialisme en France, 1789–1945.* 4th ed.; Paris: Marcel Rivière, 1946.

Mimin, Pierre. *Le socialisme municipal devant le Conseil d'Etat (critique juridique et politique des régies communales).* Paris: Recueil Sirey, 1911.

Noland, Aaron. *The Founding of the French Socialist Party, 1893–1905.* (Harvard Historical Monographs, no. 29.) Cambridge: Harvard University Press, 1956.

————. "Individualism in Jean Jaurès' Socialist Thought," in *Ideas in Cultural Perspective.* Ed. Philip P. Wiener and Aaron Noland. New Brunswick: Rutgers University Press, 1962.

Nomad, Max. *Aspects of Revolt.* New York: Bookman Associates, 1959.

Philip, André. *Pour un socialisme humaniste.* Paris: Plon, 1960.

Ramadier, Paul. *Le socialisme de Léon Blum.* Paris: Librairie des municipalités, 1951.

Stafford, David. *From Anarchism to Reformism: A Study of the Political Activities of Paul Brousse within the First International and the French Socialist Movement, 1870–90.* London: Weidenfeld and Nicolson, 1971.

Suarez, Georges. *Briand, sa vie, son oeuvre.* Vol. 1: *Le révolté circonspect, 1862–1904.* Vol. 2: *Le faiseur de calme, 1904–1914.* Paris: Plon, 1938.

Willard, Claude. *Le mouvement socialiste en France (1893–1905): les guesdistes.* Paris: Editions sociales, 1965.

Wohl, Robert. *French Communism in the Making, 1914–1924.* Stanford: Stanford University Press, 1966.

Zévaès, Alexandre. *Histoire du socialisme et du communisme en France de 1871 à 1947.* [Paris]: Editions France-Empire [1947].

Other Sources

Alpert, Harry. *Emile Durkheim and His Sociology.* ("Studies in History, Economics, and Public Law," no. 445.) New York: Columbia University Press, 1939.

Andler, Charles. *Vie de Lucien Herr (1864–1926).* Paris: Rieder, 1932.

Arendt, Hannah. *The Origins of Totalitarianism.* 2d ed., enlarged; New York: Meridian Books, 1958.

Aubery, Pierre. *Milieux juifs de la France contemporaine à travers leurs écrivains.* Paris: Plon, 1957.

Bréal, Auguste. *Philippe Berthelot.* ("Les contemporains vus de près," 2d ser., no. 4.) Paris: Gallimard, 1937.

Byrnes, Robert F. *Antisemitism in Modern France.* Vol. 1: *The Prologue to the Dreyfus Affair.* New Brunswick: Rutgers University Press, 1950.

Challaye, Felicien. *Péguy socialiste.* Paris: Amiot-Dumont, 1954.

Chapman, Guy. *The Dreyfus Case: A Reassessment.* London: R. Hart-Davis, 1955.

Chastenet, Jacques. *La Belle Epoque: la société sous M. Fallières.* [Paris]: Bibliothèque historique mondiale [1958]. Originally published as *La France de M. Fallières.* Paris: Arthème Fayard, 1949.

————. *Histoire de la Troisième République.* Vol. 3: *La République triomphante, 1893–1906.* Paris: Hachette, 1955. Vol. 4: *Jours inquiets et jours sanglants, 1906–1918.* Paris: Hachette, 1957.

Delhorbe, C[écile]. *L'affaire Dreyfus et les écrivains français.* Paris, 1932.

Friedrich, Carl J. *Totalitarianism.* New York: Grosset & Dunlap, 1964.

Halasz, Nicholas. *Captain Dreyfus: The Story of a Mass Hysteria.* New York: Simon & Schuster, 1955.

Halévy, Daniel. *Charles Péguy et les Cahiers de la Quinzaine.* Paris: Payot, 1918.

Jefferson, Carter. *Anatole France: The Politics of Skepticism.* New Brunswick: Rutgers University Press, 1965.

Johnson, Douglas. *France and the Dreyfus Affair.* New York: Walker, 1967.

Klein, Viola. *The Feminine Character: History of an Ideology.* Foreword by Karl Mannheim. New York: International Universities Press, 1949.

Labori, Mme. Marguerite-Fernand. *Labori, ses notes manuscrits, sa vie.* Paris: Victor Attinger, 1947.

Leroy, Maxime. *Les premiers amis français de Wagner.* Paris: Albin Michel, 1922.

Lewin, Kurt. *Resolving Social Conflicts: Selected Papers on Group Dynamics.* Ed. Gertrud Weiss Lewin. Foreword by Gordon W. Allport. (A publication of the Research Center for Group Dynamics, University of Michigan.) New York: Harper, 1948.

Marrus, Michael R. *The Politics of Assimilation: A Study of the French Jewish Community at the Time of the Dreyfus Affair.* Oxford: Oxford University Press, 1971.

Masur, Gerhard. *Prophets of Yesterday: Studies in European Culture, 1890–1914.* New York: Macmillan, 1961.

Parsons, Talcott. *The Structure of Social Action: A Study of Social Theory with Special Reference to a Group of Recent European Writers.* 2d ed.; Glencoe, Ill.: Free Press, 1949.

Prélot, Marcel. *Cours d'histoire des idées politiques.* Paris: Les cours de droit, 1959.

Roblin Michel. *Les juifs de Paris: démographie—économie—culture.* Paris: A. et J. Picard, 1952.

Schmitt, Hans A. *Charles Péguy: The Decline of an Idealist.* Baton Rouge: Louisiana State University Press, 1967.

Seignobos, Charles. "La séparation des pouvoirs," *Revue de Paris*, 15 February 1895.

Silvera, Alain. *Daniel Halévy and His Times: A Gentleman–Commoner in the Third Republic*. Ithaca: Cornell University Press, 1966.

Smith, Robert John. "The Ecole Normale Supérieure in the Third Republic: A Study of the Classes of 1890–1904." Ph.D. dissertation, University of Pennsylvania, 1967.

Soulié, Michel. *La vie politique d'Edouard Herriot*. Paris: Armand Colin, 1962.

Thibaudet, Albert. *La République des professeurs*. ("Les écrits," ed. Jean Guéhenno.) Paris: Bernard Grasset, 1927.

Tonnelat, Ernest. *Charles Andler, sa vie et son oeuvre*. ("Publications de la Faculté des lettres de l'Université de Strasbourg," fasc. 77.) Paris: Les belles lettres, 1937.

INDEX

Lenéru, Marie: Blum on, 224
"Lettres sur la réforme gouverne-
mentale," 154
Lévy-Bruhl, Lucien, 236
Leygues, Georges: Blum on, 141
Librairie Georges Bellais, 125. *See
also* New Society of Bookselling
and Publishing
Libre Parole, La, 95
Ligue des Patriotes, 102
"Livre de mes amies, Le," 33
Lois scélérates, 141–43
Longuet, Charles, 110
Loti, Pierre: Blum on, 174
Loubet, Emile, 102
Louÿs, Pierre, 29, 97; Blum and,
25; Blum on, 67
Lugné-Poë, Aurélien-Marie, 206

Maeterlinck, Maurice, 30; Blum on,
232
Mallarmé, Stéphane, 30, 42, 43, 62;
Blum on, 232
Malon, Benoît, 110, 127, 146
Margueritte, Paul and Victor, 173
Marinetti, F. T.: Blum on, 227
Maritain, Jacques, 233
Marxism, French, 109–14, 118, 119,
120, 132–33, 137, 146, 150–52,
165–66, 181, 199. *See also* Blum,
Léon; Guesde, Jules; Parti
Ouvrier Français; Parti Socialiste
de France; Socialist congresses;
Socialists
Mathieu, Félix, 141
Mathiez, Albert, 127
Matin, Le, 96, 156, 229; Blum and,
205, 207–8, 213, 229
Mauriac, François, 235
Maurras, Charles, 63, 236
Mauss, Marcel, 155
"Méditation sur le suicide d'un de
mes amis," 32
Méline, Jules, 101; ministry of, 96
Menard-Dorian, Mme., 130
Mendès, Catulle, 14
Mercure de France, 35, 41, 43
Metchnikoff, Elie, 196, 197

Michel, Henry, 18
Michel, Louise, 87
Milhaud, Edgar, 155
Millerand, Alexandre, 108, 121,
127, 132, 133, 134–38, 140, 154,
157, 160, 165; Blum on, 140,
150–51
Mirbeau, Octave, 42, 155, 204;
Blum on, 210, 216
Moch, Gaston, 98
Monfort, Eugène, 179
"Monopoles, Les," 144
Moréas, Jean, 30; Blum on, 63
Morice, Charles, 30
Mouvement socialiste, Le, 127
Muhlfeld, Lucien, 40, 41, 97

Natanson, Alexandre, 31, 44
Natanson, Louis-Alfred [pseud. Al-
fred Athis], 31, 41, 44, 155
Natanson, Thadée, 31, 41, 42, 44;
and Dreyfus affair, 97–98; Blum
on, 216
Naturism: Blum on, 57–58, 68,
214–15
New Society of Bookselling and
Publishing, 125–31, 134–35, 141,
155, 156, 163; Blum and, 126–31,
144
Nietzsche, Friedrich, 237–38
Noailles, Anna, comtesse de, 98;
Blum on, 177–78, 232
Nomad, Max, 119
Notes critiques, 127
"Nouvelles conversations avec
Eckermann," 22–23, 49–50, 69,
92, 107, 115, 139, 144, 161, 165,
171–72, 182–83, 187
*Nouvelles conversations de Goethe
avec Eckermann*, 182–85

Palewski, Gaston de, 204
Parnassians, Blum and, 65
Parti Ouvrier Français (POF), 109–
11, 132, 136, 139–40. *See also*
Guesdists
Parti Ouvrier Socialiste Révolu-
tionnaire (POSR), 110